A LITERARY HISTORY OF SPAIN

General Editor: R. O. JONES
Cervantes Professor of Spanish, King's College, University of London

THE MIDDLE AGES
by A. D. DEYERMOND
Professor of Spanish, Westfield College, University of London

THE GOLDEN AGE: PROSE AND POETRY
by R. O. JONES

THE GOLDEN AGE: DRAMA
by EDWARD M. WILSON
Professor of Spanish, University of Cambridge
and DUNCAN MOIR
Lecturer in Spanish, University of Southampton

THE EIGHTEENTH CENTURY
by NIGEL GLENDINNING
Professor of Spanish, Trinity College, University of Dublin

THE NINETEENTH CENTURY
by DONALD L. SHAW
Senior Lecturer in Hispanic Studies, University of Edinburgh

THE TWENTIETH CENTURY
by G. G. BROWN
Lecturer in Spanish, Queen Mary College, University of London

SPANISH AMERICAN LITERATURE
SINCE INDEPENDENCE
by JEAN FRANCO
Professor of Spanish and Portuguese, Stanford University, California

CATALAN LITERATURE
by ARTHUR TERRY
Professor of Spanish, The Queen's University, Belfast

A LITERARY HISTORY OF SPAIN

SPANISH AMERICAN LITERATURE SINCE INDEPENDENCE

A LITERARY
HISTORY OF SPAIN

SPANISH AMERICAN

LITERATURE

SINCE INDEPENDENCE

JEAN FRANCO

Professor of Spanish and Portuguese
Stanford University, California

LONDON · ERNEST BENN LIMITED

NEW YORK · BARNES AND NOBLE BOOKS

First published 1973 by Ernest Benn Limited

25 New Street Square · Fleet Street · London · EC4A 3JA

and Barnes & Noble Books · 10 East 53rd Street · New York 10022

(a division of Harper & Row Publishers Inc.)

Distributed in Canada by

The General Publishing Company Limited · Toronto

© Jean Franco 1973

Printed in Great Britain

ISBN 0 510-32295-6

ISBN 06-4922383 (USA)

Paperback 0 510-32296-4

Paperback 06-4922375 (USA)

FOREWORD BY THE GENERAL EDITOR

SPANISH, the language of what was in its day the greatest of European powers, became the common tongue of the most far-flung Empire the world had until then seen. Today, in number of speakers, Spanish is one of the world's major languages. The literature written in Spanish is correspondingly rich. The earliest European lyrics in a post-classical vernacular that we know of (if we except Welsh and Irish) were written in Spain; the modern novel was born there; there too was written some of the greatest European poetry and drama; and some of the most interesting works of our time are being written in Spanish.

Nevertheless, this new history may require some explanation and even justification. Our justification is that a new and up-to-date English-language history seemed called for to serve the increasing interest now being taken in Spanish. There have been other English-language histories in the past, some of them very good, but none on this scale.

Every history is a compromise between aims difficult or even impossible to reconcile. This one is no exception. While imaginative literature is our main concern, we have tried to relate that literature to the society in and for which it was written, but without subordinating criticism to amateur sociology. Since not everything could be given equal attention (even if it were desirable to do so) we have concentrated on those writers and works of manifestly outstanding artistic importance to us their modern readers, with the inevitable consequence that many interesting minor writers are reduced to names and dates, and the even lesser are often not mentioned at all. Though we have tried also to provide a usable work of general reference, we offer the history primarily as a guide to the understanding and appreciation of what we consider of greatest value in the literatures of Spain and Spanish America.

Beyond a necessary minimum, no attempt has been made to arrive at uniform criteria; the history displays therefore the variety of approach and opinion that is to be found in a good university department of literature, a variety which we hope will prove stimulating. Each section takes account of the accepted works of scholarship in its field, but we do not offer our history as a grey consensus of received opinions; each contributor has imposed his own interpretation to the extent that this could be supported with solid scholarship and argument.

ix

Though the literature of Spanish America is not to be regarded simply as an offshoot of the literature of Spain, it seemed natural to link the two in our history since Spanish civilisation has left an indelible stamp on the Americas. Since Catalonia has been so long a part of Spain it seemed equally justified to include Catalan literature, an important influence on Spanish literature at certain times, and a highly interesting literature in its own right.

R.O.J.

PREFACE

ANYONE ACQUAINTED ONLY with the literature of the major Western countries will find the organisation of this Spanish American volume strange indeed. In histories of European literature, most attention is devoted to the past, to Golden Age Spain, Shakespearian England, or the French neo-classical period. However much emphasis is placed on modern literature, this is always seen in the context of past greatness. In contrast, the literature of what is now known as the 'developing' world observes different patterns. Africa, the Caribbean, Latin America have gone through the experience of colonisation. Print culture came to them as an imposition of conquering Europe and became the mark of an élite as against the non-print culture of serfs and slaves. As a result, certain polarities which are present in European literatures between folk and élite traditions are intensified and recurrent. The gulf between African, Amerindian, Afro-Caribbean on the one hand and the European-derived cultures of the élite is so wide as to split them off into almost mutually exclusive spheres. The élite literary tradition, alternatively wooing and rejecting the folk, expresses itself in the antinomies of provincialism and cosmopolitanism, barbarism and civilisation, the native and the European. This kind of pattern makes it imperative to study Latin American literature alongside other 'third world' cultures.

The historical development of such cultures is not at all comparable to that of Europe. For obvious reasons, colonisation creates a literature which is directed towards the metropolis rather than the home environment, which is estranged. Excellence may require that the author lose his national identity in order to immolate himself in the 'universal' tradition of the metropolis. Ruiz de Alarcón, the Mexican who became famous as a dramatist in seventeenth-century Spain, is one example. But ultimately it is of little importance whether we consider Ruiz de Alarcón to be Spanish or Mexican. What is important, is the inhibition which the colonial situation places on writers not willing or able to accept such immolation. There were other factors, too, which made a free development of literature in Spanish America difficult, factors such as the discouragement of literature in Indian languages or of certain genres, the novel for instance. For this reason, the present study begins with Independence; the colonial period being studied primarily in the light of later developments. Further, greatest emphasis is placed on the contemporary period and on certain representative authors and texts, since the present is the most important period of Spanish American literature.

The essay as a special genre has been omitted despite its importance. The scope of this book does not include the history of ideas and the essays mentioned—Sarmiento's *Facundo*, Rodó's *Ariel*, Octavio Paz's *Laberinto de la soledad*—are included for their influence upon imaginative literature. A detailed look at the essay would obviously have carried the study over into history, sociology, and other related disciplines. But though the essay has been left aside, the myth patterns which have been projected onto Latin America have not. Both the primitivist myth and the related myth of the 'immaturity' of the American continent which Europe projected from the Conquest onwards had a profound effect on the way the inhabitants of the Americas saw themselves and ultimately on the myth patterns of their literatures. Latin America was both a Utopian ideal, an innocent state of primitive goodness, but also a plunderable El Dorado. To be on the receiving end of this myth was to be an innocent child or an immature adolescent best guarded against himself. European attitudes to Latin America placed the continent in a cycle of frustration, doomed always to aspire, never to reach. In literature, the frustration is reflected in patterns of despair, in circular and enclosed novels. The present study sets out to explore some of these patterns and concentrate attention on matters of style and form. A short list of texts and critical studies accompanies each chapter, but all students of Spanish American literature will find the following helpful:

Anthologies

Apart from the anthologies mentioned in the reading list there are several big anthologies published in the United States, for example:

Anderson Imbert, Enrique and Florit, Eugenio, *Literatura hispano-americana* (New York, 1960)

Flores, Ángel, *Historia y antología del cuento y la novela en Hispanoamérica* (New York, 1959)

There are also several histories of literature published in Britain and the United States:

Alegría, Fernando, *Historia de la novela hispanoamericana*, 3rd ed. (Mexico, 1966)

Anderson Imbert, Enrique, *Historia de la literatura hispanoamericana*, 2 vols. 3rd ed. (New York, 1961)

Henríquez Ureña, Pedro, *Las corrientes literarias en la América Hispana* (Mexico, 1949)

Torres-Rioseco, A., *La novela en la América Hispana* (Berkeley, 1939)

——, *La gran literatura iberoamericana*, 2nd ed. (Buenos Aires, 1951)

CONTENTS

THE COLONISED IMAGINATION

THAT SPANISH AMERICA WAS for three centuries part of Spain's colonial empire is a fact that no student of its literature can possibly ignore. In the course of two or three generations between 1492 and the middle of the sixteenth century, the great Inca and Aztec empires were reduced to fragments, their religion, culture, economy, and history converted almost to nothing. In their place, all over the Americas arose the outward signs of the conquerors' civilisation—the government buildings, the houses of Spanish officials, the church —all grouped round the central plaza of the towns. Monarchy and Church and their respective hierarchies of officials institutionalised the political and religious lives of the inhabitants. And those whom they did not bring into their fold—nomadic Indians, isolated rural communities—could be ignored or allowed to exist at the margin of civilisation as long as they did not destroy the machine whose dual purpose was, on the one hand, to ensure the regular supply of precious metals to the royal coffers and, on the other, to bring to America the true Catholic faith and the stability of paternalistic government. Indian cultures did not die entirely; in many parts of Latin America; in Peru, Bolivia, Guatemala, parts of Mexico, and the southern cone, the survival of Indian languages ensured the survival of customs, folk-tales, songs. But these lay outside the central cultural tradition of the colonial period and only marginally influenced it.

By 1533, the Spanish Empire already had the structure that was to remain essentially unaltered until the end of the eighteenth century. There were two vast viceroyalties: that of New Spain whose centre was Mexico City but which stretched from California almost to Panama and took in the Caribbean islands; the Viceroyalty of Peru covered the whole of South America. This empire was highly centralised under the supreme body, the Council of the Indies, established in 1524, and this body was directly accountable to the king and always met in Spain. The high officials of the Spanish colonial hierarchy were also born in Spain so that their identification with the interests of the mother country was ensured. Creoles, or Spanish American citizens who were born in America and of Spanish descent, could only participate as members of the lower echelons, in the *cabildos* or town councils, for example.

The Church, on the other hand, was by no means so unanimously identified with Peninsular interests. Large land grants made the Church wealthy and powerful, but it also had a missionary task which brought it into close contact with the indigenous inhabitants of the New World. Missionaries learnt Indian languages, collected evidence about the histories and civilisations that had existed in America before their arrival, and they mitigated in many cases the worst treatment of the Indians.[1] The protest of the Dominican Fray Bartolomé de las Casas (1474-1566) against the treatment of the Indians of the islands of Santo Domingo and Cuba in his *Brevísima relación de la destrucción de las Indias* (1552) achieved wide renown (and incidentally helped to create the Black Legend of Spanish colonial cruelty). Las Casas championed the Indian cause at a celebrated debate in Valladolid held in 1550 and 1551, in which he successfully maintained that the Indians were rational creatures and not natural slaves. He argued that they should therefore be converted by peaceful methods and should not be bought or sold.[2] In 1537, Las Casas went to Central America and there, in Vera Paz (now in northern Guatemala), he helped to set up an experimental community in which Indians were converted to Catholicism and then taught useful skills. He was one of the first of many paternalistic friars; the Jesuits too were to set up similar communities in their South American missions.[3] The best and most dedicated of such missionaries regarded the Americas as the ideal Christian community in potential because of the fact that the natives were still untainted by European luxury and its attendant vices. The negative aspect of the Church's sway over Latin America was the extreme narrowness of criteria and the sanctions which visited those who strayed from the restricted doctrinal path. Censorship and the Inquisition made an early appearance in the New World, the efforts of the latter being mainly directed against those who tried to import and read forbidden books and those who held to the remnants of pre-Christian belief.[4]

The economic life of the colony was at first based on exploitation of the silver and gold mines; later there was a development of large estates or *haciendas* worked by peon labour organised on semi-feudal lines. However, the progress of agriculture was curtailed by the monopolistic policy of Spain which for long allowed trading only in certain goods and then only between the ports of Seville and Cádiz in the Peninsula and Vera Cruz, Cartagena, and Porto Bello in the New World.

Although Spain's monopolistic control of her colonies was not fundamentally different from that of other colonising powers, it was perhaps more rigidly exercised. Further, there was a parallel restriction of the imaginative and spiritual life of the colonies whose isolation from the main currents of European thought was aggravated. It should be borne in mind that Spain's own culture, brilliant at the end of the sixteenth and at the beginning of the seventeenth centuries, gradually became more and more provincial and impoverished. When transmitted to the colonies, it was little more than the attenuated reflection of a marginal culture.

Spanish American intellectuals were either churchmen and missionaries or the sons of landowners and officials: the education of both had been in the hands of the Church. Their literary tradition was classical and Spanish. They thought in terms of classical literary categories—the ode, the epic, the elegy—or of forms popular in Spain, such as the sonnet, the folk-song and ballad, the comedy or the religious play (the *auto*). The themes also tended to be conventional —the pastoral, the love poem, the religious sonnet. But why was it that such literary works were so often lifeless and uninspired? Was Spanish America lacking in talent? It is true, of course, that the *conquistadores* were not writers and intellectuals but men of action, but many of the early settlers were. Many Spanish writers emigrated to the New World, among them Gutierre de Cetina (1520 or 22-1557), the dramatist González de Eslava (1534?-1601?), and the novelist Mateo Alemán (1547-after 1613). So talent there was. But in a colonised society it is not always easy for talent to express itself. The imagination is also colonised, that is, it cannot draw its sustenance from immediate experience but tends to be parasitic on the developments of the metropolitan society. However, even in a colonised culture, reality cannot be shut out entirely. And although Spaniards and American-born writers of Spanish descent made great efforts to fit this reality into the categories familiar to them, yet circumstances often forced them into new ventures.

Perhaps the clearest illustration of this situation was the fact that potential novelistic material tended to be diverted into other channels. Novels could not be imported or published in the New World since the Indians had to be guarded from a fantasy literature that might make them doubt religious truths.[5] Hence spicy anecdotes which could well have made a picaresque novel or a collection of Boccaccio-like stories were presented as if they were part of a historical record. Such a book is *El carnero* (1636) by a Colombian, Juan Rodríguez Freile (1566-1640?), who purported to record early post-Conquest history but in reality related scandal.

The novel, then, scarcely existed in colonial America. The theatre, the most popular literary genre in seventeenth-century Spain, was in the Americas overwhelmingly devoted to religious themes and was used as an instrument of indoctrination. Though some secular drama was performed, it is significant that America's most talented dramatist, Ruiz de Alarcón, earned his reputation in Spain and lived in that country for most of his adult life. Poetry, less restricted by censorship and the demands of the public, was the most flourishing of the genres. Juan de Castellanos (1522-1607) in New Granada, Bernardo de Balbuena (1568-1627) in Mexico, and Francisco Terrazas (1525?-1600?), also of Mexico, are representative of the competent but minor poets of the period. Bernardo de Balbuena wrote pastoral poetry in imitation of Theocritus and Virgil; composed an epic poem, *Bernardo* (1624), in imitation of Ariosto; and another poem, *La grandeza mexicana* (1604), which was a celebration of the Spanish Empire on which the sun never set. Here there is certainly no suggestion that untrammelled nature and the noble savage are superior to civilisation. Spain's glory is to have brought her institutions and pomp to the New World:

> Y admírase el teatro de Fortuna
> Pues no ha cien años que miraba en esto
> Chozas humildes, lamas y laguna;
> Y sin quedar terrón antiguo enhiesto,
> De su primer cimiento renovada
> Esta grandeza y maravilla ha puesto.

To write lyric poetry was the common courtly accomplishment throughout the colonial period. To write an epic was to raise one's claims. Yet the outstanding American epic was written not by a creole[6] but by a Spaniard, Alonso de Ercilla y Zúñiga (1533-1594), whose *La Araucana* (published in three parts in 1569, 1578, and 1589) was written during the long struggle against the Araucanian Indians of Chile. Perhaps to highlight the courage of the Spaniards, Ercilla emphasised the strength, courage, and nobility of his Indian opponents. Here, for instance, is his description of Caupolicán, the young Indian chief who is acclaimed leader after an ordeal—a theme that was later taken up by the Modernist poet Rubén Darío.[7]

> Era este noble mozo de alto hecho,
> varón de autoridad, grave y severo,
> amigo de guardar todo derecho,
> áspero y riguroso, justiciero;
> de cuerpo grande y relevado pecho,
> hábil, diestro, fortísimo y ligero,
> sabio, astuto, sagaz, determinado,
> y en casos de repente reportado.

In other words, he has all the qualities of the best Spaniard. Translations of *La Araucana* were used by Southey in the Romantic period and inspired European poems on the 'noble savage' theme, as well as Latin American imitations, of which the best known is *Arauco domado* (1596) by Pedro de Oña (1570-1643?), who was born in Chile. Yet the tenor of *La Araucana*, as well as its high style and its conclusion—the conversion of Caupolicán to Christianity before his death—demonstrate that Ercilla, like Balbuena, was more concerned with celebrating Spain's success than with justifying the Indian.

With the exception of *La Araucana* and its imitations, however, the clash of the Old World and the New, and the myths and legends that arose as a result of the struggle, were not to find their way into the conventional literary genres. The epic of the Conquest was composed in other forms—in the logbooks, in the records of discoveries, in letters, chronicles, and histories, even in polemic. The logbooks of Columbus, the *Cartas de relación* of Hernán Cortés, unsophisticated and unshaped by artistic endeavour, describe a leap into the unknown of staggering proportions. Works such as these set the mythopoeic pattern of Latin American literature, in which the themes of the journey and the quest were to predominate. The conquerors became legendary heroes. Cortés in Mexico and Pizarro in Peru faced numerically superior forces and immense natural hazards and therefore took on a magical aura. In the most famous of the chronicles of the Conquest, the *Historia verdadera de la conquista de la Nueva España* (1632) by Bernal Díaz del Castillo (1492-1581?), a soldier in the ranks of Cortés, each gesture and event is an archetype, the original enactment of an American myth. Here we meet Doña Marina, whom the Indians called Malinche and who acted as guide and interpreter, and was mistress of Cortés. Nowadays she is the symbol of the betrayal of the Indians to the Spaniards. Here we meet Moctezuma, vainly trying to buy off the Spaniards with gold but only arousing their greed; and, with Díaz del Castillo, we experience the first sight of a civilisation so fabulous that it can only be compared to the *libros de caballerías*.

> nos quedamos admirados, y decíamos que parecía a las cosas de encantamiento que cuentan en el libro de Amadís, por las grandes torres y cúes[8] y edificios que tenían dentro en el agua, y todos de calicanto, y aun algunos de nuestros soldados decían que si aquello que veían si era entre sueños, y no es de maravillar que yo escriba aquí de esta manera, porque hay mucho que ponderar en ello que no sé como lo cuente; ver cosas nunca oídas, ni aun soñadas, como veíamos.

'Things never heard of nor even dreamed of' fill these records of the Conquest. Never were a group of men so conscious of making history and more than history. Events such as the death of Moctezuma and of his son Cuauhtémoc in Mexico, the betrayal and death of

Atahualpa in Peru, were to become sources of legend and literature almost as fertile as the Trojan wars. And even before they entered the mythology of America, they formed the subject of innumerable plays and stories in seventeenth- and eighteenth-century Europe.[9]

These sixteenth-century chroniclers, men such as Bernal Díaz del Castillo; Pedro Cieza de León (1519 or 22-1560) who wrote of the conquest of Peru; Agustín de Zárate (?-after 1560), author of *Historia del descubrimiento y conquista del Perú* (1555); Gonzalo Jiménez de Quesada (1499-1579), chronicler of the discovery and conquest of New Granada; and Fray Gaspar de Carvajal (1504-84) who first described the Amazon; or Álvar Núñez Cabeza de Vaca (1490?-1559), author of *Naufragios y comentarios*, in which he wrote of his adventures as a captive in the hands of Indians; all these and many others presented an imaginative vision of the New World and in their different ways offered insights into a clash of races and cultures that was hitherto unprecedented.[10]

There was, however, one sixteenth-century writer who dramatised in his life and writings the conflicting elements—indigenous and Hispanic—which were to form Spanish America. This man was the 'Inca' Garcilaso de la Vega (1539-1616), son of an Inca noblewoman and a Spanish *conquistador*, and author of the *Comentarios reales*, an invaluable and moving document of the Inca empire of South America.

In 1560, the Inca left his native Cuzco for Spain, where he was befriended by paternal relatives. The last twenty years of his life were lived in Córdoba. In many ways, he was the typical sixteenth-century man of letters and one of his most important works was the translation into Spanish of the *Dialoghi d'amore* by the neo-Platonist León Hebreo. In 1605, he published *La Florida del Inca*, an account of the adventures of Hernando de Soto, the discoverer of Florida, and one of the first imaginative descriptions of the New World. But it was his *Comentarios reales que tratan del origen de los Incas*, which appeared in 1609 (a second part with the title *Historia general del Perú* was published posthumously in 1617), which was to achieve European renown, providing source material for plays, novels, and works on the noble savage theme.[11]

The *Comentarios reales* describes manners, communications, social and political organisation, intellectual life, and the historical events of the Inca régime. An invaluable record of Inca culture, it included transcriptions of songs and prayers which would otherwise have been lost. The Inca was a conscientious historian and was at pains, in the opening pages of the work, to show how he had come by his specialised knowledge.

Yo nací ocho años después que los españoles ganaron mi tierra, y como lo he dicho, me crié en ella hasta los veinte años, y así vi muchas cosas de las que hacían los indios en aquella su gentilidad, las cuales contaré, diciendo que las vi. Sin la relación que mis parientes me dieron de las cosas dichas y sin lo que yo vi, he habido otras muchas relaciones de las conquistas y hechos de aquellos reyes; porque luego que propuse escribir esta historia, escribí a los condiscípulos de escuela y gramática, encargándoles que cada uno me ayudase con la relación que pudiese haber de las particulares conquistas que los Incas hicieron de las provincias de sus madres.

The Inca was above all concerned with justification, with showing that the Inca empire could be compared with those of Rome and Greece and that its religion was not far removed from monotheism and hence was ripe for the Christian faith. Although he judged the civilisation of his mother's race from the point of view of a man who had acquired the superior outlook of Western Christendom, nevertheless circumstances forced him to be broader in vision than many of his contemporaries. He rejected Latin in favour of the vernacular Spanish when it came to translating Quechua poetry and was not ashamed to declare his ignorance of the classical tongue:

Para los que no entienden indio ni latín, me atreví a traducir los versos en castellano, arrimándome más a la significación de la lengua que mamé en la leche, que no a la ajena latina, porque lo poco que de ella sé lo aprendí en el mayor fuego de las guerras de mi tierra, entre armas y caballos, pólvora y arcabuces, de que supe más que de letras.

It is plain that he is aiming at a public wider than an academic one and that he himself is deeply involved in stressing the glory and achievements of a native Peruvian civilisation which Europeans were all too ready to condemn as pagan and barbaric.

Inadvertently, he helped to tip the balance in another direction, by promoting the myth of the noble savage. For instance, Jean-François Marmontel's well-known novel Les Incas (1777), based largely on material from Garcilaso, was to portray noble, disinterested, if at times misguided, Indians at the mercy of avaricious Spaniards. But whatever its subsequent fortunes, the Inca's work represents the appearance on the literary scene of a totally new human type—the *mestizo*, the man of mixed European and American blood.

Once the Conquest was completed, the intellectual task was not merely one of description, but also that of fitting the variety and strangeness of the New World into acceptable and recognisable forms. Garcilaso, for this reason, never allows the reader to forget that the customs he is describing are similar to customs in Greece and Rome.

Thus, speaking of the Inca attitude to thunder and lightning, he declared: 'Lo mismo sintieron dello que la gentilidad antigua sintió del rayo, que lo tuvo por instrumento y armas de su dios Júpiter'. What the Inca attempted intuitively, others tried scientifically. The most ambitious attempt to confront the new material of America with traditional knowledge was made by the Jesuit Father José de Acosta (1539-1600), author of the *Historia natural y moral de las Indias*. Father Acosta lived in the province of Peru from 1570, the year of his arrival in the New World, and visited Mexico before his return to Spain in 1587. A polymath, thoroughly grounded in the writings of the ancients, he was a man of insatiable curiosity and was devoted to detailed study of the phenomenal world. But above all he was concerned with the problem of matching his experience in the New World to the learning of the ancients with which his Jesuit training had made him familiar. Like Garcilaso, he too stresses the direct knowledge he has of the continent he is describing, grounding himself not on theory, as so many of his contemporaries did, but on careful observation and commonsense deductions. Thus, for instance, he argues that the ancients cannot have discovered the Americas because they had no lodestone and therefore could not have made the journey. He also argues that the American Indians must have arrived in the Americas by way of the Bering Straits. Again and again, he is forced to challenge the authority of Aristotle who, for instance, had maintained that the 'burning zone' near the Equator was not habitable, whereas Father Acosta knew from first-hand experience that it was 'commodious, pleasant, and agreeable'. This reasonable and honest man also upheld the dignity of the indigenous inhabitants of the Americas. He refused to consider them merely as savages, showing that they had government and civilisation, which, had they been known, would have been esteemed as much as those of the ancients. He deplored the greed and haste of the conquerors who destroyed men they could not understand and who treated them as animals:

> ... como sin saber de esto entramos por la espada sin oírles ni entenderles, no nos parece que merecen reputación las cosas de los indios sino como de caza habida en el monte y traída para nuestro servicio y antojo. Los hombres más curiosos y sabios que han penetrado y alcanzado sus secretos, su estilo y gobierno antiguo, muy de otra suerte lo juzgan, maravillándose que hubiese tanto orden y razón entre ellos.

Father Acosta urges the study of Indian culture even if only for political reasons:

> Que demás de ser agravio y sinrazón que se les hace, es en gran daño por tenernos aborrecidos como a hombres que en todo, así en

lo bueno como en lo malo, les somos y hemos siempre sido contrarios.

The *Historia natural* constitutes a thorough revision of knowledge concerning the New World and a re-examination of the writings of the ancients in the light of this knowledge. Through Acosta's work, we can appreciate the great shattering of European intellectual structures that occurred with the discovery of America. However, his sympathy for the Indian and his culture was by no means unusual, for the Jesuits often identified themselves with their converts, and during the years of their missionary activities in the Americas gradually became the apologists of the Indian. Indeed, it is partly from their writings that Rousseau's idea of natural man came to be formed.

The conflict with the metropolitan culture was not only experienced by missionaries, but by all those who were concerned with intellectual exploration. Nobody felt the contradictions more acutely than the major literary figure of the colonial period, the Mexican nun Sor Juana Inés de la Cruz (1648-95). Her position was even more difficult because of the fact that she was a woman and therefore had fewer options open to her. Indeed, there were only two real alternatives—marriage or the Church. At an early age, and after a brief period of service at the viceregal Court in Mexico, she became a nun for reasons which she explained in a letter known as *Respuesta a Sor Filotea de la Cruz* (1691):

> Entréme religiosa, porque aunque conocía que tenía el estado cosas (de las accesorias hablo, no de las formales) muchas repugnantes a mi genio, con todo, para la total negación que tenía al matrimonio, era lo menos desproporcionado y lo más decente que podía elegir en materia de la seguridad que deseaba de mi salvación; a cuyo primer respeto (como al fin más importante) cedieron y sujetaron la cerviz todas las impertinencillas de mi genio, que eran de querer vivir sola, de no querer tener ocupación obligatoria que embarazase la libertad de mi estudio, ni rumor de comunidad que impidiese el sosegado silencio de mis libros.

Her entry into the convent did not bring her complete tranquillity. Throughout her life, the demands of an unquiet intellect led her to try and express her conflicts in every kind of writing—in poetry including *romances*, *redondillas*, *liras*, *silvas*, *villancicos*, meditative poetry (the *Sueño*); in drama—including *sainetes*, *loas*, *autos*, and secular *comedias*; and in religious polemics and prose-writings.

As a poet, she was more intellectual than lyrical. Her poems usually argue a point, her great preoccupation being the extent and limitations of intellectual knowledge. One of her ballads, for instance, has the title 'Acusa la hidropesía de mucha ciencia, que teme inútil aun para saber y nociva para vivir'. The ballad ends:

> Aprendamos a ignorar,
> Pensamiento, pues hallamos
> Que cuanto añado al discurso,
> Tanto le usurpo a los años

—a sentiment that seems to be in contradiction with her own passionate love of the sciences. Her rational outlook extends to her emotions, as the titles of some of her *romances* and *redondillas* show. For instance, in one of her poems she summarises the theme as follows: 'En que describe racionalmente los efectos irracionales del amor'; and another 'Que resuelve con ingenuidad sobre problema entre las instancias de la obligación y del afecto'. The struggle between reason and irrationalism is one of her favourite themes and often represented through an ingenious play of contradictions:

> En dos partes dividida
> tengo el alma en confusión,
> una esclava a la pasión
> y otra a la razón medida.

In other poems, the contradiction is expressed as a dispute between quarrelling lovers or between love rivals—between Fabio and Silvio, or Feliciano and Lisardo.

One of Sor Juana's most ambitious poems, *El Sueño*, aptly illustrates both her genius and her limitations. Although describing the poem as an imitation of Góngora, she lacks the Spanish poet's sensuality and plasticity. Hers is an intellectual approach. In the poem's description of the soul enveloped in sleep, the poet is more concerned with sleep as a physical phenomenon than with the irrational dreamworld of which it is the threshold.

> el cuerpo siendo, en sosegada calma,
> un cadáver con alma,
> muerto a la vida y a la muerte vivo,
> de lo segundo dando tardas señas
> el del reloj humano
> vital volante que, si no con mano,
> con arterial concierto, unas pequeñas
> muestras, pulsando, manifiesta lento
> de su bien regulado movimiento.

Sor Juana's fascination with technical details overrides lyricism and poetic rhythm. She chooses words such as 'reloj', 'vegetativo', 'arterial', 'volante' for their exactness, and there is perhaps more science than poetry in her description of the regulated clockwork of the body.

This is not to undervalue Sor Juana, but rather to marvel at the ingenious way she managed to pursue her intellectual interests despite
the limited options open to her.

She was also a prolific playwright, though she never experimented
beyond the conventions of contemporary Spanish drama. But she
wrote both comedies of intrigue, like the witty and ingenious *Los
empeños de la casa,* and *autos* like *El divino Narciso,* a charming
pastoral which personified Human Nature in its search for salvation.

Sor Juana's great friend, the sharer of her intellectual interests,
was the polymath Carlos Sigüenza y Góngora (1645-1700), whose
writings cover the fields of anthropology, history, mathematics, astron-
omy, contemporary journalism, and poetry. Though he had more
opportunities than Sor Juana to pursue the sciences, he was also
inhibited by living in a colonial society, far from the centres of
advanced learning, and he was destined to be something of a mute
inglorious Newton. Trained as a Jesuit, he left the order and took
up a chair of mathematics, but unlike contemporary British scientists,
whose theoretical work was not pursued in a void, Sigüenza y Góngora found himself working almost alone. To the literary historian,
he is mainly of interest as Mexico's first novelist, author of *Los infortunios de Alonso Ramírez* (1690), rather than for his poetry, which
is on the whole pedestrian.

Both Sor Juana Inés de la Cruz and Sigüenza y Góngora are
examples of writers whose imagination was fettered by their provincial
environment which offered them little scope for their talents. Not
only did they live in areas remote from Spain, but they were dependent on a metropolis whose intellectual life already lagged behind that
of other European countries. Nevertheless, there were positive aspects
of colonial society from which they also benefited. The convent undoubtedly provided the kind of shelter and justification that Sor
Juana needed for her single life and there must have been other
women in her position. In Colombia, for instance, there was a fine
lyric poetess, the Venerable Mother Francisca Josefa del Castillo y
Guevara (1671-1742), who, though less intellectual than her Mexican
counterpart, was more lyrical in her Christian poetry.

The other Viceroyalty, with its capital in Lima, Peru, seemed
even further removed than Mexico from intellectual progress,
although there were periods when the viceregal Court there attained
great pomp and brilliancy. However, in comparison with Mexico,
there is a greater conservatism. The satirical poetry of Juan del Valle
Caviedes (1652?-92) lashes the middle-class upstart doctors. In the
shelter of his convent, Diego de Hojeda (1571-1615) wrote his
Christian epic, *La Christiada* (published 1611), which began with the
Last Supper and ended with the Crucifixion. Often writers in Lima
earned their greatest glory from good imitation rather than origin-

ality. Juan de Espinosa Medrano ('El Lunarejo'; 1632-88) wrote *culterano* prose and published an *Apologético en favor de don Luis de Góngora*. And one of the great figures of colonial Lima, Pedro de Peralta Barnuevo (1663-1743), was far more defensive in the face of the new learning than his Mexican counterparts. He is now chiefly remembered for his epic *Lima fundada* (1732), though he also wrote plays.

The style of the colonial period is often loosely referred to as Baroque because both in the fine arts and literature there was a love of ingenuity of form. However, the use of this term tends to obscure some rather interesting differences between the intellectual life of different centres during the colonial period. Why, for instance, does Mexico produce more unorthodox thinkers than Peru?—men like Fray Servando Teresa de Mier (1765-1827) who would even deny Spain the glory of having brought Christianity to the New World. This is a neglected area of comparative study. Even in the comparatively superficial state of our present knowledge of the colonial period, there are fascinating contrasts between Mexico and Peru.

The exaggeration of Baroque ornament in the churches of Spanish America is often attributed to the influence of Indian craftsmen. In literature, however, there are too few *mestizo* or Indian writers for this to be the case, although both in Mexico and Peru, the subdued Indian race could never be entirely excluded from culture. Both Garcilaso and El Lunarejo were *mestizos*. In Peru, Quechua continued to be spoken and there was a continuous tradition of poetry in that language.[12] A testimony of the vigour of Quechua culture is not only the poems collected by modern scholars, but also the survival of a strange hybrid drama, *Ollantay*, whose structure is Spanish but which was written in Quechua.

Throughout the colonial period in Spanish America, forces were at work which would undermine or come into conflict with the imported culture. The mixture of races, the remoteness of country areas, the different forms of life and social structure—that of the gaucho, for instance—which arose out of the nature of the environment, the concentration of the cultured élite in scattered urban enclaves—all these factors contributed to the creation of two cultures and the persistence of these two cultures down to the present. Urban culture, especially in the major centres, looked towards Europe; its communications were with Europe as much as or more than with its own hinterland. In the countryside older social structures persisted—the feudal *hacienda*, the nomadic tribe, the Jesuit community, the *ayllu* or collective which had its origin in pre-Columban Inca society, the *cacique* or local boss who could raise an army of retainers whenever necessary. Such primitive organisations coexisted with the structures imposed by the Crown and the Council of the Indies, and were not suppressed as long as they did not conflict with the interests of the Empire. And in these areas, literature tended to be as archaic as the social structures. Literature was oral whether it took the form of gaucho ballad or plantation song or country tale. Towards the end of the nineteenth century, in an essay called *Nuestra América*,[13] José Martí was to analyse the two cultures—that of natural man and that of the 'imported book'—and was to urge the intellectual élite to be guided by the former rather than the latter. Even today, the breach is not healed. Spain's empire left an indelible mark both on the physical appearance of the continent, on its towns and buildings, and on its literature. Spanish language and tradition were the foundation of Spanish American literature, but the absorption of American experience and its transmutation into art was a far more daunting task than it first seemed. From the Independence movement onwards, we shall observe how hard was the writer's struggle to free himself from his colonised imagination and how urgent was the quest for authenticity. The quest partly accounts for the importance of the essay. Martí's *Nuestra América*, Sarmiento's *Facundo*, the essays of Alfonso Reyes and Octavio Paz in twentieth-century Mexico, or of Ezequiel Martínez Estrada in the Argentine, represent different stages in that long search for identity which the trauma of Conquest and Colonisation made inevitable.

Cultural dependence was not solely a matter of influences, whether Spanish or French. Dependence was also translated into the myth-structures of Spanish American literature. Created out of the search for El Dorado, Latin America was the object of Europe's expansion. What Europe saw as the unlimited horizon was for Spanish America the closed circle. There was nowhere for *them* to go. Hence, though the journey pattern becomes one of the most common structures of Spanish American literature, the journey tended to be circular or frustrated. In dependent countries progress is cut off, the linear is false, there is a tendency to look backwards to try and find authenticity in a past Golden Age. In this the myth of the Indian was to play an important part. Though his culture was fragmented and broken, in remote areas there was a remarkable persistence of language and belief which the Church itself frequently encouraged. It was the Franciscan Bernardino de Sahagún (1500-90) who salvaged a vast body of Indian lore in his monumental *Historia general de las cosas de la Nueva España*; it was a priest, Father Ximénez, who translated and preserved for posterity the Maya Bible, the *Popol Vuh*. From accidentally preserved remnants such as these, post-Independence writers were to create nostalgias for this other 'innocent' culture untainted by conquest. The frustrated journey, the Golden Age of the Indian, the myth of El Dorado were myths created in the colonial period which were to live on long after Independence. It is in the study of these broader patterns of structure that we can often observe the manner in which the shards of European literature were incorporated into the new artefacts of Spanish American culture.

NOTES

1. There is a succinct chapter on the Church and missions in J. H. Parry, *The Spanish Seaborne Empire* (London, 1966), chapter 8.
2. The controversy is described by L. Hanke, *Aristotle and the American Indians* (London, 1959). See also the same author's *Bartolomé de las Casas. Bookman. Scholar. Propagandist* (Philadelphia, 1949).
3. Pierre-François-Xavier Charlevoix, *Histoire de Paraguay* (Paris, 1756). A more recent and entertaining account of the missions is that of R. B. Cunningham Graham, *A Vanished Arcadia. Being some account of the Jesuits in Paraguay 1607-1767*, rev. ed. (New York, 1924).
4. I. A. Leonard's *Books of the Brave*, 2nd ed. (New York, 1964), gives an account of the importation of books and the evasion of censorship and restrictions.
5. ibid.
6. *Creole* here and elsewhere refers to the American-born people of Spanish descent, as opposed to *mestizo* (part Indian and part Spaniard), Indian, negro, and mulatto.
7. 'Caupolicán' was published in the 1890 edition of Darío's *Azul*.
8. Cués—temple. The word is of Caribbean origin, according to Acosta as quoted by R. H. Humphreys, *Tradition and Revolt* (London, 1965).
9. H. N. Fairchild, *The Noble Savage. A Study in Romantic Naturalism* (New York, 1928). G. Chinard, *Amérique exotique et le rêve exotique dans la littérature française au XVIIe et au XVIIIe siècles* (Paris, 1926).
10. For some account of European attitudes to non-Europeans see E. H. P. Baudet, *Paradise on Earth. Some thoughts on European images of non-European man* (New Haven and London, 1965).
11. Fairchild, op.cit.
12. There are examples of Quechua poetry in J. M. Arguedas, *Poesía quechua* (Buenos Aires, 1966).
13. 'Nuestra América' is included in a selection of Martí's work compiled by J. Torres Bodet, *Nuestra América* (Mexico, 1945).

READING LIST

This chapter is simply an introduction which attracts attention to tendencies in the colonial period which were to affect post-Independence literature. For a more extended study of the colonial literature, see Raimundo Lazo, *Historia de la literatura hispanoamericana, I. 1492-1780* (Mexico, 1965). There is a well-written general survey by Mariano Picón Salas, *A Cultural History of Spanish America from Conquest to Independence* (Berkeley and Los Angeles, 1960). On Mexico, I recommend Irving A. Leonard, *Baroque Times in old Mexico* (Ann Arbor, 1959) which is written with gusto. On Peru, there is an ample discussion of colonial literature in Luis Alberto Sánchez, *La literatura peruana*, 6 vols. (Buenos Aires, 1951). Those interested in pre-Conquest literature can consult two anthologies of poetry: J. M. Arguedas, *Poesía quechua* (Buenos Aires, 1966) and M. A. Asturias, *Poesía precolombina* (Buenos Aires, 1960)

Texts

Acosta, Padre José de, *Obras*. Estudio preliminar y edición del P. Francisco Mateos (Madrid, 1954)

Cabeza de Vaca, Álvar Núñez, *Naufragios y comentarios*, 4th ed., Colección Austral (Buenos Aires, 1957)

De las Casas, Bartolomé, *Tratados* (Mexico, 1966)

Díaz del Castillo, Bernal, *Historia verdadera de la conquista de la Nueva España* (Mexico, 1960)

Ercilla, Alonso de, *La Araucana* (Santiago de Chile, 1956)

Garcilaso de la Vega, 'El Inca', *Comentarios reales*, 6th ed., Colección Austral (Buenos Aires, 1961)

Juana Inés de la Cruz, Sor, *Obras completas*, 4 vols. (Mexico, 1962)

——, *Poesía, teatro y prosa*, ed. Antonio Castro Leal (Mexico, 1944)

——, *Antología*, ed. Elias L. Rivers (Salamanca, 1965)

Sigüenza y Góngora, Carlos de, *Los Infortunios de Alonso Ramírez*. In the anthology *La novela de México colonial*, ed. Antonio Castro, 2 vols. (Mexico, 1964)

Some poetry of the colonial period is included in the anthology compiled by Marcelino Menéndez y Pelayo, *Antología de poesía hispanoamericana* (Madrid, 1893-95)

Historical material and critical texts on separate authors

Garibay, A. M., *La literatura de los aztecas* (Mexico, 1964)

Hanke, Lewis, *The Spanish Struggle for Justice in the Conquest of America* (Philadelphia, 1949)

Kirkpatrick, F. A., *Los conquistadores españoles*, 7th ed., Colección Austral (Buenos Aires, 1960)

León-Portilla, Miguel, *The Broken Spears. The Aztec Account of the Conquest of Mexico* (London, 1962)

Parry, J. H., *The Spanish Seaborne Empire* (London, 1966)

Paz, Octavio, 'Sor Juana Inés de la Cruz' in *Las peras del olmo* (Mexico, 1957)

Pfandl, Ludwig, *Sor Juana Inés de la Cruz, La Décima Musa de México* (Mexico, 1963)

Roggiano, A., 'Momentos de la poesía en los primeros centros culturales de la colonia', *En este aire de América*, primera serie (Mexico, 1966)

Wolf, Eric R., *Sons of the Shaking Earth* (Chicago, 1959)

Chapter 1

INDEPENDENCE AND LITERATURE

'Pocas veces ha presentado el mundo un teatro igual al nuestro para former una constitución que haga felices a los pueblos'
(Mariano Moreno)

1. THE FIRST STEPS

THE BREATH OF INDEPENDENCE was felt in Spanish America before the republics were emancipated from Spanish rule. In the eighteenth century, there was already an awareness of separate destiny from that of Spain, and this awareness was reflected, though fitfully, in colonial culture. This new spirit did not come into existence spontaneously. Spain herself was undergoing change. Charles III, believing that the Church was an obstacle to progress, initiated an attack on church privilege and in 1767 had the Jesuits expelled from Spain and the Spanish colonies. With the Jesuits went one of the supports of colonial society, for not only did they hold vast territories in South America, but they were also the most active educationalists and missionaries. Their expulsion converted them into the opponents of Spain and their powerful propaganda was directed against colonial rule and monarchy as an institution. Paradoxically, the period in which colonial power was brought into question was also one in which the viceregal Courts, especially in Lima, attained great splendour. Lima during the viceregency of Amat (1761-65) was a splendid society of theatres, café life, allegorical spectacles, and bull-fights.

It is often the case that a period of reform, by raising expectation, increases the chance of more violent revolution. In eighteenth-century Spanish America, there were several uprisings against the Spanish Crown, like the famous rebellion of the Indian Tupac Amaru in Peru, a rebellion crushed with savage ferocity in 1781. And as soon as the social and political structures weakened, the repressive machinery began to function more savagely. The Inquisition, never as efficient in the colonies as in Spain, increased its activities and directed its attentions to the Jesuits and to forbidden books, especially

16

the works of Rousseau and Voltaire, which might foster scepticism or rebellion. The colonists, at the very moment when they were eagerly seeking new ideas, were more exposed to danger for embracing them. In such a period of transition, imaginative literature was least in men's minds. The tract, the lampoon, and the newspaper, the first examples of which appeared in the colonies in the later part of the century, provided a more direct outlet for criticism and the expression of grievances. One of the favourite ways of attacking the Spanish government, however, was by means of the *pasquín*, a lampoon pinned to the door of a public building or some other prominent place. Here, for instance, is one which appeared in Cuzco:

> Ya en el Cuzco con empeño
> quieren sacudir, y es ley,
> el yugo del ajeno Rey
> y coronar al que es dueño.
>
> Levantarse americanos!
> tomen armas en las manos
> y con osado furor,
> maten, maten sin temor
> a los ministros tiranos.[1]

The Spanish officials made a determined attempt to stamp out such subversive ideas and in 1782, after the rebellion of Tupac Amaru, they prohibited Garcilaso's *Comentarios reales*, presumably because the book roused dangerous feelings of pride in a pre-colonial past. On the other hand, the Inquisition was increasingly impotent against the march of science. An attempt to bring the naturalist José Celestino Mutis (Colombia; 1732-1808) to book for believing in the Copernican system failed. Moreover, increased travel between Europe and the colonies made the suppression of new ideas impossible. News of the North American colonies' emancipation or of the French Revolution could not simply be suppressed and an increasing number of creoles who visited Europe acted as carriers of the revolutionary ideas. The wandering revolutionary is characteristic of the period, men like Fray Servando Teresa de Mier (1765-1827), whose hatred of the Spaniards was carried to such lengths that he declared that they had not brought the gospel to the Americas, but that this had already been known in pre-colonial times, having been introduced by Saint Thomas. In 1794, after a sermon in which he preached this doctrine, he was forced to flee from Mexico. His turbulent life was recorded in his *Memorias*. More directly influential in the Independence movement was the Venezuelan Francisco Miranda (1750-1816), the indefatigable traveller who visited Russia and the Courts of Europe to find support for the Independence struggle and who was to die in a Spanish prison.

Just as important were the European travellers who now began to arrive in the former Spanish colonies insatiably curious about a region which the Spaniards had so effectively insulated from the rest of the world. The most famous of these was Alexander von Humboldt, a German philosopher who brought scientific rigour to his observation of the peoples, the flora, fauna, and geology of the continent, and who revealed the vast untapped resources. His *Voyages* (1814-29) confirmed the opinion of many creoles that Spain had failed to make use of the continent's potential and, having failed, should retire from the scene leaving the land in the hands of those with an interest in its development.[2]

Economic frustration was probably the major cause of creole discontent at the end of the eighteenth century and was aggravated by their awareness of the expansion enjoyed in North America after Independence. But the ideology of emancipation came from Europe and was inspired by the *Social Contract* of Rousseau and the ideas of Montesquieu. Rousseau's concept of a General Will and Montesquieu's 'spirit of the law' invested both power and institutions elsewhere than in monarchy and metropolis.

Nevertheless, Independence when it came was precipitated by outside events. The French Revolutionary War, Napoleon's invasion of Spain, the free *Cortes* of Cádiz which met in 1812 and proclaimed a liberal constitution, and the liberal revolution against Fernando VII in 1820, each of these events had its repercussion on some stage of the Independence struggle, which, however, was more protracted in some parts of the Spanish Empire than in others. Achieved with little difficulty in the Plate region, Independence came as the result of a long and bitter struggle in Venezuela and the Andean region.

The Wars of Independence began in curious circumstances. In 1806, during the Napoleonic War, a British fleet was encouraged to sail to Argentina from South Africa and to attempt the invasion of the hemisphere. The invasion was repelled by the colonists, who gained self-confidence in the fight. But it was Napoleon's invasion of Spain and the Spaniards' struggle against the French which had the most far-reaching results, for once the legitimate monarch had been overthrown, America's legal bond was also dissolved. The cities of Caracas and Buenos Aires immediately threw off royal rule. In 1811 Venezuelan Independence was declared, but the Spaniards defended the territory, and in 1812 Simón Bolívar, leader of the Independence army, was forced to retire from the field. He returned in 1814, was again defeated, and was successful only on a third expedition which from 1816 operated from a base in Angostura and gradually conquered New Granada (now Colombia) and Venezuela.

The Argentine *coup* was more successful, for the Spaniards were not so interested in defending the undeveloped territory. From this

centre, the liberation of the southern part of the continent under the
leadership of José de San Martín (1778-1850), the most upright of
leaders, was planned. The whole of Spanish America was virtually
liberated when Bolívar destroyed the last major Spanish resistance in
Peru at the battle of Ayacucho in 1824.

Mexican emancipation followed a somewhat different course. Here
there had been a social revolution in 1810 when a priest of Dolores,
Miguel Hidalgo, led a ragged force of Indians against the Spaniards,
was captured, and executed. Hidalgo was defeated by the creole con-
servatives as well as by the Spaniards, and when Mexican Independence was finally achieved, it was as a result of a conservative *coup* led
by Iturbide who had himself crowned emperor.

The Independence movement had thus many different facets—
conservative in Mexico, liberal in the Plate region where men like
Mariano Moreno (1778-1811) represented the most enlightened thinking on democracy and race. In his introduction to an edition of the
Social Contract, Moreno paid tribute to the immortal Rousseau:

> ... quizá el primero, que disipando completamente las tinieblas,
> con que el despotismo envolvía usurpaciones, puso en clara luz
> los derechos de los pueblos, y enseñándoles el verdadero origen
> de sus obligaciones, demostró las que correlativamente contraían
> los depositarios del gobierno.

Moreno's words express the highest hopes of the ex-colonists, that
of forming a new type of society based on the reason and justice of
Rousseauesque man.

As has already been indicated, the period of Independence was
not a period of great literature: nevertheless, there appeared works
whose authors showed a new consciousness of environment, works
which were not directly imitative of European fashion. One of these
was by a Spaniard, an official of the colonial bureaucracy who lived in
Lima. This was Alonso Carrió de la Vandera (*c.* 1715- after 1778),
who was first *corregidor* then an inspector of posts in Peru. Under
the pseudonym Concolorcorvo he wrote a guide for travellers, *El
lazarillo de ciegos caminantes* (Lima, 1776) which was first published
with the false date of 1773 and a false place of publication (Gijón,
Spain). Why the subterfuge? It was simply that his travel guide
included some explosive sentiments about certain aspects of Spanish
rule and the author thought to dispel criticism by putting the controversial opinions in the mouth of an anonymous traveller who until
recent years was invariably identified with the Indian Don Calixto
Bustamante who was Carrió de la Vandera's travelling companion.[3]

Carrió de la Vandera did not simply set out to give people information about travelling conditions on the long and difficult road from
Buenos Aires to Lima, although this was necessary enough. He also

wished to make the point that the inhabitants of the New World would do better to study their own land rather than to worry so much about what was going on in Europe. The guidebook was one of the first works by a Latin American writer to survey populations of towns, customs of inhabitants, and to describe actual conditions on the road. This for instance is Concolorcorvo's account of the routine of travel:

> A las cuatro de la tarde se da principio a caminar y se para segunda vez el tiempo suficiente para hacer la cena, porque en caso de estar la noche clara y el camino sin estorbos, vuelven a uncir a las once de la noche y se camina hasta el amanecer, y mientras se remudan los bueyes hay lugar para desayunarse con chocolate, mate o alguna fritanguilla ligera para los aficionados a aforrarse más sólidamente porque a la hora se vuelve a caminar hasta las diez del día. Los poltrones se mantienen en el carretón o carreta con las ventanas y puerta abiertas, leyendo u observando la calidad del camino y demás que se presenta a la vista. Los alentados y más curiosos montan a caballo y se adelantan o atrasan a su arbitrio.

The guidebook includes one of the first descriptions of the *gauderíos* or gauchos of Montevideo and the surrounding countryside. Like all subsequent observers, Concolorcorvo is impressed by the freedom and lack of conventionality of the life they lead as they ride from one ranch to another, eating at the host's table and then departing to the next ranch. But he is impressed too by their skill at catching horses with the 'bolas', the leather-bound stones on thong ropes which formed one of the principal weapons of the gaucho.

> Si pierden el caballo o se lo roban, les dan otro o lo toman de la campaña enlazándolo con un cabestro muy largo que llaman *rosario*. También cargan otro, con dos bolas en los extremos del tamaño de las regulares con que se juega a los trucos, que muchas veces son de piedra que forran de cuero, para que el caballo se enrede en ellas, como asimismo en otras que llaman ramales, porque se componen de tres bolas, con que muchas veces lastiman los caballos, que no quedan de servicio, estimando este servicio en nada, así ellos como los dueños.

Here we have the carefree creole life, a subject of embarrassment to nineteenth-century authors who saw it as an obstacle to progress. Concolorcorvo, however, still identified himself with the Spaniard as against the indigenous inhabitants of the New World and the negro. He draws a distinction between the civilised Indians living under the dominion of the Spaniards and the wild nomadic pampa Indians who can only be conquered by being outnumbered.

> Lo cierto es que no hay otro medio con los indios bárbaros que el de la defensiva e irlos estrechando por medio de nuestra multiplicación.

The negro is more 'grosero' than the Indian:

> Su canto es un aúllo. De ver sólo los instrumentos de su música se inferirá lo desagradable de su sonido.

and their dances positively indecent:

> ... se reducen a menear la barriga y las caderas con mucha deshonestidad, a que acompañan con gestos ridículos, y que traen a la imaginación la fiesta que hacen al diablo los brujos en sus sábados.

Carrió de la Vandera, therefore, while urging a closer study of the people and the environment in which the Spanish American lived, betrayed the limitations of the imperial mentality. All that surpassed his understanding was the work of the devil. *El lazarillo de ciegos caminantes* is ultimately concerned more with the efficient working of the colonial empire than with criticising its foundations.

Northrop Frye, the literary critic, remarks that 'Literary shape cannot come from life; it comes only from literary tradition, and so ultimately from myth'. In a colonised society, as we have seen, this literary tradition is imposed from without. The myths are alien. Eighteenth-century Europe projected onto the Americas two contradictory myths—that of Utopia inhabited by noble savages and the contrary myth, that of inferior peoples who must be civilised.[4] The Utopia myth implies a literary structure of quest, of search, and it is significant that one of Spanish America's first original literary works is a picaresque novel in which the quest for Utopia is one of the themes. This novel is *El Periquillo Sarniento* (1816) by the Mexican writer José Joaquín Fernández de Lizardi (1776-1827). Generally regarded as the first Latin American novelist,[5] he was the son of a doctor, and largely self-taught. He supported Hidalgo's premature independence uprising and in 1812 founded a journal, *El Pensador Mexicano* (1812-14), devoted to the revolutionary cause. The failure of the independence movement brought increased repression to Mexico and Fernández de Lizardi was several times imprisoned for his outspoken views. Perhaps for this reason, he turned to the novel, seeing this as a method of criticising the government without falling under the immediate displeasure of the censorship. It is indeed significant that all his novels, from *El Periquillo Sarniento* to *La Quijotita y su prima* (1819) and the posthumously published *Don Catrín de la Fachenda*, were written before censorship was lifted and before Independence. After Independence, Fernández de Lizardi turned to what appeared to be his preferred medium—the press. He became editor of the government paper, *La Gaceta del Gobierno*, and in 1826 founded his own journal, *Correo Semanario*.

Fernández de Lizardi's novels reflect the new values of a middle-class, underprivileged creole and criticise those of the coloniser. These values are presented within the structure of the picaresque, a genre which the author borrowed from Spain and which was traditionally concerned with the adventures of low-life characters parasitic on society. Generally too, the picaresque novel is a story of downfall and repentance. Fernández de Lizardi borrowed the structure and placed the hero's downfall within the framework of the colonial institutions—Church, monasteries, law courts, army, and university. In *El Periquillo Sarniento*, the title of the novel refers to the hero's nickname and means, literally, 'The Itching Parrot', a graphic symbol of the parroting or imitation which was the chief weakness of a colonised society. The hero is essentially a victim of the colonial system, and his over-indulgent but wrong-headed family is an exact symbol of the indulgent paternalistic administration.

Father and mother are humble citizens, unable to give the youth an income, only able to offer him education and advice. The schools he attends are either too strict or too lenient and there is an aristocratic prejudice against teaching trades or useful knowledge. Moreover, an indulgent and permissive mother prevails against a more realistic father so that the child is sent to university rather than apprenticed to a tradesman. University education teaches him nothing and he emerges with a degree and no more knowledge of sciences than the most superstitious of his fellow-countrymen. When his father dies, he finds that he has no place in society, for he has not inherited wealth. Only the monastic orders, the army, or the priesthood are open to a man without a profession. He tries the first, but has not the necessary discipline to stand its austerity. He ruins his mother, who dies in poverty, and then sinks rapidly to the lower ranks of society, becoming a gambler, a quack doctor, sexton, a government official, and an army recruit. With the army he leaves for the Philippine Islands and on his return finds himself shipwrecked on an island where men have found the secret of good government. None of these experiences really reforms him and he finally almost comes to grief as a member of a bandit gang, only finding time to repent shortly before his death.

The plot and the characterisation of *El Periquillo Sarniento* are clumsy by modern standards, but the novel is not simply to be evaluated on these grounds. Fernández de Lizardi gives an extremely vivid picture of all aspects of colonial society. His apostrophes, his declaration of intentions, his haranguing of the reader are frequently tedious, as is his constant appeal to classical authors for support even on comparatively trivial matters.

As against this, Fernández de Lizardi has real merits. He shows us what it was to go to school in colonial Mexico, what the insides of monasteries and prisons and hospitals were like. Even the language and jokes of the period are faithfully recorded. Here, for instance, is his description of the gamblers' breakfast:

> Por ahora sábete que hacer la mañana entre esta gente quiere decir desayunarse con aguardiente, pues están reñidos con el chocolate y el café, y más bien gastan un real o dos a estas horas en *chinguirito* malo[6] que en un pocillo del más rico chocolate.

This has the ring of authenticity, as does his description of the over-crowded hospitals:

> A otro día me despertaron los enfermeros con mi *atole*[7] que no dejé de tomar con mas apetencia ... a poco rato entró el médico a hacer la visita acompañado de sus aprendices. Habíamos en la sala como setenta enfermos, y con todo eso no duró la visita quince minutos. Pasaba toda la cuadrilla por cada cama, y apenas tocaba el médico el pulso al enfermo, como si fuera ascua ardiendo, lo soltaba al instante, y seguía a hacer la misma diligencia con los demás, ordenando los medicamentos según era el número de la cama.

Every aspect of colonial society is equally corrupt. The notary regards the law not as a set of rules to be observed but as 'antiguallas'. The apothecary is in collusion with the doctor to exploit the patients, and drugs are watered or improperly dispensed. Monks go to feasts, and dances, the sacristan robs the dead. Beggars prey on the Catholic obligation to give charity and learn how to cheat and counterfeit sickness and lameness in their beggars' school.

But Fernández de Lizardi is not content with depicting abuses. His novel must show the path to enlightenment, and little by little a coherent and reasoned programme of reform emerges. Naturally enough, the author could not openly denounce the Spaniards as the main cause of disaster, but he could express his belief in the self-determination of nations. Interestingly, he expressed this by putting his opinions in the mouth of a negro, a man whom Periquillo meets in the Philippines and who argues that, since each nation is peculiar and distinct, all have an equal right to develop the institutions and laws proper to them. Discrimination, says the black man, has its roots in 'la altanería de los blancos y ésta consiste en creerlos inferiores por su naturaleza, lo que, como dije, es una vieja e irracional pre-ocupación'. Thus at one blow, the author exposes the irrational nature of discrimination and by extension shows that Latin American societies ought not to be considered inferior to those of Europe. The negro's impassioned outburst is also an attack on Europeo-centralism.

Luego, si cada religión tiene sus ritos, cada nación sus leyes y cada provincia sus costumbres, es un error crasísimo el calificar de necios y salvajes a cuantos no coinciden con nuestro modo de pensar, aun cuando éste sea el mas ajustado a la naturaleza.

The conclusion of the negro's outburst is a triumphant vindication of human dignity:

De lo dicho, se debe deducir: que despreciar a los negros por su color y por la diferencia de su religión y costumbres es un error; el maltratarlos por ellos, crueldad; y el persuadirse a que no son capaces de tener almas grandes que sepan cultivar las virtudes morales, es una preocupación demasiado crasa.

The Indians, among whom El Periquillo works for a time as a quack doctor and later as a government official, are equally outspoken against the abuses practised on them. The village which suffers from his lack of medical knowledge eventually expels him, whilst that in which he cheats when acting as an official sends a delegation to Mexico to complain against exploitation. It is little wonder that the last book of *El Periquillo Sarniento* could not be published in its author's lifetime. Not only does it include the inflammatory views of the black man but also the author's picture of an ideal society. In the tradition of the eighteenth-century Utopian novel, so popular in Europe, El Periquillo is shipwrecked and finds himself on an island. Having learned the language of the inhabitants, he learns that it is an island on which everybody works. Here there is no idle aristocracy, and education is empirical in method. Laws are understandable to everyone and are rigorously applied. Thus Periquillo's Utopia is a bourgeois democracy based on hard work and application, and therefore quite different from the parasitic aristocratic society of colonised Mexico.

Fernández de Lizardi was to take up the theme of decadent aristocracy in a novel, *Don Catrín de la Fachenda*, which was not published during his lifetime. Don Catrín is the epitome of the colonised mentality, a vain nobleman who despises work and thinks the army the only suitable career for a gentleman. But he enters into a peacetime army where battles are fought in taverns and around gaming tables. This is Don Catrín's ideal:

En pocos días me dediqué a ser marcial, a divertirme con malas hembras y los naipes a no dejarme sobajar de nadie, fuera quien fuera, a hablar con libertad sobre asuntos de estado y de religión, a hacerme de dinero a toda costa y a otras cosas como éstas, que en realidad son utilísimas a todo militar como yo.

We see here the birth of the *macho* idea so important in Mexican literature and which is really the survival of feudal virtues of valour and audacity carried over into situations where they no longer have the same meaning. Don Catrín, like Periquillo, sinks to the bottom strata of colonial society but his fate is even more tragic, for he neither glimpses Utopia nor is he given time to repent. He commits suicide.

Fernández de Lizardi wrote one novel on what was for the period the unusual theme of the education of women. *La Quijotita y su prima* (1818) exposed the unhappy consequences of educating women only for marriage and society.

Fernández de Lizardi represents the most liberal wing of Independence thinking. He advocated equal rights for all regardless of colour; the establishment of a *Cortes* (or parliament) to represent all classes; the enfranchisement of women; and complete religious freedom. For this latter principle, he was in trouble even after Independence, for he was excommunicated after publishing *Defensa de los Francmasones* in 1822 and was kept under house arrest. He made a characteristic defence in which he proudly declared that he was a poor man who had not inherited any wealth and had not committed any crime in order to escape from his poverty; he had simply wished that 'el monopolio, el lujo, y la simonía sean desterrados de la iglesia católica'.

He was an ardent advocate of personal freedom and of freedom of the press, and criticised Mexico because he believed that the poverty of the inhabitants was a threat to liberty.

He saw small hope for the Indians except through the paternalistic rule of an enlightened middle class who would help to educate them. He stood for a bourgeois ideal of progress and for bourgeois values.

His novels are an early example in Spanish America of the novelistic quest for authenticity which was to become one of the most important aspects of Spanish American literature, though what makes his novels still readable is the detail and humour with which he deploys his material. Periquillo is a far more vivid character than the anguished eponymous hero of *La peregrinación de Bayoán* (1863) by the Puerto Rican Eugenio María de Hostos (1839-1903) who also sets out in search of Independence, or the restless hero of *El cristiano errante* (1847) by the Guatemalan Juan Bautista de Irisarri (1785-1868).

Fernández de Lizardi is the most considerable literary talent of the Independence period if we confine 'literature' to the conventional genres of novel, drama, and poetry; but there was also immense journalistic and epistolary activity. Bolívar's letters, the articles of the Ecuadorian thinker Francisco Eugenio de Santa Cruz y Espejo (1747-95), can legitimately be considered as early works of literary independence.[8]

Poetry was the genre most dependent on foreign fashions and poets in the neo-classical tradition will be considered in a separate chapter. But, even here, the Independence period provides some interesting attempts to strike out in new directions. In the Plate region, for instance, the gauchesque genre sprang out of the Independence wars. Probably invented by Bartolomé Hidalgo (1788-1822), who was born of humble parents in Montevideo, the gauchesque genre drew on folk-ballads and songs such as the *cielito* and converted them into satirical poems. Hidalgo wrote *Diálogos* in which two men speaking in gaucho dialect discussed in verse the events of the time, bitterly criticising abuses and injustice. They represent an authentic creole voice.

In Peru, one Independence poet turned to Indian tradition in his search for new forms. This was Mariano Melgar (1791-1815) who, in his brief life, abandoned the priesthood, took part in the struggle against the Spaniards, and was executed on the field of battle, at Umachiri. He wrote poems in the form of the Indian song, the *yaraví*, of which the following love poem is an example.

> Vuelve, que ya no puedo
> vivir sin tus caricias,
> vuelve, mi palomita,
> vuelve a tu dulce nido.
>
> Mira que hay cazadores,
> que, con afán maligno,
> te pondrán en sus redes
> mortales atractivos;
> Y, cuando te hayan preso,
> te darán cruel martirio;
> no sea que te cacen;
> huye tanto peligro,
> vuelve, mi palomita,
> vuelve a tu dulce nido.

Melgar, who was of mixed blood, was not simply using the *yaraví* as a picturesque verse form. Like many writers of the period, he realised that the Indian was oppressed, and in one of his verse fables, 'El cantero y el asno', he drew a parallel between the ass who is brutalised by beating and the Indian. Both appear stupid because they have been stunned into this state.

Fernández de Lizardi, Melgar, and Mariano Moreno are examples of some of the most enlightened thinking of the Independence period. We find similar liberal aspirations in many of the letters of Bolívar who, however, saw something that many of his contemporaries missed —the fact that the newly-independent republics had inherited not freedom to march towards a glorious future but a chaos of conflicting forces which would prevent them from moving at all.[9]

II. THE NEED FOR STANDARDS

Between 1810 and 1830, most of the modern Latin American republics came into being. Though their boundaries often coincided with those of the captain-generalcies of the colonial period, their existence as separate nations had no precedent. Having rejected Spain and Spanish tradition, they must start from new beginnings. The first area to emerge as an independent state was Argentina and its first name—the United Provinces of the Río de la Plata—indicated the loose federal nature of the new republic. One of its provinces, Paraguay, was itself to become a separate state and the eastern part of the republic, known as the Banda Oriental, was occupied for some years by Brazil and emerged after the occupation as the independent republic of Uruguay. A similar process of fragmentation was to divide Chile from Peru, Colombia from Venezuela. The provinces of Central America, which had formed a Central American Union which lasted until 1839, separated into the states of Guatemala, Nicaragua, Honduras, El Salvador, and Costa Rica.

The dream of democracy, like the dream of federation, was soon shattered. The leaders of the Independence movement—Bernardo O'Higgins in Chile, Antonio José de Sucre in Bolivia, Dr Francia (José Gaspar Rodríguez) in Paraguay, Agustín de Iturbide in Mexico, and Simón Bolívar in New Granada tended to take over the direction of the new states and almost invariably became autocrats. Elected parliaments and democratic machinery could not be created overnight, and in those countries where representative government functioned, it often became farcical. The very nature of the Spanish empire had restricted the political expression of the creole. When Spanish structures were destroyed, all that was left were powerful local interests with no central scaffolding. Thus was formed the pattern that was to prevail in most Spanish American countries until well into the twentieth century—the threat of anarchy, the restoration of order by a strong *caudillo* who exploited the state for his personal ends, and during those periods when no *caudillo* emerged, the instability of governments which, even when legally elected, fell quickly at the first *coup d'état*. Iturbide and Antonio López de Santa Ana in Mexico, General Rosas in Argentina, Dr Francia in Paraguay, General Páez in Venezuela, General Sucre in Bolivia, and O'Higgins in Chile—these were the new men who took over the states and ruled them with a strong arm, while intellectuals such as Andrés Bello, Esteban Echeverría, Domingo Sarmiento, Juan Bautista Irisarri found it difficult or impossible to get their rational projects accepted.[10]

Within a decade of Independence, the intellectuals of Latin America were forced to ask themselves one question. Why the failure? The answers they offered were diverse but tended to fall into two main categories—the lack of tradition; and economic and political backwardness inherited from the years under Spanish rule. In this chapter, we shall be concerned with the first of these answers, with the attempt to establish traditions where none had hitherto existed except the hated tradition of Spanish rule.

In considering the question of tradition, we should bear in mind that the creation of the Latin American republics coincided with the period of Romanticism in Europe and that the intellectuals of the continent were profoundly affected by Romantic assumptions. Romantic aesthetic theory had replaced the old idea of 'schools' of literature with the more dynamic idea of literary 'movements'. Writers such as the Schlegels had shown that nations passed through stages of culture, the classical stage being succeeded by a Romantic period. Even where writers were not necessarily influenced directly by such theories, there does seem to have been an assumption that humanist standards must be created in order to provide models, much as classical culture had provided models for Europe. Disillusioned with the Church, most Latin American intellectuals of the nineteenth century believed that a humanist code could be established which would serve as a moral guide, and some of the prominent writers concerned themselves precisely with this—Andrés Bello, Juan Montalvo of Ecuador, down to José Enrique Rodó of Uruguay, whose work was influential well into the twentieth century.[11] Characteristic of this tendency is Andrés Bello who, writing in *El Repertorio Americano*, a magazine published in London in 1826-27, defined the task of the new generation of intellectuals as:

> hacer germinar la semilla fecunda de la libertad, destruyendo las preocupaciones vergonzantes con que se le alimentó desde la infancia; establecer el culto de la moral; conservar los nombres y las condiciones que figuran en nuestra historia, asignándoles un lugar en la memoria del tiempo; he aquí la tarea noble, pero vasta y difícil, que nos ha impuesto el amor de la patria.

Bello was an admirer of Herder, and was anything but a stuffy imitator of classical literature, yet because he felt that the new nations needed a humanist moral code, his work has an archaic ring about it. As we shall see, he is characteristic of the contradictory directions that Romantic influence took in Latin America.[12]

Classical writers formed the most obvious model for this moral literature, partly because most intellectuals had received their early education almost entirely in the classics. There was, however, another problem which faced writers: the absence of any sense of nationality in countries of such recent origin. Here again, Romanticism offered a solution. The historical novel was in vogue and was regarded by many writers as the ideal instrument for creating a sense of national pride.[13] Thus Bartolomé Mitre, the Argentine writer and politician (1821-1906), in the introduction to his novel *Soledad* (1847) writes:

> La novela popularizaría nuestra historia echando mano de los sucesos de la conquista, de la época colonial, y de los recuerdos de la guerra de independencia.

Moralising poetry and the historical novel, then, are two instruments through which post-Independence writers tried to set standards and create traditions in the intellectual vacuum that followed the expulsion of the Spaniards.

III. THE LESSONS OF POETRY

Andrés Bello (1781-1865) is a writer whose work faithfully reflects the ideals of the Independence period. A polymath, he wrote books on international law, geography, on grammar and spelling, and was author of a history of Venezuela.

He was born in Venezuela and spent his early years in that country, where he became a disciple of Humboldt, and read Rousseau as well as classical authors. His father was a civil servant and his formative years were spent under the guidance of a tutor, Fray Cristóbal de Quesada, an outstanding Latin scholar. He was far from sharing the hatred of many of his contemporaries for Spain and appreciated the civilising role of the mother country in the New World. Yet when the *cabildo* of Caracas proclaimed independence, Bello was sent to London on a diplomatic mission on behalf of the junta and therefore remained in the British capital until 1829. In London Bello lived by teaching and by doing secretarial work, and he also founded two literary journals, *La Biblioteca Americana* (1824) and *El Repertorio Americano* (1825-27). It was during this period that he published two major poems, *Alocución a la poesía* and *La agricultura de la zona tórrida*. In 1829, he left for Chile, on the invitation of the government, and there threw himself into the task of educating the new élite. He became director of the *Instituto Nacional*, published his *Principios de Derecho de Gentes* and his *Ortología y métrica de la lengua castellana* (1835), and in this way made a practical contribution to what he saw as the major task of the leaders of the young republic—that of raising educational standards and establishing the rule of law. He tried to encourage the study of the natural sciences and urged that doctors be held in higher esteem. However, the work for which he is probably most famous in the Spanish-speaking world is his *Gramática de la lengua castellana destinada al uso de los americanos* (1847), a pioneer work destined not to sever American

Spanish from Peninsular Spanish but rather to create a common standard. He was one of the first of many writers to see that a general literary Spanish could act as an important cohesive factor, a spiritual tie of the Hispanic peoples. But there was little that did not come to the attention of this indefatigable man—the condition of prisoners, the situation of solicitors, the protection and encouragement of the theatre. For many years a member of the Chilean Senate, he helped to draw up legislation on weights and measures and other matters, and also to draw up a civic code. In 1843, when the University of Chile was founded, he helped to draw up the statutes and he became its first Rector.

Although, while in Chile, Bello became involved in a polemic over Romanticism and took sides against some of the more enthusiastic supporters of that movement, he denied that art was to be found

en los preceptos estériles de la escuela, en las inexorables unidades, en la muralla de bronce entre los diferentes estilos i jéneros, en las cadenas con que se ha querido aprisionar al poeta a nombre de Aristóteles i Horacio.[14]

Recent criticism has destroyed the over-simple classification of Bello as a 'neo-classicist' totally opposed to Romanticism. In London he came to know the poetry of the Romantic movement and was one of the first Spanish Americans to do so. His reading of Romantic authors was wide and according to at least one critic his attitude was dictated by discrimination, not by hostility.[15] Even so, an examination of his poetry reveals the structures of earlier rhetoric and his preferred subject is the ancient theme of the goodness of nature and the corruptibility of man.

Alocución a la poesía is an invocation to the muse of poetry which he invites to leave the Courts of Europe and to settle in America. Europe has been invaded by utilitarian philosophy and is threatened by a decline in values:

donde la libertad vano delirio,
fe la servilidad, grandeza el fasto,
la corrupción cultura es apellida.

But in America, virgin Nature still reigns. Writing in the gloom of London, Bello's descriptions of his native Venezuela are idyllic:

o reclinado acaso
bajo una fresca palma en la llanura,
viese arder en la bóveda azulada
tus cuatros lumbres bellas,
¡oh Cruz del Sur!

And he points out that, though America's spacious solitude is scarcely touched by man, yet it has already given birth to heroes such as San Martín and Bolívar who can be compared to the heroes of old.

The *Alocución* 'names' American nature and brings it into the universal rhetoric of Western civilisation. The elevated and noble tone and the coupling of classical references with regional touches are similar in intention to the Inca Garcilaso's comparisons of the Incas and the Romans. In both cases, the author is trying to absorb new matter into the framework of the known. Adjectives such as 'carmín', 'cándida', and nouns like 'nieve' and 'ambrosía' are often associated with plants unknown in Europe, such as the cotton plant or sugar cane:

> donde cándida miel llevan las cañas
> y animado carmín la tuna cría
> donde trémola el algodón su nieve
> y el ananás sazona su ambrosía:

In *La agricultura de la zona tórrida*, this naming takes on almost voluptuous overtones. Palm, yucca, banana are described in all their florid splendour:

> Tendida para tí la fresca parcha
> en enramadas de verdor lozano,
> cuelga de sus sarmientos trepadores
> nectáreos globos y franjadas flores;

La agricultura is, however, not simply descriptive. It is a didactic poem which praises simple country life in contrast to 'el ocio pestilente ciudadano'. In it Bello condemns those who have exploited the land without giving anything in return, and he begs the inhabitants of America to leave their city prisons, to disdain luxury, and seek 'durables goces' which can only be found in the calm and the pure air of the countryside. With Independence achieved, swords can be turned into ploughshares:

> cerrad, cerrad las hondas
> heridas de la guerra: el fértil suelo
> áspero ahora y bravo,
> al desacostumbrado yugo torne
> del arte humana, y le tribute esclavo.

'Honour the countryside and the simple life' is Bello's message. In spirit, he is near to Fernández de Lizardi. Both were concerned with upholding values more constructive than those of the old colonial aristocracy.

Both were concerned with instilling the value of hard work and honest toil, both exemplified the nascent middle-class emphasis on effort and peaceful reform. Both too have recourse to archaic literary forms. Fernández de Lizardi revives the picaresque at a time when it is dead in Spain. Bello revives the Virgilian and classic forms at a time when in Spain and Europe as a whole freer forms were replacing them. But his Latinate forms and vocabulary were deliberately chosen for their dignity and universality.

Two other didactic writers of the period merit attention. José Joaquín Olmedo (1780-1847) was a friend of Bello's and like him played an important part in the Independence movement. He attempted to write the heroic poem of Independence, the poem that would immortalise the victory of Bolívar. His *La victoria de Junín, Canto a Bolívar* (1825) has reminiscences of all his favourite classical authors. Bello admired the poem and wrote glowingly of the 'entusiasmo sostenido, variedad y hermosura de los cuadros'; it was enriched, he believed, by the author's reading of classical authors and he also approved of the didacticism, the 'sentencias esparcidas con economía y dignas de un ciudadano que ha servido con honor a la libertad antes de cantarla'.[16] The poem is hard to read today, but we should bear in mind that the nineteenth century prized lofty intentions. His picture of Bolívar is idealised, a shining statue deliberately made to give the impression of a classical figure.

> Tal el héroe brillaba
> por las primeras filas discurriendo.
> Se oye su voz, su acero resplandece,
> do más la pugna y el peligro crece.
> Nada le puede resistir ... Y es fama
> —¡oh portento inaudito!—
> que el bello nombre de Colombia escrito
> sobre su frente, en torno despedía
> rayos de luz tan viva y refulgente
> que, deslumbrado el español, desmaya,
> tiembla, pierde la voz, el movimiento,
> sólo para la fuga tiene aliento.

It is not historical accuracy that is in question here, but the figure of Bolívar that must be presented to posterity.

The weight of classical example which formed such an important part of any young intellectual's reading is also patent in the work of José María de Heredia (1803-39), a Cuban writer who spent much of his life in exile. Cuba was not to be liberated until 1898, so Heredia belonged to those unfortunate generations who fought unsuccessfully for a cause. He lived the life of a Romantic exile, first in the United States and then in Mexico. The themes of his poems are often Romantic—the ruins of a pyramid in 'En el teocalli de Cholula',[17] wild nature in his poem 'A Niágara'. But though the Niagara invites him to annihilate himself in its impetuous torrent,

Heredia draws a traditional conclusion from the poem;

> ¡Niágara poderoso!
> ¡Adiós! ... Adiós! Dentro de pocos años
> Ya devorado habrá la tumba fría
> A tu débil cantor. ¡Duren mis versos
> Cual tu gloria inmortal! ¡Pueda piadoso,
> Viéndote algún viajero,
> Dar un suspiro a la memoria mía!
> Y al abismarse Febo en occidente,
> Feliz yo vuele do el Señor me llama,
> Y al escuchar los ecos de mi fama,
> Alce en las nubes la radiosa frente.

As in the poetry of Andrés Bello, the native setting serves as a point of departure for the traditional theme of *sic transit gloria mundi* or *ubi sunt?*

IV. THE DIDACTIC ESSAY: JUAN MONTALVO

The humanist standards which Bello sustained in his poetry perhaps more properly belonged to the essay form. Throughout the nineteenth century, the polemical essay formed one of the most important literary genres of the continent and most novelists and poets published essays at some period of their lives. One of the most famous of such essayists was Juan Montalvo (1832-89), celebrated for his bitter attacks on the theocratic government in Ecuador of García Moreno (1859-75), a dictator who combined fanatical Catholicism with repressive methods. In opposition to García Moreno, Montalvo adopted a liberal position and attempted to set up a humanist moral code in his *Siete tratados* (1882). In his essay on 'Nobility', he upholds the view that true aristocracy cannot be based on inheritance or wealth, but on nobility of character. He looks forward to a democracy of equality of opportunity led by noble characters:

> Los filósofos preven el triunfo de la república universal, los bardos le sueñan, los profetas la anuncian, a amables sabidores que muestran al género humano en puras formas la prefiguración de su felicidad. El mundo será republicano, y por tanto democrático. Chateaubriand y Lamartine, aristocráticos y realistas, lo han dicho. Estos cisnes son las dos palomas de Dodona; Apolo nunca engañó a su sacerdotisa.

What immediately springs to the attention in the work of this liberal writer is the archaic style, sprinkled, despite the references to Chateaubriand and Lamartine, with classical references and Spanish structures more reminiscent of the seventeenth than the nineteenth century. The very titles of his treatises have a Senecan ring and one of the works for which he is most famous, *Capítulos que se le olvidaron a Cervantes* (1895), is a moral updating of *Don Quixote* which imitates Cervantes's style but cloaks Montalvo's own brand of neo-Stoicism. Always aware of the classical model, he named his polemical outbursts against the government of Veintimillia, *Catilinarias* (1889). Contemporary writers have attacked the myth of Montalvo's style, accusing him of vanity and pomposity.[18] Nevertheless he is a man who epitomises the nineteenth-century Latin American intellectual, for he was forced into the position of liberal and opposition spokesman while temperamentally being a conservative. He is an excellent example of a writer who took a self-consciously noble stance which he thought posterity would applaud and who failed precisely because he imitated the past and could not create new values for the present.

This chapter has been concerned with two seemingly contradictory factors—revolution and tradition. On the one hand there was the critical realism that arose in the period of opposition to Spain; on the other the assertion of standards by certain Spanish American writers like Bello, Olmedo, and Montalvo who felt that there was a universal humanism to be reflected in the literature of the New World. Unfortunately, as the Argentine experience was to show, this humanism was only available to an élite.

NOTES

1. Luis Alberto Sánchez, *La literatura peruana*, IV, 102.

2. An English translation was published in seven volumes (1814-29) with the title *Personal Narrative of Travels to the Equinoctial Regions of the New Continent during the years 1799-1804*.

3. There is a discussion of the evidence for Carrió de la Vandera's authorship by M. Bataillon in a French edition of *Lazarillo de ciegos caminantes*, Travaux et mémories de l'Institut de Hautes Études de l'Amérique Latine, No. 8 (Paris, 1962).

4. For the view that America was inhabited by inferior species, see Antonello Gerbi, *Viejas polémicas sobre el nuevo mundo. En el umbral de una conciencia americana*, 3rd ed. (Lima, 1946).

5. Many scholars would dispute that Fernández de Lizardi was the 'first' and point to narratives of the colonial period such as Sigüenza y Góngora's *Los infortunios de Alonso Ramírez* as proto-novels, but none before *El Periquillo* have real literary form.

6. A poor-quality liquor made from sugar-cane.

7. Maize-porridge.

8. His main work is embodied in his dialogues on philosophical and allied themes, *El nuevo Luciano*, of which there is a recent edition published in the series Clásicos Ecuatorianos (Quito, 1944).

9. For a brief account of Bolívar's views, see William Spence Robertson, *Rise of the Spanish-American Republics as told in the lives of their liberators*, Collier paperback (New York, 1961).

10. This does not refer to Bello who had considerable influence in Chile after 1829. The situation changed for the Argentinians after the fall of Rosas in 1852.

11. Rodó's work belongs to the history of ideas rather than to the present survey. There is a full discussion of his influence in the *Obras completas* (Madrid, 1957) which has a good introduction by E. Rodríguez Monegal. There is an English edition of his major essay, *Ariel* (Cambridge, 1967) edited by G. Brotherston.

12. See below, Chapter 3, for further discussion of this topic.

13. Part of the polemic is included in N. Pinilla (ed.), *La polémica del romanticismo en 1842* (Santiago, 1945).

14. From a speech on the occasion of the foundation of the University of Chile, 1843, and included in G. Arciniegas, *El pensamiento vivo de Andrés Bello* (Buenos Aires, 1946).

15. E. Rodríguez Monegal, *El otro Andrés Bello* (Caracas, 1969).

16. *Repertorio Americano* (October 1826).

17. *teocalli*—pyramid.

18. Montalvo's work has been criticised by the young generation of Ecuadorian critics; but he was for many years considered to be the epitome of the liberal intellectual. See, for instance, Rodó's essay, 'Montalvo', in *El mirador de Próspero*.

READING LIST

Anthologies
Menéndez y Pelayo, Marcelino, *Antología de poetas hispanoamericanos*, 4 vols. (Madrid, 1893-95)
E. Caracciolo-Trejo (ed.), *The Penguin Book of Latin American Verse* (London, 1971)

Texts
Bello, Andrés, *Obras completas*, 15 vols. (Santiago, 1881-93)
——, *Andrés Bello*, ed. J. C. Ghiano (Buenos Aires, 1967)
——, *Antología de Andrés Bello*, ed. and introduction by Pedro Grases (Caracas, 1949)
Blanco Fombona, Rufino, *El pensamiento vivo de Bolívar*, 3rd ed. (Buenos Aires, 1958)
Bolívar, Simón, *Obras completas*, 2 vols. (La Habana, 1947)
Concolorcorvo, *El lazarillo de ciegos caminantes*, 2nd ed. (Buenos Aires–Mexico, 1946)
——, *El lazarillo: a guide for inexperienced travellers between Buenos Aires and Lima 1773*, trans. D. Kline (Urbana, 1965)
Fernández de Lizardi, José Joaquín, *Obras* (Mexico, 1965)
——, *El Periquillo Sarniento* (Mexico, 1959)
Heredia, José María de, *Poesías completas*, 2 vols. (La Habana, 1940-42)
Hidalgo, Bartolomé, selection of poems included in *Poesía gauchesca*, ed. J. L. Borges and A. Bioy Casares (Mexico, 1955)
Montalvo, Juan, *Siete tratados* (Paris, 1912)
——, *Capítulos que se le olvidaron a Cervantes* (Paris, 1921)
——, *Juan Montalvo*, ed. Gonzalo Zaldumbide (Quito, 1959)
Olmedo, José Joaquín, *Poesías completas* (Mexico, 1947)

Historical and critical works
Ghiano, J. C., *Análisis de las Silvas Americanas* (Buenos Aires, 1957)

González, Manuel Pedro, *José María Heredia, primogénito del romanticismo hispano* (Mexico, 1955)

Grases, Pedro, *Doce estudios sobre Andrés Bello* (Buenos Aires, 1950)

Humphreys, R. A. and Lynch, John (eds.), *The Origins of the Latin American Revolution (1808-1826)* (New York, 1965)

Lira Urquieta, Pedro, *Andrés Bello* (Mexico–Buenos Aires, 1948)

Madariaga, Salvador de, *The Fall of the Spanish American Empire* (London, 1947)

Moses, Bernard, *The Intellectual Background of the Revolution in South America, 1810-24* (New York, 1926)

Nicholson, Irene, *The Liberators* (London, 1969)

Robertson, William Spence, *Rise of the Spanish American Republics* (New York, 1961)

Rodríguez Monegal, Emir, *El otro Andrés Bello* (Caracas, 1969)

Whitaker, A. F. (ed.), *Latin America and the Enlightenment*, 2nd ed. (Ithaca, 1961)

Chapter 2

CIVILISATION AND BARBARISM

Allí la inmensidad por todas partes, inmensa la llanura, inmensos los bosques, inmensos los ríos, el horizonte siempre incierto, siempre confundiéndose con la tierra entre celajes y vapores tenues que no dejan en la lejana perspectiva señalar el punto en que el mundo acaba y principia el cielo.

(Sarmiento)

THE IMMENSITY OF THE ARGENTINE PAMPA described in these words by Domingo Sarmiento was an important theme in the early literature of the River Plate region. The solitude and the empty spaces seemed to annul human effort. And on the coast the eyes discovered another vastness—that of the river which was as immense as a sea:

La mirada se sumerge en la extensión que ocupa el río, y apenas puede divisar a la distancia la incierta luz de algún que otro buque de la rada interior.

Thus the characters in Jose Mármol's novel, *Amalia*, trapped in the city of Buenos Aires by an oppressive dictator, feel themselves surrounded by an even more menacing enemy—the great natural spaces of river and pampa. Argentine writers felt themselves lost in the geographical space of the land around, lost among alien peoples—alien gauchos, wild Indians, or coastal negroes and mulattos, lost in a cultural vacuum, faced with the prospect of creating a culture with no tradition to guide them.

The problem was aggravated by the political situation when, after the failure of the first liberal government, which was unable to assert control over the provinces, a period of chaos and civil war began. The pattern that was to become classic in Latin America was now set. A strong man emerged to salvage the country from anarchy: Juan Manuel Rosas, who was first of all elected Governor of Buenos Aires (1829-32), then undertook a campaign against the Indians, and then became Governor of the whole nation (1835-52). Cleverly manipulating the rivalries of local bosses, Rosas was accused by his opponents of running the country as if it were a cattle farm. He was indeed a

37

wealthy *estanciero* and took pride in his skill as a horseman and his ability to round up and brand cattle as well as the most skilful gaucho. There is no doubt that he exercised a reign of terror through the secret police or *mazorca* and that he drove the liberal or unitarian opposition into exile. Yet the weight of the liberal polemic against him should not blind us to his merits. One of his predecessors, the liberal Bernardino Rivadavia, had been quick to try and secure his country's progress by granting concessions to foreign countries and by borrowing money from abroad. Rosas, on the other hand, chose a different path, one more akin to the Paraguayan dictator, Dr Francia. His intention was to protect the cattle interests; and he did not encourage foreign investment or immigration. In the eyes of the liberal intellectuals, his great sin was that he kept the country in a barbarous pastoral state instead of encouraging its incorporation into the era of industry and progress. But Rosas was to remain in power until 1852 and we have the phenomenon of an Argentine literature that arises in large measure out of a movement of protest against the dictator. The 'generation of exiles' included some of the most brilliant men of the day: Juan Bautista Alberdi (1810-84), whose *Bases*[1] is one of the fundamental documents on which the Argentine constitution was based; Domingo Sarmiento, a largely self-taught journalist, teacher, and politician who was to become President of Argentina in 1868; Esteban Echeverría, Romantic poet and one of the founders of the *Asociación de Mayo*, an anti-Rosas organisation; José Mármol, Romantic poet and novelist. With Alberdi, who is primarily of interest as a political writer, we shall not be concerned here; the other three are among the pioneers of Argentine literature.

I. ESTEBAN ECHEVERRÍA (1805-51)

The career and writings of Esteban Echeverría epitomise the dilemmas and difficulties which faced the post-Independence intellectual. He was born in Buenos Aires in 1805 and grew up the spoiled son of a widowed mother. In 1825, he went to Europe and studied at the Sorbonne where he read not only writers such as Pascal, Montesquieu, and Chateaubriand but also contemporary English and French Romantic writers. At the beginning of 1830 he returned to Buenos Aires with great hopes, and in one early poem even preached the decadence of Europe compared with the New World. But the hopes were shortlived. 'Al volver a mi patria, cuántas esperanzas traía'—he wrote later—'pero todas estériles; la patria ya no existía'.[2] Nevertheless, for a short period before Rosas became absolute ruler, there was a semblance of literary activity in clubs, *tertulias*, and meetings in which poems were read and the new doctrines of the Romantics discussed. During this period. Echeverría published his *Rimas* (1837). As Rosas began to secure his power, the poet helped found the *Asociación de Mayo* for which he drew up the manifesto, later published in book form as *Dogma socialista*. Despite the name, this is a liberal document which set out the ideals of the *Asociación de Mayo* —ideals of free assembly, universal suffrage, respect for the freedom of the individual. But no sooner was the *Asociación de Mayo* formed than Echeverría was obliged to go into exile, first to his own country estate of La Tala and afterwards to Montevideo where, cut off from the source of his income, he lived in poor circumstances. He died in 1851, without returning to Buenos Aires.

Echeverría's literary theories are to be found in his essay *Fondo y forma en las obras de imaginación* (published posthumously). The ideas in this essay are influenced by the Romantic theorist A. W. Schlegel and by Herder whose works had appeared in French in 1827. Echeverría shows that moral ideas are universal, but that climate, customs, and forms of government each contributed to the originality of nations. In Latin America, which is without a classical heritage, poetry must have the variety and vigour of tropical vegetation

> ... ninguna forma antigua le cuadra, y henchida de savia y sustancia como la vegetación de los trópicos, debe brotar y crecer vigorosa y multiforme, manifestando en la variedad, contraste y armonía de su externa apariencia, todo el vigor y fecundidad que en sí entraña.[3]

Caught up as he was in a political struggle, Echeverría's literary works are comparatively slight. He is best known for a long narrative poem, *La cautiva*,[4] and for a short story, *El matadero*, which was published posthumously.

La cautiva centres on one of the legendary figures of nineteenth-century Argentina—the white woman who was captured by Indians and forced to become concubine of a chief. The occurrence was common enough. Lucio Mansilla, who visited the Indian tribes in 1870, met several *cautivas* and William Henry Hudson, the English writer whose youth was spent in Argentina, based one of his best stories, *María Riquelme*, on such a person. But Echeverría's poem is Romantic in conception—the poetic narration of a flight from the Indian tents and an unsuccessful bid to reach civilisation. But note how Argentine circumstance reverses the usual Romantic *escapes* from civilisation. We are not in industrialised Europe where lovers must find refuge in the countryside. The flight here is *from* barbarism. And although the loneliness of the pampa is evoked in terms of the 'sublime' of contemporary European Romanticism, there are also elements of fear and horror in the natural environment which totally mar its beauty. A description of a pampa fire, for instance, emphasises the loathsome force of wind and elements.

> Lodo, paja, restos viles
> De animales y reptiles
> Quema el fuego vencedor,
> Que el viento iracundo atiza:

The animal and reptile world are all part of the hostile force which is nature.

The poem centres upon a Romantic heroine, María, who represents the most delicate of civilisation's products, brought face to face with the most brutal of natural forces. Captured by the Indians, she kills the chief rather than succumb and then, on discovering that her husband is captive, also helps him to escape. There is certainly no hint of noble savage in Echeverría's picture of the drunken Indians:

> Mas allá alguno degüella
> Con afilado cuchillo
> La yegua al lazo sujeta,
> Ya la boca de la herida
> Por donde ronca y resuella,
> Ya borbollones arroja
> La caliente sangre fuera,
> En pie, trémula y convulsa.
> Dos o tres indios se pagan.
> Como sedientos vampiros,
> Sorban, chupan, saborean
> La sangre ...

This is a primitive energy which is in total contrast to the impotence of the white hero Brian who is first glimpsed tied between four lances. Throughout the poem, Brian plays a purely passive role and is more helpless even than María. He almost refuses to run away with her for fear that her honour has been stained. Nor does he make a better showing once they leave the Indian camp, for nature has a repulsive rather than a beautiful aspect. They find themselves in a 'páramo yerto' with 'feos, inmundos despojos de la muerte'. The lovers, though in flight, often appear curiously immobile:

> En el vasto pajonal
> Permanecen inactivos.
> Su astro, al parecer, declina
> Como la luz vespertina
> Entre sombra funeral.

Despite the eruptions of violence—there is a pampa fire and an encounter with a tiger—it is this impression of inactivity and help-lessness which is overwhelming. Fittingly Brian dies calling deliriously for his lance, a weapon he has never been able to use in the course of the poem. María, the more active of the two, has no will left once her man has gone and she too dies heartbroken on learning that her son had also perished.

The poem is not a literary masterpiece and is more of interest for what it tells us about Echeverría than for any intrinsic beauty. Certainly the contrast between the savage energy of Indian and nature and the passiveness and impotence of the white couple appears to reflect not the sturdy values of a pioneer civilisation but the tired resignation of a dying race. The vital forces of the poem are those which Echeverría fears, not those which he wishes to prevail. *La cautiva* forms a complete contrast in style to Echeverría's story *El matadero*, although the theme of the two works—the confrontation of an idealistic but impotent white race with a powerful, cruel, indigenous element —is similar. In the poetry, there has to be idealisation, for as Echeverría explained in the introduction to his *Rimas*:

> El verdadero poeta idealiza. Idealizar es sustituir a la tosca e imperfecta realidad de la naturaleza, el vivo trasunto de la acabada y sublime realidad que nuestro espíritu alcanza.

The prose work, on the other hand, is realistic, modelled on the *costumbrista* literature which purported to give a faithful depiction of types. Like his Spanish model, Larra, Echeverría transcends the picturesque and makes his *costumbrismo* the pretext for a savage attack. It was this directness that made him unable to publish *El matadero* in his lifetime, although it was probably written soon after Rosas's oppression of the Unitarian opposition in 1840.

The story is set during the floods of the Lenten season when animals could not be brought into the slaughterhouse, thus causing famine on top of fasting. Echeverría, liberal and anti-clerical, takes the opportunity to expose the Church's collusion with the Rosas régime and is savagely ironic about the 'intestine war between the conscience and the stomach' which their ordinances bring about. However, he continues:

> no es extraño, supuesto que el diablo, con la carne suele meterse en el cuerpo, y que la Iglesia tiene el poder de conjurarlo; el caso es reducir al hombre a una máquina cuyo móvil principal no sea su voluntad sino la de la Iglesia y el gobierno.

But though Echeverría attacks directly as in the above passage, he also uses symbolism to heighten the effect. The slaughterhouse is Argentina under Rosas, the workers—negroes and mulattos—are barbarian forces dedicated to the slaughter of everything that comes their way. They are so brutal that they play with balls of flesh and fight together like the dogs around them:

De repente caía un bofe sangriento sobre la cabeza de alguno, que de allí pasaba a la de otro, hasta que algún deforme mastín lo hacía buena presa, y una cuadrilla de otros, por si estrujo o no estrujo, armaba una tremenda de gruñidos y mordiscones.

Notice that it is the 'deforme mastín' who wins the prize. Echeverría does not spare his feelings about the blacks and mulattos. The violence of dogs, of children, and of men is similar to the violence of the country as a whole.

Violence, cruelty, and hypocrisy are the prevailing forces, but they are not the only ones. Echeverría now introduces defiance in the form of a proud bull 'emperrado y arisco como un unitario' which escapes, is recaptured, and, in a primitive rite, is slaughtered and the testicles, the symbol of its potency, are given to the chief butcher, Matasiete. As they finish the slaughter, a young man passes on horseback and is seen to be riding with a European saddle. He is dragged off his mount and his hair is cut as a punishment. As he shouts his protest against these men whom he compares to animals, the butchers torment him more and more until he dies of haemorrhage brought on by his anger.

El matadero reflects a similar impotence against the forces of violence as La cautiva. The young Unitarian is held powerless by the butchers and forced to submit to humiliating torments. The reader cannot help being struck by the parallel of this young man, choked by his own rage, and Echeverría and his generation. Perhaps he himself suffered the feeling that verbal assaults on Rosas were finally useless. Certainly, in El matadero he attempted to use literature as a weapon. Yet there is the curious feature that in both his major works, the forces of barbarism and civilisation are unequal, the former being vigorous and dynamic, the latter weak, effeminate, reduced to verbal gestures.

II. DOMINGO SARMIENTO (1811-88)

Domingo Sarmiento, unlike Echeverría, was not a member of the landed class. His father was owner of a mule train and a native of San Juan. 'He nacido en una familia que ha vivido largos años en una mediocridad muy vecina de la indigencia', he wrote in his Recuerdos de provincia (1850). Educated by a priest, he worked for a time as a shop assistant, a job that gave him leisure to educate himself 'sin maestros ni colegios'. He learned languages during periods of exile and, by joining a literary society in 1839, he came into contact with contemporary French literature. Born in 1811, almost at the same time as the independent republic of Argentina, Sarmiento identified his own rise with that of the nation of which he was to become President. When he came to write *Mi defensa* in 1843, he even divided his biography into stages: 'la historia colonial' of the family followed by 'la vida de la república naciente', 'la lucha de los partidos', 'la guerra civil', 'la proscripción', 'el destierro'.

Sarmiento was still a young man when he found himself drawn into political struggle in his native province of San Juan. He was forced to go into hiding and then in 1831 into exile in Chile where he stayed until 1836. His return to Argentina was brief; in 1840 he again fled to Chile and this country remained his base until the fall of Rosas in 1852. During his exile, Sarmiento helped to found a teachers' training college and took part in a polemic on behalf of Romanticism. He travelled too, both to Europe and to the United States, a country for which he had great admiration, and whose success he attributed to the moral qualities instilled by Puritanism.

The work on which Sarmiento's literary reputation rests is a polemical essay, *Civilización y barbarie. Vida de Juan Facundo Quiroga, y aspecto físico, costumbres, y hábitos de la República Argentina.* The essay, published in 1845 at a time when the Chilean government was about to accept an ambassador from Rosas, was clearly intended to act as a counterweight. It is possible, as some critics have pointed out, that Sarmiento incorporated into the essay certain 'cuadros de costumbres': descriptions of Argentine types such as the *baquiano* (pathfinder) and the *payador*, which he had written as separate studies. Certainly the structure would seem to owe much to de Tocqueville's *Democracy in the United States* and the ideology to the ideas of Montesquieu and Herder.

Facundo sets out to show how 'barbarism' became institutionalised in Argentina during the Rosas régime. In the introduction to the first edition, Sarmiento explains that Facundo Quiroga, the local chieftain whose biography he writes, and the more powerful Rosas who was to have Facundo assassinated, represent incarnations of certain aspects of the national state, Rosas being the more sophisticated version of these. Facundo was 'provinciano, bárbaro, valiente, audaz'; his successor, Rosas, 'organiza lentamente el despotismo con toda la inteligencia de un Maquiavelo'. Sarmiento's essay is therefore both an analysis of the Rosas phenomenon and a weapon against him. Why then write the biography of Facundo Quiroga and not of the more powerful Rosas? Firstly because Sarmiento knew Quiroga, the gaucho who had become ruler of his native province, and he could therefore draw upon his own memories and anecdotes he had heard. Secondly, because he believed that Facundo was the 'expresión fiel de una manera de ser de un pueblo, de sus preocupaciones e instintos'. If Rosas represented the institutionalisation of barbarism, Facundo represented its spontaneous expression. He was therefore the 'representative man' of his time. For this reason, Sarmiento divides his study into two parts—a description of the land or the 'theatre' in which the characters are going to act and secondly the chief actor 'con su traje, sus ideas, su sistema de obrar'.

The dramatic analogy is not a gratuitous one. Sarmiento sees events in terms of conflict: the conflict of man and nature, of settler and Indian, of city and country, barbarism and civilisation. It is also a drama between good and evil. For Sarmiento the good life is associated with commerce from which civilisation and culture grow. Argentina possesses two notable natural features—rivers, the natural routes of trade, under-utilised in that nation; and the pampa on which civilisation has as yet made little impact and on which life takes on the aspect of oriental desert nomadism. Here is the home of the gaucho and the Indian, the home of barbarism, in contrast to the cities which are centres of culture and progress.

For Sarmiento, the Indian of Argentina is outside the pale. The gaucho symbolises 'barbarism'—a term which Sarmiento uses as a blanket to cover all the evils from which his nation suffered. Civilisation means *sociabilidad,* the rule of law, the inviolability of private property. To achieve *sociabilidad,* men must have relations regulated by a mutually agreed code of behaviour; they must recognise the existence of a common good as well as of their own individual wishes. Barbarism is the negation of *sociabilidad.* The gaucho is schooled to habits of self-dependence in the solitude of the pampa. He has his own law and morality and self-survival comes first. Having no needs, he has no reason for thinking of the common good.

> El gaucho no trabaja; el alimento y el vestido lo encuentra preparado en su casa; uno y otro se lo proporcionan sus ganados, si es propietario; la casa del patrón o pariente, si nada posee.

The gaucho does whatever it occurs to him to do spontaneously. If he feels like watching the rodeo, he sits there and watches. If he wants to join in: 'desciende lentamente del caballo, desarrolla su lazo y lo arroja sobre un toro que pasa con la velocidad del rayo a cuarenta pasos de distancia; lo ha cogido de una uña, que era lo que se proponía, y vuelve tranquilo a enrollar su cuerda'.

As has often been noted, Sarmiento is often unwittingly the devil's advocate in these passages which describe the skills of the gaucho. *El rastreador* (the tracker), *el baquiano* (the pathfinder), *el gaucho malo* (the outlaw), *el cantor* (the singer) arouse ill-concealed enthusiasm in the writer who marvels at the natural poetry and the natural skills that have arisen in the heart of the plains. The contrast to this 'medieval' form of society is offered by the cities, the home of culture and refinement, now rapidly degenerating because of the growing power of the forces of barbarism.

Against this background, Sarmiento sets the personality and career of Juan Facundo Quiroga, the gaucho who came to control many of the provinces of the interior. Born in the province of La Rioja, Facundo is the negation of all the qualities that his compatriot Sarmiento appears to represent. He rejects education, becomes the wild outlaw who fights in the *montonera* (i.e., the gaucho cavalry that fought against the Spaniards), and emerges as a permanent rebel against law, order, and religion. 'Jamás se ha confesado, rezado ni oído misa'—or so legend proclaimed.

Unlike Sarmiento, who emphasised his self-education, Facundo lived as he was born, as a natural man.

La vida a caballo, la vida de peligros y emociones fuertes, han acerado su espíritu y endurecido su corazón; tiene odio invencible, instintivo contra las leyes que lo han perseguido.... contra toda esa sociedad y esa organización a que se ha sustraído desde la infancia.

This natural man rose to power when a governor of La Rioja, Don Nicolás Dávila, used him in his bid for power and then tried to dispense with his services. Quiroga killed Dávila and took control of La Rioja.

From this point onwards, Sarmiento traces the career of Facundo Quiroga, the battles he wins and loses to gain control over the cities of the interior. At the same time, the comparison and contrast with Rosas and his institutionalised form of barbarism is ever present. Facundo kills when the spirit moves him, Rosas systematically; Facundo destroys cities instinctively, Rosas's destruction is conscious.

Facundo's own fall occurs at the very moment of Rosas's definitive rise to power. In 1835, Quiroga is sent by Rosas on a mission to the interior. As soon as he reaches the pampa, his barbarous spirit reasserts itself:

Apenas ha andado media jornada, encuentra un arroyo fangoso que detiene la galera. El vecino maestro de posta acude solícito a pasarla; se ponen nuevos caballos, se apuran todos los esfuerzos y la galera no avanza. Quiroga se enfurece y hace uncir a las varas al mismo maestro de posta.

Shortly afterwards he is ambushed and he and his whole party are killed, apparently by a gaucho outlaw Santos Pérez, probably on orders from Rosas. The final section deals with the institutionalisation of barbarism by the Rosas régime—the establishment of the secret police, and of the Rosas terror. Finally comes the positive aspect: Sarmiento's own proposals for the future. Immigration and industrialisation are shown to be necessary conditions for Argentina's prosperity.

Allison Williams Bunkley, author of *The Life of Sarmiento*, has seen *Facundo* as a great Romantic work. 'The titanic figures of Facundo

Quiroga, Rosas, and their gauchos are literary characters to compare with many of the great titans of Romanticism'. However, as in *La cautiva*, there are elements in *Facundo* that distinguish it from European Romanticism. The natural man, Facundo, cannot be blamed, but neither can he be admired. Nor is Sarmiento in flight back to nature from the alienating effects of urban civilisation. For him, the city is still the centre of culture, of social virtues, and of law and order. But powerful the essay certainly is, carried along by the dynamic of the conflict, and frequently using a present tense that adds to the urgency and actuality of the narration. Certainly, for generations it affected Argentinians' analysis of their society[5].

Sarmiento differs from many nineteenth-century thinkers and writers in that he was given the opportunity to put into practice many of his ideas. After the fall of Rosas he took an active part in educational reform in the Buenos Aires region, and on becoming President in 1868 he managed, despite a state of civil war and much opposition, to create schools, encourage immigration, and build railroads. In 1874, he retired to private life. His last major work was *Conflictos y armonías de las razas en América* (1883), in which he attributed the difficulties of Latin America to inherent racial defects. The Europeanising of Argentina was the only solution.

In many ways, Sarmiento is the typical nineteenth-century liberal intellectual. In formation and outlook he is European, measuring the progress of his own country in relation to Europe and the United States. Among his most revealing works are his travel notes. A great admirer of the practical side of the English character epitomised by Cobden, he reserves his greatest enthusiasm for France and for the Frenchman:

> Sus ideas y sus modas, sus hombres y sus novelas, son hoy el modelo y la pauta de todas las otras naciones; y empiezo a creer que esto que nos seduce por todas partes, esto que creemos imitación, no es sino aquella aspiración de la índole humana a acercarse a un tipo de perfección, que está en ella misma y se desenvuelve más o menos, según las circunstancias de cada pueblo[6].

If he feels admiration for the French, his most intense interest seems to be aroused by the United States. Here was an American nation that appeared to be on the way to greatness. Sarmiento realises that it does not answer to his idea of perfection, but neither is it a deformed monster. 'La más joven y osada república del mundo' he calls it, and compares it to ancient Rome[7].

Reading these travel accounts, we can appreciate the enormity of the task that the nineteenth-century liberal intellectual saw before him. 'Civilisation' established in Europe and the northern parts of America was still absent from the barbarous and as yet empty pampa.

III. JOSÉ MÁRMOL (1817-71)

The third of the group of writers who was to give literary expression to the theme of civilisation and barbarism was José Mármol, the poet who was briefly imprisoned during the Rosas terror during the year 1840 and then escaped to Montevideo where he wrote his novel *Amalia* (1851). The novel is a romantic love story set in the grotesque reality of the Rosas régime. It is a story which even more than *El matadero* reveals the prejudices and ideals of the liberal intellectual. The story is slight; Eduardo Belgrano is wounded when trying to escape from Buenos Aires to join the rebels against Rosas. His friend Daniel Bello rescues him and takes him to the home of his cousin, the widow Amalia, where he is to be kept in hiding until he recovers. Both Daniel and Amalia play a double game, pretending to support Rosas but in reality plotting against him. But during the course of the novel, the net closes irrevocably around the three; Amalia and Eduardo fall in love and marry on the eve of a projected escape, but are ambushed by a group of Rosas's supporters who kill them as well as Amalia's faithful servant, Pedro.

The star-crossed lovers are of little interest, being conventional elements in a novel in which the political denunciation and the relation of the atrocities of the Rosas régime occupy the foreground. Like Echeverría, Mármol identifies barbarism with the racial element; the 'civilised' are a little group of intellectuals, pupils of a certain doctor, Alcorta:

> Desde la cátedra él ha encendido en nuestro corazón el entusiasmo por todo lo que es grande: por el bien, por la libertad, por la justicia.

Daniel Bello, a kind of Argentinian Scarlet Pimpernel, is the most dynamic of the civilised characters, but Eduardo Belgrano, like Echeverría's Brian, plays the passive role of wounded hero throughout the novel. He and Amalia are clearly victims, almost always in hiding; and dying, characteristically, in an ambush. From the first, these civilised people are presented as being besieged by hostile elements, by the pampa and the river which surround the city with their solitude:

> La ciudad, a dos o tres cuadras de la orilla, se descubre, y solo el rumor monótono y salvaje de las olas anima lúgubremente aquel centro de soledad y de tristeza.

The mulatto, the negro, and the gaucho who now dominate society are simply the human expressions of this wildness. Characteristically it is the urban 'gaucho', Merlo, who betrays Eduardo at the beginning of the novel. The negroes are almost all in the pay of Rosas and the mulattos, among whom civilisation is possible because they want to better themselves, have also in some cases been prostituted by the régime. Rosas, for example, has an imbecile mulatto as a pet buffoon and scapegoat. His régime is based on ignorance and on exploitation of the worst instincts, and especially on the envy of the poor for the rich. Thus of the negro, Mármol says:

> El odio a las clases honestas y acomadadas de la sociedad era sincero y profundo en esa clase de color: sus propensiones a ejecutar el mal eran a la vez francas e ingenuas; y su adhesión a Rosas leal y robusto.

In contrast, the refined and European character of the opponents of Rosas is a guarantee of their moral superiority. Belgrano is described as 'very pale', of distinguished background (a relative of General Belgrano), 'corazón valiente y generoso e inteligencia privilegiada por Dios y enriquecido por el estudio'. He is thus an aristocrat, unjustly forced into flight by the barbarism of Rosas. Daniel Bello attending a meeting of Rosas supporters is described as 'el hombre más puro de aquella reunión y el hombre más europeo que había en ella'. Apart from these two elements there exists the gaucho of the pampa, whom Mármol describes in terms reminiscent of *Facundo*:

> La soledad y la Naturaleza han puesto en acción sobre su espíritu sus leyes invariables y eternas y la libertad y la independencia de los instintos humanos se convierten en condiciones imprescindibles de la vida del gaucho.

But the gaucho is represented as the menacing force at the city gate: 'está rodeando siempre, como una tempestad, los horizontes de las ciudades'.

The novel is totally Manichean in its division of the forces of good and evil. Rosas is the evil demiurge who has created a city of darkness. His very house is dark:

> En el zaguán de esa casa, completamente obscuro, había tendidos en el suelo y envueltos en su poncho, dos gauchos y ocho indios de la Pampa, armados de tercerola y sable, como otros tantos perros de presa que estuviesen velando la mal cerrada puerta de la calle.

> Un inmenso patio cuadrado y sin ningún farol que le diese luz, dejaba ver la que se proyectaba por la rendija de una puerta a la izquierda, que daba a un cuarto con una mesa en el medio, y unas cuantas sillas ordinarias ...

The darkness and rustic simplicity in which Rosas lives are in startling contrast to the beauty, the civilised luxury, and light which surrounds Amalia:

> Dos grandes jarras de porcelana francesa estaban sobre dos peque-
> ñas mesas de nogal con un ramo de flores cada una; y sobre cuatro
> rinconeras de caoba brillaban ocho pebeteros de oro cincelado, obra
> del Perú, de un gusto y de un trabajo admirables.

Enlightenment is here closely associated with objects. These objects are produced by a highly developed commercial system and hence depend on *sociabilidad*. Once again the Argentinian Romantic celebrates the community over the individual and the universal stamp which commercial organisation places on its products. It is self-sufficient individualism which is reflected in the poverty and rusticity of Rosas's house.

The work of Echeverría, Sarmiento, and Mármol can be grouped together because they share a common definition of civilisation and of barbarism. All three differ from the European Romantics in putting social organisation above the whims of the individual, in seeing the city as the centre of civilisation and the countryside as the home of barbarism. All three tend to give a racial bias to their definition of barbarism and to define civilisation in terms of the achievements of European industrial societies. Finally, in all three, the slender prospects of civilisation tend to be incarnated in weak or impotent men. Paradoxically the energy of a work like *Facundo* springs from the very forces that it was attempting to negate.

Not all the literature of this period was inspired by this absolute dichotomy between the Europeanised forces of light and the Indian or gaucho forces of darkness. The Indian, however, was to remain the great unknown, almost unconsidered as a human being, the victim of frontier vendetta and war which slowly drove him south. At the end of the Desert Campaign of 1879, the Indian tribes of Argentina were virtually exterminated and ceased to exist as a threat. As in the United States, the railway proved to be the great enemy of the Indian; wherever its lines stretched, Indian power terminated before the insatiable demand of the white man for land. The railway and the barbed-wire fence transformed the life of the pampa; once property was secure and inviolable, not only the Indian but the nomadic gaucho disappeared, to be replaced by the farmhand or cowboy. Gaucho customs and folklore were to linger as nostalgic memories.

IV. LUCIO MANSILLA (1831-1913)

It is precisely at this moment of transition from a nomadic pastoral community to a settled and increasingly industrialised one that two works appear which entirely reverse Sarmiento's categories of civilisation and barbarism. These two works are Hernández's poem *Martín Fierro* and the account of a journey among Indians recounted by Lucio Mansilla in his *Una excursión a los indios ranqueles* (1870). Mansilla, son of a family which had enjoyed eminence during the Rosas régime and which therefore suffered an eclipse after 1852, was an interesting and complex person, unique in the apology he frequently makes for the redskin. Mansilla is no idealiser of the noble savage. His expedition was made in an attempt to secure concessions from the Indians peacefully so that railways could be built. But despite his distaste for the dirt and sordidness of the villages, he does note some Indian virtues and is frequently critical of 'civilisation' which, unlike Sarmiento, he does not see as an undiluted benefit. Whereas Sarmiento wished to bring the civilisation and progress of Europe to the pampa, Mansilla sees progress in moral terms; Christianity is superior in its teaching to paganism, but this superiority must be proved by example. Thus Mansilla makes an effort to understand the Indians in order to persuade them of the virtues of Christianity. For instance, he cuts his toenails in public to gain their confidence. He then sets out to demonstrate his Christian spirit by lifting up a man ill with smallpox. Despite the revulsion he feels for the body, he insists on placing the man upon a conveyance, feeling rewarded as he does so by the sentiment that 'Aquel fue un verdadero triunfo de la civilización sobre la barbarie; del cristianismo sobre la idolatría'. But in certain aspects, he himself is forced to recognise that the Indians are nearer to the spirit of Christianity than the creoles. Their hospitality and their generosity puts 'Christian' society in the shade. And he is honest enough to admit that much of the so-called barbarism of the Indians is simply an aspect of their poverty, for one can find the same habits among the poor whites.

The truth of the matter is that Lucio Mansilla found himself in a dilemma that never occurred to Sarmiento. His very mission amongst the Indians was a dubious one. He is the instrument of Sarmiento's own government which wished to secure the assent of the Indians so that railways could be constructed across their territories, but both the Indians and Mansilla himself realised that the coming of the railroad was bound to disrupt and even destroy Indian life. When Mansilla met the chiefs, he realised the misery of this once noble race and became conscious of the ignominy of their living on charity from a hostile government. And he has the honesty to admit that he has changed his opinion on race. Formerly he believed in the superiority of the Latins. Now, he declares 'Pienso de distinta manera'. Bad governments of whatever race have evil effects, and moral forces always predominate over the physical. Hence the true Christian must act in an exemplary manner at all times.

The pathos of Mansilla's book, however, arises from the powerlessness of Christian example in the face of economic forces. All the Christian example in the world would not prevent the land-hungry creoles from driving into Indian territory and this both they and the Indians realised. Sarmiento's concept of civilisation and not Mansilla's was to triumph.

V. JOSÉ HERNÁNDEZ (1834-86)

Tragic too was the fate of the gaucho. Like the Indian, he represented a stage of human society that Western society had surpassed. His nomadic life could not survive the establishment of big estates and of meat-packing and exporting on an industrial basis. The gaucho like the Indian was doomed. By the twentieth century, traditional gaucho life survived only in externals in clothing, in the *bombacha* or wide baggy pants, the leather apron or *chiripá*; in song and literature, in certain attitudes of *machismo* and *hombría*. José Hernández's poem *Martín Fierro* captures gaucho life at the very moment of disappearance. However, it was no isolated phenomenon. The author drew on two existing traditions: that of a satirical urban poetry in gaucho dialect—the gauchesque—and that of folk-poetry of the pampa which was of mixed Indian, Spanish, and even negro origin.

The gauchesque tradition was initiated by a Uruguayan poet of the Independence period, Bartolomé Hidalgo (1788-1822), who composed a kind of political lampoon using the dialect of the gaucho and the rhythms of popular song. Hidalgo's most characteristic poems are in the form of the *cielito*, a gloss with a chorus, 'Cielito, cielito que sí'; and in the form of the dialogue in which two gauchos exchange opinions in verse and comment, sometimes satirically, on the events of the day. The genuinely popular appeal of this poetry is illustrated by the fact that Hidalgo sold his poems on the streets. In the hands of his successors, Hilario Ascasubi (1807-75), who wrote under the pseudonym of Aniceto el Gallo, and Estanislao del Campo (1834-80), gauchesque poetry became increasingly satirical. Ascasubi, for instance, wrote bitter political satires, directed against Rosas. Only later did gauchesque poetry become in any way the expression of the sentiments of the gaucho. Hernández's friend, the Uruguayan Antonio Lussich (1848-1928), published his *Tres gauchos orientales* in 1870, just before *Martín Fierro*. Here the gaucho is no longer the mere mouthpiece for a political campaign that has little direct bearing on gaucho life. He is much closer in his feelings and language to the genuine gaucho of the *Banda Oriental* (Uruguay)[8]. Thus literary convention and reality begin to converge. In *Martín Fierro*, the gauchesque tradition survives in the complaints against the government, in satirical passages, and in the verse form of the more primitive parts of the poem[9]. But Hernández, unlike the other gauchesque poets, also achieved an artistic expression of the essence of gaucho life and was able to transform the traditional popular theme of the *gaucho malo* into a universal and tragic expression.

Born in Buenos Aires in 1834, José Hernández was related, on his mother's side of the family, to Don Juan Martín de Pueyrredón, who led the gaucho cavalry against the invasion of the English in 1806-07. Hernández's father worked as an administrator of cattle estates (he worked for Rosas at one period) and José spent part of his childhood in the country where he grew up as a gaucho. When he reached manhood, he joined the army but later trained himself as a parliamentary reporter. Early on in his career, he began to support the federalist cause against the Unitarians and for a time was forced to emigrate to Brazil. In his articles, Hernández set himself up as the champion of the countryside which he claimed had been neglected and repressed by the city. One of the greatest abuses, he believed, was the recruitment of country-dwellers for service on the frontier against the Indians.

Out of these discontents the poem *Martín Fierro* emerged. In the preface to the eighth edition published in 1878, Hernández declared:

> Ese *gaucho* debe ser ciudadano y no paria: debe tener deberes y también derechos, y su cultura debe mejorar su condición.

However, the hero of the poem, Martín Fierro, is more than a gaucho. He is a *payador*, or singer, who is proud of his inventiveness and most important he is an outlaw, an outsider from society. The poem presents the story of his misfortunes, related by himself. Conscripted to serve on the frontier against the Indians, he deserts, finds that his family have disappeared, and from then on becomes a 'tigre', motivated by hatred of law and order. The present sad state of the gaucho, he contrasts with a legendary Golden Age:

> Ricuerdo ¡qué maravilla!
> cómo andaba la gauchada
> siempre alegre y bien montada
> y dispuesta pa el trabajo:
> pero hoy en el día ... ¡barajo!
> no se la ve de aporriada.

The dissolution of the Golden Age comes about through social forces which not only bring the exploitation of man by man, but also attack the dignity of the individual. Service at the frontier undermines Martín Fierro's dignity as a man by depriving him of the horse and weapons by which gaucho manhood is defined. A fight with the Indian restores this lost manhood, but only momentarily. Soon afterwards he is ignominiously tied to the stake as a punishment for asking for pay. Once again his human dignity is destroyed. Martín Fierro incarnates the values of *hombría* pitted against all those forces—exploitation, corruption, injustice—which threaten the individual. He incarnates also the values of the frontier, values of courage, self-reliance, and independence, as against what Sarmiento would regard as the values of civilisation—rule of law, social organisation, and commerce.

The second part of the poem, the *Vuelta*, published in 1878 merely reaffirms these basic patterns. The culmination of the second part is the *payada* or song contest between Martín Fierro and a *moreno,* brother of the negro he had slain in the *Ida*. In this display of the skill of the gaucho poet, the two men reaffirm the suffering and the struggles of man and place these in a cosmic setting. The form of the contest—the unanswerable questions—is an example of the riddle-song found in most archaic cultures, a 'knocking on the door of the Unknowable' as Huizinga calls it and it was also a ritualistic way of doing down the opponent.[10]

The poem has had a strange fortune among critics. For many years, its popularity among the masses was almost seen as a guarantee of inferiority by the cultured élite. But in the early years of this century, opinions began to be expressed in its favour. For the Spanish critic Unamuno, it expressed the spirit of the *conquistadores.*[11] For the Modernist poet Leopoldo Lugones, it was the epic of Argentina,[12] and the radical nationalist Ricardo Rojas saw it as the supreme national poem.[13] For the contemporary writer Jorge Luis Borges, it is more akin to the novel than to the epic. Perhaps, however, categories are less important than the phenomenon itself. Sarmiento, Echeverría, Mármol, despite their virtues, still had a colonised imagination. They could not see Argentina moving in any direction other than that of the European norm. Hernández went deeper. He intuitively grasped the vastness of the forces at work and he came down on the side of forces that were doomed—independence, manhood, courage—virtues of a heroic age which the nineteenth century was in the process of destroying, and which it tried to ignore. It was not until José Martí that a Spanish American writer attempted to find virtues in the barbarism that European civilisation utterly condemned.

NOTES

1. The full title of the work was *Bases y puntos de partida para la organización política de la república argentina* (Buenos Aires, 1852).

2. Quoted by Juan María Gutiérrez in the 'notas biográficas' which preface vol. V of *Obras completas de Esteban Echeverría* (Buenos Aires, 1874).

3. 'Fondo y forma en las obras de imaginación', *Obras completas,* V, 78-80.

4. Included in the first edition of *Rimas* (Buenos Aires, 1837).

5. For example, Ezequiel Martínez Estrada, *Radiografía de la pampa,* 2 vols. (Buenos Aires, 1942).

6. *Viajes en Europa, Africa y América* (Buenos Aires, 1956).

7. ibid., pp. 262-78.
8. All the gauchesque poets mentioned here are amply represented in *Poesía gauchesca* (see reading list).
9. There is a discussion of these points in E. Martínez Estrada, *Muerte y transfiguración de Martín Fierro,* 2 vols., 2nd ed. (Buenos Aires–Mexico, 1958).
10. Johan Huizinga, *Homo Ludens* (London, 1970).
11. *Revista española,* I (1895).
12. *El Payador* (Buenos Aires, 1961), p. 19.
13. Ricardo Rojas, *Historia de la literatura argentina,* 9 vols. (Buenos Aires, 1960).

FURTHER READING

Texts

Echeverría, Esteban, *Dogma socialista y otras páginas políticas* (Buenos Aires, 1958)
——, *La cautiva y El matadero,* 7th ed. (Buenos Aires, 1962)
——, *El matadero et La cautiva de Esteban Echeverría, suivis de trois essais de Noé Jitrik* (Paris, 1969)
Hernández, José, *Martín Fierro,* 8th ed. (Buenos Aires, 1953)
Mansilla, Lucio V., *Una excursión a los indios ranqueles,* 3rd ed. (Buenos Aires, 1947)
Mármol, José, *Amalia* (Buenos Aires, 1944)
Poesía gauchesca, ed. J. L. Borges and A. Bioy Casares, 2 vols. (Mexico, 1955)
Sarmiento, Domingo, *Facundo; Civilización y barbarie* (Buenos Aires, 1958)

Historical and critical texts

Anderson, Imbert, Enrique, 'Echeverría y el socialismo romántico', in *Escritores de América* (Buenos Aires, 1954)
——, *Genio y figura de Domingo Sarmiento* (Buenos Aires, 1967)
Borges, J. L., *El Gaucho Martín Fierro* (London, 1964)
Carilla, E., *El romanticismo en la América hispánica,* rev. ed., 2 vols. (Madrid, 1967)
Halperín Donghi, Tulio, *El pensamiento de Echeverría* (Buenos Aires, 1951)
Jitrik, Noé, *Muerte y resurrección de 'Facundo'* (Buenos Aires, 1968)
Martínez Estrada, Ezequiel, *Meditaciones Sarmientinas* (Santiago de Chile, 1968)
——, *Muerte y transfiguración de Martín Fierro,* 2 vols. (Mexico, 1958)
Onís, Federico de, *España en América* (Universidad de Puerto Rico, Río Piedras, 1955)
Rojas, Ricardo, *Historia de la literatura argentina,* 9 vols. (Buenos Aires, 1960)

Chapter 3

THE INHERITANCE OF ROMANTICISM

Desdeñábamos todo lo que a clasicismo tiránico apesta, y nos dábamos un hartazgo de Hugo y Byron, Espronceda, García Tassara y Enrique Gil.

(Ricardo Palma)

THAT CHANGE OF SENSIBILITY which is called Romanticism embraced among its sometimes contradictory aspects an intense subjectivity, a quest for originality, a belief in national genius, the flight from the city to the countryside, the exploration of a visionary world of dream and the subconscious, the release from constraint whether moral or formal, the exaltation of spontaneity, and the celebration of liberty. Which of these aspects was most important tended to vary according to national circumstances. In Latin America, still fresh from Independence, it was the idea of originality, of national genius, which most speedily gained currency. Aesthetic and formal considerations were less pressing.

Romanticism came to Latin America, as Ricardo Palma implies, in a diluted form, by way of Spanish and French influence.[1] Long after the battles had been won and lost in Europe, when Realism was the new vanguard, Latin Americans fought shadowy campaigns and still regarded Romanticism as the modern movement *par excellence*. Chile in the 1840s saw Sarmiento and other Argentine exiles upholding Romanticism against the reservations of Andrés Bello.[2] When Echeverría wrote his *Dogma socialista* in the 1830s, he identified Romanticism with the modern attitude as compared with the old-fashioned Spanish traditionalism.[3]

But most of all Romanticism inspired writers to create their own national cultures. They were conscious of living in lands and among people who had, as yet, no literature. As Juan León Mera wrote in the preface to his novel *Cumandá*, America was as yet an undiscovered continent.

Razón hay para llamar vírgenes a nuestras regiones orientales: ni la

55

industria y la ciencia han estudiado todavía su naturaleza, ni la poesía la ha cantado, ni la filosofía ha hecho la disección de la vida y costumbres de los jívaros, zapados y otras familias indígenas y bárbaras que vegetan en aquellos desiertos, divorciados de la sociedad civilizada.

We find Echeverría, Sarmiento, Alberdi, and Mitre making similar claims for the Plate region.[4]

To propose originality was easier than to execute it, however. The quest for a new national culture inevitably brought the Romantic writer up against the contradictions of his position in an under-developed country, in which originality meant backwardness. To embrace modernity meant to reject natural man, to attempt to control nature. And 'modernity' in the European sense could simply be a disastrous state of neo-colonialism. Neither could the Romantic writer always detect where the freedom he sang ran over into chaos. Romanticism, which in Europe responded to industrialisation, in Latin America ironically emphasised underdevelopment. That is why when studying Latin American Romanticism it is necessary to look below the surface to the hidden—and ultimately very traditional—structures.

I. THE HISTORICAL NOVEL AND THE 'TRADICIÓN'

The novel was a genre which had no past in Latin America. There was no tradition of the novel and writers simply imitated what was most popular in contemporary Europe—namely the historical novels of Walter Scott. In doing so, they were conscious of a national project—that by fictionalising history, they were also reinterpreting it in the new light of Independence. They believed therefore that their work had a didactic function, to indoctrinate the people in their national tradition. The result was inevitably a test-tube novel, one written for ideological reasons and all too often unreadable. They are historical tracts, sweetened with a romantic intrigue that is frequently absurd or monstrous. In *La novia del hereje* (1846) by Vicente Fidel López (Argentina; 1815-1903), a historian and politician, the substance lies behind the scaffolding of an unbelievable love affair between a noble English pirate and a Peruvian maiden. In novels such as *Amalia* the texture is rich enough to support the conventions of the plot, but such examples are very rare. The author's message was usually discernible in his very choice of period. The Mexican Eligio Ancona (1836-93) depicted the struggles of the indigenous civilisations against the Spaniards and set his novels, *La cruz y la espada* (1864) and *Los mártires de Anáhuac* (1870), at the time of the

Conquest. The Cuban woman Romantic writer, Gertrudis de Avel-
laneda (1814-73) in *Guatemocín* (1846) also described the Conquest.
In such novels, the theme is inevitably the defeat of the indigenous
race and the loss of paradise. The most successful of these Indianist
historical novels is *Enriquillo* (1882) by Manuel de Jesús Galván
(Dominican Republic; 1834-1911), which is a very careful historical
reconstruction based on contemporary documents. The plot, through
the usual love story of thwarted love, is more skilfully blended with the
historical material. It concerns the love of an Indian chief Enriquillo
who is befriended by Bartolomé de las Casas, and his cousin Mencía
who is part Indian, part Spaniard.

The structure of *Enriquillo* does, of course, imply a view of the
Conquest that is coloured by Catholicism. Christian enlightenment
prevails and finally checks the worst instincts of those who only think
of exploiting the Indians. But this is an idealisation of history. The
Indian disappeared from Santo Domingo because of exploitation and
for Galván to end his novel on an optimistic note betrays an attempt
to present Spanish colonisation in the best possible light. We shall find
that it is a general characteristic of the Romantic novel in Latin
America to idealise reality, and this idealisation springs from nostalgic
traditionalism rather than from a forward-looking Utopianism.

This generalisation would seem to apply less to historical novels
set in the colonial period, novels such as those of the Mexican Justo
Sierra O'Reilly (1814-61), *La novia del hereje* by Vicente Fidel López,
El Inquisidor Mayor (1882) by Manuel Bilbao (1828-95), whose main-
spring is an attack on Catholic obscurantism. Yet none of these transcends anachronism. It is only with the *tradición*, a genre which is
considered later in this chapter, that the colonial period can be
re-evaluated.

The most obvious choice of period for the historical novelist was
that of Independence, for it was near enough in time to be vivid, and
by its very nature the Independence struggle implied a national theme.
A novel such as *Juan de la Rosa* by the Bolivian Nataniel Aguirre
(1843-88), which portrayed the heroic fight of the people of Cocha-
bamba, had a degree of vividness and actuality that was lacking in the
reconstructions of the remote pre-Columban societies. The question
still arises as to whether the material would not have been better em-
ployed in a straightforward historical work. Most writers, however, believed that by using the novel form they had a freer hand and were
more likely to get their ideas across to people. The Uruguayan novelist
Eduardo Acevedo Díaz (1851-1921) wrote a series of novels on the
entire campaign of the Uruguayans, first against Spain and then against
the Brazilian occupation, believing that he had ordered the material
according to 'una luz superior a nuestra lógica'. In the preface to the
first novel of the series, *Ismael* (1888), he wrote that the novel was

superior to straight history because of the vision it gave, not simply of the past, but of the national future.

Acevedo Díaz's historical novels comprise the trilogy *Ismael, Nativa* (1890), and *Grito de gloria* (1893); and a fourth novel, *Lanza y sable,* written as late as 1914, continues the story into the Independence period, during the rule of the *caudillos,* and especially of one man, the *archicaudillo* Fructuoso Rivera who, like Sarmiento's Facundo, destroys civic order in the name of personal rule.

The weakness of Acevedo Díaz—one he shared with all the writers of historical novels mentioned here—lies in the routine nature of his language. We have only to compare Martí's vivid, concrete description of General Páez[5] with the Uruguayan's more conventional representation of the lands left desolate by guerrilla warfare:

> Las campañas antes tan hermosas, rebosantes de vida, estaban. ahora mustias, llenas de desolación profunda. Creeríase que un ciclón inmenso las hubiese devastado de norte a sur y del este al occidente, sepultando hasta el último rebaño bajo las ruinas del desastre.
>
> Soplaba como un viento asolador sobre los campos; la gran propiedad parecía aniquilada. No se veía ya numerosos los ganados agrupados en los valles o en las faldas de las sierras.

The conventional adjectives and the colourless verbs take some of the force from the description. The author and the reader are passive observers of an empty scene.

Language was the critical factor, what in the last resort separated the mediocre imitation from the genuine creation. The historical novel generally failed in this respect. True originality could not spring solely from material. It was the invention of a new genre, the *tradición,* which exploited a more colloquial language, that enabled historical writing to rise above mediocrity.

The *tradición* was the creation of one man, the Peruvian Ricardo Palma (1833-1919), who achieved a genuinely new vision of the historical past by drawing on two existing literary antecedents—the art of oral story-telling, which had never been lost in Latin America, and the *costumbrista* sketch. *Costumbrismo* was a style of writing which had been developed in nineteenth-century Spain and which consisted of depictions of folk-types. Palma, however, was not content simply to accept existing precedents.

Palma began his career as a poet and a dramatist, but his interest in history and in historical documents seemed to have turned his attention towards the writing of 'traditions' based on anecdotes and incidents that he himself discovered in the national archives. Although in youth he appears to have nursed political ambitions and also had wanted to be a serious historian, his lack of success in both these fields

led him to take refuge in creative writing. In 1872 he had published
his first series of *Tradiciones peruanas*, the fruit of twelve years labour.
They represented a consolation, as he explained to the historian
Vicuña Mackenna: 'me retiré a cuarteles de invierno, es decir, busqué
refugio y solaz en la historia y en la literatura'.[6] From this point onwards he published his 'traditions' at frequent intervals despite the fact
that in 1882, during the Chilean occupation of Lima, he lost both his
personal library and saw the Chilean troops destroy the National
Library. In 1883, he was made Director of the new National Library
and played a major role in building up a new collection until his enforced resignation to give way to Manuel González Prada in 1912.

Palma stands quite apart from other Romantic writers in nineteenth-
century Latin America in his attitude to his art. His contemporaries
among historical novelists invariably believed that literature was
didactic. Their novels were intended to be history lessons and to
instil a sense of nationality. Not so the 'traditions' of Palma. For him,
as for Gautier, art was neither moral nor utilitarian, a view that was
later to endear him to Rubén Darío. Indeed, long before Darío confessed his love of the seven deadly sins as well as of the seven
theological virtues, Palma wrote 'ya vivo con Cristo, ya estoy con
Satanás'. This 'amorality' perhaps gave him a more objective vision of
the past:

> La pluma debe correr ligera y ser sobria en detalles. Las apreci-
> aciones deben ser rápidas. La filosofía del cuento o consejo ha de
> desprenderse por sí sola, sin que el autor la diga.[7]

Palma looks to the past, then, not to draw moral lessons but for sheer
enjoyment of human foibles. He likes to see human ingenuity exercised
against authority, law, religious and social sanctions. Perhaps, for this
reason alone, he preferred the colonial period, a time of strict conventions and protocol, the period of viceroys and Inquisition and therefore
extremely fertile in transgressions and hypocrisy. His attitude is one
of ironical appreciation of events which, seen across the abyss of time,
lose the power to shock. Here, for instance, is a portrait of a 'lady of
pleasure' who, had she been a contemporary of Palma, could hardly
have been treated with such good-humoured indulgence:

> Leonorcica Michel era lo que hoy llamaríamos una limeña de
> *rompe y rasga,* lo que en los tiempos del virrey Amat se conocía
> por una mocita del *tecum* y de las que se amarran la liga encima de
> la rodilla. Veintisiete años con más mundo que el que descubrió
> Colón, color sonrosado, ojos de más preguntas y respuestas que el
> catecismo, nariz de escribano por lo picaresca, labios retozones, una
> tabla de pecho como para asirse a ella un náufrago. La moza, en fin,
> no era *boccato di cardenale,* sino *boccato* de concilio ecuménico.[8]

The use of the diminutive at the beginning sets the burlesque tone. The reader is invited not to identify himself with Leonorcica but to share the author's familiarity with a person who is no lady. His description of her as 'wearing the garter above the knee' and of 'knowing more of the world than Columbus' has exactly the right lightness of touch. Without the value-loaded implications of the word 'prostitute', Palma's portrait conveys the attractions and the excessive familiarity of the girl. The portrait is unlike a *costumbrista* sketch in that Leonorcica is not presented as a type. She is a lively individual whose large comfortable breasts (a plank to a drowning man) and quick tongue have nothing in common with the languid Limeñan society beauties. The portrait is rounded off with a saucy dig at the clergy (she is a mouthful not simply for a cardinal but for a whole ecumenical council), which is not only amusing but tells us about Leonorcica's relations with the relaxed and licentious creole priests. People are no better than they should be, such is the general impression left at the end of the *tradición*.

In painting the portrait of a Leonorcica, Palma was dealing with matters which his contemporaries considered unfit for literature, and not all his work could be published in his lifetime. However, the humour did allow Palma to broach topics which could certainly not have been the subjects of serious literature of the period, and not only sexual topics but also matters such as race relations and the corruption of the clergy. Compare, for instance, a *tradición* called 'La emplazada' on the subject of race with the Cuban anti-slavery novel *Cecilia Valdés* (see below, pp. 63-4). In *Cecilia Valdés*, a mulatto girl falls in love with a white man with tragic consequences, as this was a taboo relationship in the society of the time. In 'La emplazada', a white widow takes a mulatto lover because he happens to be the most attractive man within reach. The story ends tragically because her chaplain is jealous of the mulatto and carries slanderous tales about him to the widow. The widow cruelly punishes her lover and, in revenge, he forecasts the exact hour of her death. She becomes 'La emplazada' whose death mysteriously occurs exactly when it was predicted, but it is jealousy not race relations that causes the tragedy. Moreover, the tragic ending is simply an excuse, an anecdote which allows Palma to present a saucy intrigue. The widow, Verónica, is never a tragic character, being described as 'jamón mejor conservado, ni en Westfalia'. Her relations with the mulatto are presented as a natural outcome of the situation, the reader's complicity having been secured in the following manner:

> Y como cuando el diablo no tiene que hacer, mata moscas con el rabo, y en levas de amor, no hay tallas, sucedió lo que ustedes sin ser brujos ya habrán adivinado.

'Idle hands make idle work', 'All's fair in love and war', these proverbial sayings enshrine ancient lore and knowledge of human nature. By passing it off in this way, Palma could seduce the reader into accepting an outrageous situation.

Palma's pleasure is in the story told for sheer entertainment, as it might have been told by the old men of a village before the days of mass entertainment. As he was the first to admit, he drew directly on living tradition, sometimes his anecdote being nothing more than a version of a popular folk-tale. An example of this is the popular tale of the outwitting of the devil which two other Latin American writers, Tomás Carrasquilla and Ricardo Güiraldes, were also to use.[9] In all three versions, the wily, apparently slow provincial is more than a match for the evil one, but Palma's version, 'Desdichas de Pirindín', has a particularly vivid picture of a sad and defeated devil leaving town:

> Resuelto, pues, a irse con sus petates a otra parte, dirigióse a la acequia de la cárcel, rompió la escarcha, lavóse cara y brazos con agua helada, pasóse los dedos a guisa de peine por la enmarañada guedeja, lanzó un regüeldo que, por el olor a azufre, se sintió en todo Pasco y veinte leguas a la redonda, y paso entre paso, cogitabundo y maltrecho, llegó al sitio denominado Uliachi.

The humour here is in the picture of an all too human devil whose supernatural powers cannot relieve the misery of a cold winter's morning when he leaves the jail. Only the belch is supernatural. It is as if Palma is saying 'We all know that the devil does not exist but it is amusing to imagine that he does'. It is this scepticism which distinguishes Palma from his contemporaries who, because they were more directly involved in beliefs and ideologies, were unable to take a detached stance that so often characterises good art.

II. THE THWARTED LOVERS OF THE NOVELA SENTIMENTAL

A glance at the titles of many Romantic novels of the nineteenth century reveals a marked preference for feminine protagonists. In Argentina we note *Soledad* (1847) by Bartolomé Mitre (1821-1906) and *Esther* (1851) by Miguel Cané (1812-63); in Colombia, *María* (1867) by Jorge Isaacs (1837-95) and *Manuela* (1889) by Eugenio Díaz (1804-65); *Clemencia* (1869) by the Mexican Ignacio Altamirano (1834-93); *Cecilia Valdés* (1892) by the Cuban Cirilo Villaverde (1812-94); *Cumandá* (1879) by the Ecuadorian Juan León Mera (1832-94); and *Amalia* by the Argentinian José Mármol (1815-71).[10]

To read these novels is to discover a repeated plot pattern—that of love thwarted by class or racial divisions. Latin Americans placed their own interpretations on the European *Paul et Virginie*. Their heroines are a new type of woman, like the *mestiza* Manuela, the mulatto woman Cecilia Valdés, the Jewish girl María, the creole girl Cumandá who is educated by Indians. Through these heroines, whose love affairs usually ended in tragedy, the author expressed a sense of nationhood cruelly thwarted by outside factors. The heroines are identified with the indigenous, often they are spokeswoman for the author's own commitment on behalf of the national genius opposed to foreign imitation.

Consider, for instance, this description of Manuela, which emphasises qualities quite different from those of the languid Victorian heroines:

> Verdaderamente que Manuela estaba seductora ese día. Su brazo, no muy blanco a la verdad, pero carnudo y sombreado por el vello, se desplegaba con elegancia hasta la mitad de la mesa, llevando y trayendo la pesada plancha, de cuyos movimientos se resentía su delgada cintura; su pecho se avanzaba en ocasiones sobre la mesa, sin más adornos que su fina camisa de tira sencilla, y es sabido el influjo favorable de la naturaleza de todos los climas calientes para la conservación de la lozanía, aun en las mujeres de alguna edad; bien es que nuestra heroína no pasaba todavía de los diez y siete.

What strikes the reader in this description is the attempt to get away from the European stereotype. The dark hair on the girl's arms, her very occupation—ironing—removes her from the aristocratic or the idealised Northern blonde. We find the similar departure from stereotype in the portrait of the 'bronze Venus', Cecilia Valdés, and in the picture of the *mestiza* mother of Juan de la Rosa, eponymous hero of the Bolivian historical novel mentioned previously. The protagonist's mother, 'Rosa la linda encajera', is described as having

> dientes blanquísimos, menudos, apretados, como solo pueden tenerlos las mujeres indias de cuya sangre debían correr algunas gotas en las venas.

Even Jorge Isaac's María has more of the oriental than the Western woman.

> María me ocultaba sus ojos tenazmente; pero pude admirar en ellos la brillantez y hermosura de los de las mujeres de su raza ...

Equally some male heroes are non-European. There is Enriquillo,[11] for instance, and there are the unattractive, inarticulate heroes of Ignacio Altamirano's *El zarco* (1901) and *Clemencia,* in both of which an 'ugly hero' of obvious Indian descent proves himself more noble than the handsome stereotype.

But to reject the European stereotype was only a timid first step and by no means implied that the author had altogether freed himself from values imposed from without. If we examine one of the best 'thwarted love' novels of the nineteenth century, *Cecilia Valdés*, we shall see that the author's attitude to race was fraught with conflict. Cirilo Villaverde who wrote the novel was, in his way, a remarkable and enlightened person. Involved in the Mina de Rosa Cubana conspiracy of 1848, he was sentenced to death by garroting, although the sentence was later commuted to one of life imprisonment. In 1849, he fled from prison and succeeded in reaching the United States where, except for a brief return to Cuba in 1858, he remained in exile for the rest of his life. Begun in the 1830s, his novel was only published in its final form in 1882 when the events the author described had already passed into history.

The 'plot' of the novel is conventionally Romantic. The heroine falls in love with a man who, unknown to her, is her half-brother. The father, ashamed of his past, refuses to acknowledge her as his daughter and hides the relationship, thus precipitating the tragedy. The incestuous love affair is consummated. Cecilia becomes pregnant, and on hearing of her lover's marriage, plots to kill the bride, but the man she sends to execute this vengeance is Pimentón who is also in love with her and who kills the lover instead of the girl. Mistaken identities, a heroine of unknown origin, love and vengeance : all these are common features of Romantic plot. What puts the novel outside the conventional framework are the race relations which are involved, for Cecilia is the daughter of a Spanish father and a black mother, the thwarted love affair with her half-brother reflects an unconscious taboo on the part of the author who could not possibly envisage the affair between the races as ending in anything but tragedy.

But all relationships in a colonial and essentially a racist society are doomed to failure, or tragedy. Cecilia's father regards his slaves as 'bultos' or 'fardos' and prefers to risk the loss of a few slaves thrown overboard rather than the loss of a ship during a storm; his son's generation regard the black and mulatto girls as sexual merchandise. They are prepared to make conventional marriages but they find real enjoyment in the dance halls and bars frequented by the coloured population. This sexual pleasure which comes from relationships with inferiors is paralleled by the inhumanity with which Cecilia's father treats his personal slaves. He is prepared to whip a slave for disobedience and cannot see what is wrong when slaves are tortured for running away. The indignity of slavery is that one set of human beings have the right to take possession of another group and treat them as objects. But freed slaves or free mulattos or slaves who try to educate themselves are equally victims of this society. Cecilia is condemned to semi-prostitution, the educated slave Dionisio becomes an outcast, and a slave who shows off his knowledge of sugar manufacture on the plantation earns the enmity of the white boss's son, who cannot bear to admit that a black man can be in any way superior to him.

Cecilia Valdés anticipates Afro-Cubanism of the twenties in showing two contrasted societies, one vital and black, one moribund and white. On the one hand there are the carriage drives, and the receptions of the aristocracy and the white middle class, the best of whom are the students whose more advanced ideas come into conflict with parental values. But below this surface there throbs the real life of Havana, with its popular balls and the African music. Here, for instance, the author describes the black man's traditional skills as a musician:

> Afinados los instrumentos, sin mas dilación rompió la música con una contradanza nueva, que a los pocos compases no pudo menos de llamar la atención general y arrancar una salva de aplausos, no solo porque la pieza era buena sino porque los oyentes eran conocedores; acierto éste que creerán sin esfuerzo los que sepan cuán organizada para la música nace la gente de color.

Feeling is lacking in this kind of writing because the author's documentary purpose takes priority. But despite the flatness of the language, the novel has real merits, not the least of which is its searching presentation of race relations.

Cumandá by the Ecuadorian Juan León Mera deals with the problem of race in a manner very different from *Cecilia Valdés*, as might be expected from a writer who lived in the puritanical climate of Quito during the theocratic dictatorship of García Moreno. Born in the provincial town of Ambato, Juan León Mera was a supporter of the dictator and an enemy of Montalvo. A politician as well as a writer, he represents a conservative strain of Romanticism, influenced by Chateaubriand and, like Chateaubriand, deriving from a Catholic tradition and outlook. In these writers, the 'noble savage' theme does conflict with Catholic dogma. Like the Jesuits, whose missionary reports in the seventeenth and eighteenth centuries helped to propagate the identification of the Indian with natural man, these writers believed that civilisation corrupts and that the unspoiled Indians of the Americas are therefore potentially better Christians than the more sophisticated Europeans. Moreover, like many sincere Catholics, both writers doubted the policy of colonisation, seeing this as a force of evil both for the coloniser and the colonised.

The plot of *Cumandá* is a clumsy imitation of *René*. The heroine, a beautiful Indian girl, falls in love with Carlos Orozco, son of a Spanish landowner turned priest. Several times this child of nature is able to save her lover from death, but her tribe's hatred of the white man brings about their separation, and she is betrothed and married against her will to a chief. On his death, she is expected to immolate herself according to the custom. Despite her efforts to escape, both she and Carlos die; only after her death is it discovered that she is the lost daughter of Orozco and Carlos's half-sister.

The novel avoids the identification of the Indian as the child of nature. The Indian tribes are cruel, vengeful, and ignorant, with the exception of Cumandá who is really of Spanish descent. However, the novel is of interest for its criticism of the exploitation of the Indians which has come about through colonisation. The father of Carlos and Cumandá is a man who had treated his Indian labourers as objects to the point where they rise in rebellion and massacre his family, except for himself, Carlos who is away at school, and Cumandá who is carried off to live in the tribe. But like the Jesuits, Mera believes that Christianity is the one force which can temper the greed of the exploiter and moderate the cruelty of the Indians who are savage only because ignorant of good and evil. Thus the author apostrophises the Indian:

> Vuestra alma tiene mucho de la naturaleza de vuestros bosques: se la limpia de las malezas que la cubren, y la simiente del bien germina y crece en ella con rapidez: pero fáltale la afanosa mano del cultivador, y al punto volverá a su primitivo estado de barbarie.

Nature in itself is neither good nor evil. It reflects man's passions and fears, as when Cumandá flees through the dark jungles which are lashed by high winds:

> Espantosa navegación. Negro el cielo, pues hay todavía nubes tempestuosas que se cruzan veloces robando a cada instante la escasa luz de las estrellas; negras las aguas; negras las selvas que las coronan, y recio el viento que las hace gemir y azota la desigual superficie de las olas, el cuadro que la naturaleza presenta por todos lados es funesto y medroso.

The parallel with Chateaubriand is evident and yet it is also superficial. Cumandá is running away from barbarism towards civilisation, unlike René who is in flight from civilisation. But the civilisation towards which Cumandá strives is not Echeverría's or Sarmiento's but the ideal of the Spanish missionaries who, like Mera, believed:

> Cada cruz plantada por el sacerdote católico en aquellas soledades, era un centro donde obraba un misterioso poder que atraía las tribus errantes para fijarlas en torno, agregarlas a la familia humana y hacerlas gozar de las delicias de la comunión racional y cristiana.

This is a viewpoint that would have been perfectly acceptable in the seventeenth century.

The concept of nature found in a novelist like Mera is undoubtedly nearer to Chateaubriand than to the reality of the jungle. It was not until the twentieth century that the Latin American writer was to see the jungle in all its horror. Influenced above all by French Romantics, writers such as Juan León Mera and Jorge Isaacs regarded nature as a reflection of divine Providence, repeating in its structures ideal patterns. This view of a divinely ordained nature informs the idyllic landscapes of *María*, a novel influenced by Bernardin de Saint-Pierre's *Paul et Virginie*. The author, Jorge Isaacs, was of Jewish origin and of a family which had recently emigrated to Colombia from the British island of Jamaica. He was a member of the literary group *El Mosaico* which helped him publish his novel *María*, which like many other Romantic novels of the period represents a conservative and Christian strain of Romanticism.

The story of María is narrated by Efraín, a landowner's son who, after years away at boarding school, returns to the family estate to find that his sisters and his cousin María are no longer children. He and María fall in love in the idyllic surroundings of a landscape in which it is always spring, always flowering, and with the 'sublime' vista of the Andes in the distance:

> se veían las crestas desnudas de las montañas sobre el fondo estrellado del cielo. Las auras del desierto pasaban por el jardín, recogiendo aromas, para venir a juguetear con los rosales que nos rodeaban. El viento voluble dejaba oír por instantes el rumor del río. Aquella Naturaleza parecía ostentar toda la hermosura de sus noches, como para recibir a un huésped amigo.

Nature here is a garden, an adornment. Every element in nature is in harmony—mountain, wind, river. And as long as men know their station, they too live in harmony and happiness:

> Viajero años después por las montañas del país de José, he visto, ya a puestas del sol, llegar labradores alegres a la cabaña, donde se me daba hospitalidad; luego que alababan a Dios ante el venerable jefe de la familia, esperaban en torno del hogar la cena que la anciana y cariñosa madre repartía; un plato bastaba a cada pareja de esposos, y los pequeñuelos hacían pinicos apoyados en las rodillas de sus padres.

This is a genre painting of the happy peasant, contented with his lot. The harmony depends on a landowning class who are sufficiently paternalistic to represent a force of social cohesion. The paternalistic landowner educates, protects, and maintains racial harmony even in remote areas where there is no other law and order. Efraín's father is the embodiment of this ideal, strong but kind, merciful to the slave girl, Nay, whom he buys in order to set free (an action which effectively ties her to the family). What elevates Efraín's father to this ideal is, however, the Christian religion which he has adopted and which is superior as a moral force to the Judaism which had been the family religion. Nevertheless, the story is a tragedy. María's health is fragile and she dies when Efraín goes away to study in England. The passions, proper to adolescence, must disappear and give way to the mature virtues of discipline and responsibility.

Thus behind the 'original' façade of the Spanish American Romantic novel, traditional values are reinforced rather than shaken. Race relations and man's place within the framework of nature are unaltered. The hierarchy of the natural world, the scale of racial types and social classes, still has the white Catholic landowner at its peak. In Argentina, this nostalgia for stable, hierarchical values is particularly significant. In the early years of the century under Rosas, landowners and *caudillos* were aligned against the forces of modernity and the intellectuals; but in the late nineteenth century, after the first period of European immigration, the writer began to feel a sense of nostalgia for the land insofar as it represented all that was most traditionally Argentinian. Typical of this outlook is the work of Joaquín V. González (1863-1923), journalist, politician, and author of a series of descriptions and sketches of the Andean region which he called *Mis montañas*. As Romantic in its manner as *María* or *Cumandá*, *Mis montañas* was written in a prose that often recalled that of Sarmiento, although the author was far from sharing Sarmiento's distinction between civilisation and barbarism. For González, nature does not represent the threat of anarchy but is a temple, the reflection of a divine harmony:

> Y qué soledad tan llena de ruidos extraños. Qué harmonía tan grandiosa la de aquel conjunto de sonidos aunados en la altura en la profunda noche. El torrente que salta entre las piedras, los gajos que se chocan entre sí, las hojas que silban, los millares de insectos que en el aire y en las grietas hablan su lenguaje peculiar, el viento que cruza estrechándose entre las gargantas y las peñas, las pisadas que resuenan a los lejos, el estrépito de los derrumbaderos, los relinchos que el eco repite de cumbre en cumbre, los gritos del arriero que guía la piara entre las sombras densas, como protegido por genios invisibles, cantando una vidalita lastimera que interrumpe a cada instante el seco golpe de su guardamonte de cuero, y ese indescriptible, indescrifrable solemne gemido de viento en las regiones superiores, semejante a la nota de un órgano que hubiera quedado resonando bajo la bóveda de un templo abandonado: todo esto se escucha en medio de esas montañas; es su lenguaje, es la manifestación de su alma henchida de poesía y de grandeza.

Each element of nature in this description—the torrent, the insects, the wind, man himself—has its own musical scale, its own language. What is undecipherable to man has its meaning in the harmony of the whole, within the 'temple' of creation. Although the work consists of a series of loosely-connected sketches, each essay—on flora, fauna, on human types and places, on crops and customs—reinforces the message of harmony. The work of the man who tills the land is one more note in the hymn of creation:

Qué quintas aquellas y cómo el trabajo unido de toda una genera-
ción era coronado por la tierra fecunda. Cómo reinaban el bullicio y
la vida en aquella aldea habitada por una aristocracia de limpio
pergamino, por familias que habían ilustrado su nombre en la
historia local, y habían fundados su hogar común con la noble y
asidua labor agrícola.

Like Mera and Jorge Isaacs, the writer orders his universe into a
hierarchy with untamed nature at the base. The aristocrats of the
earth are those who work the land from generation to generation.
Gutiérrez's ideal is a return to the primitive Christian community—
the basis of which, he believes, is already there in the 'municipio'. And
once again, it is Catholicism that is destined to form the cohesive link
between peoples of different races and give dignity to human life.

The examples of Romantic writing we have studied in this chapter
are among the best afforded by the nineteenth century. They give an
indication of the nature of Romantic influence which inspired 'original'
themes but was conservative in essence. The authors are for the most
part traditional and Catholic in outlook. Only by understanding this,
can we appreciate how revolutionary was Modernism in its break with
Catholic tradition.

III. POETRY

The influence of Romanticism was as important to poetry as to prose.
Echeverría had declared that it penetrated beneath the surface aspects
of life:

> es la voz íntima de la conciencia, la sustancia viva de las pasiones,
> el profético mirar de la fantasía, el espíritu meditabundo de la
> filosofía, penetrando y animando con la magia de la imaginación los
> misterios del hombre, de la creación y la providencia.[12]

Yet this influence proved more revolutionary in theory than in practice.
Poets concentrated on originality of subject-matter and the translation
of Byronic or Hugoesque themes into a Latin American context. And
as in prose-writing, patriotism, the Indian, nature provided the 'original'
themes. Condors instead of eagles, the Andes instead of the Alps, and
Niagara or Tequendama instead of the waterfalls of Europe.

Poetry like fiction was still considered, before Modernism, to have
a didactic function. This helps to account for the popularity of the
long poems on national themes, poems like *Tabaré* by the Uruguayan
José Zorrilla de San Martín (1855-1931) and like *Gonzalo de Oyón*
by the Colombian Julio Arboleda (1817-61). *Tabaré* (1886) told the
story of 'una raza muerta'—the *charrúa* tribe—which had disappeared

from the face of Uruguay in the years following the Conquest. The poet assumes the voice of the dead race, thus restoring them to their place in history (as Neruda was to do with Incas in his 'Alturas de Machu Picchu'). Zorrilla de San Martín, a fervent Catholic, believed that only through the mediation of Catholicism could these races have been saved from extinction. Zorrilla de San Martín's patriotic poem is a justification of Spanish conquest and of the establishment of the Catholic faith in America:

> España va; la cruz de su bandera,
> Su incomparable hidalgo;
> La noble madre raza, en cuyo pecho,
> Si un mundo se estrelló, se hizo pedazos.

Liberty is the theme of an Argentine patriotic poem, *El nido de condores* by Olegario Andrade (1839-82), which describes San Martín's crossing of the Andes. Here the condor and the 'sublime' Andean peaks are symbols of freedom and of human aspiration. They nest in the topmost summit:

> Todo es silencio en torno. Hasta las nubes
> van pasando calladas,
> Como tropas de espectros que dispersan
> Las ráfagas heladas.

Andrade's poem stems from the same tradition as that of Olmedo, a tradition of heroic poetry intended to enshrine national heroes. It is during this period, after all, that the words of many of the national anthems were written, with their calls to death, glory, and acts of heroism.

The long poem, however, dealt with other themes than the heroic or the patriotic legend. Bello's 'Oda a la agricultura' created another tradition—that of the Virgilian celebration of the cattle and the corn of America, of man's peaceful pursuits. The Colombian poet Gregorio Gutiérrez González (1826-72) wrote *Memorias sobre el cultivo del maíz en Antioquía* (1866) which, despite the title, is not a farmer's handbook but a poem which describes the cultivation of corn from the clearing and burning of the land to the harvest. The poet's vision of a harmonious and peaceful life lived on the land is not unlike that of Isaac or Joaquín González.

> Lanza la choza cual penacho blanco
> La vara de humo que se eleva recta;
> Es que antes que el sol y que las aves
> Se levantó, al fogón, la cocinera.

> Ya tiene preparado el desayuno
> Cuando al peón más listo se despierta;
> Chocolate de harina en coco negro
> Recibe cada cual con media arepa.

The very regularity of the hendecasyllable with the caesura almost invariably breaking the middle of the line creates an effect of repeated day-to-day activity, almost of security. And the vocabulary is full of homely touches, with its references to *coco* and to the *arepa* or maize cake. In this way, the poet creates a sense of ordered, domestic activity on which a Christian community must rest.

Even in lyric poetry, the treatment of these major themes is not different. There are patriotic lyrics, poems on Indian themes such as the *Cantos de Netzahualcoyotl* by the Mexican José Joaquín de Pesado (1801-61), and—most popular of all—the pastoral idyll set in the American countryside: poems such as 'Bajo el mango' by the Cuban José Jacinto Milanés (1814-63) or the *Escenas del campo y de la aldea de México* by José Joaquín de Pesado. The latter wrote *costumbrista*-type lyrics describing cockfighting and markets:

> Están en limpias esteras
> Naranjas de oro encendidas
> Limas cual cera, y teñidas
> De vivo carmín las peras.[13]

There is nothing in these lines which could not have been written by a seventeenth-century Spaniard except, perhaps, for the reference to oranges. In phrases such as *limpias esteras* and *vivo carmín*, the adjective appears to have no function other than that of filling the line. But the importance of order and regularity is paramount. Pesado's compatriot, Manuel José Othón, some of whose best poetry was written during the Modernist period, mostly wrote poetry descriptive of Mexican scenes, such as the *Himno de los bosques* (1891); in 1902 he published his *Poemas rústicos*.

Having examined the prose-writing and the poetry influenced by Romanticism in Latin America, we must conclude that order was more important to the writers than freedom, tradition more important than exploration, authority more important than subjectivism. Novelists and poets were concerned with the creation of oases of order and calm in anarchic societies, with conservation rather than revolution. Bearing this in mind, we are better prepared to understand the importance of Modernism and the revolutionary nature of poets such as Martí and Darío who ventured outside order and perceived new depths.

It was Ortega who pointed out the popularity of Romanticism, its achievement of mass circulation.[14] In Latin America, though there was no mass public, some of the most sentimental of Romantic works took a hold on the popular taste. Romantic sensibility became sentimentality. And literature became associated with the arousal of feeling. It was against this that the avant-garde of the twenties reacted with such vehemence.

NOTES

1. J. M. Oviedo, *Genio y figura de Ricardo Palma* (Buenos Aires, 1965), p.40. Influences are discussed by E. Carrilla, *El romanticismo en la América hispánica*, rev. ed., 2 vols. (Madrid, 1967).

2. N. Pinilla, op. cit.

3. E. Echeverría, *Dogma socialista y otras páginas políticas* (Buenos Aires, 1958).

4. Leopoldo Zea discusses originality and Romanticism in *The Latin American Mind* (Norman, Oklahoma, 1963).

5. José Martí, 'Un héroe americano', *Obras completas* (La Habana, 1964), VIII, 211-19.

6. Quoted by J. M. Oviedo, op. cit., p.85.

7. ibid., p. 153.

8. The *tradición* from which the quotation is taken is 'Rudamente, pulidamente, mañosamente', set in the year 1768.

9. Tomás Carrasquilla in 'En la diestra de Dios Padre' and Güiraldes in one of the tales told by Don Segundo Sombra in his novel of that name.

10. For a general study of these Romantic novels, see M. Súarez-Murias, *La novela romántica en Hispanoamérica* (New York, 1964).

11. Hero of the novel *Enriquillo* by Manuel de Jesús Galván.

12. 'Fondo y forma en las obras de imaginación', *Obras completas*, V.

13. 'Escenas de campo y de la aldea en Méjico' included in Menéndez y Pelayo, *Antología* ...

14. *La deshumanización del arte*, 5th ed. (Madrid, 1958), p.3.

READING LIST

Anthologies

Menéndez y Pelayo, M., *Antología de poetas hispanoamericanos* (Madrid, 1893-95)

E. Carracciolo-Trejo, *The Penguin Book of Latin American Verse* (London, 1971)

Texts

Acevedo Díaz, Eduardo, *Ismael*, prologue by Robert de Ibáñez (Montevideo, 1953)

——, *Nativa*, prologue by E. Rodríguez Monegal (Montevideo, 1964)

——, *Grito de gloria* (Montevideo, 1964)

——, *Lanza y sable* (Montevideo, 1965)

Aguirre, Manuel, *Juan de la Rosa*, 5th ed. (La Paz, 1964)

Altamirano, Ignacio Manuel, *El zarco, La navidad en las montañas* (Mexico, 1960)

——, *Clemencia y La navidad en las montañas* (Mexico, 1964)

Díaz Castro, Eugenio, *Manuela*, 2 vols. (Paris, 1889)

Galván, Manuel de Jesús, *Enriquillo* (New York, 1964)

González, Joaquín V., *Mis montañas*, ed. G. Ara, 7th ed. (Buenos Aires, 1965)

Gutiérrez González, Gregorio, 'Memorias sobre el cultivo del maíz en Antioquía', included in Menéndez y Pelayo, *Antología* ...

Isaacs, Jorge, *Obras completas*, I (Medellin, 1966)

Mera, Juan León, *Cumandá* (Buenos Aires, 1961)

Palma, Ricardo, *Tradiciones peruanas completas* (Madrid, 1964)

Villaverde, Cirilo, *Cecilia Valdés* (La Habana, 1953; also La Habana, 1964)

Zorrilla de San Martín, José, *Tabaré*, with introduction by Pablo Groussac, 44th edition (Montevideo, 1896)

Historical and critical texts

Arciniegas, G., *Genio y figura de J. Isaacs* (Buenos Aires, 1968)

Carrilla, E., *El romanticismo en la América hispánica*, rev. ed., 2 vols. (Madrid, 1967)

Cometta Manzoni, Aida, *El indio en la poesía de América española* (Buenos Aires, 1958)

Echeverría, E., *Obras completas* (Buenos Aires, 1874)

Meléndez Concha, *La novela indianista en Hispanoamérica (1832-89)* (Río Piedras, Puerto Rico, 1961)

Oviedo, José Miguel, *Genio y figura de Ricardo Palma* (Buenos Aires, 1965)

Rodríguez Monegal, E., *Vínculo de sangre* (essays on Acevedo Díaz) (Montevideo, 1958)

Suárez-Murias, Marguerite C., *La novela romántica en Hispanoamérica* (New York, 1964)

Zea, Leopoldo, *The Latin American Mind* (Norman, Oklahoma, 1963)

Chapter 4

REALISM AND NATURALISM BEFORE 1914

THE THEME OF THIS CHAPTER presents difficulties, for in Spanish American (as in European) literature, it is often hard to make very sharp distinctions between the Romantic and the Realist. European Realism was, in its origins, an attempt to describe contemporary life, particularly contemporary urban life, as opposed to the historical, exotic, or imaginary. Yet both Flaubert and Balzac wrote historical novels as well as realistic works. Moreover, in many Realist novels, the plot conventions are inherited from Romantic fiction.

Because of these difficulties, I am adopting a view of Realism which may not be generally applicable. In most of the novels I discuss in this chapter, structures are similar to those of the Romantic novel except in one important respect—they represent 'degraded' versions of the ideal. The tragic outcome of ideal love is matched in the Realist novel by the tragic fate of the prostitute. The forces that part lovers in the Realist novel are corrupt social forces—class or money—rather than nature or religion. Nature is transformed from a benevolent manifestation of the divine into a malevolent energy.

Romanticism and Realism in Spanish American writing have, nevertheless, one common ancestor—*costumbrismo*. The depiction of types and of typical scenes often formed the substance of novels with Romantic or Realist plot as the scaffolding.

And Realist writers often described their work as *costumbrista*. Lucio Vicente López (1848-94), for instance, gave his novel *La gran aldea* (1884), the subtitle of 'costumbres bonaerenses'. Paul Groussac (Argentina; 1848-1929) described *Fruto vedado* (1884) as 'costumbres argentinas'. However, it would be extremely difficult to draw an exact demarcation line between Realism and *costumbrismo,* and I have preferred to subsume all attempts to depict the external world and society with verisimilitude under the category of Realism. I have chosen to draw the line between the idealised representation of reality found in the Romantic novel and the degraded version of the Realist novel.

The word 'degraded' is not, however, intended as a moral judgement. Rather it corresponds to the primitive meaning of the word which has implications of 'going down'. The Realist was aware of

73

changes in society which implied a loss of quality. Thus when the Argentine essayist Miguel Cané (1851-1905) writes, 'Nuestros padres eran soldados, poetas y artistas; nosotros somos tenderos, merca-chifles y agiotistas',[1] he is monitoring changes for the worse, his attitude being plainly explicit in his use of the word 'mercachifle'. This is precisely the kind of evaluation we meet in the Spanish American Realist novel.

Naturalism is also difficult to distinguish from Realism. The influence of Zola gave rise to many imitations in Spanish America, but in reality is difficult to isolate in any particular school. In the imitators of Zola, there is, perhaps, a greater emphasis on determinism either of environment or heredity. But the moral message is always uppermost. Among Mexican Realist and Naturalist novelists, for instance, law, order, good citizenship, the middle-class virtues are shown to be superior to personalism and disorder. Emilio Rabasa (1856-1930), for instance, wrote four *novelas mexicanas*: *La bola* (1887), *La gran ciencia* (1887), *El cuarto poder* (1888), and *Moneda falsa* (1888) in order to expose politics and the press and the dishonesty of the middle class; José López Portillo y Rojas (1850-1923) in *La parcela* (1898) lays the onus for reform on a more enlightened and morally irreproachable landowning class, and implies that the state of Mexico depends not on the social and economic structures but on the moral qualities of the landowners. Federico Gamboa (1864-1939), in *Suprema ley* (1896) and *Santa* (1903), was primarily concerned with the hypocrisy of the middle classes.[2] Elsewhere in Latin America, the moral preoccupation is uppermost at this period. In Argentina, for instance, José María Miró (pseudonym Julián Martel; 1867-96), in his novel *La bolsa* (1891), denounces greedy speculation which he identifies with the penetration of foreign (i.e., Jewish) elements into national life.[3] It is not my purpose to discuss these novels in detail but merely to select one or two of the best examples of Naturalist and Realist writing as illustrations.

There remains one geographical point to be made relating to the concentration of Naturalist and Realist novels in Argentina and Mexico. The preoccupation of writers in both these cities with change and tradition is explicable since both places underwent modernisation and were self-consciously 'progressive'.

What characterises Spanish American Realism, however, is a strong moral tone. Consider, for instance, *La gran aldea*, a novel by the Argentine writer Lucio Vicente López (1848-94). The novel purports to describe the customs of Buenos Aires, a city which had only recently been declared the capital of the republic, and in which foreign investment and the industrialisation of meat-production and packing had brought about the change from 'gran aldea' to modern city. The author, through the downfall of the central characters, exposes the evil results of their 'insaciable deseo de lujo y refinamiento', and the moral degeneration this brought about in day-to-day relationships. Here, for instance, we have the contrast between the family store and the modern business:

> ¡Oh, qué tiendas aquéllas! Me parece que veo sus puertas, su vidriera tapizada con los últimos percales recibidos, cuyas piezas avanzaban dos o tres metros a la exterior, sobre la pared de la calle; y entre las piezas de percal, la pieza de pekín lustrosa de medio ancho, clavado también en el muro, inflándose con el viento y listo para que la mano de la marchanta apreciase la calidad del género entre el índice y el pulgar, sin obligación de penetrar a la tienda.
>
> Aquélla era buena fe comercial y no la de hoy en que la enorme vidriera engolosina los ojos sin satisfacer las exigencias del tacto que reclaman nuestras madres con un derecho indiscutible.

Honesty and trust between people, physical contact between the customer and the goods she was buying are contrasted with the immoral advertisement of the modern shop. And the characters are punished for succumbing to modernity. The narrator's uncle who, on the death of a nagging wife, had married a much younger woman, finds that his new wife is only interested in a life of pleasure. He becomes the passive author of tragedy when, during his wife's absence at a ball, he dozes off; fire breaks out and their child is burned to death. The spendthrift wife, the scheming gold-digger, the innocent child victim recur in many novels of this type as symbols of the moral degradation of the new society and the suffering it brings.

I. EUGENIO CAMBACERES (1843-88)

Eugenio Cambaceres, the Argentinian Naturalist, was the author of two novels which combined the condemnation of luxury and the wickedness of the city with the tragedy of heredity. In one of these, *Sin rumbo* (1885), there was an additional theme—that of the influence of German pessimism, then a philosophical fashion, upon the lives and attitudes of people. The protagonist's ideals had been undermined by reading authors such as Schopenhauer, who convinces him that individual life has no purpose beyond the betterment of the species. This attitude kills any regard he might have for others, or any sense of the dignity of human life. Since he is a landowner's son, this position has class implications, for he seduces a country girl on his estate, tires of her, and abandons her for the more sophisticated pleasures of the city and the venal love of an opera-singer, Amorimi. As in many novels of this type, the protagonist comes to an unpleasant end. Disillusioned with the city, he returns to the countryside where he finds that his former mistress has died, leaving him the illegitimate daughter whose upbringing he now undertakes. But accident intervenes. The child falls ill and dies, and the father, with no hope left for the future, commits suicide in one of the most repulsive scenes in Spanish American literature. The novel works out to an extreme conclusion, the consequences of the individual's loss of faith and moral guidance. In another of his novels, *En la sangre* (1887), the consequences of hereditary defects are explored with equal thoroughness. Genaro is the son of an avaricious immigrant whose only concern is for making money. He lives a completely sordid life totally devoted to material ends, conforming to the Argentine stereotype of the Italian, which is very different from the Italian stereotype in Europe.[4] Genaro becomes a cold-blooded social climber. At school, he cheats at examinations. As an adult, he seduces a girl to get her to marry him and then spends her father's money. At the end of the novel, he is as brutish and miserly as his father had been. In neither novel is escape or alternative action offered. Once the formula has been set out, the conclusion inevitably follows. In other words, Cambaceres chooses only one possible pattern in the structure of his novels, a pattern of cause and effect, of linear development. The metaphor or analogy which is closest to his structure is that of the biological programming in which the organism develops according to innate tendencies. But the possibilities for Cambaceres's characters are narrower even than those which a growing plant has; in fact, they are reduced to two– purposeless survival or death.

These novels are no masterpieces. But they do offer an interesting comment on the cultural climate of the period. They have closed and deterministic structures which were perhaps appropriate to countries where modernisation was to bring greater dependence on the big industrial powers and was to reduce rather than extend possibilities of self-determination.[5]

II. ALBERTO BLEST GANA (1829-1904)

The Chilean writer Alberto Blest Gana combines social observation with Romantic plot conventions (the hero of obscure birth, for instance). He had modelled himself during his apprentice years on Balzac, whose work he came to know when studying at a French military academy. Later he wrote:

> Desde un día que leyendo Balzac hice un auto-da-fe en chimenea, condenando a llamas las impresiones rimadas de mi adolescencia, juré ser novelista y abandonar el campo literario si las fuerzas no me alcanzaban para hacer algo que no fuesen triviales y pasajeras composiciones.[6]

From his first successful novel, *La aritmética en el amor* (1860), he set out to show the forces behind Chilean society, interpreting these in the manner of Balzac. *La aritmética en el amor* follows the fate of a young man, Fortunato, who wants to climb up the social scale by making a wealthy marriage. In the course of his upward climb, he sheds a tiresome relationship with the poor but honest Amelia and plays off a couple of wealthier girls against one another. But the novel falls between cynicism, which Blest Gana has not the nerve to take to its extreme, and a romantic happy ending. The faithful Amelia wins back her bruised and defeated lover and conveniently comes into money so that he is not obliged to suffer too much for his calculations. The author has broken with Romanticism just enough to be persuaded that love does not make the world go round, but the final fusion of financial success with lover's happiness is extremely naïve:

> Su herencia, unida a la de Amelia, componía la suma de cien mil pesos: estos y su amor bastaban para asegurarles una felicidad duradera en este valle de lágrimas y de risas.

The plot and conclusion are absurd, yet one can understand why the novel won a prize, for it was the first work to attempt a portrayal of contemporary Chilean characters. The difficulty occurred when Blest Gana attempted to stencil the Balzacian situation upon Chilean society. Balzac's typical hero uses cynical methods to triumph in a corrupt world; as long as he is prepared to accept the degraded values, upward mobility is possible. But in Chile, there was comparatively little social mobility. The landed oligarchy held the country tightly and Blest Gana's Realism consists therefore in sketches of typical scenes and people against which the adventures of the protagonist appear gratuitous rather than necessary. *Martín Rivas* (1862) exemplifies these difficulties. Martín Rivas is a more consistent character than Fortunato and wins a rich wife through patience, honesty, constancy, and love despite the disadvantages of his poor, provincial background. But here again the hero's adventures are often contingent. For instance, at the climax of the novel, Leonor, the heroine, saves Martín from execution to which he is sentenced for taking part in the unsuccessful *Sociedad de la Igualdad* rebellion.[7] Martín's reasons for joining the rebellion have nothing to do with ideology. He joins out of loyalty to a friend, so that the rebellion, instead of forming an integral part of the novel, is merely a sensational plot device. Once again, the 'Realism' consists in scenes of Chilean life, the depiction of impoverished members of the middle classes (for whom both respectable marriage and legitimate work seem impossible), and descriptions of the dances and popular songs, the military parades which formed the Sunday entertainment, the September Independence celebrations.

Of the three novels of this early period, *El ideal de un calavera*

(1863) is the most successful. The hero, Abelardo Manríquez, is a poor provincial; caught up in an anti-government conspiracy and executed. The tragic ending, the frustrations of Abelardo in the course of the novel, are in sharp contrast to the Romantic treatment of previous heroes, and Blest Gana's French sources are less evident. Abelardo is a Romantic who idealises a married woman, Inés, but because of her unattainability, turns his attention to the daughter of an impoverished middle-class family. This picture of a frustrated *demi-monde* excluded from power, unable to rise socially, has dark overtones which are quite lacking in *Martín Rivas* but which would seem more in keeping with the theme. This middle sector is thrust aside by their superiors but is also separated from the classes below, from the domestic servants and the *huaso* or peasant. Abelardo's psychology also arises naturally out of a situation of frustration. He is given to crazy practical jokes (that is why he is a *calavera*) and the final conspiracy seems the last desperate resort, a tragic, misfired *calaverada*.

What mars Blest Gana's writing in all of his novels is the poverty of his literary language. His apprenticeship was served before Modernism imposed new standards of style and his prose continually falls into an uninspired flatness and cliché. He does not seem to have been affected by Modernism, although, after a long period in the diplomatic service in which he wrote little or nothing, he enjoyed a second period as a novelist. During this time he wrote *Durante la Reconquista* (1897), a historical novel set on the eve of Independence; *El loco Estero* (1909), a novel which recalled the Santiago of his youth; and *Los transplantados* (1904), on the Jamesian theme of American innocence victimised by European sophistication. In each of these novels, the theme has potentialities which the language betrays. Take, for instance, the graceless pedantry which often mars *El loco Estero*:

> El ñato **Díaz.**
> Aquel nombre, con su calificativo chileno de lo que el diccionario de la lengua llama chato, pareció ejercer sobre ellos una fascinación poderosa.

A dictionary definition would have had more charm. Blest Gana's language here has only one purpose—to give information—and this is a poor and limited use of language as far as literature is concerned. In the same novel, he describes two people falling in love in a coy awkward prose:

> Pocos días después de ese encuentro, en el que los ojos de ambos se revelaron sin disimulo la recíproca atracción de que al mismo tiempo se sintieron conmovidos.

This is why Blest Gana was not able to be the great Realist writer of Latin America. He is an interesting failure, a man who once or twice found his theme but had not a fine enough instrument in which to express it.

III. REALISM AND THE CONTEMPORARY INDIAN

Discussion of Realism often displaces interest from manner of writing to theme, and inevitably discussion of Realism tends to become thematic. In Spanish America, moreover, Realist theme was often Romantic theme reversed. Idealisation of the noble savage is Romantic in inspiration. Realism dwells on the degenerate conditions of the contemporary Indian.

The Indianist novel of contemporary life was, nevertheless, rare before the 1920s and there is only one example in the nineteenth century, *Aves sin nido* (1889) by the Peruvian novelist Clorinda Matto de Turner, whose work was influenced by the ideas of Manuel González Prada. Wife and then widow of a doctor, she lived for many years in Cuzco, a town set in the heart of the Andean Indian zone, surrounded by villages which were dominated by the priest, the judge, and the landowner. Her novel is a mixture of Romantic plot and Realist detail. The story describes the fate of a pair of lovers, Manuel, the judge's son, and Margarita, daughter of an Indian couple who had been massacred for resisting the local oligarchy. Margarita is brought up by a married couple, Fernando, who has mining interests, and his wife, Lucía. They represent the enlightened middle classes who try unsuccessfully to modify the harsh social conditions in the town, but finally have to admit their defeat and return to Lima. The climax, however, is not only this failure of paternalistic enlightenment but the discovery that Margarita and her lover are half-sister and brother, both being illegitimate children of the priest. Hence the novel conveys a strong anti-clerical message both implicit in the plot and in the direct outbursts of criticism.

So far, the Realist novels we have discussed have been characterised by their very distinct moral message, whether against the corruption of luxury, or against the hypocrisies of the Establishment. But towards the end of the century, writers began to be more and more interested in questions of style and language, whether or not they came directly under the influence of the Modernists. At the same time, there was also a trend towards the depiction of rural and provincial life, known in some countries as *criollismo*.[8]

IV. TOMÁS CARRASQUILLA (1858-1940)

An example of a novelist who concentrated on provincial life and yet refused the tendency to write a 'thesis' novel in the nineteenth-century Realist manner is Tomás Carrasquilla of Colombia. Born in the province of Antioquía, he was deeply rooted in provincial life and owed the freshness of his style to the conversations, tales, and anecdotes which still formed a major source of entertainment in areas remote from the metropolis. His family, though modest, was thoroughly Hispanic, preserving in its attitudes and manners the traditional family life of Catholic Spain. They were, he said, 'más blancos que el Rey de las Españas'; and again: 'Todos ellos eran gentes patriarcales, muy temerosos de Dios y muy buenos vecinos'.[9] His novels reconstruct the simple life of these provincial families whose dramas and tragedies were played out in obscurity, whose main enemy was boredom, the kind of rainy season boredom that made Carrasquilla turn to the writing of stories. His first novel, *Frutos de mi tierra* (1896), is a picture of provincial life, more highly structured than a *costumbrista* sketch, and less insistently moral in tone than many Realist novels. Yet the theme has moral implications, for this story, like his more ambitious historical novel *La marquesa de Yolombó*, is that of honest provincialism ruined by the metropolis. In *Frutos de mi tierra*, the treatment is still grotesque, for it centres on the life of a sordid money-grubbing brother and sister whose fine airs make them ridiculous in their provincial environment. They are vulnerable because proud and the sister, ugly, old, and unattractive as she is, allows herself to be carried off by a flashy cousin from Bogotá who cheats her of the family fortune. An extended and far more ambitious treatment of the theme is to be found in the historical novel *La marquesa de Yolombó*[10] (1926), in which the theme of the metropolitan exploitation of the province is taken back into historical times, and set in the colonial period. Born in a mining town, the heroine is appropriately named Bárbara (patron saint of miners). She is a fiery girl, confined in the narrow colonial society in which a woman is not expected to take an intelligent interest in anything other than clothes and marriage. But Bárbara is passionately interested in the mine, and she symbolises the involvement of the creole in her own country as against the attitude of the Spaniards who wish to exploit the mine without developing the country as a whole or ploughing back profits into that society. Bárbara's mother, on the other hand, is the conventional female who accepts her own limited role:

Que trabajaran los hombres como bestias de carga, que ganasen como gentes que venden su alma al diablo; pero a las mujeres no

les cumplía sino gastarles la plata, darles hijos, levantar la familia
y alegrar la casa.

Bárbara has little option but to spend her time educating and looking
after the slaves and workers. Ignorant of politics and international
affairs, she is knowledgeable about her native region. Yet she pro-
claims her loyalty to the Spanish throne at the height of the Independence movement, sending the monarch a rich present for which she
is given the title of Marquesa. This is her undoing. She becomes
proud and arrogant, falls victim to a Spanish adventurer who, under
the pretext of loyalty to the king, steals the wealth of the mines, and
is then abandoned by him. Once again the story is one of province
and metropolis (but this time symbolised by the imperial power).
There is great consistency of style which comes from the use of the
colloquial language which is itself the mark of the author's thorough
familiarity with his region. The 'local patriotism' helps to account for
Carrasquilla's hostility to Modernism and the influence of the French
decadents.[11]

But it is in the stories that Carrasquilla exploits his folk-sources
most fully. Many of them are close to folk-tales. 'En la diestra de Dios
Padre', for instance, tells a traditional story of the peasant outwitting the devil, other versions of which we have met in the
tradiciones of Ricardo Palma and *Don Segundo Sombra*. Others are
closer to autobiography. In 'Dimitas Arias', Carrasquilla describes a
crippled schoolmaster, 'El Tullido', whose character and appearance
correspond to those of one of his own teachers. This closeness to the
source material, whether in real life or in popular legend, extends
even to writing on political themes. In 'El Padre Casafús' he captures
the fanaticism of the provinces in a story of a priest whose bad temper
alienates a powerful woman parishioner, who persecutes him to the
point of unemployment, starvation, and death by giving him the
reputation of being a 'liberal'.

Carrasquilla is at his best in 'Simón el Mago', a tale that combines
grotesque humour with a theme of provincial ingenuity and ignorance.
Simón is a boy whose mulatto nurse dabbles in witchcraft and who
instructs him in the art of flying like a witch. He follows her advice,
but ends up ignominiously in the compost heap. Carrasquilla tells his
story exactly as the villagers would have done, giving it a certain
black quality like a Goya witchcraft painting. Here, for instance,
is the nurse giving her instructions:

Pues la gente s'embruja muy facilito: la mod' es qui uno si
untan bien untao en aceite en toítas las coyunturas: se que' en la
mera camisa y se gana a una parti alta y así que' está uno encaramao
abre bien los brazos como pa volar, y dici uno; ¡pero con harta
fe! ¡No creo en Dios ni en Santa María! Y guelvi a decir hasta

que ajuste tres veces sin resollar: y entonces si avienta uno pu' el
aire y s'encumbra a la región.

We notice how faithful Carrasquilla is to the source and how carefully
he transcribes the mulatto's speech almost to the point of unintelligi-
bility. But verisimilitude is of great importance to him and he conveys
the ingenuousness of both the woman and her pupil.

This verisimilitude was carefully observed by the *criollista* writers
who emerged at the beginning of the twentieth century when there was
a widespread reaction from the 'cosmopolitanism' of the Modernist
period. *Criollismo* tended to concentrate above all on novels of rural
life. But although the authors inherited the deterministic structure of
nineteenth-century Realism, they were writing after the Modernist
period and hence were much more aware of the evocative powers of
language than an author like Blest Gana. In Chile, and in many
small Latin American countries less accessible to avant-garde
influences, *criollismo* was a movement that lasted until very recently;
but it was at its height in the years before 1918. Javier de Viana
(Uruguay; 1868-1926), Mariano Latorre (Chile; 1886-1955), both
prolific authors, are typical of the movement. In both cases they based
their stories on incidents which illustrated the harsh life of the country-
dweller. Viana described the gauchos of Uruguay and the degeneration of a rural population too unenlightened and uneducated to lift
themselves out of the trough of daily despair. Latorre described the
life of the mountaineers and fishermen of Chile. Many more examples
could be cited—the Venezuelans Luis Manuel Urbaneja Achelpohl
(1872-1937) and Rufino Blanco Fombona (1874-1944); or the Peruvian
Ventura García Calderón (1886-1959); and many short-story writers
from the Central American Republics like Ricardo Fernández Guardia
(Costa Rica; 1867-1950); but the scope of this kind of writing was
limited. The authors overwhelmingly preferred the short-story form,
partly because of the ease of publication in newspapers and periodicals at a time when native publishing houses were still rare. The
stories were usually built around an anecdote illustrative of the life
of a particular region. However, modern writers tend to point out
the inauthenticity of much 'criollista' material, especially when the
author was himself an outsider from the region and the way of life
that he was describing, because he came either from a different social
class or from the city.

But *criollismo* was a moralistic form of literature, aimed at the
conscience of the urban élite. Writers were not only describing country
people, but they wished also to remedy the social situation which
condemned the rural areas to backwardness and poverty. The stories
of the Uruguayan Javier de Viana and of his compatriot Carlos Reyles
(1868-1938) had explicit moral and national messages about the value

of honest labour on the land as a means of national regeneration. Paternalistic education of country people was expected to raise the general level of the country. The novel of the Ecuadorian Luis Martínez (1869-1909), *A la costa* (1904), in which the petty bourgeois hero from Quito begins to find dignity in the running of a coastal plantation is typical of this school of writing which demonstrated the author's awareness of the problem but was seldom instrumental in bringing about social change.[12]

The writers of this generation were by no means invariably of the élite. The Russian-born Argentine writer Alberto Gerchunoff (1884-1950) was brought up on a farming commune and wrote of this in his *Los gauchos judíos* (1910); Baldomero Lillo was a shop assistant; the Cuban writer Carlos Loveira (1882-1928), author of *Juan Criollo* (1927), was a trade-union organiser. Their social origins perhaps gave them a truer insight into the lives of the humble, but in outlook they were surprisingly similar to reformist intellectuals of the landowning élite like Carlos Reyles and Rufino Blanco Fombona. They shared a common regard for education and the printed word as an instrument for the reform of society.[13] The regionalist, Realist, and social-protest novels of the 1920s and '30s sprang directly out of this social concern of the *criollistas*.

*   *   *

The common pattern of Realist writing before 1914 is deterministic. The central theme was the conflict of modernity and traditional values, with the writer casting a critical glance at an age of progress and development which brought about not only the destruction of old institutions but the creation of new types of exploitation. The Spanish American Realist was nearer than he realised to the Romantic poet in his nostalgia for tradition and his fear of the moral anarchy that might result from the new materialism.

NOTES

1. Quoted Teresita Frugoni de Fritzsche in her introduction to Lucio Vicente López, *La gran aldea* (Buenos Aires, 1965).
2. There is a full discussion of Gamboa and of other Mexican Realists and Naturalists in John S. Brushwood, *Mexico in its Novel. A Nation's Search for Identity* (Austin and London, 1966).
3. G. Ara, *La novela naturalista hispanoamericana* (Buenos Aires, 1965).
4. The money-grubbing Italian immigrant is the stereotype found in the theatre, e.g. in the plays of Florencio Sánchez discussed in chapter 10.
5. Carlos Fuentes discusses the relationship of the static novel and a static social structure in *La nueva novela hispanoamericana* (Mexico, 1969).
6. Quoted Ricardo A. Latcham in *Blest Gana y la novela realista* (Anales no. 20, University of Chile, Santiago, n.d.).

7. The *Sociedad de la Igualdad* was a society founded by Francisco Bilboa who went into exile in 1850. The events referred to in Blest Gana's novel occurred during the armed uprising of 1851.

8. Ricardo Latcham, 'La historia del criollismo', in *El criollismo* (Santiago de Chile, 1956).

9. In the introduction to the *Obras completas* (Madrid, 1952).

10. The chronology of 'periods' of Latin American literature is always difficult. I can only justify this inclusion of a novel published in 1926 on the grounds that Carrasquilla seems to be a pre-1914 writer.

11. Nigel Sylvester discusses this briefly in *The Homilies and Dominicales of Tomás Carrasquilla* (Monograph Series, I, Centre for Latin American Studies, the University of Liverpool, 1970).

12. There is a fuller discussion of this point in 'The Select Minority: Arielism and *Criollismo*', chapter 2 of J. Franco, *The Modern Culture of Latin America* (New York and London, 1967).

13. David Viñas, *Literatura argentina y realidad política* (Buenos Aires, 1964).

READING LIST

Texts
Blanco Fombona, Rufino, *Obras selectas* (Madrid and Caracas, 1958)
Blest Gana, Alberto, *Martín Rivas* (Santiago de Chile, 1960)
——, *La aritmética en el amor* (Santiago de Chile, 1950)
——, *Los transplantados* (Santiago de Chile, 1961)
——, *El ideal de un calavera* (Santiago de Chile, 1964)
——, *El loco Estero y Gladys Fairfield* (Santiago de Chile, 1961)
Cambaceres, Eugenio, *Obras completas* (Santa Fe, 1956)
Carrasquilla, Tomás, *Obras completas* (Madrid, 1952)
Latorre, Mariano, *Sus mejores cuentos*, 14th ed. (Santiago, 1962)
López, Lucio Vicente, *La gran aldea* (Buenos Aires, 1965)
Martínez, Luis, *A la costa*, 2nd ed. (Quito, 1959)
Matto de Turner, Clorinda, *Aves sin nido* (Buenos Aires, 1889)
Viana, Javier de, *Selección de cuentos*, 2 vols. (Montevideo, 1965)

Historical and critical
Alegría, F., *Las fronteras del realismo: literatura chilena del siglo XX* (Santiago, 1962)
Ara, G., *La novela naturalista hispanoamericana* (Buenos Aires, 1965)
Brushwood, J., *Mexico in its Novel. A Nation's Search for Identity* (Austin and London, 1966)
Castro, Raúl Silva, *Alberto Blest Gana* (Santiago de Chile, 1955)
Prieto, Adolfo, *Literatura autobiográfica argentina*, 2nd ed. (Buenos Aires, 1966)

Chapter 5

TRADITION AND CHANGE: JOSE MARTÍ AND MANUEL GONZÁLEZ PRADA

'History will absolve me'. (Fidel Castro)

I. JOSÉ MARTÍ

THE CONNECTION BETWEEN the two writers considered in this section is a tenuous one. José Martí was a Cuban, the son of a humble immigrant family; Manuel González Prada, the son of a landowner, a member of the Peruvian upper class. Both were poets, but their common ground lies not so much in their style of writing as in their political militancy. We are dealing here with writers for whom literature and revolution are closely allied. To change the language was to them another way of changing attitudes.

When still in his teens, José Martí (1853-95) was sentenced to forced labour in the quarries for his part in the 1868 Independence conspiracy. The sole proof of his involvement was his connection with Rafael María Mendive (1821-86), a poet, educator, and freedom-fighter who had founded the *Revista de la Habana* and was head of the *Escuela Superior de Varones*. Mendive was one of the great humanitarians of nineteenth-century Cuba, and an important influence on the young Martí. But what undoubtedly changed Martí from being the usual student idealist to a life-long commitment as a fighter for Independence was his political sentence of forced labour. During the months before his sentence was commuted to exile, he slaved in the sun, feet and hands chained, along with old men and young boys who had been similarly sentenced. The experience of gross injustice and oppression left its mark. One of Martí's first tasks when he arrived in Spain, where he was to spend the period of exile, was to compose his essay *El presidio político de Cuba* (1871),[1] a denunciation aroused more by the sufferings of others, than by the hardship he had experienced. He has no doubt as to where guilt lies.

¡Horrorosa, terrible, desgarradora nada!
¡Y vosotros los españoles la hicisteis!
¡Y vosotros la sancionasteis!
¡Y vosotros la aplaudisteis!

85

The denunciation is hammered home with harsh facts. The list of atrocities includes the cases of children of twelve and the brutal beating of old men like Don Nicolás who had collapsed from weakness and was thrown aside senseless onto a heap of stones:

> Se le echó al pie de un montón. Llegó el sol, calcinó con su fuego las piedras. Llegó la lluvia; penetró con el agua las capas de la tierra. Llegaron las seis de la tarde. Entonces dos hombres fueron al montón a buscar el cuerpo que, calcinado por el sol y penetrado por la lluvia, yacía allí desde las horas primeras de la mañana.

Notice how Martí builds up the picture. The body is left lying among the stones of the quarry lifeless. The sun and rain beat on the senseless stones. And they also beat on the human body. The Spaniards' insensitivity to human life is implicit and does not need to be emphasised more. Man has been equated with stones, and for Martí who believed 'God was in that man', it was the supreme blasphemy. He was to remain constant to his view that human life was sacred, that the right of the human individual was liberty, and that liberty was worth sacrificing one's own life for.

Between 1871 and 1873, Martí studied in exile in Spain; in 1873, he became editor of the *Revista Universal* in Mexico; and in 1877, went to teach in the University of Guatemala. He only made one brief return to Cuba before his final fatal expedition. Most of the final years of his life were spent, first in Venezuela (until 1881) and then in the United States which he only left in 1895 to join the liberation expedition under General Máximo Gómez. On 19 May of that year, he died fighting at Boca de Dos Ríos.

Martí was one of the writers who wrote 'the most beautiful prose in the world',[2] according to Rubén Darío. Certainly his conception of the literary language was far in advance of most of his contemporaries. He had been influenced by the North American writer Ralph Waldo Emerson, for whom the word was emblematic and who wrote, 'Parts of speech are metaphors, because the whole of nature is a metaphor of the human mind'. In an age of rather windy eloquence, Martí endorsed Emerson's view of language as rooted in truth. The strongest language is often the simplest and the most concise:

> El arte de escribir ¿no es reducir? La verba mata sin duda la elocuencia. Hay tanto que decir, que ha de decirse en el menor número de palabras posibles: eso sí, que cada palabra lleve ala y color.[3]

'Ala' and 'color' refer to the ideal element in language and to its allusive powers, qualities which inflation could never produce. Martí was thus more acutely aware than most of his contemporaries, with the possible exception of the Modernists, of the potentialities of language.

But like Emerson, these potentialities were very much related to the quality of the man and of his closeness to the people who were ultimately the makers of poetry and the forgers of words. Inspiration comes to the writer from this source, and a man is nothing without the people:

> Los hombres son productos, expresiones, reflejos. Viven, en lo que coinciden con su época o en lo que se diferencian marcadamente de ella; lo que flota, les empuja y pervade.[4]

Hence the importance of sincerity in his view of poetry, by which he meant truth to one's time and situation, and to one's dignity as a human being.[5] Literature is both the 'espontáneo consejo y enseñanza de la naturaleza' and also the realm in which apparent contradiction can be resolved, and it has also a social and religious significance.[6]

If we now go back to consider Martí's views on language, on society, on man, and on poetry we find them all linked to this central core of nature, with man at its centre continually progressing through self-enlightenment. His was an optimistic creed with the long-term goal of the betterment of humanity and the short-term objective of liberating Cuba, to which all energies must be dedicated. This explains why, despite his love of poetry, he usually wrote with some more practical end in view. With rare exceptions (an unfinished novel and some short stories) almost everything he wrote in prose was for a determinate end – was purely functional—whether a newspaper article, a speech, letters to comrades and relations.

But because Martí based his hierarchy of values on truth to nature, he believed that any falseness, any cowardice or betrayal would be exposed if not to contemporaries then by posterity. The future would judge which men had worked unselfishly for the good of mankind. And he himself applied this yardstick to the heroes of the past— Bolívar, San Martín, General Páez—and to contemporaries such as General Gómez, Walt Whitman, and Emerson. His essays on these men are the finest of his prose works. He has quick sympathy for those who, however barbaric and unorthodox, see beyond their own personal comfort or salvation. Here, for instance, is General Gómez, the Cuban Independence leader:

> A caballo por el camino, con el maizal a un lado y las cañas a otro, apeándose en un recodo para componer con sus manos la cerca, entrándose por un casucho a dar de su pobreza a un infeliz, montando de un salto y arrancando veloz, como quien lleva clavado al alma un par de espuelas, como quien no ve en el mundo vacío más que el combate y la redención, como quien no le conoce a la vida pasajera gusto mayor que el de echar los hombres del envilecimiento a la dignidad, va por la tierra de Santo Domingo, del lado del Monte Cristal, un jinete pensativo, caído en su bruto como—su silla natural, obedientes

los músculos bajo la ropa holgada, el pañuelo al cuello, de corbata campesina, y de sombra del rostro trigueño el fieltro veterano.[7]

It is worthwhile considering this passage carefully, for in both style and subject-matter it is characteristic of Martí's prose work. The present tense gives the reader a sense of the actuality of the events; the rapid succession of activities is indicated by the series of gerundives–'apeándose', 'entrando', 'montando', 'arrancando'. The activity is then linked to the ideal of 'combate y redención', which gives sense to the final lines describing the now pensive horseman dressed in simple peasant clothes. Activity and appearance only have sense when related to the man's ideal of lifting people up from degradation to dignity. The moral imperative which guides the hero's life is always made patent. Thus, describing the life of the poet Heredia, Martí stresses the easy circumstances of his family in order to bring out the full nobility of a decision which is nevertheless seen as the only possible decision for an honest man:

En las ventanas dan besos, y aplausos en las casas ricas, y la abogacía mana oro; pero, al salir del banquete triunfal, de los estrados elocuentes, de la cita feliz, ¿no chasquea el látigo, y pide clemencia a un cielo que escucha la madre a quien quieren ahogarle con azotes los gritos con quien llama al hijo de su amor? El vil no es el esclavo, ni el que lo ha sido, sino el que vio este crimen, y no jura, ante el tribunal certero que preside en las sombras, hasta sacar del mundo la esclavitud y sus huellas.[8]

The passage shows us why Martí believed that it was impossible to be a happy man in an unjust society. Personal success cannot obscure social injustice. There is a vast difference here from the attitude of a Modernist like Darío who would like to disassociate himself from society and has no clear vision of a future without injustice.

Martí's attitude is also very different from Sarmiento's. For Martí, the barbarian was the man, whatever his class or education, who tacitly consented to injustice. A man like the Venezuelan 'centaur of the plains', General Páez, who was as barbarous as a Facundo, was viewed with sympathy by Martí because of his single-minded devotion to the Independence cause. That is why Martí's essay, written on the occasion of the General's death in New York, stresses the virtues of this 'natural man' and recognises the admirable side to his barbarism.[9] Martí admired energy and independence in people, and not simply physical energy but also the intellectual energy of men like Emerson or Walt Whitman (for whom he felt especial sympathy). He is as unprejudiced about Whitman's homosexuality as he is about the barbarism of Páez. For Whitman was working towards his own goal of human fraternity:

Imagínese qué nuevo y extraño efecto producirá ese lenguaje hen-
chido de animalidad soberbia cuando celebra la pasión que ha de unir
a los hombres. Reúne en una composición del 'Calamus' los goces
más vivos que debe a la Naturaleza y a la patria; pero sólo a las olas
del océano halla dignas de corear, a la luz de la luna, su dicha al ver
dormido junto a sí al amigo que ama. Él ama a los humildes, a
los caídos, a los heridos, hasta a los malvados.[10]

Martí always brought out in some way or other these ideal qualities in
the men he admired and particularly their devotion to something other
than selfish ends.

Martí's views on the social and political future of Latin America
differed in many important respects from those of his contemporaries.
His first-hand knowledge of the United States allowed him to evaluate
both the strengths and weaknesses of her civilisation: on the one hand
the opportunity she gave to individuals, the 'melting pot' of immigration; on the other hand, the aggressive intentions which were already a
threat to Latin America. His essay 'Nuestra América' sums up his
feeling that the Hispanic nations are too weak and that this weakness
derives from their division between an alienated ruling and intellectual
class and the people. He believes that Indians and negroes have to be
fully integrated into the nations and that the simple people might well
have something to teach those who try and learn from 'imported
books'. This is very different from Sarmiento's rejection of the people
and his policy of 'civilisation'. Another great difference between Martí
and his contemporaries is that he did not share their gloomy estima-
tion of multiracial societies and non-European culture. He was well
ahead of his time, for instance, in recognising the beauty of pre-
Columban civilisations. His picture of Tenochtitlán brings out the
colour and plastic beauty of that city:

¡Qué hermosa era Tenochtitlán, la ciudad capital de los aztecas,
cuando llegó a México Cortés! Era como una mañana todo el día,
y la ciudad parecía siempre como en feria. Las calles eran de agua
unas, y de tierra otras; y las plazas espaciosas y muchas; y los al-
rededores sembrados de una gran arboleda. Por los canales andaban
las canoas, tan veloces y diestras como si tuviesen entendimiento; y
había tántas a veces que se podía andar sobre ellas como sobre
la tierra firma. En unas venían frutas, y en otras flores, y en otras
jarros y tazas, y demás cosas de la alfarería.[11]

Martí's poetry is as original as his prose. In his lifetime, he published
a series of poems to his infant son, *Ismaelillo* (1882), and his *Versos
sencillos* (1891). His *Versos libres* were published posthumously. As
with the prose-writing, there is a remarkable consistency, for the poems
were 'nacidos de grandes miedos o de grandes esperanzas o de indómito

amor por la libertad, o de amor doloroso a la hermosura'.[12] His imagery is based on a dualistic view of humankind, of ideal and reality, spirit and matter, truth and falsehood, the light of consciousness and the darkness of the unconscious. Ala, cumbre, nube, pino, paloma, sol, águila, luz are recurring symbols of the ideal; abismo, cueva, hormiga, gusano, veneno are the depths. Symbolic colours—verde, plata, amarillo, negro, carmesí—afford the differing degrees of intensity and the shades of feeling.[13] In many of Martí's poems there is a subtle interplay of forces of light and forces of darkness.

The poems of *Ismaelillo* are excellent examples of this. They are based on the paradox that the weakness, innocence, and dependence of the child are his strength, for they rouse the best and most noble in the father. The child is a symbol of power and potentiality, described as a lion, a knight on a charger, a conqueror, and the defender of the father when assailed on all sides by doubts, temptations, and despair. He is the dwarf prince who brings light to the prisoner in the cave:

> ¡Venga mi caballero
> Por esta senda!
> ¡Éntrese mi tirano
> Por esta cueva!
> Tal es, cuando a mis ojos
> En imagen llega,
> Cual si en lóbrego antro
> Pálida estrella,
> Con fulgores de ópalo
> Todo vistiera.
> A su paso la sombra
> Matices muestra,
> Como al sol que las hiere
> Las nubes negras.
> ¡Heme ya, puesto en armas,
> En la pelea!
> Quiere el príncipe enano
> Que a luchar vuelva;
> ¡Él para mí es corona,
> Almohada, espuela!
> Y como el sol, quebrando
> Las nubes negras,
> En banda de colores
> La sombra trueca, −
> Él, al tocarla, borda
> En la onda espesa,
> Mi banda de batalla
> Roja y violeta.

¿Conque mi dueño quiere
Que a vivir vuelva?
¡Venga mi caballero
Por esta senda!
¡Éntrese mi tirano
Por esta cueva!
¡Déjeme que la vida
A él, a él, ofrezca!
Para un príncipe enano
Se hace esta fiesta.

The poet in the cave is like the squire of a feudal knight dependent on his lord for life and for motivation. In despair and lonely meditation in the cave, the poet is given back joy in life, militancy, energy. There is a playful irony about words like 'tyrant', 'prince', 'lord' used of the helpless child, the evil connotations of these words being quite dispelled while they retain connotations of force or moral obligation. It is, in fact, precisely the child's helplessness that gives him his power. The brilliant contrast between darkness and light recalls Plato's allegory of the cave and the ascent to the sun, as well as the struggles between darkness and light of older mythologies.

In *Versos sencillos,* the poet speaks as the 'hombre sincero', contrasting his joy in nature with the evil and complexity of civilisation:

Yo sé de Egipto y Nigricia,
Y de Persia y Xenofonte;
y prefiero la caricia
Del aire fresco del monte.

Yo sé las historias viejas
Del hombre y de sus rencillas;
Y prefiero las abejas
Volando en las campanillas.

A bee in the flower, the wind itself, are pure life, ancient civilisations are dead history; but then the poem's mood shifts suddenly from joy and sincerity to something darker:

Yo sé del canto del viento
En las ramas vocingleras:
Nadie me diga que miento,
Que lo prefiero de veras.

Yo sé de un gamo aterrado
Que vuelve al redil y expira,
Y de un corazón cansado
Que muere oscuro y sin ira.

The glories of the great civilisations which had begun the poem stand in contrast to the obscure suffering and death of the last verse. What had seemed a simple antithesis between civilisation and nature becomes something far more complex, for neither the glory of the past nor the carefree happiness reflected in nature are options for the poet who must face the possibility of a life of struggle and death without glory.

Martí's verse often has a hallucinatory or visionary quality. In the following poem, for instance, what begins as an enquiry about the mystery of the Church suddenly turns into a bizarre and sinister image of an owl:

> En el negro callejón
> Donde en tinieblas paseo,
> Alzo los ojos y veo
> La iglesia, erguida, a un rincón.
>
> ¿Será misterio? ¿Será
> Revelación y poder?
> ¿Será rodilla, el deber
> de postrarse? ¿Qué será?
>
> Tiembla la noche; en la parra
> Muerde el gusano el retoño.
> Grazna, llamando el otoño
> La hueca y hosca cigarra.
>
> Graznan dos: atento al dúo
> Alzo los ojos y veo
> Que la iglesia del paseo
> Tiene la forma de un buho.

When compared with Spanish American Romantic poetry, this is a very strange poem indeed. The poet's sense of the mystery of religion, possibly his feeling that the Church holds some key to human destiny, abruptly gives way to the description of natural life around the Church, a natural life in which the worm eats the bud and the autumn approaches with its promise of degeneration and death. The poet seems to suggest that the Church cannot account for evil, for the struggle of life, nor the change of seasons.

Sharp contrast often raises Martí's poems out of the commonplace. A brief poem, 'Iba yo remando', opens with a dazzling view of a lake, idyllic until the poet realises that there is a stinking fish at his feet, that beauty is marred by degeneration. In 'El amigo muerto', the entire situation is fantastical. The poet is visited by a dead friend still suffering from the contradictions between ideal and reality that had plagued him during his life and the dead poet (the past) has to be comforted by the living poet.

The *Versos libres* published after Martí's death are written, as the title suggests, in free verse. They are direct statements of his personal battles and convictions. In these poems, he returns obsessively to the role of poetry and to his own convictions of a man's true worth. 'Poética', 'Mi poesía', 'Cuentan que antaño' reaffirm those ideas as to nature of poetry which we have already discussed. His poetry, 'mi verso montaraz', is to be as near as possible to the sources of life and inspiration, and he fears that over-preoccupation with formal questions will kill the delicate plant. So, 'Cuentan que antaño' ends:

> Así, quien caza por la rima, aprende
> Que en sus garras se escapa la poesía.

Many poems are concerned with the quality of human life, the difference between those who dedicate themselves to selfish personal ends and the true man. Two of these, 'Odio el mar' and 'Pollice Verso', deserve special mention. In the first, the sea is a symbol of evil, 'vasto y llano, igual y frío'. Mere existence in the way that the sea exists is not enough for Martí; life must have a manifest purpose.

> Lo que me duele no es vivir; me duele
> Vivir sin hacer bien.

The sea symbolises all that is contrary to this; it is purposeless, death-dealing:

> Odio el mar, muerto enorme, triste muerto
> De torpes y glotonas criaturas
> Odiosas habitado; se parecen
> A los ojos del pez que de harto expira,
> Los del gañán de amor que en brazos tiembla
> De la horible mujer libidinosa.

The language is both obscure and powerful. Who are these monsters? The surfeited fish? The 'cold-blooded creatures' indicate something sinister, some unseen yet present evil whose eyes are compared to those of the 'labourer of love', trembling in the arms of a 'horrible' lascivious woman. There are very complex and personal tensions at work here. Possibly Martí felt that private passions could absorb the life of man, so there was nothing left of him, not even the courage of his convictions. 'Pollice Verso', subtitled 'Memoria del presidio', is Martí's confession of faith.

> Hay leyes en la mente, leyes
> Cual las del río, el mar, la piedra, el astro,
> Ásperas y fatales.

These 'laws' man must be faithful to; he must not do violence to this inner necessity and if he does so, the price is high. For man is compared to a gladiator in the arena, watched by the eyes of the people and the king who register his actions and judge accordingly:

> La brida es la ancha arena
> Y los hombres esclavos gladiadores,
> Mas el pueblo y el rey, callados miran
> De grada excelsa, en la desierta sombra ...
> Pero miran!

The 'desierta sombra' is like the unknown unpopulated area of the future whose eyes Martí feels upon himself. And he is aware of what happens to the man who throws his arms aside and chooses ease and comfort, and a worthless life.

Martí's poetry, then, must be seen in relation to his whole life and there is no separating 'Martí the man' from 'Martí the politician'. But what divides Martí most completely from Modernism is his view of man as part of a society and as part of a historical process. Man cannot deny history and cannot escape the consequences of his actions. He must live out the truth and his convictions however much suffering this involves. Not for Martí the concept of poetry as an alternative to political action. The poem is affirmation, not mask or ritual.

II. MANUEL GONZÁLEZ PRADA (1848-1918)

González Prada's life had less consistency than that of Martí, for he seems to have vacillated between periods of withdrawal and periods of political engagement. Destined by his mother for the priesthood, he spent some time at an English school in Valparaíso and there seems to have adopted the positivistic point of view and an interest in science which was to last throughout his whole life. He managed to persuade his mother to abandon her plans for making him a priest, but finding it impossible to pursue his real interests in pious, narrow, conservative Lima, he retired for eight years to the family estate where he spent his time studying and writing. He was already thirty-one when the Peruvian-Chilean war broke out, still a dilettante without direction in life. But the Chilean occupation of Lima, the crisis in Peruvian society which the war laid bare forced him into the open. He realised that the ruling class were out of touch with the people, that Peru would never be a real nation unless the Indians were integrated and educated. He therefore formed a literary circle with the slogan 'Propaganda and Attack', whose aim was the regeneration and democratisation of Peru. He also launched the *Unión Nacional* Party.

González Prada regarded Science as the liberating force, education as the door to the future, and the Church as an obstacle to the adoption of scientific attitude which would allow Latin America to progress. By allowing man to control nature, Science redeemed him from the limitations of necessity. 'Ese redentor', he called Science, 'que nos enseña a suavizar la tiranía de la Naturaleza'. Unlike the Mexican 'científicos', however, he did not put scientific education before urgent political and social reforms. One of the first tasks of a Peruvian government should be that of liberating the Indian from the 'tiranía del juez de paz, del gobernador i del cura, esa trinidad embrutecedora del indio'.[14]

González Prada's revolutionary views about the nature of Peruvian society were accompanied by an equally revolutionary conviction that the writer should be committed, that the writer's source was the people, and that both literature and language must take the culture of the folk into account:

> De las canciones, refranes i dichos del vulgo brotan las palabras orijinales, las frases gráficas, las construcciones atrevidas. Las multitudes transforman las lenguas, como los infusorios modifican los continentes.[15]

For this reason, he attacked vigorously the slavish imitation of Peninsular Spanish and urged the need for a new and vigorous literary language.

But after this early burst of 'propaganda and attack', González Prada once again withdrew from the national scene. He married a Frenchwoman, lived in Paris from 1887 to 1894, and during this period attended Renan's lectures. Meanwhile the *Unión Nacional* was dissolved and when eventually González Prada returned to Peru, he turned to more radical politics, to anarchism and the organisation of working-class movements, contributing articles to *Los Parias,* a monthly founded in 1905 by a group of artisans, and protesting vigorously at the gunning-down of workers in the Iquique strike of 1908.[16] He lived long enough (until 1919) to influence the nationalist and socialist movements of the 1920s.

González Prada was, then, intermittently a militant, but one who was less revolutionary in his prose and poetry than Martí. His prose is cruder, without the plasticity of the Cuban, and much of his poetry is escapist. The exceptions are some early poems, *Baladas peruanas,* written between 1871 and 1879, most of which remained unpublished in his lifetime. They are written in ballad metre and many are on the theme of social injustice. In *Minúsculas* (1900) and *Exóticas,* there is a kind of preciosity; he was interested in reviving old forms of verse— the triolet, rondinel, the *gacelas* (an Arabic verse form), and in experimenting in free verse. But despite the originality of form, the result is often lifeless. His best poems tend to be those which deal in some way with the senselessness of existence, though he often resolves his feelings in a kind of forced optimism.

¿Donde la firme realidad? Giramos
En medio a torbellino de fantasmas:
En el flujo y reflujo de la vida,
Somos los hombres apariencia vana.
¡Mas ni despecho ni furor! Vivamos
En una suave atmósfera optimista;
Y si es un corto sueño la existencia,
Soñemos la bondad y la justicia.[17]

'Crepuscular', in which he allows the mood of pessimism to prevail and where he effectively uses an unrhymed form, seems more convincing:

En gris de plomo se disfuma
El oro lívido y enfermo
De los ocasos otoñales;
Y lentamente baja, lentamente se difunde,
Una tristeza desolada y aterida,
Una tristeza de orfandad y tumba.[18]

This is effective poetry, in which the dying fall towards the final 'tumba' is sustained and prolonged by the middle line with its repeated 'lentamente'. But more often González Prada cannot sail successfully between the twin threats of formal experiment and meaning. He is either merely playing or being too univocal and explicit.

He is, in fact, an interesting contrast to José Martí. The latter fused personal, political, and literary life successfully into a single whole. González Prada never had such consistency—so that his prose-writing tends to be polemical and his poetry a game.

NOTES

1. José Martí, *Obras completas* (Editorial nacional de Cuba, La Habana, 1964), I.
2. Ivan A. Schulman y Manuel Pedro González, 'Resonancias martianas en la prosa de Rubén Darío', in *José Martí, Rubén Darío y el Modernismo* (Madrid, 1969).
3. *Obras completas*, XI, 196.
4. ibid., XIII, 34.
5. See the introduction to his *Versos sencillos, Obras completas*, XVI, 61-2 for a declaration of sincerity.
6. From the essay on 'Whitman' in *Obras completas*, XVI.
7. ibid., IV, 445-6.
8. ibid., V, 168.
9. ibid., VIII, 214.
10. ibid., XIII, 139.

11. ibid., XVIII, 383.
12. From the preface to *Versos sencillos* (New York, 1891).
13. I. A. Schulman, *Símbolo y color en la obra de José Martí* (Madrid, 1960).
14. *Páginas libres*, new ed. (Lima, 1966), p.51.
15. ibid., p.20.
16. ibid., p.126.
17. 'Optimismo', *Exóticas* (Lima, 1911).
18. Also from *Exóticas*.

READING LIST

Texts
González Prada, Manuel, *Minúsculas* (Lima, 1900)
——, *Exóticas* (Lima, 1911)
——, *Páginas libres*, new ed. (Lima, 1966)
——, *Baladas peruanas* (Santiago de Chile, 1935)
——, *Grafitos* (Paris, 1937)
——, *Propaganda y ataque*, new ed. (Buenos Aires, 1939)
Martí, José, *Obras completas*, 22 vols. (La Habana, 1964)
——, *Obra selecta* (Buenos Aires, 1965)
——, *Poesías completas* (La Habana, 1959)
——, *Versos*, ed. E. Florit (New York, 1962)

Historical and critical
Chang Rodríguez, E., *La literatura política de González Prada, Mariátegui y Haya de la Torre* (Mexico, 1967)
González, Manuel Pedro, and Schulman, Ivan A., *José Martí, Rubén Darío y el Modernismo* (Madrid, 1969)
Ghiano, Juan Carlos, *José Martí* (Buenos Aires, 1967)
Marinello, Juan, *José Martí. Escritor americano* (Mexico, 1958)
Schulman, I. A., *Símbolo y color en la obra de José Martí* (Madrid, 1960)
Schultz de Mantovani, Fryda, *Genio y figura de José Martí* (Buenos Aires, 1968)

Chapter 6

THE MANY FACES OF MODERNISM

El Modernismo—como el Renacimiento o el Romanticismo—es
una época y no una escuela, y la unidad de esa época consistió
en producir grandes poetas individuales que cada uno se define
por la unidad de su personalidad, y todos juntos por el
hecho de haber iniciado una literatura independiente, de valor
universal, que es principio y origen del gran desarrollo de la literatura hispano-americana posterior.   (Federico de Onís)

MODERNISM, like Romanticism and Realism, is a difficult term to
define. The movement issued no manifesto and even a cursory glance
at anthologies of Modernism reveal widely divergent styles, ranging
from the 'Parnassianism' of certain stages of Darío's writing to Symbolism or the late-flowering Romanticism of José Asunción Silva.
Modernism appears to be a convenient umbrella term which covers a
number of poets writing between the 1880s and the 1920s.

Yet it is obviously much more than a name. Juan Ramón Jiménez
described it as part of the general, spiritual crisis of the *fin de siècle*.[1]
And Federico de Onís believed that its influence extended over all
contemporary poetry.[2] Few modern critics would confine a definition
of Modernism within the limits of technical innovations.

One possible starting-point is to define Modernism in relation to
Realism and Romanticism, in other words define it as a *difference*. In
Spanish America, Romanticism had meant nostalgia for stability, for
the security of Catholic belief, and the traditional hierarchical social
system. Modernism, on the other hand, floated in the realms of un-
certainty, of loss of faith and awareness of cracks in the social order.
On the other hand, the Realist writer accepted a rigid determinism
and fell into stylistic cliché, while Modernism attempted to break out
of biological and social limitations and to create awareness through new
uses of language. In short, Modernism translated the crisis of which
Onís speaks into aesthetic terms, into literary patterns of flight and rest,
of contradiction and resolution, and into a language whose ambiguities
were able to encompass paradox and tension.

98

This new awareness could only have come about at a period when poets took the creation of a new vocabulary and new forms seriously. The pull between private and public life, between civic service and literary activity, did not disappear, but—for the first time in Spanish America—the Modernist poet tended to place literary activity higher in the hierarchy of values than political activity. The stereotype of the politician was already far more tarnished than in Bolívar's day, while conversely, Victor Hugo represented the ideal of the laureate who stood above the political hurly-burly. If, on the one hand, the poet saw himself as an outcast from society, he also saw himself as an outcast of giant stature. This legend of the poet's superiority to ordinary men, of his great vision and prophetic powers, was to sustain the humblest versifier living in the obscurity of Quito as well as Darío walking the Paris boulevards. Yet here again our picture of Modernism is paradoxical. Darío, for instance, could write a story like 'El rey burgués' in which the bourgeois king forces the poet to play the harmonium in the snow outside the palace and lets him starve to death; yet Darío himself, and Modernism in general, is hardly conceivable without the fin-de-siècle affluence that brought new standards of luxury and refinement to the continent, which created a certain modest demand for books, which financed literary magazines, and which changed the face of the bigger cities like Mexico City and Buenos Aires, giving them a European veneer. The process was a two-way one. The presence of the poets enriched an indigent literary scene, but at the same time they partook of its nouveau-riche brashness, its subservience to European fashion, and even of its bad taste. An edition of the poems of Herrera y Reissig, published in 1912 and edited by the Spanish poet Villaespesa, illustrates this aspect of Modernism delightfully.[3] The cover shows a pair of chaste lovers, the man wearing a bear-skin, the woman wearing a Roman toga. Clothed yet lascivious, the pair display their sexual intentions only within the taboos of the period, the bear-skin standing as the sign of virility in the semiotic code of sex. The Modernist was therefore a mediator between European taste and Spanish American barbarism, and at the same time could not go much beyond the taboos of his time, or at least, could not go beyond them in an overt fashion. That is why Modernist rhetoric tends to clothe contradictions and tensions rather than reveal them openly.

That the Modernist lived and suffered a spiritual crisis is undeniable. And this crisis was all the more acute in that it was compressed into a short time-span. Spanish America had remained on the margins of the literary and philosophical speculations of nineteenth-century Europe. Now within twenty years, the impact of historicism and materialism, of the new fin-de-siècle spiritualism with its exploration of the occult, of aestheticism; all these were felt at once. But this impact was mediated through print. The Modernist poet did not himself live through the technological and societal changes that were transforming human lives in Europe. At most, he observed these as a tourist. His awareness was at one remove. The experience he felt directly was that of his dependent relationship on European culture, that of his own instability and lack of tradition. What in a European writer might be rejection of science and industry was in the Spanish American a plank of tradition thrown to a drowning man. He needed European culture as an affirmation, as a genealogy to furnish his illegitimate descent with a show of respectability.

Without a rooted or stable society to fall back on, the Spanish American writer was in a vacuum. He shared with his European contemporaries a loss of traditional faith or belief in social remedies. But even more than they, he needed literature to fill up the hollows. The flight to an organic nature presented no alternative, for nature's determinism was only a cruel reminder of the fact that Spanish American man was not yet in control of his environment. Thus, the Cuban poet Julián del Casal lumps science and nature together in the determinist bag:

> En el seno tranquilo de la ciencia
>   que, cual tumba de mármol,
> guarda tras la bruñida superficie
>   podredumbre y gusanos,
> en brazos de la gran Naturaleza,
>   de los que huí temblando
> cual del regazo de la madre infame
>   huye el hijo azorado.

The security of science is the security of Death, but the arms of Nature are no better. Like the European Romantic, Parnassian, and Symbolist, the Modernist poet wanted to defy science and nature, to explore all that lay outside a deterministic pattern of heredity, growth, and decay. He celebrated sensuality and perversion, not marital love, Salome and Venus rather than the mother figure. He longed for a time more ample than that of the biological time-clock, and this art seemed to promise. Perhaps even literature could be made to last as long as marble and stone. Art is essentially the artificial, that which is made, that which is not simply life-span and organic process. Julián del Casal celebrates artifice over the shimmering attractions of the natural cosmos:

> Y el fulgor de los astros rutilantes
> no trueco por los vívidos cambiantes
> del ópalo, la perla o los diamantes

For these reasons, the need for a new literary language, freed from process, freed from the limitations of the epoch, was felt as urgent. And this urgency was something different from the preoccupation of writers such as Andrés Bello and Ricardo Palma, concerned with more direct problems of communication, or relevance. The Modernists posed the problem of language at a different level, on the level of creation. They could not use either the Castilian that belonged to a tradition that was dead to them or the local dialect of a culture that was still regional and traditional, nor could they create out of the void. Hence, once again, the importance of French and above all of French poetry.

French poetry of the nineteenth century had, by this time, succeeded in creating a definable aesthetic. Baudelaire, Verlaine, Rimbaud, and Mallarmé had triumphantly demonstrated that poetry was a field of autonomous activity, not answerable to civic demands. Art was not useful; Théophile Gautier had argued this brilliantly as early as the 1830s, when he wrote the preface to *Mlle de Maupin*. There was no need for stories or poems to drive home a moral point. Art was above all a matter of the senses. Aesthetic enjoyment was separate from what was good or bad in a moral sense. The battle did not finish there, of course, for the argument of art for art's sake was a continuing one; but by the end of the nineteenth century, poetry, at least, had very largely broken with any notion of didacticism and moral purpose.

A second Romantic notion which the French gradually abandoned was the notion that literature was necessarily the expression of the subject. With Parnassianism, there arose a theory of objective art, of themes remote from the poet's life and concerned with archetypal patterns and tensions. In order to break with this biographical reference, the Parnassian chose distant and exotic themes like the pagan world of Leconte de Lisle's *Poèmes Barbares*, the classical world of his *Poèmes Antiques*, or the poems on 'Princesses' of Théodore de Banville. These poets despoiled language of contemporary associations and brought out archetypal connotations, suggesting patterns of restriction, freedom, calm, violence:

Argentyr, dans sa fosse étendu pale et grave
A l'abri de la lune, à l'abri de soleil ...

Here the pattern and sound of words are as important as meaning. 'Pale et grave' are words which slow down the line, while the repetition that follows is the repetition of day and night. The first line freezes with the immobility of death, the second line places this within the repetitive cycle of nature.

The only relation of the Parnassians to the present was one of rejection:

Noyez dans le néant des suprèmes ennuis
Vous mourrez bêtement en emplissant vos poches.

Verlaine, Rimbaud, and Baudelaire greatly extended the sphere of awareness after the rather narrow preoccupations of the Parnassians. One of the first poets to comprehend the monstrosity of the modern, the dark areas of the human psyche, the terror of the city, Rimbaud released language from the anchor of rationality. He loosened the hawsers that tied his 'drunken boat' to objective reality.

Now the Modernist poet faced all these developments in French literature not as a series of developments, but as one great wave displayed to him on the bookshelf. Little wonder that occasionally, like Darío, he did not seem to know where to choose and was at times prophetic with Hugo, Parnassian with Leconte de Lisle, at other times as fascinated as Verlaine by 'musicality'. All of which betrays the fact that Spanish America had no such thing as a 'style' which could be developed or defined. Nor did Modernism itself develop into a recognisable 'style'. Rather it was a number of parallel impulses, obeying currents of influence and of subjective preference. That is why, in the last resort, the contribution of each separate poet has to be separately considered.

I. JOSÉ ASUNCIÓN SILVA (1865-96)

José Asunción Silva is the poet of the Modernist period who remains closest to Romantic roots. He himself rejected the label 'Modernist' and his poetry was written in isolation from that of his Spanish American contemporaries. Son of a Colombian businessman, he spent some time in Europe in 1884 and his literary heritage was European, except perhaps for the influence of Poe which probably came to him filtered through France. Yet in his short novel *De la sobremesa* he charts the story of his disillusionment with bohemianism and the emptiness of modern life. Like the hero of his own novel, he was to return home to devote himself to business in an attempt to refloat the family fortune after his father's losses in a civil war. He was dogged by bad luck. He lost a sister, Elvira, whom he adored and after a period in the diplomatic service in Venezuela many of his papers (and reputedly many poems) were lost in a shipwreck. In 1896, he committed suicide.

Miguel de Unamuno summed up his poetry admirably:

> Silva volvió a descubrir lo que hace siglos estaba descubierto, hizo propias y nuevas las ideas comunes y viejas. Para Silva fue nuevo bajo el sol el misterio de la vida; gustó, creó, el estupor de Adán al encontrarse arrojado del paraíso; gustó el dolor paradisíaco.[4]

The summary captures the main theme of Silva's poetry, the theme of Paradise lost. Childhood is the only period of life which for Silva still trails its glory:

> Infancia, valle ameno,
> De calma y de frescura bendecida
> Donde es suave el rayo
> Del sol que abrasa el resto de la vida.

This period is recaptured in the poem 'Los maderos de San Juan', in which to the tune of the nursery rhyme,

> Aserrín
> Aserrán
>
> Los maderos de San Juan
> Piden queso, piden pan.

the child rocks on the 'rodillas duras y firmes de la Abuela', secure and happy for the only time in its life. The Abuela reminds us of his sad and inevitable future, the time of 'angustia y desengaño'.

The glimpse of Paradise is only occasional. Most of Asunción Silva's poetry is of night and death. Both 'Una noche' and 'Día de difuntos'—his best-known poems—are meditations on these themes. The first contrasts the warm, perfumed night in which he had once walked in perfect communion with his sister, Elvira, with the coldness and horror of his loneliness after her death. The images of the first walk are of the delight of the senses of 'perfumes' and 'murmullo de alas', but with death the images from nature are those of horror and coldness:

> Por la senda caminaba,
> Y se oían los ladridos de los perros a la luna,
>
> A la luna pálida,
> Y el chillido
> De las ranas.
>
> Sentí frío, era el frío que tenían en la alcoba
> Tus mejillas y tus sienes y tus manos adoradas
>
> Entre las blancuras níveas
> De las mortuorias sábanas.

If we compare this poem on death with poems by Darío or Jaimes Freyre on similar themes, we observe vast differences. Asunción Silva does not use symbols but describes a landscape reflecting mood in the Romantic manner. His originality is less in the imagery than in the form of his poetry which, far more than Darío's, breaks with traditional metres and stanzas, attaining a sinuous, flowing musicality. In 'Día de difuntos', the influence of Poe is evident in the form and in the rhythm which, as critics have pointed out, recall 'The Bells'.

> Allá arriba suena,
> Rítmica y serena,
> Esa voz de oro.

The poem imitates the sonorous chimes of the great bells which toll on the day of the dead and the jocular rhythms of a chiming clock which measures human time, ephemeral, swift, charged with speedy oblivion. Human time tinkles out against eternal time:

> Las campanas plañideras
> Que les hablan a los vivos
> De los muertos!

Disappointment, disillusion, the presence of death in life are never far from the surface of Asunción Silva's poetry. There is a strong sense of the vanity of existence which he sometimes expresses in the form of irony:

> Trabaja sin cesar, batalla, suda,
> vende vida por oro;
> conseguirás una dispepsia aguda
> mucho antes que un tesoro.

But ultimately he is an isolated figure, one who suffered the tragedy of isolation and whose poetry remained thin and Romantic perhaps because of his lack of contact with a greater world outside himself and outside Bogotá.

II. JULIÁN DEL CASAL (1863-93)

Julián del Casal represents the Modernist tendency to escape from contemporary life in its most extreme form. He died at an early age of tuberculosis and not unnaturally his poetry is dark with the anticipation of death. The son of a Spanish Basque family whose money had been sunk in a sugar plantation, he lived in very comfortable circumstances until the family fortune was lost when he was still a child. Suddenly he was the poor boy at a Jesuit school where all the other students were rich, an experience that perhaps generated in him his aristocratic poses and his exaltation of poetry.

In the languorous *fin-de-siècle* atmosphere of exotic Havana, he cultivated other exoticisms, celebrating Japanese women in his poetry and creating an 'oriental' atmosphere around him. As a contemporary wrote:

Quiso rodearse, penetrarse, saturarse de las sensaciones reales, voluptuosas de aquella exótica y lejana civilización. Leía y escribía

en un diván en cojines donde resaltaban, como en biombos, y
múnsulas y jarrones, el oro, la laca, el bermellón. En un ángulo,
ante un ídolo búdico ardían pajuelas impregnadas de serrín de
sándalo. Amaba las flores, preferentemente el crisantemo, la ixora,
amarylis, myosotis, el ilang, los clorílopsis ... Preocupábanle asuntos
como éste : si la Princesa Nourjihan, en el imperio del Gran Mogol,
fue la que descubrió el perfume sacado de la esencia de las rosas y
le adoptó por favorito.

What an effort this seems, what a superlative evasion. Physically, he
was unable to make the escape, for he only once went abroad, and
to Madrid, not to Paris. His illness affected his life-style, perhaps
increased his impression of being trapped, 'rodeado de paredes altas,
de calles adoquinadas, oyendo incesantemente el estrépito de coches,
ómnibus y carretones'.[5]

Casal published two collections of poetry: *Hojas al viento* (1890)
and *Nieve* (1892). He knew and met Darío during the latter's brief
stay in Havana on his way to Spain for the 1892 celebrations and,
as in Darío, the erotic and the sensual erupt into his poetry. Indeed
Casal's poetry moves along on the contradictory tensions of sensual
perception and rejection of the phenomenal world. His poems
addressed to women are sometimes celebrations of sensuality, sometimes celebrations of the ideal, but translated, in a curious way,
the racial divisions of the society in which he lived. Observe, for
instance, the poem 'Quimeras':

> Si sientes que las cóleras antiguas
>   surgen de tu alma pura,
> tendrás, para azotarlas fieramente,
> negras espaldas de mujeres nubias.

White refinement and black slavery—but also black sensuality. In
'Post Umbra' sexual sin is incarnated in the black woman. The
stereotype was transmitted to Darío who, during his brief stay in
Havana, also wrote a poem addressed to a famous courtesan, 'A la
negra Dominga'.

> Vencedora, magnífica y fiera
> con halagos de gata y pantera
> tiende al blanco su abrazo febril,
> y en su boca, do el beso está loco,
> muestra dientes de carne de coco
> con reflejos de lácteo marfil.

Here is the magnificent savage, uninhibited by European taboos, and
captured with far more vigour than in Casal's more languid lines.
Indeed, this is a fantasy that Casal found it hard to entertain. Instead

he turned his imagination away from the tropical and the African to a cool, snowbound Europe. Snow is a symbol of purity, of distance and remoteness from sordid reality. Summer and heat represent purity sullied like the dusty 'Paisaje de verano':

> Polvo y moscas. Atmósfera plomiza
> donde retumba el tabletear del trueno
> y, como cisnes entre inmundo cieno
> nubes blancas en cielo de ceniza.
> El mar sus ondas glaucas paraliza,
> y el relámpago, encima de su seno,
> del horizonte en el confín sereno
> traza su rauda exhalación rojiza.
> El árbol soñoliento cabecea,
> honda calma se cierne largo instante,
> hienden el aire rápidas gaviotas,
> el rayo en el espacio centellea,
> y sobre el dorso de la tierra humeante
> baja la lluvia en crepitantes gotas.

Contrast these lines with Asunción Silva's 'Una noche . . .', in which nature reflected human sentiment. Casal's landscape is a landscape without man, a play of elements, of rain, light, calm, and movement. Trees and birds, clouds and sky, are subject to hidden forces and man has no part in it. At the same time, Casal sees these forces as being in antithetical relationships. Dark sky, brilliant lightning, white clouds, muddy background, calm, still scenery, darting birds, solidity of earth, discreteness of rain—all these compose a landscape of contrasts and tensions.

In common with many Modernist poets, Casal's vision of experience was idealistic. The phenomenal world is all too imperfect, something from which to escape, even by means of drugging oneself. So in 'La canción de la morfina', he writes:

> Y venzo a la realidad
> ilumino el negro arcano
> y hago del dolor humano
> dulce voluptuosidad.

If not drugs, then art:

> el alma grande, solitaria y pura
> que la mezquina realidad desdeña
> halla en el Arte dichas ignoradas.

The world of the imagination becomes the only goal of existence, that which enables him to withdraw from the society of man and from societal relationships:

> Libre de abrumadoras ambiciones,
> soporto de la vida el rudo fardo,
> porque me alienta el formidable orgullo
> de vivir, ni envidioso ni envidiado,
> persiguiendo fantásticas visiones
> mientras se arrastran otros por el fango
> para extraer un átomo de oro
> del fondo pestilente de un pantano.

Human society is conceived only in terms of competition, ambition, envy. In part this reluctance to engage may be attributable to Casal's illness which is reflected in the many poems that deal with death. This death he faced without any kind of religious faith, as he hints in 'Flores'.

> Marchita ya esa flor de suave aroma,
> cual virgen consumida por la anemia,
> hoy en mi corazón su tallo asoma
> una adelfa purpúrea, la blasfemia.

Virgin purity and faith have gone, leaving only the flower of sin and blasphemy in his breast. Perhaps, however, blasphemy does imply a faith, even if only negatively. In 'Tristissima Nox', however, we glimpse a spiritual desert:

> Noche de soledad. Rumor confuso
> hace el viento surgir de la arboleda,
> donde su red de transparente seda
> grisácea araña entre las hojas puso.
>
> Del horizonte hasta el confín difuso
> la onda marina sollozando rueda
> y, con su forma insólita, remeda
> tritón cansado ante el cerebro iluso.
>
> Mientras del sueño bajo el firme amparo
> todo yace dormido en la penumbra
> solo mi pensamiento vela en calma,
>
> como la llama de escondido faro
> que con sus rayos fúlgidos alumbra
> el vacío profundo de mi alma.

The poem opens on a note of solitude and ends with emptiness. Nature itself conveys a feeling of weariness and greyness, the spider's web and the repetitive sound of the waves reinforce monotony. But within the greyness there is a point of consciousness and light—the poet himself—but his consciousness, far from giving meaning to the nightscape, is itself invaded by emptiness. There is no source of comfort either in the external world nor in the world of nature. Perhaps that is why the art object takes on supreme importance. In Casal's collection *Nieve*, there are many poems which describe paintings, such as the ten sonnets dedicated to Gustave Moreau, and these paintings in turn depict myth figures—Prometheus, Galatea, Helen of Troy, Hercules, Venus, Jupiter, and Europa. Casal's poems thus distil an experience already mediated through myth and through art. They are thrice removed from life. The same is true of his 'Japanese' poems, like the one addressed to 'Kakemono':

> Hastiada de reinar con la hermosura
> Que te dio el cielo, por nativo dote,
> pediste al arte su potente auxilio
> para sentir el anhelado goce
> de ostentar la hermosura de las hijas
> del país de los anchos quitasoles
> pintados de doradas mariposas
> revoloteando entre azulinas flores.

Woman is here transformed into a work of art. She is decoration, rather than organism.

Casal is the supreme example of the Modernist poet who refuses to engage with everyday experience, whose refuge is in an exotic world of his own creation, in the defiance of nature through art. And art is the only religion left to him in the spiritual desert in which he spent the years of his lonely struggle with death and disease.

III. SALVADOR DÍAZ MIRÓN (1853-1928)

At first sight, it is hard to understand how Salvador Díaz Mirón comes to be numbered among the Modernists. Perhaps his inclusion in Modernist anthologies has much to do with the fact that he wrote at the end of the nineteenth century and less to do with the style in which he wrote. His poetic language is rhetorical, his themes incline towards Naturalism. Of all the poets of the period, he is the one who is closest in spirit to the Realist or Naturalist novel and whose deterministic view of the world comes nearest to theirs.

Born in the province of Vera Cruz, he was destined for a brilliant political career and served in the legislature. At this period, he saw himself as a Mexican Hugo, the political and literary voice of the masses. Addressing himself to the French poet, he declared:

> La historia
> no ha producido en los mayores siglos
> gloria que pueda superar tu gloria.

And in 'Sursum', a poem dedicated to Justo Sierra, the educationalist and politician, he identifies the poet with the highest point of progress in the climb towards a higher level of human consciousness. The poet is able to face truth without flinching, able to face the lost paradise of faith. However much he may suffer personally, he imbues humanity with hope by keeping a Utopian vision before their eyes:

> ha de contar la redentora utopia,
> como otra estatua de Memnón que suena
> y ser, perdida la esperanza propia,
> el paladión de la esperanza ajena.

The poet then signifies sacrifice of self to the greater vision of the future, a view which is plainly historicist in perspective and hence radically different from the anti-historicism of much Modernist poetry.

In 1892, Salvador Díaz Mirón reached the turning-point of his life. In this year, he killed an opponent in self-defence during an election campaign, and, as a result, spent four years in prison, the fruit of which was the collection *Lascas* (1901). The optimistic, rhetorical language of the earlier poetry is now greatly modified. Men are no longer Romans fighting triumphantly in the arena of life. The landscape has darkened. Death, night, the prison haunt the verse. Where poems are social in theme, they border on the grotesque as in 'Ejemplo', which describes a hanging body on a gibbet. And though there is still rhetoric and cliché, the poet concentrates on formal perfection:

> Forma es fondo, y el fausto seduce
> si no agranda y tampoco reduce.

But finally what marks Salvador Díaz Mirón off most distinctly from his contemporaries is his inability to escape into a private vision or into the world of art. He sees man without illusion, but has no counter-vision. Thus in the ironically-titled 'Idilio', he describes a girl, a child of nature in the tropical landscape of Vera Cruz province, but cannot see her nor her setting in terms of natural idyll. Nature cannot transcend itself:

> Y un borrego con gran cornamenta
> Y pardos mechones de lana mugrienta,
> Y una oveja con bucles de armiño
> —la mejor en figura y aliño—
> se copulan con ansia que tienta.

Nature does not select on grounds of refinement. The ram with its dirty fleece copulates with the cleanest sheep. The girl who grows up among the animals gives herself to the first comer as soon as she feels the stirrings of sexual desire. The sinister consequences of this blind acceptance of the natural instincts are implied by the buzzard hovering in the heavens.

> Y en la excelsa y magnífica fiesta,
> y cual mácula errante y funesta
> un vil zopilote resbala,
> tendida e inmóvil el ala.

To accept 'the natural' on the sexual plane, it also follows that one must accept the struggle for life in which the buzzard preys on lesser animals and carrion. And there is nothing outside this for Díaz Mirón.

IV. MANUEL GUTIÉRREZ NÁJERA (1859-95)

'Un poeta atormentado por el deseo de la felicidad' according to Justo Sierra.[6] Manuel Gutiérrez Nájera was also the most cosmopolitan of Modernist poets though he never left his native Mexico. He was the most libertine too, though he reportedly was small, ugly, and poor. His father was a journalist and Manuel's first job was in a department store, but his talent quickly opened a career in journalism to him. He contributed to *El Porvenir*, *El Liberal*, and *La Voz*, and was one of the founders of a famous Modernist magazine, the *Revista Azul*, which published translations of Whitman, Tolstoy, Gautier, and Daudet.

Gutiérrez Nájera translated the luxury, refinement, and frivolity of Paris during the nineties into Mexican terms. In the preface to his *Poesías completas*, his friend and admirer, Justo Sierra, described how natural his 'afrancesamiento' was, given the fact that Mexican educated classes tended to be educated through France and French culture:

> Como aprendemos el francés al mismo tiempo que el castellano, como en francés podíamos informarnos y todos nos hemos informado, acá y allá, de las literaturas exóticas, como en francés, en suma, nos poníamos en contracto con el movimiento de la civilización humana y no en español, al francés fuimos más directamente.[7]

Contemporaries most admired Gutiérrez Nájera for his serious philosophic poems such as '¿Para qué?' and 'Ondas muertas', in which he perceived the universe as an irrational force; but the poems which the modern ear finds more attractive are those which reflect a 'gay nineties' hedonism. In 'En un cromo', for instance, the poet adorns the 'Gather ye Rosebuds' theme in the cynical contemporary manner:

Niña de la blanca enagua
Que miras correr el agua
Y deshojas una flor,
Más rápido que esas ondas,
Niña de las trenzas blondas,
Pasa cantando el amor.

Ya me dirás, si eres franca,
Niña de la enagua blanca,
Que la dicha es el amor,
Mas yo haré que te convenzas,
Niña de las rubias trenzas,
De que olvidar es mejor.

If it were not for this modern mood, the poem would verge on
pastiche. The poet always plays very close to the borderline of bad
taste and perhaps in 'La Duquesa Job' skirts very close to the borderline. The 'Duque Job' was one of Gutiérrez Nájera's pseudonyms and
the 'duquesa' is his mistress whom he portrays as being as charming
and lively as any French courtesan, but with some Mexican spontaneity to add piquancy to the character:

Ágil, nerviosa, blanca, delgada
Media de seda bien restirada
Gola de encaje, corsé de crac!
Nariz pequeña, garbosa, cuca,
Y palpitantes sobre la nuca
Rizos tan rubios como el cognac.

This is more Toulouse-Lautrec than Gustave Moreau. The verse has
a light skipping metre which matches the frivolity of the subject.
A brilliant, occasional poet with a fine ear, Gutiérrez Nájera was not
able to translate his skill into poems on more serious topics.

V. RUBÉN DARÍO (1867-1916)

Y en la playa quedaba, desolada y perdida,
una ilusión que aullaba como un perro a la Muerte.[8]

All the conflicting currents that flow into the Modernist movement
erupt in the work of Darío, who coined the term 'Modernist' and
whose restless journeyings between America and Europe served as
a link between poets of different nationalities—Lugones and Jaimes
Freyre in Buenos Aires, Julián del Casal in Cuba, the poets of Central America and Chile, and those of Spain. His poetry reflects the
restlessness of his life. He absorbed many influences from Parnas-

sianism to Symbolism, from Hugo and Gautier to Leconte de Lisle and Eugenio de Castro. He experimented with all types of verse form from the pastiche of the *Dezires y Layes* to the sixteen-syllable line sonnet and Latin hexameters. His celebration of refinement and sophistication, his doubts and loss of faith, the elevation of poetry to a religion, the transmutation of flux and contradiction into an aesthetic harmony—all these aspects of Modernism, found singly in other poets, come together in Darío.

He was born in 1867 in Metapa, Nicaragua, of parents who separated when he was a child. He was brought up by a grandmother, taken as a young prodigy to Managua, the Nicaraguan capital, and there began his career as a poet when still in his early teens. Invited to San Salvador, he began to read French poetry, particularly that of Hugo. But the event that lifted his life out of the provincial limitations of civic poetry was his visit to Santiago de Chile in 1886. Santiago, 'sabe de todo y anda al galope',[9] he declared, for this was his contact with a metropolis, with a large modern city, with sophisticated society. Still hesitant and unsure of himself, he veered between the social poetry of 'A un obrero' to poems addressed to Hugo. But it was in Santiago that he published the handful of poems and stories with the title *Azul* (1888) and so attracted the attention of the internationally famous Spanish critic Juan Valera.[10] Though neglected and snubbed at this stage in his career, he had some powerful and wealthy friends who encouraged his reading of contemporary French writers such as Catulle Mendès, and Gautier. His 'Canto épico a las glorias de Chile' (1887) which celebrated the Chilean naval victory over Peru, however, shows that he still saw himself as a civic poet. It was a role that he was to reassume at intervals, just as he would always be ready to serve in an official capacity, when called upon to do so. He was not a man like Martí whose life was ruled by a single principle, but a man who wavered between a number of different projects. If today he was the civic poet, tomorrow he would be a lonely outcast, if today he celebrated sensual love, tomorrow he would see himself as a man laden down with religious guilt.

But Santiago was the definitive experience. There was an ideal now of sophistication, of refined living which could only be cultivated in big cities. Above all, provincialism must be left behind, howling after him like the lost illusion in the poem 'Marina', written in 1898. The poem is worth meditating on. It is not one of Darío's best-known ones and he makes the shocking mistake of thinking that it was Achilles not Ulysses who blocked his ears against the sirens; nevertheless, there is much of his most intimate self in the picture of the boat sailing gaily towards Cythera, bidding farewell to the 'peñascos, enemigos del poeta' and the coasts 'en donde se secaron las viñas' and shutting his ears to the memories of the past. Certainly the provincial Rubén

Darío who arrived in an ill-cut suit to conquer Santiago was soon to be buried in the depths of memory. His place was taken by a man of international reputation who, after a brief return to Central America and two marriages, spent five years in Buenos Aires, working for the most important of Latin American newspapers, *La Nación*. In 1900, he went to live in Paris, a city he had loved since his first visit there, and in 1907, he was made Nicaraguan representative in Madrid. During all this period, during which he made frequent journeys backwards and forwards between America and Europe, when he was the centre of Hispanic literary life, the one trace of provincialism that remained was perhaps his affair with Francisca Sánchez, a Spanish woman of the people by whom he had a child. The metropolis, the Cythera to which he so happily set sail, was symbolised by Europe, above all by the Paris of the nineties. He was at home in a world that ended in 1914. But by then he was already an alcoholic, a sick man who tried to find religious peace in Mallorca, and who, as his life neared its end, found himself almost penniless. His last journey to America was the *via crucis* of a defeated soul. He wrote:

> Yo no puedo continuar en Europa, pues ya agoté hasta el último céntimo. Me voy a América Latina lleno del horror de la guerra.[11]

So ended the life of the man for whom Europe had symbolised so much. In flight from a war-torn continent, he died on reaching Nicaragua in 1916 and did not live to see the transformation of values that the twilight of Europe implied for younger generations.

After the early poetry, much of it of a civic and occasional nature, Darío's major publications are *Azul* (1888), a collection which appeared in an enlarged second edition in 1890; *Prosas profanas* (1896), which also was published in an enlarged second edition in 1901; *Cantos de vida y esperanza* (1905), *El canto errante* (1907), *Poema del otoño y otros poemas* (1910), and *Canto a la Argentina* (1914). His contribution to prose-writing, which was considerable, will be discussed later in this chapter.

Although all his life Darío remained a divided and conflicting personality, these conflicts became increasingly explicit after the publication of *Prosas profanas*. The poetry of *Azul* is still Romantic in inspiration, Hugoesque in its celebration of carnal love linked to a cosmic harmony, and in its depiction of evil as the struggle for life. Romantic, too, is the containment of the poetry within a seasonal cycle—'Primaveral', 'Estival', 'Otoñal', and 'Invernal'. In the first of these poems—'Primaveral'—springtime is joy in life and life is still superior to art. The poet rejects the artificial:

> No quiero el vino de Naxos
> ni el ánfora de asas bellas,

> ni la copa donde Cipria
> al gallardo Adonís ruega.
> Quiero beber el amor
> sólo en tu boca bermeja
> ¡Oh amada mía! Es el dulce
> tiempo de la primavera.

Here the poet rejects all mediation between himself and enjoyment. The tone is that of the 'Song of Songs'. Sexual love is sacred, the incarnation of divine love, not in conflict with it. In 'Estival', the poet celebrates animal love in a way that is quite different from Salvador Díaz Mirón's grim picture of animality. The tragedy of 'Estival' is not that animals obey their instincts but that man suppresses the animal. The female tiger is shot by a prince on safari, a gratuitous act of destruction which introduces evil and disharmony into the world of nature. 'Otoñal' celebrates nostalgia. 'Invernal' the sophistication of modern love which can defy the seasons, since the lovers can take refuge from the elements in 'lechos abrigados', covered with 'pieles de Astrakán'. But the four poems should be considered together as four aspects of love. Only in the first poem, however, are instincts and fulfilment in perfect harmony with the natural cycle.

In *Prosas profanas*, Darío declines to draw parallels between love and the natural cycle. He feels himself separated from nature, perhaps protected from it by art. 'A través de los fuegos divinos de las vidrieras historiadas', he wrote, 'me río del viento que sopla afuera, del mal que pasa'. And in the opening poem of the collection, 'Era un aire suave', Eulalia, the archetypal *belle dame sans merci*, gives herself to the poet rather than to more noble lovers. Poetry now mediates between Darío and the crudeness of experience. Harmony is achieved within the poem and is formalised in descriptions of sculpture, music, gardens, and manners. Hence, with the passage of time, Darío draws nearer to Julián del Casal, putting more and more objects in front of himself as if trying to cover up the emptiness of the world.

> Los tapices rojos de doradas listas,
> cubrían panoplias de pinturas y armas,
> que hallaban de bellas pasadas conquistas,
> amantes coloquios y dulces alarmas.

And sometimes this piling-up of objects borders on vulgarity, an ever-present threat in Modernism. Here, once again, is the panther-skin, not worn by a noble savage but by a Victorian in fancy dress:

> E iban con manchadas pieles de pantera,
> con tirsos de flores y copas paganas,

las almas de aquellos jóvenes que viera
Venus en su templo con palmas hermanas.[12]

Indeed it is the genius of Darío that he did not transcend his period,
but that he expressed its tastes, its gropings, and limitations with
absolute fidelity and that he lived out in his own life the sense of
guilt that came from having overthrown traditional religious and moral
restraints. In this respect, it is revealing to read *Los raros*, a collection of essays on Edgar Allan Poe, Leconte de Lisle, Paul Verlaine,
Léon Bloy, and others and which were written contemporaneously
with the poems of *Prosas profanas*. These essays show more clearly
than the poems how deeply tinged with guilt Darío's feelings were,
even when he was dealing with sensuality on a purely literary level.
Mark, for instance, his description of Rachilde:

> Trato de una mujer extraña y escabrosa, de un espíritu único
> esfíngicamente solitario en este tiempo finisecular; de un 'caso'
> curiosísimo y turbador: de la escritora que ha publicado todas sus
> obras con este pseudónimo 'Rachilde'; satánica flor de decadencia,
> picantemente perfumada, misteriosa y hechicera y mala como un
> pecado.

Despite the 'scandal' of his life and his blatant bohemianism, there
is a certain timidity in Darío, a fear of transgressing, that is patent in
his portrait of Rachilde, and of others among *Los raros*. Perception of
this helps us to understand the fact that he clothed his verse, that he
opted for a process of refinement, of transmutation of experience into
mythical or musical terms rather than for a poetry of self-revelation.
In *Prosas profanas* and *Cantos de vida y esperanza*, the majority of the
poems—'Coloquio de los centauros', 'El cisne', 'Leda', for instance—
clothe the poet's conflicting impulses by evoking figures of Greek
mythology and by containing ambiguous drives within a mythological
framework. The centaurs are offspring of gods and of humans, the
swan is a god in disguise since this was the form Jupiter took to rape
Leda. The mythological figure of the centaur, part human, part animal,
reconciles aspects which in life are simply contradictory. In this way,
a poem could be made to reflect the conflicts between sexual impulse
and the aspiration to transcend the purely animal—and at the same
time to resolve the tensions. Thus in 'Coloquio de los centauros',
the voices of the centaurs speak of the dangers of sexual love and of
the beauty and power of Venus:

> princesa de los gérmenes, reina de las matrices,
> señora de las savias y de las atracciones.

Venus is both pure and impure:

> Tiene las formas puras del ánfora, y la risa

del agua que la brisa riza y el sol irisa;
mas la ponzoña ingénita su máscara pregona:
mejores son el águila, la yegua y la leona.

The poem forces on the reader an attention to conflict and yet
is the harmony towards which man strives. The music of the verse,
the balanced lines and sounds (la brisa riza y el sol irisa) are external
manifestations of a divine equilibrium,[13] which the poet, of all men,
is best able to perceive:

El vate, el sacerdote, suele oír el acento
desconocido; a veces enuncia el vago viento
un misterio, y revela una inicial la espuma
o la flor; y se escuchan palabras de la bruma.
Y el hombre favorito del numen, en la linfa
o la ráfaga, encuentra mentor:—demonio o ninfa.

Darío, in this section of the poem, sees the poet as the mediator
between a divine unity and the phenomenal world, at once empowered
to monitor the universe and at the same time to maintain a sense of
underlying harmony. That is why his poetry breaks away from a
Romantic depiction of nature as simply a background against which
a human morality play is enacted. Instead he sees nature and art as a
cosmic harmony which includes animal, human, and divine. Art
idealises nature and at the same time reveals its hidden message
which links the seemingly chaotic manifestations to the divine pattern.
Man is not degraded by his animal nature, as long as he keeps this in
harmony with the spiritual. And nature when read properly signals
a heavenly order. So, in 'La espiga', he writes:

Con el áureo pincel de la flor de la harina
trazan sobre la tela azul del firmamento
el misterio inmortal de la tierra divina
y el alma de las cosas que da su sacramento
en una interminable frescura matutina.

This is different from Julián del Casal's Manichean presentation of
ideal and sensual love. The divine here is within nature and sensually
manifest. The earth is 'divine', objects have souls. The rape of Leda
by Jupiter in the form of a swan becomes for the poet as significant a
moment in time as the godhead's incarnation in human form as Christ,
and the event is proclaimed as an annunciation:

Antes de todo, ¡gloria a ti, Leda!
Tu dulce vientre cubrió de seda
el Dios. ¡Miel y oro sobre la brisa!
Sonaban alternativamente
flauta y cristales, Pan y la fuente.

¡Tierra era canto: Cielo, sonrisa!

Ante el celeste, supremo acto,
dioses y bestias hicieron pacto.
Se dio a la alondra la luz del día,
se dio a los buhos sabiduría,
y melodía al ruiseñor.
A los leones fue la victoria,
para las águilas toda la gloria,
y a las palomas todo el amor.

Pero vosotros sois los divinos
príncipes. Vagos como las naves,
inmaculados como los linos,
maravillosos como las aves.

En vuestros picos tenéis las prendas
que manifiestan corales puros.
Con vuestros pechos abrís las sendas
que arríba indican los Dioscuros.

Las dignidades de vuestros actos
eternizadas en lo infinito,
hacen que sean ritmos exactos,
voces de ensueño, luces de mito.

De orgullo olímpico sois el resumen,
¡oh blancas urnas de la armonía!
Ebúrneas joyas que anima un numen
con su celeste melancolía.

Melancolía de haber amado,
junto a la fuente de la arboleda,
el luminoso cuello estirado
entre los blancos muslos de Leda.[14]

The event announced in the opening lines is the incarnation of divinity
in the extremely sensual animal form. The divine becomes part of the
world of nature. Art and nature, 'flauta y cristales', join in celebration
of the union in which earth and heaven partake—'Tierra era canto:
Cielo, sonrisa'—where the very balance of the lines reflects harmony.
And this harmony is symbolised throughout nature. Each animal or
bird, being an emblem of an ideal attribute as well as a living creature,
and the swan, being the most divine of all birds, symbolise harmony
itself. Swans are 'immaculate as linen', pure, for though Jupiter raped
Leda, this act is seen not as a descent from a pure ideal but as an
archetypal act. So the swans too are 'eternizadas en lo infinito' through
'the dignity' of their acts. The note of melancholy on which the poem

ends is not out of key with this joyful communion, for the poem describes a gentle descent from heaven to earth, and the divine, incarnate in animal form, partakes of temporality and hence must be imbued with 'heavenly sadness'.

'Leda' is one of Darío's most fully realised poems, one in which the temporal and the eternal are successfully balanced, in which the conflicts between animal and divine, sensual and ideal, cease to be conflicts. Though the mid-line caesura divides two different spheres, yet the equal halves hold the two spheres in harmony.

The idealisation of the sensual is only one aspect of Darío's poetry which is infinitely varied. He is attracted at times to the purely pictorial, as in 'Sinfonía en gris mayor', an attempt to create a word-etching, a mood poem. There is the attempt to imitate a musical effect in 'Marcha triunfal', and in the collections *Cantos de vida y esperanza* and *El canto errante,* there is even a poetry of direct statement when his anguish was too great for him to contain it in symbol. So, he speaks directly of 'el horror':

> de ir a tientas, en intermitentes espantos,
> hacia lo inevitable desconocido.

In such poems, the harmony tends to break. 'No obstante', for instance, after a magnificent beginning:

> ¡Oh terremoto mental!
> Yo sentí un día en mi cráneo
> como el caer subitáneo
> de un Babel de cristal

ends lamely 'Hay, no obstante, que ser fuerte . . .' At other times, even during these late, dark years, he captures the sense of joy in beauty which had informed the poetry of *Prosas profanas*, but in 'Nocturno', 'Thanatos', and other poems he broods on death and fear. Even consciousness seems too painful because of the suffering it brings:

> Dichoso el árbol que es apenas sensitivo
> y más la piedra dura, porque ésta ya no siente,
> pues no hay dolor más grande que el dolor de ser vivo,
> ni mayor pesadumbre que la vida consciente . . .

Darío has a totally different side to him, however, than any of these. He was also a civic poet who wrote poems on political themes either to celebrate national events or to criticise, in the Hugo manner: 'to write his protest', as he put it, 'on the swan's wing':

> Mañana podremos ser yanquis (y es lo más probable); de todas maneras, mi protesta queda escrita sobre las alas de los inmaculados cisnes, tan ilustres como Júpiter.[15]

It is said that Darío had been stung by Rodó's remark that he was not the poet of America;[16] but whether influenced by Rodó or not, his view of the poet as mediator between the ideal world and the phenomenal world did not exclude the writing of poetry on political themes. He was to praise Theodore Roosevelt for his defence of poetry and believed that the practice of poetry was more than ever necessary as an antidote to the modern world. In the preface to *El canto errante*, he wrote:

> Otros poderosos de la tierra, príncipes, políticos, millonarios, manifiestan una plausible deferencia por el dios cuyo arco es de plata, y por sus sacerdotes o representantes en una tierra cada día más vibrante de automóviles ... y de bombas.

Ideally poetry should be prophetic, according to Darío. It should expose the mental cliché and open the way to new ideas. And he felt that if Modernism had any importance, it was in this respect as a trail-blazer:

> No es, como lo sospechan algunos profesores o cronistas, la importancia de otra retórica, de otro *poncif*, con nuevos preceptos, con nuevo encasillado, con nuevos códigos. Y, ante todo, ¿se trata de una cuestión de formas? No. Se trata, ante todo, de una cuestión de ideas.

Nevertheless, in the poems on political themes, though he uses symbols, his language is often more direct. 'A Roosevelt', '¿Qué signo haces, oh Cisne?', 'A Colón' have little room for ambiguity. 'A Colón', written in 1892, but not published in any collection before *El canto errante*, describes in explicit terms the disaster which discovery implied to America.

> Duelos, espantos, guerras, fiebre constante en nuestra senda ha puesto la suerte triste: Cristóforo Colombo, pobre Almirante, ruega a Dios por el mundo que descubriste.

Both 'A Roosevelt' and 'Salutación del optimista' are influenced by the ideas of Rodó, who had contrasted the materialism of the Anglo-Saxon with the supposed lack of materialism in the Latin race. Following this lead, Darío celebrates 'la América ingenua que tiene sangre indígena'. However, Darío's attempts to dignify the political theme through an emblematic or symbolic use of language does not get beyond the stereotype of masculine/aggressive versus female/artistic notions, nor beyond an emotive rhetoric which rests on the assumption that weakness is virtue. There is nothing inherently impossible about writing political poetry and if Darío fails, it is because he does not feel the problem with any great immediacy. This is just as true of his civic poetry, like the *Canto a la Argentina*, which takes a Whitmanesque model but lacks Whitman's vital link with the people he is celebrating. Darío (we suspect) is much more concerned with what the Argentine oligarchy would like to hear in the year of the centenary celebrations:

¡Que vuestro himno soberbio vibre,
hombres libres en tierra libre!

As a political prophet, Darío was a failure. As a barometer of the tastes of his period and of what Juan Ramón Jiménez referred to as the spiritual crisis of the time, he is much more reliable. He registered the varied avant-garde impulses of the time, attempted to salvage art from commercialism and the dead hand of verisimilitude; he refined and transmuted. In one sense, he performed a service akin to Garcilaso, domesticating the exotic in order to make available new areas of feeling. And as a man of the period, he felt its religious and moral crisis deeply. That is why his verse is not simply the slavish imitation of fashion, but a genuine reflection of doubt and anguish. Because he was a man who liked to assume roles, he tended to externalise his attitudes —was now courtier, now bohemian, now lay-brother, now portrayed in all the splendour of diplomatic regalia. This makes him sometimes difficult to write about, since his poetry is as contradictory as the roles he assumed, varying from the direct statement of 'Dichoso el árbol que es apenas sensitivo' to the allusions and symbols of 'Coloquio de los centauros'. And both attitudes were sincere. He had as much need for self-expression as he had to link himself to a literary tradition of swans, princesses, and myth. Being a Latin American, too, made him eclectic. He was Parnassian, Symbolist, decadentist, nativist, and did not have to commit himself to any single school, but felt free to draw on all.

If much of Darío's poetry now appears dated, if we have lost the taste for classical mythology which acts as the support for many of his poems, there can be no doubt as to his historical importance. Because of his personality, because of the continental scope of his activity and his international reputation, he acted as the catalyst of the artistic elements of his time. He can be regarded as the first truly professional writer of Latin America and it is thanks to his example that its literature developed a more serious concern for form and language.

VI. JULIO HERRERA Y REISSIG (1875-1910)

'Respiraba la poesía, se alimentaba de poesía, paseaba sobre la poesía';[17] thus the critic Enrique Anderson Imbert speaks of the Uruguayan poet Herrera y Reissig. This member of a traditional oligarchic family was not without political ambitions, before the failure of the family fortunes left him without resources. Though Anderson

Imbert suggests that he was quite without interest in 'la realidad
práctica', this does not seem to be entirely true. Rather the apparent
lack of interest arose out of disappointment and disillusion from which
he only escaped in poetry. So like Julián del Casal, poetry was very
much a refuge, an imaginary castle in which he could draw up the
drawbridge between himself and the world, rather as he did when he
climbed up to the 'Torre de los Panoramas', the attic room in which
he lived. In his successive publications, *Las pascuas del tiempo* (1900),
Los maitines de la noche (1902), *Los éxtasis de la montaña* (1904-07),
Sonetos vascos, and *La torre de las esfinges* (1908), he invented and
peopled a world of idealised and yet grotesque landscapes. In his
poetry, the tensions are nearly all externalised. Consider, for instance,
the following sonnet, 'La iglesia':

> En un beato silencio el recinto vegeta.
> Las vírgenes de cera duermen en su decoro
> de terciopelo lindo y de esmalte incoloro
> y San Gabriel se hastía de soplar la trompeta.
>
> Sedienta, abre su boca de mármol la pileta.
> Una vieja estornuda desde el altar del coro ...
> Y una legión de átomos sube un camino de oro
> aéreo, que una escala de Jacob interpreta.
>
> Inicia sus labores el alma reverente
> Para saber si anda de buenas San Vicente,
> con tímidos arrobos repica la alcancía ...
>
> Acá y allá maniobra después con un plumero.
> mientras, por una puerta que da a la sacristía
> irrumpe la gloriosa turba del gallinero.

The poet is talking about the death of God, but he does it by
describing the emptiness of the church with its waxed virgin, dusty
atmosphere, the bored Saint Gabriel waiting without conviction for the
last trump, the empty font, and the aged 'beata'. The church is
drained of life. Energy is elsewhere—in nature, and the 'gloriosa
turba' of the hencoop. On the one hand is boredom and stagnation,
transmitted through verbs like 'vegeta', 'se hastía'; on the other, the
eruption of the hallelujah chorus of the hens.

Herrera y Reissig often expresses nostalgia for the innocence of the
past, especially of the rural life of the past—'¡Oh campo siempre
niño!', he wrote, '¡Oh patria de alma proba!'—yet he is deeply preoccupied with change. Sometimes he tries to abolish change, to concentrate on the archetypal, setting his poems in an eternal present.
But he is also deeply aware of something that is irrevocably past. The
very title, *Los parques abandonados*, suggested that something had

ended, that the modern world was one of separation, absence, and pain. In 'La sombra dolorosa', he talks of the communication of two people 'unidos por un mal hermano', but even this feeling of union is shattered by the sound of a train which breaks the mood and accentuates feelings of loneliness and separation:

> manchó la soñadora transparencia
> de la tarde infinita el tren lejano,
> aullando de dolor hacia la ausencia.

The train is not simply a convenient 'futurist' image but an exact symbol of progress made at the cost of suffering and solitude. The audacious metaphor is characteristic. Take, for instance, the sonnet 'La noche' which has fourteen-syllable lines instead of the usual hendecasyllable and which is even more original in its imagery.

> La noche en la montaña mira con ojos viudos
> de ciervo sin amparo que vela ante su cría;
> y como si asumieran un don de profecía
> en un sueño inspirado hablan los campos rudos.
>
> Rayan el panorama, como espectros agudos,
> tres álamos en éxtasis. Un gallo desvaría
> reloj de media noche. La gran luna amplía
> las cosas, que se llenan de encantamientos mudos.
>
> El lago azul de sueño, que ni una sombra empaña,
> es como la conciencia pura de la montaña ...
> A ras de agua, tersa, que riza de su aliento,
>
> Albino, el pastor loco, quiere besar la luna.
> En la huerta sonámbula vibra un canto de cuna ...
> Aúllan a los diablos los perros del convento.

The sonnet opens with images of loss, of negativity. There is night with its wounded deer's eyes. But night brings out unconscious, irrational forces. The cock, symbol of time and natural order, crows at midnight, the moon enlarges things; and the only human element is a mad shepherd, whose name, Albino, suggests purity, and who wishes to kiss the moon, a symbol of chastity. The poem inverts our sense of order, presents a nightscape in which daylight laws are inapplicable. Reason has been exiled. Irrationality is all that remains—and this, years before Dada, years before the surrealist movement, though, of course, long after German Romanticism which had made the nightscape commonplace. But certainly Herrera y Reissig went much further than Darío towards perception of unconscious forces and he successfully conveys a sense of unprotected isolation in his poems.

VII. RICARDO JAIMES FREYRE (1868-1933)

Jaimes Freyre, a Bolivian poet, was a friend of Darío's and co-founder with the Nicaraguan of the *Revista de América*, a magazine published in Buenos Aires in the 1890s. He was destined to have a distinguished career as a diplomat, teacher at the University of Tucumán, and Chancellor of the Bolivian Republic. He was a notable political speaker and wrote a treatise on Castilian prosody, *Leyes de la versificación castellana* (1912) as well as being author of a historical work, *La historia del descubrimiento de Tucumán*.

As a poet, Jaimes Freyre's reputation rests on *Castalia bárbara*, a collection which he published in 1899, and which evoked a mythology and landscape of the North rather similar to that of Leconte de Lisle's *Poèmes Barbares*, which was probably the initial source of inspiration. The theme is the conflict between a pagan world and Christian values. Like Herrera y Reissig, Jaimes Freyre tends to see the modern world as a desert, a snow-covered steppe, as in 'Las voces tristes', from which the warmth and comfort of human contact have disappeared. The pagan world has analogies with our world, but was more heroic. The pathos of the Valhalla warriors he describes lies in their heroic though fruitless death without hope of resurrection. For instance, 'Havamal' from *Castalia bárbara* is a Christ-figure for whom there is no saving God:

Yo sé que estuve colgando en el árbol movido por el viento
durante nueve noches,
herido de lanza, sacrificado a Odín.
Yo sacrificado a mí mismo
(en aquel árbol, del cual nadie sabe
de qué raíces nace)—
No me dieron un cuerno para beber, ni me alcanzaron pan.
Miré hacia abajo, grité fuerte,
recogí las runas y después caí hacia atrás.

The death parallels the passion save that the agony is longer. Like Christ, he is given a lance wound and refused sustenance, but he is not resurrected. The tension in the poem arises because of the inevitable comparison with Christ and Christ's salvation. Certainly the two worlds are locked in conflict. In 'Eternum Vale', the pagan gods flee with the coming of the 'silent God with outstretched arms'.

Un Dios misterioso y extraño visita la selva,
Es un Dios silencioso que tiene los brazos abiertos.
Cuando la hija de Thor espoleaba su negro caballo,
Le vio erguirse de pronto, a la sombra de un añoso fresno

Y sintió que se helaba la sangre
Ante el Dios silencioso que tiene sus brazos abiertos.

The pagan world was one of aggression and violence, the Christian vision is one of submission and love, and yet perhaps a daunting experience. The daughter of Thor is frozen, not warmed, by the sight of this submissive God and possibly there are Nietzschean overtones in the confrontation of a heroic age with the God of the 'slave religion'.

Jaimes Freyre also published a collection, Los sueños son vida, in which he abandoned the Nordic framework but without succeeding in attaining a new poetic vision. His verse is technically skilful but narrow in range.

VIII. LATER MODERNISM

The divergent aspects of Modernism were intensified after 1900. There would be little point in discussing all the manifestations in detail, for some of the most prolific poets are the most disappointing. The Mexican Amado Nervo (1870-1943) was mainly concerned with religious crisis and experience. There is the rather frigid perfection of the Colombian Guillermo Valencia (1873-1943) and the forceful 'masculine' poetry of José Santos Chocano (Peru; 1875-1934). In Uruguay there is the remarkable woman poet Delmira Agustini (1886-1914).

Unusual for a woman poet of the period Delmira Agustini was obsessed by erotic themes and tends to be remembered for the fact that she was murdered by her husband rather than for her poetry. The erotic obsession nowadays seems less daring than quaint. In Los cálices vacíos, sex symbols obtrude obviously and she constantly reflects an acceptance of her role as sexual object, dependent on the all-powerful male.

Y hoy río si tú ríes, y canto si tú cantas;
y si tú duermes, duermo como un perro a tus plantas.

The language of her poetry often falls into sensationalism, as in her Cuentas de sombra:

Los lechos negros logran la más fuerte
Rosa de amor; arraigan en la muerte.
Grandes lechos tendidos de tristeza,
Tallados a puñal y doselados
De insomnio ...

It is all a little heavy-handed and rhetorical; to find a new poetic language for the sexual theme, we have to turn to Ramón López Velarde, whose poetry will be discussed later in this chapter.

If we think of Delmira Agustini as a 'feminine' poet, then the Peruvian José Santos Chocano was certainly aggressive and masculine. He was also one of the first Latin American writers to try and use a system of American referents in his poetry. At his best he evoked the Peru of the colonial period or, as in *Alma América*, paints American nature. In 'El sueño del caimán', for instance, we can see how the Modernist princess becomes curiously transformed into an enchanted prince imprisoned in the crocodile's scales.

> Inmóvil como un ídolo sagrado,
> ceñido en mallas de compacto acero,
> está ante el agua extático y sombrío,
>
> a manera de un príncipe encantado
> que vive eternamente prisionero
> en el palacio de cristal de un río ...

The immobility and the scaly coat are seen as limitations in the animal. The theme of biological limitation was quite common among Modernists and Darío's centaurs and swans are often symbolic of this. But here is an attempt to take this out of a European literary tradition and place the theme in American terms. When we turn to poets such as Carlos Pezoa Véliz (Chile; 1879-1908) or Leopoldo Lugones (Argentina; 1874-1938), we find this rooting of common Modernist themes within the American scene carried to a far more intense level. Pezoa Véliz broods on death in a concretely Chilean setting. Lugones began his career with *Las montañas del oro* (1897), a Hugoesque epic; was influenced by Samain and Laforgue in *Los crepúsculos del jardín* (1905) and *Lunario sentimental* (1909); and only in *Odas seculares* (1910) turns to the American scene. In *Lunario sentimental*, he anticipates the humour of avant-garde poetry with a light and often comic parody of the moonlight scenes dear to Romanticism. He thus parodies his literary tradition in lines like the following:

> Sobre la azul esfera
> Un murciélago sencillo
> Voltejea cual negro plumerillo
> Que limpia una vidriera

in which he divests the bat of any sombre associations to make it into a humble feather-duster.

With the *Odas seculares*, written for the centenary of Argentine Independence in 1910, there was, however, a return to the tradition of Andrés Bello and Gregorio Gutiérrez González, the tradition of descriptive bucolic verse extolling the virtues of rustic life. In *El libro de paisajes* (1917), the style again changes. Here are descriptions of different moods and seasons of the countryside, 'Tormenta', 'Lluvia', etc., in which nature alone speaks, as, for instance, in 'La granizada':

> Sobre el repicado cinc del cobertizo,
> Y el patio que, densa, la siesta calcina,
> En el turbio vértigo de la ventolina
> Ríen los sonoros dientes del granizo.
>
> Ríen y se comen la viña y la huerta.
> Rechiflan el vidrio que frágil tirita,
> Y escupen chisguetes de saltada espita
> Por algún medroso resquicio de puerta.
>
> Junto al marco rústico, donde pía en vano,
> Refúgiase un pollo largo y escurrido.
> Volcado en el suelo yace un pobre nido.
> En el agua boya la flor del manzano.
>
> Con frescor de páramo el chubasco azota.
> Cenizas de estaño la nube condensa.
> Y al lúgubre fondo de la pampa inmensa,
> Desgreñados sauces huyen en derrota.

There is nothing here that could not be found in one of the *Sonetos vascos* of Herrera y Reissig, with the exception of the 'pampa inmensa'. This and perhaps the violence of the storm are the only indications that the poem is set in Argentina. But the indications *are* there. And the emphasis, too, has changed from the poems of Herrera y Reissig, for here is not a nature which offers man a guide, an external code of references, but nature as a devouring and hostile force from which even the willow trees flee in defeat. There is an indication here of the growing awareness of writers that Spanish American nature cannot be described in the same terms as European nature. But Leopoldo Lugones does not always present such a desolate picture. In 'Día clara', American nature can also offer a scene of harmony:

> En la gloria del sol palpita el mundo
> Y alzan su arquitectónica armonía
> Blancas nubes en que de azul profundo
> Sus bellas torres embandera el día.
>
> Celebra el gallo con viril porfía
> Aquel oro solar que arde en su gola,
> Y en su cántico excelso se gloria
> Empenachado por la verde cola.

Ciñe cada guijarro una aureola.
Oloroso calor exhala el heno.
Remueve el bosque un grave azul de ola.
El día es como el pan, sencillo y bueno.

As in many poems by Lugones, the effect is like that of a landscape-painting but one in which each element is separated—sky, cock, pebble, wood, stand out as discrete aspects, fused only in the poem and perhaps simply consummated in the poet's final image of the day 'simple and good like bread'. But the consummation is not communion. And we are far indeed both from Darío's incarnation of God in nature and from the Romantic pathetic fallacy. Rather nature is presented as a set of items which present themselves to the senses, perceived in turn and then like the bread consumed and gone.

Most of Lugones's later poems are either pastoral or ballad in form, and reinforce the impression of a rather deliberate and intellectual appreciation of country life. He published *Poemas solariegos* (1927) and a collection of ballads, *Romances del Río Seco* (1938) appeared after his death by suicide in 1938.

Lugones, along with the Mexican Ramón López Velarde and the Argentinian Baldomero Fernández Moreno, represents the 'mundonovista' or localist current of Modernism, for they attempted to root their poetic language in a province or region, rather than to hook up with the European network as Darío had done. To term their poetry regionalist is, however, misleading. Their themes did not differ from Modernist themes of time and death, though their poetic landscape was not the same.

Ramón López Velarde (1888-1921) published his first collection of poetry, *La sangre devota*, in 1916, at the height of the Mexican Revolution. *Zozobra* appeared just after the end of the revolutionary fighting in 1919 and a posthumous collection, *El son de corazón*, was published in 1932. Born in the provinces, his poetry expresses the conflict between metropolitan and provincial values,[18] and his poetic technique rests on a basic sincerity which he felt verse must transmit:

> Yo anhelo expulsar de mí cualquier palabra, cualquier sílaba que no nazca de la combustión de mis huesos.[19]

To achieve this 'combustión de huesos', the poet must have experienced and observed intense feeling, and there must be a pitiless stripping of non-essentials. Mere decoration can have no place.

> La quiebra del Parnaso consistió en pretender suplantar las esencias desiguales de la vida del hombre con una vestidura fementida. Para los actos trascendentales—sueño, baño o amor,— nos desnudamos. Conviene que el verso se muestre contingente, en paragón exacto de todas las curvas, de todas las fechas: olímpico

y piafante a las diez, desgarbado a las once; siempre humano.[20]

The faithfulness of language to feeling sometimes resulted in abrupt changes of tone from the exalted to the familiar or jocular, as in 'Tenías un rebozo de seda'.

> ... en la seda me anegaba
> con fe, como en un golfo intenso y puro,
> a oler abiertas rosas del presente
> y herméticos botones del futuro.
>
> (En abono de mi sinceridad
> séame permitido un alegato.
> Entonces era yo seminarista
> sin Baudelaire, sin rima y sin olfato.)

The abrupt change of mood, the introduction of an ironic note, makes reading Ramón López Velarde an acid experience. There is little sweetness, except in nostalgia, in the poems he wrote to his early idealised 'Fuensanta' or his memories of the pure provincial women.

> Ingenuas provincianas: cuando mi vida se halle
> desahuciada por todos, iré por los caminos
> por donde vais cantando los más sonoros trinos
> y en fraternal confianza ceñiré vuestro talle.

In his early poems 'Fuensanta' is a promise of purity and salvation, though modern readers have to put these words in their true context, for both 'purity' and 'salvation' had meaning for the poet and were not empty shells. Even when drained of faith, the Church has presence and power to work in him. Contrast this poem, for instance, with Herrera y Reissig's 'La iglesia':

> Mi espíritu es un paño de ánimas, un paño
> de ánimas de iglesia siempre menesterosa;
> es un paño de ánimas goteado de cera,
> hollado y roto por la grey astrosa.
>
> No soy más que una nave de parroquia en penurias,
> nave en que se celebran eternos funerales,
> porque una lluvia terca no permite
> sacar el ataúd a las calles rurales.
>
> Fuera de mí, la lluvia; dentro de mí, el clamor
> cavernoso y creciente de un salmista;
> mi conciencia, mojada por el hisopo, es un
> ciprés que en una huerta conventual se contrista.

The initial image is a striking one. Instead of a 'paño de lágrimas', he refers to his soul as a 'paño de ánimas' as if his soul has been worn out with compassion and he is dead inside. Yet the edifice of religion is very much there, shoring up whatever remains of his inner life. What sense of moral order exists in his world, exists because structured according to a pattern of purity and fall, sin and repentance. The poem 'La bizarra capital de mi estado', a series of amusing or ironic vignettes of the state capital, culminates on a more exalted note as he evokes the cathedral and its bell:

> y al concurrir, ese clamor concéntrico
> del bronce, en el ánima del ánima,
> se siente que las aguas
> del bautismo nos corren por los huesos
> y otra vez nos penetran y nos lavan.

The 'señoritas', 'católicos', and 'jacobinos' of the town are nothing more than discrete entities without the cathedral and the bell which bestow the communion of faith upon society. Even without faith, the waters of baptism bind people more intimately than any other force. Similarly in 'Mi prima Águeda', where the poet recalls a first love for his cousin, and the mixture of sensuality and fear that she arouses, the emotions gain in strength because they are referred to a system of values in which to wear mourning (as the cousin does) has powerful implications of death and of the danger of sin. One of López Velarde's most powerful poems on the theme of sensuality is 'Hormigas', in which the language is almost unbearably tense.

> A la cálida vida que transcurre canora
> con garbo de mujer sin letras ni antifaces
> a la invicta belleza que salva y que enamora,
> responde en la embriaguez de la encantada hora
> un encono de hormigas en mis venas voraces.

> Fustigan el desmán del perenne hormigueo
> el pozo del silencio y el enjambre del ruido,
> la harina rebanada como doble trofeo
> en los fértiles bustos, el Infierno en que creo,
> el estertor final y el preludio del nido.

The language is grand, Latinate, and bestows an impression of opulence on the verse. Life is voluptuous and carnal; there is the biological urge, the cycle of death, but there is something else too— the 'hormigas', the blind, stinging power of his sensuality which could never be so powerful if he did not see his beloved's mouth as both communion and gate of hell:

> tu boca, que es mi rúbrica, mi manjar y mi adorno,

> tu boca, en que la lengua vibra asomada al mundo
> como réproba llama saliéndose de un horno

and the contradictory sensations that it provokes:

> ha de oler a sudario y a hierba machacada,
> a droga y a responso, a pabilo y a cera.

The mouth is life and death, crushed grass and shroud. The poet can only know experience through enjoyment and hence by risking salvation. The words have the high-powered Latin rhetorical quality of prayer as if something as strong as prayer were needed. Hence the closing lines:

> Antes de que tus labios mueran, para mi luto,
> dámelos en el crítico umbral del cementerio
> como perfume y pan tósigo y cauterio.

In all the poems there is the suggestion of enjoyment snatched from the very gates of hell. And there is a strongly liturgical suggestion about the language.

López Velarde's most famous poem is 'Suave Patria', a poem with 'acts' and 'intervals' which celebrates Mexico, but has nothing at all in common with Darío's dithyrambic *Canto a la Argentina*. The opening lines, indeed, have a Byronic irony, as the poem acknowledges that it is a little embarrassing to write civic poetry:

> Navegaré por los olas civiles
> con remos que no pesan, porque ven
> como los brazos del correo chuán
> que remaba la Mancha con fusiles.
>
> Diré con una épica sordina:
> la Patria es impecable y diamantina.

The poem represents a kind of demystified patriotism, as the poet explains at the beginning of the Second Act:

> Suave Patria: te amo no cual mito
> sino por tu verdad de pan bendito.
> como a niña que asoma por la reja
> y la falda bajada hasta el huesito.

It is this homely, everyday aspect of his country that he regards as its truth:

> sé siempre igual, fiel a tu espejo diario.
> Patria, te doy de tu dicha la clave:

The 'patria' is very much like the 'catedral', a foundation, strongly

laid, of the impressions and faith of childhood. For this reason, the
Revolution is seen in one of his best-known poems, 'El retorno
maléfico', as a destructive wind. This did not imply a political attitude,
but an attitude towards his own childhood which now belonged to
another age. The poem evokes a return visit to a native village:

> Mejor será no regresar al pueblo,
> al edén subvertido que se calla
> en la mutilación de la metralla.

But the strange maps that the shooting has made on the walls remind
the poet not of larger events but of his own 'esperanza deshecha'.
The violence that has occurred is a violence that has separated him
from the past, now evoked in the rusty doorlocks, the ancient doors,
and the medallions on the porch. What has gone is his own youth
and all hope of fulfilment, while around him a new life goes on,

> campanario de timbre novedoso;
> remozados altares;
> el amor amoroso
> de las parejas pares;
> noviazgos de muchachas
> frescas y humildes como humildes coles.

All nature and humanity seem to be paired, reinforced by the tautology
of 'parejas pares' and by the repetition of the adjective 'humilde'.
The Revolution has not changed the life of the village, but time *has*
changed his own life, reducing it to nostalgia as he hears:

> alguna señorita
> que canta en algún piano
> alguna vieja aria;
> el gendarme que pita ...
> ... Y una íntima tristeza reaccionaria.

The biological life-force and the Christian promise of an after-life
conflict with great intensity in the poetry of López Velarde. And
though his language is drawn from Christian and literary tradition,
he is far less dependent than Darío on existing literary symbols and
myths. He really took Modernism into a wholly new direction when
he rooted the conflicts in a Mexican provincial setting, and he did
so without indulging himself in a *costumbrista*-type regionalism.

López Velarde has an Argentine counterpart in Baldomero Fernández Moreno (1886-1950), a poet of Spanish descent who lived in
tension between an idealised Spain remembered from the childhood
years he spent there and a bare, poor New World. His language is
spare and simple. Far less intense than López Velarde, his poetry

reflects the rootlessness he felt in the New World, the need for the security of traditional ways of life. In 'Tráfago', he wrote:

Me he detenido enfrente del Congreso
y en medio del urbano remolino
he soñado en un rústico camino
y me he sentido el corazón opreso.

Una tranquera floja, un monte espeso,
el girar perezoso de un molino,
la charla familiar de algún vecino,
¿no valen algo más que todo eso?

This is finally what places Fernández Moreno with the Modernist rather than the avant-garde, despite the fact that their work overlaps in time.

IX. MODERNIST PROSE-WRITING

Modernism cannot be left behind without a brief consideration of the transformation that Darío, Gutiérrez Nájera, and their successors brought about in prose-writing. Even Romantic writers such as Echeverría had used a logical structure that appealed to the intellect rather than to the senses. Darío and Gutiérrez Nájera were among the first of Spanish American writers to use prose-writing simply to build up a mood. Most of Darío's stories are either allegories illustrating the conflict between the artist and society or they are word paintings—'Acuarela', 'Paisaje', 'Un retrato de Watteau', 'Naturaleza muerta', 'Aguafuerte'. One of his characteristic landscapes depicts the meeting of two lovers in a park and is simply a description of the scene:

Y sobre las dos almas ardientes y sobre los dos cuerpos juntos, cuchicheaban, en lengua rítmica y alada, las aves. Y arriba el cielo, con su inmensidad y con su fiesta de nubes, plumas de oro, alas de fuego, vellones de púrpura, fondos azules flordelisados de ópalo, derramaba la magnificencia de su pompa, la soberanía de su grandeza augusta.

The texture of the prose gives the impression of voluptuous opulence —'fiesta de nubes', 'plumas de oro', 'flordelisados de ópalo'. Darío is here concerned with enriching the texture to the maximum. There is no anecdote, no thread except a mood of sensuality. Similarly the stories of Gutiérrez Nájera, though they often retain an element of anecdote or even a moral, are primarily mood pieces. With Modernism, descriptions of nature come into their own, to be enjoyed for their own sake and not because they underline a message or contribute very directly to the theme. Leopoldo Lugones's novel *La guerra gaucha* (1905), for instance, evokes scenes of the Independence war but places the anecdotes in a carefully observed natural setting. The following is a description of the pampa storm:

> Llovía y llovía ...
> Por el cielo plúmbeo rodaban las tormentas, una tras otra, sus densidades fulginosas. Algún trueno propagaba retumbos. Incesantemente cerníase la garúa convertida vuelta a vuelta en cerrazones y chubascos. Sobre el azul casi lóbrego de la sierra, flotaban nubarrones de cuyo seno descolgábase a veces una centella visible a lo lejos, como una linterna por un cordón ...

There is a difference between this description and that of Darío, apart from the obvious ones. Darío is creating an imaginary landscape or at least embroidering on a real one. Lugones is attempting verisimilitude with only the occasional metaphor—'como una linterna por un cordón'—to lift the description. Both descriptions were intended to appeal to the senses. But Darío's example was to give rise to new styles of non-realistic writing, including the 'fantastic' short story and novel, including the early stories of Quiroga where the achievement consisted in creating imaginary rather than realistic landscapes. It gave rise also to the 'artistic' novel and story, in which exact, even precious, language was as important as plot-novels like *La gloria de don Ramiro* (1908) by Enrique Larreta (1875-1961), which is set in the time of Philip II and concerned with the persecution of the Moors and the co-existence of Moors and Christians in Spain. The novel is not only a skilful piece of historical evocation, but it allows the novelist great scope in descriptions of the sights and sounds of a sixteenth-century Spanish city, the sense impressions of colour and contrast between the repressive Christian beliefs and the sensuous Moors. Contrast, for instance, the following description with the cliché adjectives found in the nineteenth-century Romantic novel:

> Afuera en la ciudad, torvo sosiego de siesta castellana. La luz del mediodía arde rabiosa en los pétreos paredones, caldea los hierros, requema el musgo de los tejados.

Neither 'rabiosa' nor 'pétreo' would have been used in the Romantic novel. Modernist too is the appreciation of objects, of fine glass and cloth. Whereas the Romantic novelist reserved his lyric flights for natural scenes, Larreta likes the luxury of civilised living:

> Habia góticos terciopelos que se plegaban angulosamente, terciopelos acartonados y finos del tiempo de Isabel y Fernando, donde una línea segura iba inscribiendo el tenue contorno de una granada

sobre el fondo verde o carmesí; donosas telas de plata que parecían aprisionar entre la urdedumbre un viejo rayo de luna; brocados y brocaletes amortecidos por el polvillo del tiempo, a modo de vidriera religiosa.

Larreta is here concerned with age and tradition, but the impression is created through the appearance of the cloth, the faded threads, the threadbare embroidery, the dim colours. The passage also refers back to the theme of the novel, for the Moorish worker has left his mark on the cloth destined for Catholic use. The description evokes rather than states. Unlike the Realist novel with its unequivocal message, Larreta's prose is allusive. This type of Modernist prose-writing was to create a counter-tradition to that of the Realist, with its emphasis on instrumentality and functionalism of prose. On the negative side, this led to a kind of preciosity. In Pedro Prado's allegorical novel *Alsino* (1920) or the stories of Abraham Valdelomar (Peru; 1888-1919),[21] there is a certain self-conscious 'fine writing' which can be over-obtrusive. But on the positive side, this meant a regard for language and texture, a sensitivity to subliminal effects which was to be very fruitful. The major Realist writers of the 1920s—Ricardo Güiraldes and Horacio Quiroga—were able to combine verisimilitude and careful observation with attention to the quality of writing, a combination that makes their work far superior to that of a Blest Gana or a Cambaceres, in whose novels the prose is often too clumsy. And it was Modernism that achieved this shift of emphasis from prose-writing as a function to formal qualities. Certainly the work of present-day writers such as José Lezama Lima and Alejo Carpentier would be inconceivable without this Modernist break-through.

NOTES

1. *El Modernismo. Notas de un curso*, ed. R. Gullón and E. Fernández Méndez (Mexico, 1962).

2. *Antología de la poesía española e hispanoamericana*, 2nd ed. (New York, 1961).

3. This is the edition published in Madrid (1911) with an introduction by Francisco Villaespesa.

4. From an essay by Unamuno included in José Asunción Silva, *Poesías completas* (Madrid, 1952).

5. Quoted J. M. Monner Sans in his *Julián del Casal y el modernismo hispanoamericano* (Mexico, 1952), pp. 27-8.

6. Justo Sierra, introduction to *Obras de Manuel Gutiérrez Nájera* (Mexico, 1896), p. xiii.

7. ibid., pp. vii-viii.

8. Darío, 'Marina' (1898), included in the 1901 additions to *Prosas profanas*.

9. Quoted A. Torres-Rioseco in *Rubén Darío. Casticismo y americanismo* (Cambridge, Mass., 1931), p. 13.

10. Max Henríquez Ureña, *Breve historia del modernismo*, 2nd ed. (Mexico, 1962), pp. 93-4.

11. Quoted Torres-Rioseco, op. cit., p. 102n.

12. 'Garçonnière', from *Prosas profanas*.

13. R. Gullón, 'Pitagorismo y Modernismo', *Mundo Nuevo*, 7 (1967), and J. Franco, 'Rubén Darío y el problema del mal', *Amaru* (1967).

14. From *Cantos de vida y esperanza*.

15. 'Palabras liminares', *Prosas profanas*.

16. 'Rubén Darío. Su personalidad literaria. Su última obra' in a preface to *Prosas profanas y otros poemas* (Paris, 1908), and also in E. Rodó, *Obras completas*.

17. E. Anderson Imbert, *Historia de la literatura hispanoamericana*, I, 384.

18. O. Paz, 'El lenguaje de Ramón López Velarde', in *Las peras del olmo* (Mexico, 1957).

19. A. Phillips, *Ramón López Velarde* (Mexico, 1962), p. 123; from an essay by López Velarde, 'La derrota de la palabra', in *El don de febrero y otras prosas* (Mexico, 1952).

20. Phillips, op. cit., p. 123.

21. For some consideration of Valdelomar as a story-writer, see Earl A. Aldrich, *The Modern Short Story in Peru* (Madison-Milwaukee-London, 1966).

READING LIST

There are several anthologies of Modernist poetry. Gordon Brotherston (ed.), *Spanish American Modernista Poets* (Oxford, 1968); García Prada, Carlos, *Poetas modernistas hispanoamericanos* (Madrid, 1956); Onís, Federico de, *Antología de la poesía española e hispanoamericana (1882-1932)* (Madrid, 1934). A new selection edited by José Emilio Pacheco has been published by U.N.A.M. (Mexico, 1970)

Texts

Agustini, Delmira, *Poesías completas*, 3rd ed. (Buenos Aires, 1962)
Casal, Julián del, *Poesías completas* (La Habana, 1945)
——, *Poesías*, 3 vols. (La Habana, 1963)
——, *Prosas*, 3 vols. (La Habana, 1963)
Darío, Rubén, *Obras poéticas completas*, 10th ed. (Madrid, 1967)
——, *Cuentos completos de Rubén Darío*, ed. Ernesto Mejía Sánchez, with an introduction by Raimundo Lida (Mexico–Buenos Aires, 1950)
——, *Los raros* (Buenos Aires–Mexico, 1952)
Díaz Mirón, Salvador, *Poesías completas*, 3rd ed. (Mexico, 1952)
Fernández Moreno, Baldomero, *Antología*, 6th ed. (Buenos Aires, 1954)
González Martínez, Enrique, *Antología poética*, 3rd ed. (Buenos Aires–Mexico, 1944)
Gutiérrez Nájera, Manuel, *Poesías completas*, 2 vols. (Mexico, 1953)
——, *Cuentos completos* (Mexico, 1958)
Herrera y Reissig, Julio, *Poesías completas*, 3rd ed. (Buenos Aires, 1958)
Jaimes Freyre, Ricardo, *Poesías completas* (Buenos Aires, 1944)
Larreta, Enrique, *La gloria de don Ramiro*, in *Obras completas* (Madrid, 1958)
López Velarde, Ramón, *Poesías completas y el minutero* (Mexico, 1952)
Lugones, Leopoldo, *Obras poéticas completas*, 3rd ed. (Madrid, 1953)
——, *La guerra gaucha* (Buenos Aires, 1946)
Nervo, Amado, *Obras completas*, 2 vols. (Madrid, 1955-56)

Silva, José Asunción, *Poesías completas* (Madrid, 1952)
Valdelomar, Abraham, *Cuentos y poesía*, ed. Augusto Tamayo Vargas (Lima, 1959)
Valencia, Guillermo, *Obras poéticas completas* (Madrid, 1955)

Historical and critical
Alonso, Amado, *Ensayo sobre la novela histórica. El modernismo en La gloria de don Ramiro* (Buenos Aires, 1942)
González, Manuel Pedro, *Notas en torno al modernismo* (Mexico, 1958)
——, with I. A. Schulman, *José Martí, Rubén Darío y el Modernismo* (Madrid, 1969)
Gullón, Ricardo, *Direcciones del modernismo* (Madrid, 1963)
Henríquez Ureña, Max, *Breve historia del modernismo*, 2nd ed. (Mexico, 1962)
Mejía Sánchez, Ernesto, *Estudios sobre Rubén Darío* (Mexico, 1968)
Monner Sans, J. M., *Julián del Casal y el modernismo hispanoamericano* (Mexico, 1952)
Onís, Federico de, *España en América* (Río Piedras, 1955)
Phillips, A. W., *Ramón López Velarde* (Mexico, 1962)
Rodríguez Fernández, Mario, *El Modernismo en Chile y en Hispanoamérica* (Santiago, 1967)
Salinas, Pedro, *La poesía de Rubén Darío*, 2nd ed. (Buenos Aires, 1958)
Schulman, I. A., *Génesis del modernismo* (Mexico, 1968)
Shaw, D. L., 'Modernism. A Contribution to the Debate', *BHS*, XLIV (1967)
Torres, Edelberto, *La dramática vida de Rubén Darío*, 2nd ed. (Mexico, 1956)
Torres-Rioseco, A., *Rubén Darío. Casticismo y americanismo* (Cambridge, Mass., 1931)

Chapter 7

REALISM AND REGIONALISM

Lo que sufrí cuando no sabía si una página brillante pertenecía a la última novela mala o a la primera buena.

(Macedonio Fernández)

Until comparatively recently, the Realist and regionalist novels were considered to be characteristic modes of prose-writing in Spanish America and literary histories generally culminated with studies of writers such as Ricardo Güiraldes, Rómulo Gallegos, and Horacio Quiroga. Since 1940, the picture has changed. The contemporary generation has turned against novels of documentation and oversimplified protest fiction. Inevitably, it is critical of the styles of the past. As Carlos Fuentes writes:

La tendencia documental y naturalista de la novela hispanoamericana obedecía a toda esa trama original de nuestra vida: haber llegado a la independencia sin verdadera identidad humana, sometidos a una naturaleza esencialmente extraña que, sin embargo, era el verdadero *personaje* latinoamericano:[1]

Though Fuentes feels that this was a necessary stage, he also considers the documentary novel a mark of underdevelopment and dates the maturity of the Latin American novel from the first works which show ambiguity and complexity. His strictures are characteristic of the contemporary generation.[2] Yet this makes it all the more necessary to situate the Realist novel in a historical perspective. *Doña Bárbara, El mundo es ancho y ajeno, Don Segundo Sombra* were the first novels from Spanish America to attract notice in Europe and North America. The very qualities which the present generation reject —the descriptions of a hostile landscape, of exotic peoples, and social injustices—were precisely the ones which most interested the European and North American reader. Even the static quality was as much a part of the prevailing ideology, as we shall see, as 'simultaneity' and 'disponibility' are of ours. What has happened is that the world has changed. An unambiguous presentation of material, a pretence of objectivity, is no longer possible.

The term 'Realism' may not be the most adequate to describe the phenomena discussed in this chapter. The West Indian novelist Wilson Harris talks of the 'novel of persuasion' and this is a good term.[3] If I have chosen to keep the term 'Realist', it is because I think that this still has relevance in that it presupposes an objective order (which may not be a social order but a natural one) against which the individual is measured. In Spanish America, most early Realists were influenced by positivism, and what is more, by a kind of positivism that was even more rigidly deterministic than European positivism. When we remember, for instance, the case of Francisco Bulnes, who set out a theory that maize-eating peoples were inferior to wheat-eaters,[4] we gain some idea of how helpless intellectuals of sixty or seventy years ago felt in relation to 'forces', 'laws', 'phenomena' which they believed governed their existence and that of their societies. The novelists of the time did not see their characters in terms of freedom and ambiguity, but rather as a particular development of a universal law. The reader's only role was to follow the development as passive observer who was bound to accept the author's foreordained conclusions. This type of 'closed' Realism is illustrated, in this chapter, by the work of two writers, Mariano Azuela (Mexico; 1873-1952) and Manuel Gálvez (Argentina; 1882-1962).

I. MARIANO AZUELA

Mariano Azuela was an established novelist before the outbreak of the Mexican Revolution in which he, like the majority of his fellow-countrymen, was involved. Trained as a doctor, he was imbued with a positivistic outlook and his early novels—*María Luisa* (1907), *Los fracasados* (1908), and *Mala yerba* (1909)—were apprenticeship novels which dealt with social evils in the Naturalist manner. In 1911, just after the outbreak of the Revolution, he published *Andrés Pérez, maderista*, the story of a journalist who was drawn into the Revolution on Madero's side. Though not outstanding as a novel, *Andrés Pérez* foreshadows one of Azuela's later preoccupations with opportunism and the compromise of the ideal.

The three works which best exemplify Azuela's Realism are all 'novels of the Revolution'. They are *Los de abajo* (1916), *Los caciques* (1917), and *Los moscas* (1918). In all three novels, the Revolution gives individual life a new significance. This is especially true of *Los de abajo*. Although the novel deals with the rise of a single leader, Demetrio Macías, from rebel peasant to revolutionary general, it is more than a close-up study of one man. Demetrio's band is a cross-section of the revolutionary forces and their complex fate is traced to the inevitable end. Nevertheless, the novel begins and ends with Demetrio, for it is he who typifies the strengths and weaknesses of the movement. With admirable economy, Azuela compresses the motivation of the protagonist and his virtues and defects into two brief scenes. Macías is presented as a spontaneous child of nature, though perhaps more Hobbesian than Rousseauesque in his behaviour. He is all unreflecting activity, his peasant background having deprived him of any opportunity of the education that would give him general ideas. He never sees beyond the immediate present. His most positive characteristic, apart from blind courage, is his passion for the land and his superiority over the Federal troops derives from his intimate knowledge of the terrain. Like all guerrilla leaders, he can count on the support of the villagers, his ascendancy being based on his valour and ability as a fighter. The other members of the band are presented with equal economy; all represent different types of revolutionary fighter—the kulak who could not progress in pre-Revolutionary society, the landless peasant, the petty criminal like Cordorniz who had robbed and hence had to become a fugitive from justice. The band is also joined by Luis Cervantes, a medical student who had deserted from the Federal side, partly from cowardice, partly because he had heard that plunder was to be had among the rebels. A more calculated evil character than the peasants, he is conditioned by his petty bourgeois background which has given him the instinct to save his own skin at any price. The peasant will die fighting, but Cervantes is essentially the survivor. Even during victorious engagements, he hangs back and he comes to the fore only when words and rhetoric are needed. He pimps for Demetrio, plunders a diamond after the successful capture of a town, and with this, finally escapes to Texas where he continues his studies and is undoubtedly destined to return as one of the 'new men' of the post-Revolutionary era. But there are those who are lower than Cervantes in the scale of moral values, notably the prostitute La Pintada and her lover, the 'Güero' Margarito, both products of an urban environment. 'Güero' indeed is the most sinister character in the novel and illustrates Azuela's conviction that the Revolution acted as a cover for criminal and mentally unbalanced characters. He represents the worst of the *lumpenproletariat*, being a sadist and pervert, capable of killing an old woman who refuses to sell him food, and a raper of virgins. One of the few hopeful indications in the novel is that this evil character hangs himself as the Revolution draws to a close, as he is obviously unable to face up to a society in which his crimes might be punished.

Los de abajo uses typical characters in order to draw a graph of values. There is a simple, abused peasantry with the virtue of courage but totally ignorant of anything except immediate tactics. There are the corrupted members of the lower classes, corrupted in most cases because they have been introduced to the false commercial values of urban society. There are the intellectuals who are either 'survivors' like Cervantes and therefore unscrupulous or idealists like Alberto Solís, who dies at the battle of Zacatecas. Solís's idealism is also found among the peasants, in Camila, the ingenuous girl who falls in love with Cervantes and is offered by him to Demetrio whose faithful follower she becomes. As ignorant as Macías, she has nevertheless an ideal that goes beyond the mere satisfaction of land hunger.

Where *Los de abajo* differs from many present-day novels is in the 'closed' fate of most of the characters. None have any choice of action, but all seem trapped in a predetermined circuit. Even Solís, the most intelligent of all, is incapable of influencing the forces around him and is killed by a stray bullet. The structure as well as the characterisation is deterministic. The events follow a course analogous to that of the Revolution: what is at first a spontaneous local uprising with the advantage of surprise over the enemy gathers strength until all the factions unite in the revolutionary force which destroys the common enemy at the battle of Zacatecas. But the triumph leads to disintegration of the armies and to infighting between Villa and Carranza, from which the latter emerges as the most powerful. Those who do not join him are slowly liquidated and scattered.

Azuela's style is characterised by its conciseness. Not a word is wasted. Even descriptions of nature have a function in the economy of the novel. Consider, for instance, this passage which describes the countryside just before Demetrio's death:

> Fue una verdadera mañana de nupcias. Había llovido la víspera toda la noche y el cielo amanecía entoldado de blancas nubes. Por la cima de la sierra trotaban potrillos brutos de crines alzadas y colas tensas, gallardos con la gallardía de los picachos que levantan su cabeza hasta besar las nubes.

The renewal of life is unaffected by human events. Ultimately Demetrio's fate is of little consequence.

The direct speech is yet another indication of the determining forces in human life. Each type of discourse is the voice of a social class and therefore represents a conditioning. That is why some characters—Camila and Luis Cervantes—are not easily able to communicate. Camila speaks with the crudest of peasant accents, but words really represent feelings for her:

> Oye, curro ... Yo quería icirte una cosa ... Oye, curro, yo quiero que me repases *La Adelita* ... pa ... a que no me adivinas pa qué? Pos pa cantarla muncho, muncho, cuando ustedes se vayan.

Cervantes, on the other hand, uses a journalistic rhetoric where words

are intended to confuse. Like Camila, Demetrio speaks with an
'authentic' peasant voice, though his language is functional rather
than affective.

To summarise, *Los de abajo* is a good example of a closed novel
in which every element, every technique is used to reinforce a simple,
deterministic pattern. The pleasure in reading it comes not from
ambiguity or surprise but from expectancy fulfilled. *Los caciques* and
Las moscas follow a similar pattern. The first is set in the period of
the Madero Revolution (1910-12), during which there existed more
rhetoric than actual change of social structure. As one of the characters,
Rodríguez, remarks:

> La revolución de Madero ha sido un fracaso. Los países gober-
> nados por bandidos necesitan revoluciones realizadas por bandidos.

The small town in which the novel takes place is dominated by the
Del Llano brothers whose power over the community is absolute.
They are shopkeepers, local capitalists who lend money at high
interest. The story centres on their control over the town, even after
the Madero Revolution, and the manner in which they ruin a rival,
Don Juan Viñas, who becomes involved in a business deal with them.
The novel has thus a much more limited range of interest than
Los de abajo, being almost entirely concerned with the middle classes
and the petty bourgeoisie. The one intelligent and far-seeing character,
Juan Rodríguez, is killed by paid assassins of the Del Llanos before
the second stage of the Revolution reaches the town. The novel exposes
the weakness of any movement that depends on a class whose ideals
are clouded by economic interests. The powerful capitalists like the
Del Llanos have no interest in changing the social system, while
the lesser and more enlightened capitalists are caught between big
monopoly and the radical demands of the lower classes. It is Viñas's
son and daughter who, after his ruin, prepare the way for Revolution,
but only because they are driven to anarchistic revenge against the
men who had ruined their father.

Las moscas, the third novel written by Azuela during the Revolutionary period, is more caricaturesque and ironic than the previous
novels. The structure is carefully contrived by the author who builds
the novel around a train journey from Mexico City to the north at a
period when supporters of Villa and counter-revolutionaries were
alike fleeing from the city before the victorious troops of Obregón.
The passengers on the train have one thing in common—all are
parasites on society: from Marta, the widow of a porter of the National
Palace, and her children, to the General with his camp followers, and
Ríos the ex-bureaucrat. The one exception is the Doctor who is the
disabused observer of the undignified flight. The train, so often a
symbol of progress, is here a kind of animal plagued by the parasitic

insects on its back. But the atmosphere is one of comedy rather than tragedy and the moral problem concerns cowardice, not heroism.

Azuela's novels offer us a complete picture of the Revolution, but it is a picture which affords only one perspective. His novels represent the Revolution as a force unleashed by oppression. The middle classes who should have been in control had failed to give enlightened leadership. Instead they had succumbed to their passions and for this retribution inevitably followed. No other interpretation is possible. The reader's enjoyment arises from a sense of completeness, of loose ends neatly tied together.

Azuela's career as a writer continued until recently. In 1918, he had published a novel, *Las tribulaciones de una familia decente*, whose theme was the adaptation of a family to the new conditions of post-Revolutionary society, a theme that has obvious links with that of *Las moscas*. Later novels, including *La malhora* (1923), *La luciérnaga* (1932), and *Nueva burguesía* (1941), were influenced by contemporary novelistic experiment without, however, achieving the openness which characterises most modern writing. His reputation was to remain that of a Realist novelist whose material was the Revolution.[5]

II. MANUEL GÁLVEZ (ARGENTINA; 1882-1962)

Manuel Gálvez was one of the most prolific of Latin American Realist writers, and like Azuela's his outlook was conditioned by positivism. As a student, he wrote a thesis on the white-slave traffic and his novels were often related to specific social problems. *El mal metafísico* (1916), for instance, analysed the death of Romantic idealism in the harsh environment of Buenos Aires. The protagonist, Riga, was a product of the Arielist generation, the founder of a magazine called *La idea moderna*, which he hoped would be instrumental in forming more idealistic attitudes. But he is destined to fail and to die an early death, a victim of 'el mal metafísico':

> la enfermedad de soñar, de crear, de producir belleza, de contemplar ...

Nacha Regules (1918) offers another version of the theme of lost ideals, being the story of a woman forced into prostitution.

It is the environment which triumphs over Gálvez's characters. In one of his best novels, *La maestra normal* (1914), the provincial town in remote La Rioja conspires to crush love and natural relationships. The 'Normal School', founded on an anticlerical and positivist creed, is rumoured to be a hotbed of immorality and when a schoolteacher, Raselda, falls in love with a young outsider and is seduced by him, she is pitilessly hounded out. But it is the city itself which breeds the bigotry and tedium which in turn precipitate Raselda's downfall:

> La ciudad parecía de una dulce tristeza, a pesar del color que ponían los naranjos y las tejas sobre el fondo gris de la montaña. Por las calles no andaba sino una que otra persona. En algunas puertas, las sirvientas endomingadas, miraban como atónitas a los transeúntes. De cuando en cuando pasaba algún carruaje, lentamente, como con desgano, saltando sobre el ruín empedrado. Sus ecos se perdían en la soledad de las calles.

Life here seems to be running down. Existence is slow and without relief. Social censorship is strict and merciless. Gálvez shows that individual hopes and illusions cannot survive the indifference or active hostility of society. Like Azuela, however, he loads his dice before playing and the reader can only accept his verdict as just.

III. THE LEGACY OF THE PICARESQUE

One form of social novel which escaped the strict predetermined pattern was the picaresque. This had its roots in seventeenth-century Spain; in twentieth-century Spanish America the genre made a reappearance among a group of writers who were not only interested in low-life characters but also preferred a form which enabled them to link episodes casually around a first-person narration. The halfway house between the closed Realist novel and the picaresque is found in the novels of Roberto Payró (1867-1928), an Argentine writer with anarchist sympathies who, like Gálvez, believed that the novel was a reforming instrument. Only one of his prose works, *El casamiento de Laucha* (1906), has picaresque characteristics, but *Pago chico* (1908) is in the form of loosely connected episodes and the *Divertidas aventuras del nieto de Juan Moreira* (1910), though more conventional in form, is also episodic. The first novel, *El casamiento de Laucha*, has obvious connections with folk-tale. It tells the story of a wily *criollo*, Laucha, who conspires with 'padre Papagna' to fake a marriage between himself and a store-owner, Doña Carolina, whose money he then spends. Finally he leaves her. In this work, the outcome is just as closed as in the novels of Azuela, but the author stands in a different relation to the reader and seems, indeed, to be conspiring with him to laugh at the characters. Here, for instance, is Carolina's wedding dress, as seen by Laucha:

> Carolina se había encajado un gran traje de seda negra, con pollera de volados y bata de cadera, y se había puesto una manteleta en la cabeza, que le pasaba por detrás de las orejas y se

ataba debajo de la barba, unas caravanas larguísimas de oro que le zangoloteaban a los lados de la cara redonda y colorada, y un tremendo medallón con el retrato del finadito, de medio cuerpo.

It is true that this is Laucha talking and hence his picture of Carolina with her crimson face and the large portrait of her late husband, 'el finadito', on her bosom is deliberately grotesque, but he is also taking the reader into his confidence in a way that Azuela's characters could never do. The reader will enjoy the joke with Laucha, but his moral superiority ensures that Laucha's tricking of Carolina will be condemned. Payró is a far more moralising writer than Azuela.

Pago chico is looser in structure and indeed resembles a collection of stories around a common theme—that of the provincial town, Pago Chico (based on Bahía Blanca), with the corrupt political hierarchy of governor, police chief, political bosses, and rival newspapers. The stories display the corruption of the politicians who hold Eatenswill elections, hire strong men to protect their interests, and speculate in land. The effect is less picaresque than *costumbrista*, though it is a *costumbrismo* which dwells insistently on political types.

Payró's attack on the corrupt political system is modified by humour, though as in his description of Laucha's wedding, there is a certain condescension intermingled.

> En Pago Chico preparábase un miti, un metín, o cosa así que debía tener lugar en el antiguo reñidero de gallos, único local, fuera de la cancha de pelota, apropiado para la solemne circunstancia, puesto que el teatro—un galpón de cinc—pertenecía a don Pedro González, gubernista, que no quería ni prestarlo ni alquilarlo a sus enemigos de causa.

Payró is poking fun at provincialism, a fact that accounts for the frequent use of parody—of political speeches, or sensational newspaper articles like the following:

> ¡¡¡¡¡Miserables!!!!!
> Mañana nos ocuparemos más extensamente de este atentado brutal. Hoy la indignación nos pone mudos y a más la falta absoluta de espacio nos impide tratar el tema con la extensión que merece.

The episodes are casually linked, but together give a composite picture of the town which is the real protagonist.

Despite the title, *Divertidas aventuras del nieto de Juan Moreira* is the most serious of the three works and one which is most tightly constructed. It is the first-person narration of the rise of the politician Mauricio Gómez Herrera, nicknamed 'the grandson of Juan Moreira', by a journalist who believes him to be the urban equivalent of the old-time gaucho bandit. The novel is the least successful of Payró's three major works, being constructed around a Romantic plot theme —that of the illegitimate son who does not know the identity of his father.

IV. MARTÍN LUIS GUZMÁN (1897-)

In Mexico, the Revolution encouraged the picaresque form of writing. So many writers had witnessed fighting at first hand and had suffered the adventures of war. José Vasconcelos (1882-1959), Minister of Education during the Obregón government, contributed his own eyewitness account and the first volume had the significant title *Ulises criollo* (1936).[6] But the writer who best exemplifies this revolutionary picaresque is Martín Luis Guzmán in his novel *El águila y la serpiente* (1928). In this 'novel', the events are related by Guzmán himself. He describes his flight from Mexico City after the Huerta *coup*, his travels in search of the armies of the north, and his adventures with various revolutionary leaders like Pancho Villa whose secretary he became. Guzmán's Realism consists in his eye for significant detail and in his selection of anecdotes which convey what living in a revolution is like. The reader is seldom allowed a glimpse of important battles and engagements; instead we are told of dances held behind the lines, of train rides in which seats have to be torn up for fuel, of a movie shown to wild Revolutionary troops who pepper the screen with bullets, of Villa's spectacular escape from prison. Guzmán's disabused eye is mainly on the leaders. Carranza is described as 'un ambicioso vulgar', Villa is seen as dangerous, panther-like. In the following passage we have an effective but terrifying close-up as the narrator and Villa face one another literally eyeball to eyeball:

> La boca del cañón estaba a medio metro de mi cara. Por sobre la mira veía yo brillar los resplendores felinos de los ojos de Villa. Su iris era como de venturina; con infinitos puntos de fuegos microscópicos. Las estrías doradas partía de la pupila, se transformaban hacia el borde de los blancos en finísimas rayas sanguinolentas e iban desapareciendo bajo los párpados.

This terrible eye is shown in all its bloodshot animal detail, but the scene above all tells us about the confrontation between the intellectual and the guerrilla fighter. And not only Villa; all the Revolutionary leaders are passed in review. Rodolfo Fierro, Villa's lieutenant, is depicted, his arms exhausted from his personal execution of hundreds of prisoners. Obregón (condemned as a charlatan) and Carranza are essentially heroes with feet of clay, and neither lives up to Guzmán's ideal. Sometimes the picture is pathetic. The Zapatistas in the National Palace are diminished by its civilised splendours:

A nuestras espaldas, el tla-tla de los huaraches de dos zapatistas que nos seguían de lejos recomenzaba y se extinguía en el silencio de las salas desiertas. Era un rumor dulce y humilde. El tla-tla cesaba a veces largo rato, porque los dos zapatistas se paraban a mirar alguna pintura o algún mueble. Yo entonces volvía el rostro para contemplarlos: a distancia parecían como incrustados en la amplia perspectiva de las salas. Formaba una doble figura extrañamente, lejana y quieta. Todo lo veían muy juntos, sin hablar, descubiertas las cabezas, de cabellera gruesa y apelmazada, humildemente cogido con ambas manos el sombrero de palma.

This type of writing is very near to good reporting, the only difference being that Guzmán allows the subjective judgement to colour the picture perhaps more than a reporter would. Like a good reporter, his view of the Revolution is microcosmic; he is concerned with the detail rather than the overview.

v. JOSÉ RUBÉN ROMERO (1890-1952)

In contrast to Guzmán, Romero, also a Mexican, used the picaresque to illustrate his view of the way life is actually experienced. His major works were the fruit of a period abroad when he was appointed Mexican consul to Barcelona. They reflected his nostalgia for the provincial Mexico of his childhood. These early works are autobiographical. *Apuntes de un lugareño* (1932), *El pueblo inocente* and *Desbandada* (1934), are set during the Revolution and paint the lives of shopkeepers and local girls for whom sad monotony is suddenly shattered by violence. In *Apuntes de un lugareño*, the uneventful existence of an adolescent is darkened suddenly when he is dragged before an execution-squad from which he is only saved at the last minute. In *Desbandada*, the familiar scenes of a boy's existence—the churchtower, the shop, the village streets—are suddenly the stage for violence and killing. These novels are told in the first person by a narrator who is of the lower-middle class and who wavers between discontent with provincial life and the need for order. In *Desbandada*, for instance, the narrator is heartbroken when bandit revolutionaries destroy his home, but will not condemn the Revolution which he describes as 'un noble afán de subir'.

La Revolución como Dios, destruye y crea y, como a Él, buscámosla tan sólo cuando el dolor nos hiere.

By the time he wrote his next novel, however, the autobiographical element has become absorbed into the form of the picaresque. *Mi caballo, mi perro y mi rifle* (1936) is the story of a widow's son who lives in obscurity, resenting the oligarchy that rules the life of the small town but unable even to express his hatred. On the outbreak of the Revolution, he leaves his wife and child to join the revolutionaries and for the first time owns a horse (symbol of mobility and escape), a rifle (symbol of power), and a dog (symbol of comradeship). A brief moment of glory and then he is wounded when running away from the enemy. By the end of the Revolution, he is more of a disappointed man than ever, for he returns to find the very forces that he had fought to overthrow are back in power. He himself loses the horse, the dog, and the rifle which the Revolution had bestowed on him. He is an underdog with all the characteristic marks of a Romero protagonist—embittered, haunted by early poverty, a hater of the rich.

Romero's masterpiece is *La vida inútil de Pito Pérez*, a novel based on a real-life character. Pito is not the principal narrator, but engages in dialogue with the author himself. The novel is loosely structured, a casual collation of anecdotes, of Pito's 'philosophy', his last will and testament, his memories of the past. The eponymous protagonist is the town drunkard, the 'other' whose very existence represents a challenge to society, a hippy *avant la lettre* whose presence reminds people of their repressions and shortcomings. They treat him as a buffoon, a criminal, and they persecute him. But they cannot afford to take him seriously, for otherwise the existence of society itself would be in question. The provincial town must keep up an outward appearance, must inhibit and control its inhabitants, and whenever Pito shows up, his presence acts as an explosive agent of emotions more safely left unexpressed. Ironically, other outcasts treat him the worst and during a prison passion play, he is left hanging on the cross while the convicts mock at him. But while others are cruel to him, his own tricks are harmless. He is an adept at keeping himself alive by telling tall stories, at finding food and drink without working. He will do anything for a drink and his lack of shame does more to embarrass people than anything else:

> No, yo seré malo hasta el fin, borracho hasta morir congestionado por el alcohol; envidioso del bien ajeno, porque nunca he tenido bien propio; maldiciente, porque en ello estriba mi venganza en contra de quienes me desprecian. Nada pondré de mi parte para corregirme.

There is no question of repentance because Pito, unlike the seventeenth-century picaresque hero, is more of a saint than the people around him. He is a Christ-figure, appropriately 'crucified', and when he dies his body is thrown on a rubbish heap, though the eyes still look 'con altivez desafiadora al firmamento'.

Romero's nihilistic view of experience was shared by the Chilean novelist Manuel Rojas, who also prefers the picaresque form.

VI. MANUEL ROJAS (1896-)

Born in Chile, Manuel Rojas is one of Spanish America's outstanding Realist writers. Like Rubén Romero, his novels are based on autobiographical experiences and are told in the first person. An excellent short-story writer, his originality is very much a matter of the anecdote and the material he draws from life rather than a matter of technique. His major novels, *Lanchas en la bahía* (1932), *Hijo de ladrón* (1951), and *Punta de rieles* (1959) were written in a style that recalls that of the Spanish writer Pío Baroja. Baroja's work tries to give the impression of being the raw material of life and, moreover, of life lived casually without plan or purpose. He broke away from the rigid plot design of some nineteenth-century Realist writing and created a looser structure, one that seemed as casual and accidental as meeting people in the street. Like Baroja, Rojas chose this casual structure deliberately because he rejected the mechanistic cause and effect development of traditional Realism:

> Descubrí, con gran sorpresa, que el resultado estaba de acuerdo con mi modo natural de pensar, de divagar, de reflexionar y de recordar, un modo en que entra todo, lo lógico y lo especulativo y también lo inconsciente y lo absurdo, un modo en que a veces los seres, las cosas y los hechos pasan y vuelven a pasar, uniéndose entre si de una manera imperceptible.[7]

And in effect he broke new ground by linking this looser structure to a theme which revealed how an urban environment transforms relationships. Without the fixed social norms that the family helps to inculcate, Rojas's characters are freer and lonelier people whose relationships are a matter of the accidental comradeship of work, prison, or bar. *Lanchas en la bahía* is narrated by a young nightwatchman on a Valparaíso lighter who is sacked for going to sleep; he becomes a member of a lighterman's team, fights over a prostitute, and is arrested. The boy's relationships are with a casually-encountered friend, Rucio, and with a prostitute. In *Hijo de ladrón*, Aniceto Hevía describes adventures, friends, memories as they occur to him. The son of a Buenos Aires jewel-thief whose imprisonment ruins family life, he has also to face the death of his mother and the complete dispersal of the family. From now on he wanders across Argentina and over the Andes to Valparaíso, working as a carpenter's assistant, as a labourer, and ending as a beachcomber. The comradeship of work and prison replaces family ties. Each step is dictated by chance rather than by a deliberate choice. As he stands watching a train move off, for instance, he is hauled on board and taken to the harvest. He is imprisoned in Valparaíso after riots whose cause is mysterious to him.

But the city which creates hardship, oppression, work also offers freedom and comradeship. Aniceto has no need to succumb to routine and take a regular job but can accept the freedom of the beach-combers' life and their friendship in lieu of the ties of family. It is all the same in the end:

> Todos viven de lo que el tiempo trae. Día vendrá en que mirare-mos para atrás y veremos que todo lo vivido es una masa sin orden ni armonía, sin profundidad y sin belleza, apenas si aquí o allá habrá una sonrisa, una luz, algunas palabras, el nombre de alguien, quizá una cancioncilla. ¿Qué podemos hacer?

Life is all the same in the end. Thus Manuel Rojas's novel is with-out the hierarchy of values which is a characteristic of the closed Realist novel. Life is simply life. You can start at the middle, the beginning, or the end, for people are not going in any particular direction.

Picaresque Realism thus breaks through some of the limitations of closed Realism. With the exception of Payró, all the authors who used the picaresque form were deliberately defying the imposition of patterns on events. They wanted to show the casualness, the dis-orderly nature of experience and they often refused to bestow on events an evolutionary order and refused to see human progress as a goal.

VII. REALISM AND THE STRUGGLE AGAINST NATURE

Contemporary writers sometimes give the impression that man's unequal struggle against nature was the major theme of Spanish American literature before the forties. In fact, very few writers gave nature a central role in their work, and more often the destructive powers of nature were seen in the context of a preoccupation with social justice. However, realisation of the hostility of the environment and of the fragility of the civilised fringe was an important stage of Spanish American consciousness. We have to bear in mind that 'nature' and 'landscape' in a European context grew in importance as writers felt more and more separated from the organic. But for Spanish American man, the escape from an urban world was likely to lead him into the lap not of wise mother nature but of nature red in tooth and claw. The two writers who best convey the implacable hostility of the environment are the Colombian Eustasio Rivera (1889-1928) and the Uruguayan Horacio Quiroga (1878-1937).

VIII. EUSTASIO RIVERA (1889-1928)

Rivera was a teacher, lawyer, and poet whose one novel, *La vorágine*, is the prototype 'novela de la selva'. Despite faults of style and clumsy plot, the confrontation between wild nature and the preconceived ideas of the Europeanised poet-hero is dramatic and effective. The author, Parnassian in his poetry, of which he published one collection, *Tierra de promisión* (1921), Romantic in his attitude to life, adopts the metaphors and plot conventions of Romantic tradition, but shows how inadequate these are compared with reality. The protagonist of *La vorágine*, Arturo Cova, has fled from Bogotá with his mistress Alicia, and this latter-day Atala and Chactas find themselves in situations Chateaubriand never dreamed of. Once outside the city, they find there is no rule but that of the survival of the fittest. The *llanuras* are run by violent cattleherders who find Arturo's attempts to rival their *machismo* pitiful. Alicia, dazzled by the fortunes to be made by rubber-tapping, follows the *enganchador* Barrera into the jungle and is hotly pursued by Arturo who, however, finds that this new environment breaks down not only his cliché ideas of nature but even his own personality and sense of identity. He has hallucinations and is drawn towards the violence which soon comes naturally to him. Nature, once the subject of poetry, is a ruthless force devouring victims in the interest of the survival of the fittest; man and the vegetable and animal worlds are prisoners in a dreary cycle of death and birth. The Indians, those 'natural men' of Romanticism, are more like the slaves of instinct than free men, even in their festivities. The force that oppresses is nature itself with the jungle as a prison from which there is little hope of escape, dominated by evil forces over which man has no control. The worst instincts of man develop to horrific proportions, for there is no civilising code to keep them in check. Hence the bloodthirsty wars of the different gangs of rubber-workers. And all around, there are the terrifying manifestations of nature's creative and destructive powers. Rivera marshals all the resources of his prose to convey his horror, as in this passage where Clemente Silva, an old man who has lost his son in the jungle, finds himself in the path of carnivorous ants and hides in the mud until they have swarmed past:

Desde allí miraron pasar la primera ronda. A semejanza de las cenizas que a lo lejos lanzan las quemas, caían sobre la charca las fugitivas tribus de cucarachas y de coleópteros, mientras que las márgenes se poblaron de arácnides y reptiles, obligando a los hombres a sacudir las aguas mefíticas para que no avanzaran en ellas. Un temblor continuo agitaba el suelo, cual si las hojarascas hirvieran solas. Por debajo de troncos y de raíces avanzaba el tumulto de la invasión, a tiempo que los árboles se cubrían de una mancha negra, como cáscara movediza que iba ascendiendo.

If we examine this passage, we find that there are two styles. Phrases like 'a semejanza de', 'cual si' prepare us for a literary description and adjectives like 'mefítica' obviously belong to this stylish writing. Again there is the scientific terminology of 'coleópteros' and 'arácnides'. In contrast, verbs such as 'hervir', nouns such as 'cucaracha' and 'cáscara', are where reality breaks through.

Human society is not seen as a civilisation in which man is set apart from nature but as an extension of the worst natural instincts. In the jungle, ex-convicts from Cayenne resort to massacre in their attempts to gain a hold of the prized rubber empire and one dreadful massacre is witnessed by a 'philosopher' who, afterwards, is struck by psychological blindness, a powerful symbol of the intellectual's impotence to prevent or influence the real lords of the backlands. Cova himself becomes more and more insensitive and finally succumbs to the law of the jungle. He kills his rival Barrera, sees his body torn by *piranhas*, and when Alicia gives birth to a premature child, the two of them escape into the jungle rather than stay to help a boatload of plague-stricken workers. They are never seen again, having been devoured by the *selva*.

La vorágine is a powerful testimony to the end of the European Romantic concept of nature in Latin America[8] and is evidently rooted in Rivera's own personal experience of the disparity between his literary education and his experiences as a lawyer and as a member of the boundary commission between Venezuela and Colombia. His novel was a landmark of Latin American literature. In it, reality broke through conventions; barbarism took over from alien forms.

IX. HORACIO QUIROGA (1878-1937)

In the stories of Horacio Quiroga, style still struggles to cope with the material, but this author did develop over the years a spare prose which exactly conveyed his stoic view of man's relation to the natural forces. This development is the more surprising since Quiroga began his career as a Modernist and even made the customary Modernist pilgrimage to Paris. On his return to Montevideo, he became a member of the literary circle *El Consistorio del Gay Saber* and wrote Modernist poetry until an accident—the involuntary shooting of a friend—changed the whole course of his life. As a result he went to live in Buenos Aires where he was befriended by Leopoldo Lugones who was then interested in the ruins of the Jesuit missions in the tropical northern territories of Argentina. Quiroga joined Lugones's expedition to the ruins as photographer, and thus discovered the tropics. Henceforward, he was to spend many years as a pioneer farmer, first in the Chaco region, then in Misiones which became the setting for most of the stories. His life was dogged by tragedy, however. His first wife killed herself and he himself committed suicide on learning that he had cancer.

Quiroga wrote novels, but his preferred genre was the short story. His first efforts were imitative of Poe, with whom he shared a preference for the bizarre, the violent, and madness, and some of his early stories—'El perseguidor', 'La gallina degollada', for instance—are in the nature of case histories. The stories were published in periodicals and only collected in *Cuentos de amor, de locura y de muerte* (1917), *Cuentos de la selva* (1918), *El salvaje* (1920), *Anaconda* (1921), *El desierto* (1924), and *Los desterrados* (1925).

Quiroga sets many of his stories in the Misiones and Chaco areas, where tropical conditions provide the background for two of his favourite themes—the demonstration of man's true worth in the face of natural hazards and the incalculability of natural forces which made it difficult for human reason or will to prevail. Both themes are found in the story 'Los fabricantes de carbón', based on an autobiographical experience and with two stoical, taciturn characters, Drever and Rienzi, as protagonists. They are engaged in experimenting with methods of burning charcoal and are constructing a furnace to this effect. Hence calculation plays a big part in the story—the measurements of the furnace, the length and width of the strips of metal used, the temperature of the area which the two men check every morning. But all these calculations prove useless in the Misiones context. Drever's daughter falls ill, so that they cannot look after their experiment properly, the temperature of the area fluctuates wildly, the Indian labourer puts the wrong wood in the furnace and sets it alight. The story does not end in tragedy and the protagonists are stoical enough to accept the vagaries of human weakness and natural phenomena. Tragedy comes when man pits his reason and will against an overwhelmingly more powerful nature. Quiroga's Realism is very close to that of Azuela and Gálvez in that he carefully constructs a chain of cause and effect which ends in the downfall of the protagonist. Where he differs from them is in his emphasis on chance or accident in human life. However, accident is always introduced, as it were, in laboratory conditions, as a new element might be introduced into a carefully controlled experiment. Consider, for instance, 'El hombre muerto', an account of the last moments of a man's life. It is a story in which Quiroga explores the nature of the 'I', of man's attempts to possess the objective world and bring it under his control, and the transformation of subject to object at the moment of death. The story is in the form of the sights, sounds, and preoccupations of a man who has just fatally wounded himself with his own machete when climbing over a wire fence. Lying on the ground where he is bleeding to death, the man can see his whole life summarised in effort—in the neat rows of banana plants, the fence which encloses them and which divides them from the sombre jungle. The man's aspirations have been objectified in these possessions which he now contemplates:

> Por entre los bananos, allá arriba, el hombre ve desde el duro suelo el techo rojo de su casa. A la izquierda, entrevé el monte y la capuera de canela. No alcanza a ver más, pero sabe muy bien que a sus espaldas está el camino al puerto nuevo; y que en la dirección de su cabeza, allá abajo, yace en el fondo del valle el Paraná dormido como un lago. Todo, todo exactamente como siempre; el sol de fuego, el aire vibrante y solitario, los bananos inmóviles, el alambrado de postes muy gruesos y algo que pronto tendrá que cambiar.

Quiroga places the reader in the position of the dying man and only allows him to observe what the dying man can observe—the red roof, the banana plants, the fence, and the road, though the reference to the 'sleeping' river hints at the unknown forces beyond the range of human perception. But unlike the dying man, the reader can understand the irony of his reactions when he notes that the wire fence will soon have to be changed. As the man approaches death, this fragile attempt to control the environment slowly gives way. The viewpoint of the story shifts from man to horse, for as the human personality dissolves, the horse instinctively feels free to cross to the other side of the fence and graze in new pastures. Implicitly the encroachment suggests that nature will once again come into its own.

Quiroga's Realism, then, does not consist of accurate psychological analysis so much as the study of human behaviour in extreme conditions. The stories almost invariably dramatise the struggle between reason and will on the one hand and hazard or nature on the other, with the dice loaded in favour of the latter. The reader's pleasure comes from the author's neat working-out of the situation rather than from allusiveness or ambiguity.

During the latter part of his life, however, Quiroga's style of short-story writing changes. *Los desterrados* consisted of less highly-structured pieces, many of them being more in the nature of character studies or odd anecdotes. The concern is with the eccentric rather than the normative, with characters such as Van Houten and the drunken Belgian Rivet, the Brazilian peasants, who were closely based on people Quiroga knew. But the major theme is still the 'end as a man'—the final grotesque contortions that precede death in a region where the pioneers have been stripped of pity and morality, where mere survival is a virtue.

X. THE VIRTUE OF NATURE

The regionalist novel in Spanish America drew sustenance from a source other than Realism. Writers seeking originality, a distinct national identity, were naturally drawn to regionalism, to all those aspects which distinguished Spanish American from European life. The definition of natural and continental characters was increasingly frequent after 1900 and especially after the appearance of the influential essay *Ariel* (1900) by José Enrique Rodó (Uruguay; 1871-1917).[9] The significance of *Ariel* was that it compared Mediterranean tradition with North American utilitarianism and favoured the former, with which Latin America was identified. For almost the first time Latin America came out better in comparison with other civilisations. After the 'bankruptcy' of Europe demonstrated during the First World War, such comparisons became more and more common and were encouraged by European or North American writers such as D. H. Lawrence, Count Hermann Keyserling, and Waldo Frank,[10] who found that spontaneous, intuitive life and organic relations still flourished in Latin America, whereas they had been crushed in industrialised and urbanised communities. What Latin Americans failed to realise, was that these comparisons were not as favourable as they seemed, for they often tended to relegate Latin America to a vulnerable pre-industrial era. But the convictions that Latin Americans were possessed of mysterious virtues that would eventually be rewarded died hard. In the twenties, we find José Vasconcelos in *La raza cósmica* (1925) forecasting an age when an Aesthetic era would replace the Technological era and when the Latin American 'cosmic race' would triumph. The arguments in such essays were often slender, but they were stimulating to literature. Writers tended to look for positive elements in the rural environment rather than lament the backwardness of the land. Sometimes this led, however, to nostalgia for the old feudal order, as in *Las memorias de Mamá Blanca* (1929) by Teresa de la Parra (Venezuela; 1891-1936) or *Gran señor y rajadiablos* (1948) by the Chilean writer Eduardo Barrios (1884-1963). However, even in the works of writers more critical of country life such as the Argentinian Benito Lynch (1885-1951) and the Uruguayan Enrique Amorím (1900-60) there is a suggestion that the authentic national spirit has more to do with rural than with urban life.[11]

This regionalism which balanced rural against urban, native against foreign values produced one outstanding work, *Don Segundo Sombra* (1926) by Ricardo Güiraldes (Argentina; 1886-1927).

XI. RICARDO GÜIRALDES

Güiraldes was the son of a landowner who had first-hand acquaint-
ance with gaucho life. As a member of a wealthy family, he was
equally acquainted with Paris, Europe, and even the East. Throughout his life, he travelled extensively and was a friend of many European writers, especially of Valéry Larbaud.[12] Hence he is not simply
a primitivist but a highly sophisticated writer whose *Don Segundo
Sombra* was the culmination of a literary career.

From the first, he was interested in a form of writing that could
express the essence of Argentina and hence of certain disappearing
values. His first publication was a collection of stories, *Cuentos de
muerte y de sangre* (1915), which were brief sketches of historical
characters and anecdotes based on people he had met in the Argentine countryside. During the same year, he published a collection of
poems, *El cencerro de cristal*, and in 1917 his first novel, *Raucho*,
'Momentos de una juventud contemporánea'. *Raucho* was Güiraldes's
spiritual autobiography, the story of his sense of alienation in a European environment and his return to the native land and the quietism
which is true experience. His tendency to mysticism was reflected both
in his poetry and in the lyrical novel *Xaimaca* (1919).

Don Segundo Sombra represents the confluence of all his earlier
influences—the stoic quietism, the rejection of modernity, the love
of the pampa. Fabio Cáceres is an illegitimate orphan, a 'guacho' who
is brought up by two unsympathetic maiden aunts in a small town
where he becomes something of a vagabond and delinquent. He is an
Argentine Huck Finn who hangs round the bars and spends his
time fishing instead of going to school. Into this futile existence
rides Don Segundo Sombra, a cattle-driver for whom the boy con-
ceives an immediate admiration. He runs away from home and is taken
in hand by the gaucho, trained in gaucho skills and in stoical acceptance of life. At the end of the novel he is 'more than a man'; he is a
gaucho. And he is no longer an orphan. The father who had refused
to recognise him dies and leaves him his ranch. The outcast has
become a member of society.

But *Don Segundo Sombra* is not simply a cowboy adventure.
Fabio's training is a spiritual exercise and like all spiritual exercises
the physical preparation is an essential first step. In the first days
with his tutor, Fabio has to learn to control his impulses, to work
as a member of a team, and to forget his individual pride. He
distances himself from the pleasures of the world, not by avoiding
them but by learning to be indifferent to them.

Fabio's spiritual education is effected away from the distractions
of women, society, and civilisation. Society is never more than a

negative force—the barkeepers of his native town, judges and lawyers who complicate life unnecessarily and are the butt of some of Don Segundo Sombra's stories, women who are the most dangerous of distractions. Fabio has to learn not only to control himself as a gaucho, but also to meet the more subtle difficulties that these forces introduce into adult life. However, there is no simple nature/society antinomy in the novel. Nature is an indifferent force; a mere struggle for life which human beings must transcend. The novel several times shows us nature in the raw—wild herds of cattle where the breed has degenerated; the ghastly sea-crabs waiting to prey on other animals. Man must tame nature, but he can only do it by learning how to control his own instincts.

Neither is *Don Segundo Sombra* an apology for the *macho* creed. Several times in the book characters meet the *macho* challenge and there are knife fights. But Don Segundo Sombra, himself, does not need to affirm his masculinity in this way. He is too sure of himself and never seeks a fight, nor does he seek to avoid one. But for him a duel over a woman is the worst and most futile form of human vanity. By refusing this conventional challenge and response, Don Segundo Sombra reaches a high stage of spirituality, transcending mere instinctual reactions:

> Don Segundo me daba la impresión de escapar a esa ley fatal, que nos cacheteaba a antojo, haciéndonos bailar al compás de su voluntad.

Only when Fabio too reaches this stage can he be said to be a man and a gaucho, and at this point Don Segundo Sombra, his work done, disappears from his life.

The language of the novel is both highly literary in the narrative passages and regional in the speech of Don Segundo Sombra:

> Aura pa la izquierda ... Aura pa la derecha ... Aura de firme no más, hasta que recule.

The structure is that of the *bildungsroman*: the story evolves with the boy's life with retrospective pauses at the beginning of the novel, in the middle, at the end in which Fabio takes stock of his progress. These stages represent the three stages of his evolution as summed up in the following passage:

> Primero el cuerpo sufre, despúes se azonza y va, como sin tomar parte, adonde uno lo lleva. Despúes, las ideas se enturbian; no se sabe si se llegará pronto o no se llegará nunca. Mas tarde las ideas, tanto como los hechos, se van mezclando en una irrealidad que desfila burdamente por delante de una atención mediocre. A lo último, no queda capacidad vital sino para atender a lo que

uno se propone sin desmayo; seguir siempre. Y se vive nada más que por eso y para eso, porque todo ha desaparecido en el hombre fuera de su propósito inquebrantable. Y al fin se vence siempre ... cuando ya a uno la misma victoria le es indiferente.

A treatise on mysticism is not very different. Güiraldes simply transposes the physical mortification and the subordination of the self to the 'propósito' into gaucho terms. Thus his regionalism is very different in intent from that of Quiroga, for instance. For Quiroga the physical and natural world is the dominant force. For Güiraldes it must be overcome. And his choice of the regional setting arises from a conviction that this spiritual goal can best be attained in societies where the distractions of an urban and industrialised society do not yet exist. He is thus closer than he at first sight may seem to the seventeenth-century Jesuit missionaries who believed that the remote Americas were a better soil for Christianity than corrupt Europe.

XII. RÓMULO GALLEGOS (1884-1969)

At first sight, Gallegos appears to be a very different writer from Güiraldes, but the message of his novels is remarkably similar. He was a Venezuelan of modest provincial background who grew up during years of dictatorship and who, under the influence of the 'Arielist' generation, became convinced that his country must be educated into modernity. He therefore became a school-teacher and only gradually won a reputation as a novelist with the appearance of his third novel, *Doña Bárbara*, in 1929. His important novels were written during a period of self-imposed exile from the dictatorship of Vicente Gómez, on whose fall he served briefly as Minister of Education. In 1946, he was elected President of the Republic, but was quite incapable of balancing the opposing forces in national life and was soon deposed.

The theme of national regeneration is central to his life and work, but he resembles Güiraldes in that he too believed that there must be a spiritual transformation before Venezuela could achieve good government. But his apprenticeship was a long one. His first novel, *Reinaldo Solar* (1920), catalogued the desperate attempts of the eponymous hero to reconcile private and public action. He wishes to regenerate both himself and Venezuela, but fails in both. But after writing this, Gallegos came to believe that his country needed a more positive guidance and in his second novel, *La trepadora* (1925), which centred on the rise to power and wealth of a mulatto, he attempted to isolate, through the optimistic outcome of the story, the positive factors in national life. He foresaw a time when the civilised and traditional white aristocracy would be infused with the energy of the mulatto and so give rise to a stronger breed. In his first successful novel, *Doña Bárbara*, Gallegos moved away from this rather mechanistic racial presentation of the conflicting forces and set his stories among the cowboys and cattle-ranchers of the plains. Doña Bárbara, symbol of barbarism, comes into conflict with Santos Luzardo whose lands she encroaches upon. Both 'barbarism' and 'civilisation' have their defects. Doña Bárbara depends on violence and lawlessness to get her way. Santos Luzardo lacks any intimate knowledge and love of the land he has inherited. Once again the conflict is solved by marriage. Doña Bárbara's daughter, the 'child of nature', Marisela, is educated by Santos Luzardo who then marries her, and she and her children will combine the energy of the savage with the polish of civilisation.

Gallegos's chief concern, therefore, is the utilisation of a primitive energy which thus far had acted as a centrifugal and destructive force so far as national life was concerned. Living as he did in a period of dictatorship, he could only place his hopes in a distant future and as time went on, his conviction that regeneration could only come about by means of a thorough spiritual transformation seems to have deepened. His novel *Cantaclaro* (1934) presented the plains region of Venezuela devastated by civil war, its people only too ready to sink their hopes in Messianic cults, in charismatic leaders or bandit chiefs. *Cantaclaro* is almost the case history of the primitive rebel, but the final conclusion is one of sadly wasted energies. Not until *Canaima* (1935) does Gallegos see the way to spiritual regeneration.

In this novel, Marcos Vargas undergoes all the human experiences that the jungle regions of the Orinoco can offer—he becomes a mule-driver, is involved in a *macho* vendetta during which he kills a man; he becomes foreman of a rubber plantation; and he hunts for gold. This is a Don Segundo Sombra transported to the wilder and more unruly tropics. And Marcos Vargas has not one but several *gurus*. There is Juan Solito, whose magic can stop animals in their tracks and who has the power of disappearing into the natural surroundings. There is Gabriel Ureña, who takes the road to civilisation by farming his lands in defiance of the local *caciques*. There is Count Giaffero whose theory is that man must cleanse himself from time to time of the dirt of civilisation. All three of these mentors are concerned with 'inner' man, with private rather than with public experience. The *macho* code implies the exacerbation of the ego drives and this, for Gallegos, is one of the chief evils of the country. When Marcos Vargas kills his rival, the Cholo Parima, he is conforming to the regional stereotype and only gradually comes to realise that he has taken the wrong path. It is nature itself that shows him the way to spiritual salvation. He learns to subordinate his ego, to sublimate his destructive drives, and finally, in the last stage of his spiritual experience, he goes to live among Indian tribes. But unlike *Don Segundo Sombra*, the story of Marcos Vargas is largely one of wasted energies, of great potentiality which is doomed to be dissipated in a country which has not yet learned how to use the national resources because individuals have not learned to subordinate their ambitions and ego drives to a more impersonal goal. Untidy and rambling, the novel does reflect its theme of energy and conveys the feeling of a landscape that is still at the dawn of time:

> Verdes y al sol de la mañana y flotantes sobre aguas espesas de los limos, cual la primera vegetación de la tierra al surgir del océano de las aguas totales; verdes y nuevos y tiernos, como lo más verde de la porción más tierna del retoño más nuevo, aquellos islotes de manglares y borales componían, sin embargo, un paisaje inquietante, sobre el cual reinara todavía el primaveral espanto de la primera mañana del mundo.

In *Pobre negro* (1937) the author returned to the racial theme to tell the story of the black rebel Pedro Miguel Candelas, who became a guerrilla leader. In this and most of his subsequent novels, wasted potential is the major theme.

Regionalism in both the novels of Gallegos and in the *Don Segundo Sombra* of Güiraldes is deployed in a quest structure which links personal realisation with national regeneration. In both authors, the region (pampa, plain, or jungle) is either pre-societal or has a society which is still tribal. It thus offers an untrammelled area for the individual, in contrast to the towns and to the representatives of national order—the judges, lawyers, political bosses. For both authors, individual regeneration takes priority and both incarnate their values in symbolic characters—Don Segundo Sombra, Juan Solito, etc. Unlike the novels of Azuela and Gálvez, where external forces are beyond the individual's control and finally crush him, Gallegos and Güiraldes both show that, in some cases, the individual can transcend his animal nature and that the wild, untamed natural life of Latin America, far from being prejudicial to the spiritual life, may actually be more conducive to this than urban civilisation with its false and degraded values.

XIII. DOCUMENTARY AND SOCIALIST REALISM

Most of the Realist and regionalist writing discussed in this chapter has been didactic, some of it overtly so. However, there is one form of South American writing in which the message is of overriding importance, and that is protest writing either in a documentary form or in the form of Socialist Realism as defined by the 1934 Writers' Congress in Paris under the influence of Zhdanov. For Zhdanov, the purpose of literature was to further or support revolution. Novels should reflect class forces and since the communist knew the final outcome of the class struggle, he should concentrate on positive elements, not simply on the tragedy of exploited workers. Zhdanov's positive force was the proletariat—a class that scarcely existed in Latin America unless one counted plantation-workers. Latin American communists tended to seek equivalents in the Indians or among miners, dockers, and other small proletariat groups. Difficult as it was to apply to a Latin American context, Socialist Realism was actively encouraged by left intellectuals, especially by *Amauta*, the magazine founded by José Carlos Mariátegui (1895-1930), founder of the Peruvian Communist Party;[13] by some members of the Argentine *Boedo* group of writers;[14] and by the Mexican Left. Intellectuals like Mariátegui were inspired by the loftiest of ideals and yet, it must be confessed that Socialist Realism reaped very poor results in a Latin American context.

It would in fact be tedious to list protest and Socialist Realist novels, many of which are too poor and unsophisticated to merit attention. They can only be justified on the grounds that they provided the reader with information which, in the absence of organised sociological surveys, would not otherwise have been available to him.

Protest fiction has its roots in the anti-slave novel of nineteenth-century Cuba and in Clorinda Matto de Turner's pioneer Indianist work, *Aves sin nido*. After 1900, humanitarian protest writing increased as an offshoot of the almost general reformist mood of the time, a mood that stimulated the foundation of the 'Asociación Pro-Indígena' in Peru in 1909. This was the period which saw the publication of *Sub terra* (1904) and *Sub sole* (1907), the two collections of short stories in which the Chilean Baldomero Lillo (1867-1923) exposed the sufferings and alienation of the coal-miners. In 'El chiflón del diablo', he presented a gloomy and powerful vision of industrial exploitation which owed much to the influence of Zola. Chile was in fact to produce a rich crop of protest fiction; *El roto* (1920) by Joaquín Edwards Bello (1887-) even included statistics of the incidence of tuberculosis and alcoholism, and the novels of Juan Marín described the life of workers in remote and unknown areas of the country.[15] The Peruvian *Amauta* group, which included César Falcón and María Weisse, exposed labour conditions and attacked imperialism. Even César Vallejo contributed to Socialist Realism with a novel *Tungsteno* (1931) which described the Indian mine-labourers. In Bolivia, documentary Realist writing centred on the tin-mines and on the Chaco war. Augusto Céspedes (1904-), whose work is among the best of this type, published *Sangre de mestizos* (1936), a series of powerful vignettes of the jungle war in which more men died of thirst and disease than of bullet wounds. In *Metal del diablo* (1946), he described the rise to power of the tin millionaire Patiño, who is a scarcely disguised central character.

Ecuador's Realist writers came mostly from Guayaquil and many belonged to the Communist Party. Their theme was often the lives of the *montuvios* (the *mestizo* inhabitants of the coastal regions) who provided the labour force for rice plantations, docks, and fishing. The school of Guayaquil Realists produced a number of excellent writers, notably José de la Cuadra (1904-41), who wrote a treatise on the *montuvios*, a number of well-made short stories, and a novel, *Los Sangurimas* (1934),[16] which effectively told a vendetta story set against the half-wild background of the Ecuadorian plains. The other writers of his generation, many of whom earned a reputation abroad, were Demetrio Aguilera Malta (1909-), Enrique Gil Gilbert (1912-), Alfredo Pareja Diezcanseco (1908-), and Jorge Icaza, whose work will be considered in connection with Indianist writing.

Realism in Colombia was more obviously polemical and propagandist, centring on the *violencia* which broke out in the forties. *Siervo sin tierra* (1954) by Eduardo Caballero Calderón (1910) and the same author's *El Cristo de espaldas* (1953) are two of the best novels on this theme.

In Argentina, Max Dickman (1902-), Leonidas Barletta (1902-), and Lorenzo Stanchina (1900-) initiated the proletarian novel of the twenties which was, however, totally eclipsed by the more avant-garde writing of Roberto Arlt, Macedonio Fernández, and Jorge Luis Borges.

If this brief survey appears critical of Socialist Realism and protest fiction, it is not to deny that it marked an important stage in Spanish American literature and for some time acted as a substitute for the non-existent social survey. Destined for militants and the politically conscious, the novels were rarely read by the public for which they were intended. With the appearance of works like Oscar Lewis's *Children of Sánchez*, which had a widespread influence, sociological information was diverted into documentary and non-fictional channels. The confusion of documentary with fiction always led to difficulties and in fact the tale of social exploitation was often told more eloquently in case-histories than in fictionalised situations.

It is obvious too that documentary Realism and social protest writing have a different function in countries which have undergone revolution. This was the case in Mexico during the twenties and thirties and is the case in present-day Cuba.

In Mexico, the Revolution was followed by a vigorous education campaign and an attempt to decrease illiteracy. Though the campaign was slow, it did result in producing a new public. Novelists of the thirties were certainly influenced in their writings by the belief that they were communicating with a non-intellectual public whose size was bound to grow. Mauricio Magdaleno (1906-), José Mancisidor, and Gregorio López y Fuentes (1897-), though their work was not perceptibly different from that of other Socialist Realist writers, were nevertheless living a different situation, one in which, they believed, a critical attitude to the weaknesses of the Revolution might result in change.

The situation in post-Revolutionary Cuba has been much more interesting principally because of the speedy success of the literacy campaign and the more thoroughgoing nature of the Revolution. Moreover, the Cuban Revolutionary government deliberately refused to take a dogmatic line on artistic questions and Che Guevara was openly contemptuous of Socialist Realism, which he saw as a prolongation of nineteenth-century conventions.[17] Post-Revolutionary Cuban writing has explored fantasy, science fiction, and Oscar-Lewis-type documentary. Even when fiction is more closely related to traditional Realism, as in *Los años duros* (1966) by Jesús Díaz, the style is closer to that of a Hemingway[18] (or even an Isaac Babel) than that of the proletarian novel of the thirties. But perhaps the most interesting factor in the Cuban situation is that within two years a new public was formed, a public without literary tradition or sophistication, and one which naturally wished to read about their own environment. For this public, works like *Cimarrón* (1967) by Miguel Barnet (1940-) have been published. Composed on the model of *Children of Sánchez*, *Cimarrón* was the tape-recorded memories of a runaway slave, an old man of ninety who reminisced about the past and described life in nineteenth-century Cuba. For almost the first time, Latin American literature captured the voice of the black plantation-worker.

Cimarrón is, however, witness to the fact that the social documentary novel is finally inadequate. In nearly every case a straightforward presentation of facts, case histories, or, even, as in *Cimarrón*, of personal memories is more moving than their fictional presentation. The documentary novel was all too often neither novel nor document.

XIV. THE INDIANIST NOVEL

The Indianist novel epitomises the difficulties of the Realist writer in Spanish America, particularly when his material is exotic to him. The Indian is as foreign to white and *mestizo* Latin Americans as an Armenian. His beliefs and myths are alien to European tradition and even the trained sociologist cannot guarantee that he really 'knows' the Indian. Yet the Indian has been a constant theme in Spanish

American novels since *Aves sin nido*, partly because he was the most exploited section of the community, but also because many writers took him as the symbol of native values as against foreign influence. At the same time, the coming to terms with Indian culture has been an important process in the continent's cultural history and has corresponded to the main ideological currents of different periods. Thus before the 1920s, the emphasis was on education, on ridding the Indian of his superstitions; in the 1930s, the Indian was seen as a political force and more recently there have been attempts to revaluate indigenous cultures and show that there were positive virtues in the Indian's rejection of European ways.

Raza de bronce (1919), by the Bolivian historian and writer Alcides Arguedas (1879-1946) is an example of the first stage of this process. Arguedas was a social thinker, author of an analysis of Bolivian national characteristics which he had called *Pueblo enfermo* (1909). By this date, he had also published a first version of *Raza de bronce* under the title *Wata-Wara* (1904); the final version, published in 1919, had all the elements of the typical Indianist novel—absentee landlord, brutal *mayordomo*, suffering Indians. The heroine, Wata-Wara, is raped by the *mayordomo* and then when pregnant is the object of an attempted mass rape which brings about her death. The novel ends with an Indian uprising. However, the point of view betrays the author's paternalistic attitude to the Indians, for he sees them from the standpoint of industrialised and positivist Europe. Hence their 'superstitions' have to be criticised. For Arguedas, the backwardness of Bolivia is a matter of wrong attitudes—too much humility and resignation on the part of the Indians whose beliefs are obstacles to progress, too much indifference to human feelings on the part of the *ladinos* (Spanish-speaking) and the white landowner. But because of his implicit criticism of Indian superstitions, Arguedas never comes anywhere near showing intuitive understanding of the customs he describes. The feasts, ceremonies, and the blessing of the fish of Lake Titicaca are demonstrations of ignorance.

In contrast, the following generation, while coming no nearer to the Indian mind, at least regarded him as the vanguard force against imperialism (though of course this was just as 'simplistic' as Arguedas's documentation of Indian 'superstition'). The most powerful novel of this second type was *Huasipungo* (1934) by Jorge Icaza (Ecuador; 1906-), an author who belonged to the Realist school. A prolific writer, his major novels, *En las calles* (1935), *Cholos* (1938), *Media vida deslumbrados* (1942), *Huairapamuchcas* (1948), dealt with racial and political themes. But it is *Huasipungo* that remains one of the most powerful Realist novels written in Spanish America. It presents a bitter picture of life in a *sierra* village, owned by a *ladino* landowner, Alfonso Pereira. Pereira has no resources except his lands in the

remote village which are worked by peasant labour. When his daughter
is dishonoured and the family have to retire to their country estate
for her to have the child, he raises money by signing an agreement
with a foreign company who want a road built to open the interior
for the exploitation of petroleum. Pereira thus becomes the instrument
of imperialist penetration of the country and is forced to dispossess
from their *huasipungos* (or plots of land) the already miserably poor
Indians. The inarticulate villagers, owned body and soul by landowner and priest, have scarcely the strength to resist the expropriation
which deprives them of food and homes. Their fate is epitomised in
the life of Andrés Chiliquinga, whose wife is forced to breastfeed
Pereira's illegitimate grandchild. Chiliquinga is exploited in every
possible way. He is lamed when working in the forest, fined for damage
done to crops, and when on the point of starving he gives his family
some rotten meat, his wife dies from eating it. Finally at the end of
the novel, he sees that his only course is to rebel in a last-stand
resistance against the seizure of the *huasipungos*, a resistance that is
doomed to failure.

Icaza's Indians, notwithstanding his isolation of one emblematic
character, move only in a mass. Except for mass action, their powers
are limited and they respond only to primitive drives like their blind
retreat from floods:

> En el vértigo de aquella marcha hacia una meta en realidad poco
> segura—entre caídas y tropezones, con la fatiga golpeando en la
> respiración a través de los maizales, salvando los baches, brincando
> las zarzas, cruzando los chaparros, las gentes iban como hipnotizadas.
> Hubieran herido o se hubieran dejado matar si alguien se atrevía
> a detenerles.

The vocabulary of this passage—'vértigo' 'hipnotizadas'—indicates
the irrational nature of the Indian whose acts are instinctive, blind,
lemming-like. His consciousness does not rise above the animal level.
Icaza's novel is successful in showing the desperate harshness of the
Indian's life, but ultimately fails to break out of a cliché presentation. There is, nevertheless, a crude strength about the writing which
conveys the feeling of physical distaste for the dirt and sordidness.
In a later novel, *En las calles* (1935), Icaza's attention shifts to the
cholo (or part Indian, part Spaniard). The *cholo* is seen as a potential element of progress, not because he is more admirable than the
Indian, but because he is more of an individualist, more concerned
with personal advancement. The novel is concerned with the *cholo*
protagonist, José Manuel Játiva, who first emerges as a mediator
between the Indians and the politicians of Quito, but when the Indian
protest is repressed, he himself escapes and eventually joins the police
force which is sent against an Indian uprising. Játiva is politically

conscious enough to feel remorse and self-disgust at his change, but
what Icaza depicts here and in later novels such as *Cholos, Media
vida deslumbrados,* and *Huairapamuchcas* is the difference between
the more individualistic and 'progressive' *cholo* and the mass action
of the Indians. In *Huairapamuchcas,*[19] for instance, the novel ends
when the twins who have been born of the rape of an Indian mother
by the *patrón* symbolically cut down an ancestral tree to bridge the
ravine that will take them to the road to the outside world. The fel-
ling of the tree signifies the death of backward-looking traditionalism,
but the twins' action is the expression of a force as unconscious as
that which moves the Indians.

The Peruvian novel *El mundo es ancho y ajeno* (1941) by Ciro
Alegría (1909-67) follows roughly the plot-pattern of *Huasipungo,*
but succeeds in offering a picture of greater complexity. Alegría's novel
is also about the expropriation of communal lands, but in this case
the story is presented partly through the consciousness of Rosendo
Maqui, an Indian *comunero,* and in language which conveys something of the Indian's sense of organic relationships. Rosendo is neither
Icaza's blind unconscious force nor Alcides Arguedas's superstitious
Indian:

> Su primer recuerdo—anotemos que Rosendo confunde un tanto
> las peripecias personales con las colectivas—estaba formado por
> una mazorca de maíz. Era todavía niño cuando su taita se la alcanzó
> durante la cosecha y él quedóse largo tiempo contemplando emo-
> cionadamente las hileras de granos lustrosos. A su lado dejaron
> una alforja atestada. La alforja lucía hermosas listas rojas y azules.
> Quizá por ser éstos los colores que primero le impresionaron, los
> amaba y se los hacía prodigar en los ponchos y frazadas ...

The above passage indicates that Alegría is attempting to describe
an Indian consciousness and show the relation of the Indian attitudes
and culture to the natural world. At the same time, it is also obvious
that he is explaining these to a reader for whom it may be unfamiliar.
He is therefore obliged to underline very explicitly that Rosendo does
not distinguish clearly between the personal and the collective.

Alegría faced another difficulty. As a member of a nationalist and
socialist Peruvian political party, APRA,[20] he was dedicated to the
idea of change. He wished to show society in transition, but was well
aware that the Indian commune was, to use Lévi-Strauss's term, a
'cold' society in which change could only come from the outside. The
expropriation of the land is an act which precipitates change in the
Indian community. But Alegría does not believe that the Indian can
attain political consciousness if he is living in the traditional commune.
Only when he is drawn into class struggle and learns to see his situation historically can he consciously project into the future. For this

reason, Rosendo Maqui only survives the first stage of the struggle. For, defying the expropriation, he is thrown into prison and there dies. The struggle is taken up by Benito Castro whose father had been a soldier and who has lived in the city where he becomes politicised. Other Indians achieve political consciousness through working in the mines or in the plantations. The novel thus works out solutions to problems which Icaza and Arguedas had either avoided or evaded. Indeed, the defect of Alegría's novel is in its overriding need to explain, and to demonstrate that the Indians could run a modern type of commune successfully.

Arguedas, Icaza, and Alegría all see the Indian within a political framework and judge him according to his capacity for change and progress. It was obviously a vital question in the Andean countries, though it did not necessarily make for the best novels. Indian attitudes were only successfully conveyed in literature when the Realist mode was superseded. However, even without Realism, there were closer approaches to the Indian mind. In *Balún Canán* (1957) by the Mexican novelist Rosario Castellanos (1925-) many of the difficulties that faced the Indianist novelist are avoided by having part of the novel narrated by a child of European origin who is brought up by an Indian nurse. The child's relation with the nurse establishes the Indians as human beings whose beliefs are intimately related to the environment. But Rosario Castellanos could still only present the Indian through the eyes of a non-Indian, though her procedure was perhaps more honest than the objective novelist who was not really in a position to be objective.[21] The alternative was to be thoroughly scientific. Ricardo Pozas (1910-) was also Mexican and a trained anthropologist who had spent some years doing field work in a Chamula village. His *Juan Pérez Jolote* (1952) was a reworking of the material he had gathered as an anthropologist. Told in the first person, the novel attempts to translate Indian attitudes into Castilian language. Even so, Ricardo Pozas like other Indianist writers has to account for change and development. He does this by having his narrator run away from home to work in the plantations and later he joins the Revolutionary forces. When he returns to the village, he is more *ladino* than Indian and though he once again adapts himself to the life of the community, his experience has given him the critical outlook of an outsider.

Though Pozas's novel seems to be a much more sophisticated view of the Indian than most previous Indianist novels, it is primarily an 'explanatory' novel in which structure and events are ordered according to a sociological plan—the study of how social changes in post-Revolutionary Mexico are absorbed into the life of a community.

XV. PSYCHOLOGICAL REALISM

The presentation of psychological problems is one of the least exploited veins in Spanish American writing. This is partly because 'character' is less important in the Spanish American Realist context than the total situation and because national and social questions have often been predominant. The isolation of the individual from public concern is more difficult in an environment where human development is all too often frustrated by dictatorship or social anarchy. Modernist writing had, however, encouraged the exploration of abnormal psychology. The early stories of Horacio Quiroga were often case histories. And in the twenties there emerged a number of women writers who explored feminine sensibility, writers such as the Venezuelan Teresa de la Parra in her novel *Ifigenia, Diario de una señorita que escribió porque se fastidiaba* (1924), and the Chilean writers María Luisa Bombal (1910-) and Marta Brunet (1901-67). Perhaps the one example of a writer who devoted his creative energies to the analysis of psychological types is the Chilean Eduardo Barrios (1884-1963).

Barrios from the first showed an interest in the unusual. His first novel which was in reality a *nouvelle*, explored a case of precocious sexuality. *El niño que enloqueció de amor* (1915) was in the form of a diary kept by a boy and telling of the strange feelings for a woman friend of the family. The first-person narration makes it difficult for the author to convey more than a superficial impression of the growing madness, especially as the language remains logical and analytical. One imagines the treatment the theme might have had, for instance, in post-Surrealist works. Here, for example, the boy sees a tapestry with a wild boar and immediately associates this with Jorge, the young man whom Angélica loves, and whose kiss witnessed by the child finally plunges him into madness:

> me acuerdo ... que unos caballeros hablaban mucho y se balanceaban desde los talones hasta la punta de los pies, parados alrededor de un viejo muy feo con lentes donde unos hombres medio desnudos y muy mal hechos querían cazar un jabalí muy bravo. Ese jabalí me parece ahora que es la cosa enorme que sale de los cerros. No, no sé bien. Bueno, en esto pasó un bulto por el pasadizo y ... me lo avisó el corazón, porque di un salto en la silla ... y lo vi pasar por la otra puerta del comedor, y era él, Jorge.

The language here is too rational, too linked by cause and effect to convey madness effectively. The child makes the kind of connection between the boar and Jorge which, in reality, only an outside observer would make.

Barrios's first major novel, *Un perdido* (1917), was semi-autobio-graphical and dealt with the misfit Lucho, the timid son of an army officer whose whole life is ruined because he cannot fit into the social stereotype. Faced with living up to the standard of being 'todo un hombre' which is his father's ideal, he is accused of having a 'carácter de marica' because he is something of a dreamer. There is no socially acceptable outlet for his sensibility and he becomes a drunken failure, a 'perdido'.

One of Barrios's best-known works was *El hermano asno* (1922), in which he again adopted the diary form. The story is told by Brother Lázaro, a Franciscan who has retired from the tempest of passion to the peace of the convent, but still has a daily struggle with his nature. He observes with sympathy and wonder the activities of the 'saint', the 'hermano asno' Brother Rufino, who is idolised by the women of the neighbourhood for his extremes of mortification and the love he displays for the humblest animals. But the saint has feet of clay. He attempts to rape a girl and it is the sinner, Brother Lázaro, who takes the burden of guilt upon himself and preserves the saint's reputation after his death. As in *El niño que enloqueció*, the rational language is out of key with the study of essentially irrational impulses, the analysis too lucid for the subconscious forces which it purports to present. In *Los hombres del hombre* (1950), Barrios tried to solve the problems of psychological analysis by split-ting the central character into a number of men; the different sides of his character speak with different voices. The protagonist has left his wife because of his jealous fear that their son may not be his own and the tensions of his character split up into the different fragments. Only finally does the voice of love and forgiveness triumph. Despite the sophisticated nature of this theme, it is not well handled. Barrios, like many writers in the Realist tradition, finally fails because of his inability to find an appropriate language and form.

We shall find that many of the great twentieth-century writers fall outside the Realist tradition and that contemporary authors were often to find verisimilitude more of an obstacle than a desirable goal. This does not mean that Realism is to be dismissed. Spanish Americans had to discover their own countries and themselves, and the documentary and Realist novels undoubtedly played an important part in this process.

NOTES

1. Carlos Fuentes, op. cit.
2. Mario Vargas Llosa, 'La novela primitiva y la novela de creación en América Latina', *Revista de la Universidad de México*, XXIII, No. 10 (June 1969). Also 'Primitives and creators', *TLS*, 14 November 1968.

3. Wilson Harris, *Tradition, the Writer and Society* (London–Port of Spain, 1964) and quoted Kenneth Ramchand, *The West Indian Novel and its Background* (London, 1970).

4. Francisco Bulnes, *El porvenir de las naciones latinoamericanas* (Mexico, 1899).

5. For other novels of the Revolution see the Aguilar anthology, *La novela de la Revolución Mexicana*, ed. Antonio Castro Leal, 2 vols. (Mexico, 1958-60). One of the best novels, apart from those of Azuela and Guzmán, is Rafael F. Muñoz's *Se llevaron el cañón para Bachimba*, which Anderson Imbert compares to *Don Segundo Sombra* in his *Historia de la literatura hispanoamericana*, II.

6. *Ulises criollo* is the title of the first volume of Vasconcelos's autobiography and is included in the anthology of *La novela de la Revolución Mexicana* and in Vasconcelos, *Obras completas*, 4 vols. (Mexico, 1951).

7. Manuel Rojas, *Obras completas* (Santiago de Chile, 1961), p. 28.

8. J. Franco, 'Image and Experience in *La vorágine*', BHS, 1964.

9. There is a discussion of the influence of Arielism in Martin S. Stabb, *In quest of Identity* (Chapel Hill, 1967).

10. Keyserling was author of *South American Meditations* (London, 1932). Waldo Frank wrote a number of articles and books on Latin America, especially *America Hispana. A Portrait and a Prospect* (New York–London, 1931).

11. For a fuller discussion of these writers, see chapters 3 and 4 of J. Franco, *The Modern Culture of Latin America*.

12. Letters to Valéry Larbaud are included in R. Güiraldes, *Obras completas* (Buenos Aires, 1962).

13. Eugenio Chang Rodríguez, *La literatura política de González Prada, Mariátegui y Haya de la Torre* (Mexico, 1967).

14. J. Franco, *The Modern Culture of Latin America*, chapter 5.

15. F. Alegría, *Las fronteras del realismo: literatura chilena del siglo xx* (Santiago de Chile, 1962).

16. *Obras completas* (Quito, 1958).

17. J. Franco, 'Before and After: Contexts of Cuban Writing', *Cambridge Review* (20 February 1970).

18. Hemingway influenced some Cuban writing, especially the short stories of Lino Novás Calvo (1905-).

19. The title means 'born of the wild'.

20. The initials stand for *Alianza Popular Revolucionaria Americana*.

21. A later novel, *Oficio de tinieblas* (1962), has a Tzotzil protagonist.

READING LIST

Anthology
Castro Leal, Antonio (ed.), *La novela de la Revolución Mexicana*, 2 vols. (Mexico, 1958-60)

Texts
Alegría, Ciro, *El mundo es ancho y ajeno*, 20th ed. (Buenos Aires, 1961)
Amorím, Enrique, *El caballo y su sombra* (Buenos Aires, 1945)
——, *El paisano Aguilar* (Buenos Aires, 1946)
Azuela, Mariano, *Obras completas*, 3 vols. (Mexico, 1958-60)
Barnet, Miguel, *Cimarrón* (La Habana, 1967)
Barrios, E., *Obras completas*, 2 vols. (Santiago de Chile, 1962)

Castellanos, Rosario, *Balún Canán* (Mexico, 1957)
Cuadra, José de la, *Obras completas* (Quito, 1958)
Gallegos, Rómulo, *Obras completas* (Madrid, 1958)
Gálvez, Manuel, *La maestra normal* (Buenos Aires, 1950)
Güiraldes, Ricardo, *Obras completas* (Buenos Aires, 1962)
Guzmán, Martín Luis, *Obras completas de Martín Luis Guzmán*, 2 vols.
   (Mexico, 1961)
Icaza, Jorge, *Cholos*, 2nd ed. (Quito, 1939)
——, *Huasipungo*, 2nd ed. (Buenos Aires, 1953)
——, *Huairapamuchcas* (Quito, 1948)
——, *En las calles* (Buenos Aires, 1944)
——, *Media vida deslumbrados* (Buenos Aires, 1950)
——, *Obras escogidas* (Mexico, 1961)
Lynch, Benito, *El inglés de los güesos* (Buenos Aires, 1966)
Payró, Roberto, *Pago chico*, 5th ed. (Buenos Aires, 1943)
——, *Divertidas aventuras del nieto de Juan Moreira* (Buenos Aires, 1957)
——, *El casamiento de Laucha*, 5th ed. (Buenos Aires, 1961)
Pozas, Ricardo, *Juan Pérez Jolote*, 5th ed. (Mexico, 1965)
Quiroga, Horacio, *Cuentos escogidos* (Madrid, 1962)
Rivera, Eustasio, *La vorágine*, 6th ed. (Buenos Aires, 1957)
Rojas, Manuel, *Obras completas* (Santiago de Chile, 1961)

Historical and critical

Alegría, Fernando, *Las fronteras del realismo: literatura chilena del
   siglo xx* (Santiago de Chile, 1962)
Brushwood, J. S., *Mexico in its Novel* (Austin and London, 1966)
Cometta Manzoni, Aida, *El indio en las novelas de América* (Buenos Aires,
   1960)
Dunham, Lowell, *Rómulo Gallegos, vida y obra* (Mexico, 1967)
Previtali, Giovanni, *Ricardo Güiraldes and Don Segundo Sombra* (New York,
   1963)
Rodríguez Monegal, Emir, *Narradores de esta América*, I (Montevideo,
   1969)
——, *El desterrado. Vida y obra de Horacio Quiroga* (Buenos Aires, 1968)
Rojas, Ángel F., *La novela ecuatoriana* (Mexico-Buenos Aires, 1948)

Chapter 8

POETRY SINCE MODERNISM

'la soledad, la lluvia, los caminos ...'

(César Vallejo)

AS FAR AS SPANISH AMERICAN POETRY is concerned the twentieth century begins in 1922. In this year, César Vallejo published *Trilce*. Two years later Pablo Neruda's *Veinte poemas de amor* appeared. The poetry of *Trilce* was ironic, experimental, hermetic, and yet for a long time scarcely caused a ripple on the literary scene; the poetry of *Veinte poemas* was Romantic, subjective, and it was immediately popular. But in their different ways, both poets are 'modern'. They are poets of an urban civilisation, poets who have lived to see nineteenth-century optimism and faith in progress grow sour, poets who can only stand in an ironic relationship to the traditions of the past. They are obliged to create new images and language, to discard conventional forms and syntax, and foreshorten the ground that separates poet from reader.

That this new spirit owes much to European avant-garde movements like Cubism, Dadaism, and Hispanic Ultraism is self-evident. Yet César Vallejo, Pablo Neruda, and many lesser-known poets of the period escape classification into schools or movements. The example of Cubism and Dadaism was not followed slavishly but used as an instrument of liberation. Once the storehouse of the subconscious was broken open, a whole new region of imagery and of literary energy was disclosed. The influence of European movements on the poetry of the twenties is a general influence, an encouragement to break new ground rather than to imitate this or that precept. Cubism, for instance, encouraged the study of non-European art (particularly that of the negroes) without which interest in Afro-Cubanism might not have arisen. Futurism brought the language of the modern technological world into poetry. Both Futurism and Cubism broke away from nature and organic growth and set the poem in an urban environment of synchronic, 'simultaneous' happenings. With Dadaism, art and literature were no longer considered to be sacred happenings or part of established culture, but became revolutionary, subversive, auto-destructive. With Surrealism, art became a force that could change both man and society by releasing the underground forces of creativity.[1]

The poets of the twenties were influenced by new sciences as well as by literary movements. They discovered psychology and were fascinated by the new techniques that cinema opened up with its freedom from linear developments—the use of flashback, the presentation of simultaneous happenings in widely different places, the use of visual signs instead of words.

I. EARLY EXPERIMENTS. VICENTE HUIDOBRO

The first indications of this revolution in poetry came timidly from the post-Modernists who were very sensitive to the aesthetic revolution that was going on in Europe and North America. Leopoldo Lugones, for instance, published his *Lunario sentimental* in which there were echoes of Laforgue's[2] lightness and irony. The Chilean poet Pedro Prado (1886-1952) in *Flor de cardo* explored new ranges of imagery. Carlos Sabat Ercasty (1887-) transformed Spanish rhythms and verse forms under the influence of Whitman. The long rhythmic periods found in Neruda's verse were first tried out by this Uruguayan poet:

> ¡Corazón mío, danza sobre la nave!
> Yo aguardo el instante del prodigioso escollo
> donde se estrellaran las viejas tablas.
> ('Alegría del mar')

The Mexican José Juan Tablada (1871-1945) visited Japan and on his return published Spanish versions of the *haiku,* and ideograms. His *haiku* have fresh visual images, like the 'Peces Voladores',

> Al golpe del oro solar
> estalla en astillas el vidrio del mar

or 'El insomnio':

> En su pizarra negra
> suma cifras de fósforo.

The most controversial of these early experimenters was Vicente Huidobro (Chile; 1893-1948), who claimed to have anticipated many European avant-garde ideas even before settling in Paris in 1916 and collaborating with Apollinaire and Paul Reverdy in magazines such as *Sic* and *Nord Sud.* Irrespective of the quality of his poetry, Huidobro is a key figure of his period, typical of the avant-garde spirit in his energy, particularly later in life, trying to show that he was the first concern for newness, priority, creativity.[3] He expended a great deal of modern Latin American poet and that he had invented *Creacionismo*. But in retrospect his polemics are only interesting as evidence that he was thinking on the same lines as his French, Spanish, and English contemporaries. Avant-garde movements, in general, all begin as breaks with the establishment, and all claim to be without precedent, so that Huidobro, unknowingly, was simply conforming to type.

But what does *creacionismo* mean? First of all, the poet no longer claims to be imitating the real world nor reflecting divine order. The word, freed from its instrumentality as a means of transaction, takes on magic properties. Words suggest, shock, contradict themselves, unexpectedly fuse. The poet invents by combining new words and these combinations suggest new areas of experience.

It is this 'freeing of the word' which provides the common ground of many of the twenties' avant-garde movements.

'Cada verso de nuestros poemas posee su vida individual y representa una visión inédita', wrote the Ultraists.[4]

Huidobro declared 'El hombre sacude su esclavitud, se rebela contra la Naturaleza como otrora Lucifer contra Dios',[5] and in the preface to one of his first experimental poems, 'Adán', which was dedicated to Emerson, he wrote:

Muchas veces he pensado escribir una Estética del Futuro, del tiempo no muy lejano en que el Arte esté hermanado, unificado con la Ciencia.[6]

Despite Huidobro's repeated claims of 'firsts', he produced little of real originality before arriving in France. Significantly, much early experimental verse, published under the title *Horizon carré*, was written in French. I say 'significantly' because the poet is here working not 'freely' but following existing avant-garde models, especially the poems of Apollinaire. His first experimental poems in Spanish are 'Ecuatorial' and *Poemas árticos*. The poem 'Gare' is modern in its use of the railway, the telephone, and in its reference to the First World War, but the suggestion of alienation, of frustration, is stated rather than conveyed poetically:

> La tropa desembarca
>   En el fondo de la noche
> Los soldados olvidaron sus nombres
>   Bajo aquel humo cónico
>   El tren se aleja como un mensaje telefónico
> En las espaldas de un mutilado
> Las dos pequeñas alas se han plegado.

Although Huidobro's most extreme experiments are probably the *Poemas giratorios* which are close to 'concrete poetry',[7] his outstanding work is *Altazor*, a seven-canto poem which describes modern man's fall from order to disorder, from the providential teleology to meaninglessness:

> Vamos cayendo, cayendo de nuestro cenit a nuestro nadir, y dejamos
> el aire manchado de sangre para que se envenenen los que vengan
> mañana a respirarlo.

Altazor wants what he cannot possibly have in the modern world—
faith and certainty:

> Dadme una certeza de raíces en horizonte quieto,
> Un descubrimiento que no huya a cada paso.
> ¡O dadme un bello naufragio verde!

Both love and poetry, two forms of liberation, are doomed to frustration by human limitation and the demands of time. Canto 4 begins with the urgent realisation that 'No hay tiempo que perder' and the poem ends in contradiction with the poet tasting freedom but knowing that he is limited:

> El cielo está esperando un aeroplano
> y yo oigo la risa de los muertos debajo de tierra.

The final canto dissolves into dream, in which even language breaks down, and the poem ends on a note that is part song, part outcry, and certainly destruction, with words breaking up into phonemes:

> Lalalí
>   Io ia
> i i i o
> Ai a i ai a iiii o ia

What finally separates Huidobro from Modernism and its aftermath is not so much the experiment, however, as the theme of modern man's frustrated search:

> El corazón sabe que hay un mañana atado
> Y que hay que libertar
> Y vive en sus silencios y su luz desgraciada
> Como el brillo que los faroles han robado a los árboles.

The 'mañana atado' and the frustrated journey will be common motifs in the poetry of the age. One of Vallejo's early poems is about the plight of a spider with 'innumerable feet', 'que ya no anda'. In *Residencia en la tierra* (first part, 1933; second part, 1935; third part, 1947) Neruda speaks of 'un solo movimiento', 'como una polea loca ...' The images arise out of the common realisation that uninterrupted progress is no longer a possibility. Time is running out and all men, for Huidobro, are 'entre su arena lenta y su ataúd'.

At the time of Huidobro's first experiments, there was a general awakening in Spanish America to the need for a new language and forms. For some the creation of vivid metaphors was the key; for others, stripping language of literary verbiage. There were extremes of irony and sophistication on the one hand—like the poetry of the Argentinian Oliverio Girondo (1891-1957)—and on the other the spare, deceptively simple poetry of his contemporary, Jorge Luis Borges. Borges was one of the first to understand the essence of the urban scene:

> Y quedé entre las cosas
> miedosas y humilladas,
> encarceladas en manzanas
> diferentes e iguales
> como si fueran todas ellas recuerdos superpuestos, barajados,
> de una sola manzana.[8]

Different elements are here imprisoned within the same frame; they are synchronic elements of a whole; or like memories which are not necessarily ordered chronologically. The city becomes analogous to the non-linear, to the simultaneous. The urban landscape becomes the gateway to resolution of contradiction and ultimately to quietude.

II. POETRY OF SIMPLICITY: GABRIELA MISTRAL

To move towards a poetry of simplicity would seem the obvious reaction after the ornate literary verse of the Modernists. We have already seen how the post-Modernists had abandoned exotic subject-matter in favour of the regional. Now among many poets, there was a further approach to plain, even colloquial, language, towards a kind of 'transparency of language' through which could be expressed the broader archetypal experiences. The outstanding example of this 'plain' poetry on archetypal themes was that of the Nobel prizewinner Gabriela Mistral (Chile; 1889-1957), whose poetry sprang out of frustrated love and motherhood. She uses traditional metres and verse forms, and the vocabulary is a heightened form of natural speech, but she broadens the scope of Spanish American verse and introduces new themes like the single woman's sense of being unfulfilled:

> La mujer que no mece un hijo en el regazo,
> cuyo calor y aroma alcance a sus entrañas,
> tiene una laxitud de mundo entre los brazos;
> todo su corazón congoja inmensa baña.[9]

She speaks too of her sense of vocation as a teacher and at the same time the sacrifice of personal life involved in this:

La maestra era pobre. Su reino no es humano.
(Así en el doloroso sembrador de Israel)
Vestía sayas pardas, no enjoyaba su mano,
¡y era todo espíritu un inmenso joyel![10]

Gabriela Mistral published three main collections of poetry, *Desolación* (1922), to whose subsequent editions she was to add many poems, *Tala* (1938), and *Lagar* (1954). In the first collection, frustrated motherhood was the major theme. Her collections also include nursery rhymes, cradle songs, and poems to children, and perhaps she is most successful in her empathy with children: for instance, in 'Ésta que era una niña de cera' she recaptures the child's sense of the strangeness of words:

Ésta que era una niña de cera;
pero no era una niña de cera,
era una gavilla parada en la era.
Pero no era una gavilla
sino la flor tiesa de la maravilla.
Tampoco era la flor, sino que era
un rayito de sol pegado a la vidriera.
No era un rayito de sol siquiera;
una pajita dentro de mis ojitos era.
¡Alléguense a mirar cómo he perdido entera,
en este lagrimón, mi fiesta verdadera!

In this poem, we recognise the language of nursery rhyme, the child's fancy transforming a wax child into a bundle of plants, into a sunflower. But the final comments are those of the adult. Profoundly religious, she was also the poet of death, of mourning, and of separation. The suicide of the man she loved, early in her life, imposed a sombre air on all she did and wrote, except for her children's poems. And though her poetry has not the complexity of that of Vallejo, yet there is a certain grave simplicity about the best of it.

In both her person and her poetry, Gabriela Mistral stands between two epochs. Her formation was nineteenth-century. She was the woman of hearth, children, of religious faith. But she was forced to live in a modern world; the 'natural' fulfilment of her life as a woman was denied her so that her poetry sprang out of frustration. Yet though she was born into the twentieth century, she was not yet of it, not 'modern' in the way that a Neruda or a Vallejo was modern, for her values were those of the past. This is not to belittle the poetry, simply to place it in a stream different from that which has watered contemporary movements.

Sencillista poets like Gabriela Mistral most frequently were inspired by nature. She herself had a fine appreciation of American landscapes, both of the tropical Caribbean and the *Selva austral* of Chile. Her contemporary Juana de Ibarbourou (Uruguay; 1895–) was known as 'Juana de América' and saw herself as a 'child of nature'.

> Me ha quedado clavado en los ojos
> la visión de ese carro de trigo
> que cruzó, rechinante y pesado,
> sembrando de espigas el recto camino.

The *sencillismo* practised by Gabriela Mistral was also favoured by some of the avant-garde who often combined an interest in folk-poetry with experimentalism. This was the case in Mexico and Havana, two cities with active avant-garde movements during the twenties.

III. CUBAN POETS. NICOLÁS GUILLÉN

In Havana, the period was one of political as well as literary combat, with poets often combining their literary activities with political militancy. Rubén Martínez Villena (1899-1934),[11] one of the most promising literary figures of the twenties, abandoned poetry to become one of the founders of the Cuban Communist Party. Those who continued writing often experimented with 'Futurist' vocabulary or with primitivism in their anxiety to get nearer the spirit of ordinary people. José Z. Tallet (1893–), for instance, in his 'Poema de la vida cotidiana' introduces the everyday vocabulary of office life into poetry, though the framework of the poem is still a literary rhetoric. The magazine *Revista de Avance,* founded in 1927, was the active promoter of these vanguard movements and in particular of Afro-Cubanism which combined primitivism—a celebration of the spontaneity and vitality of the Cuban negro—with *sencillismo* of language. At first mainly concerned with the picturesque elements in Cuban life, Afro-Cubanism received an added stimulus from the visit to Havana in 1931 of García Lorca. Lorca was returning from New York to Spain and had already written his *Poeta en Nueva York* which included a lament for the 'imprisoned blood' of the Harlem negro. He was a decisive influence on a young mulatto poet, Nicolás Guillén (1902–), in whose poetry the theme of the negro became more than a picturesque defiance of European values. Guillén's Afro-Cubanism was the assertion of pride in his black past, and in the suffering of his black ancestors. The culture of the negro had hitherto been underground and until the 1920s was unknown by most intellectuals. The *santería* cults, through which the folklore of Africa and even languages such as Yoruba were transmitted from generation to generation, were outside the ken of the white Cuban, until the researches of the anthropologist Fernando Ortiz and the folklorist Lydia Cabrera brought them to the surface. For the white Cuban, Afro-Cubanism brought awareness of the richness and importance of the African in Cuban life. For a mulatto like Nicolás Guillén, Afro-Cubanism provided the voice of the suppressed part of his consciousness. Now he could speak of African music in 'La canción del bongó', of the alienation of his race in 'Pequeña oda a un negro boxeador cubano', of the Yoruba songs in 'Canto negro':

> Repica el congo solongo,
> repica el negro bien negro;
> congo solongo del Songo,
> baila yambó sobre un pie.

> Mama tomba,
> serembe cuserembá

And in poems like 'Negro Bembón', 'Mulata', 'Búcate plata', he voices the sentiments of the illiterate black population, by employing Afro-Spanish dialect.

Guillén began to write on the eve of the Great Depression and in the early thirties his poetry increasingly combined the political with the racial theme. In *West Indies Limited*, he moves away from the picturesque towards the committed anger of the man who has recognised the heritage of colonialism:

> Puños los que me das
> para rajar los cocos tal un pequeño dios colérico.

His best-known poem in this collection, 'Balada de los dos abuelos', marks the mature recognition of the African and the Spanish in his blood; there is the Africa of his black grandfather:

> África de selvas húmedas
> y de gordos gongos sordos ...
>   Me muero
> (Dice me abuelo negro).
> Aguaprieta de caimanes,
> verdes mañanas de cocos.

This forces him to remember the cruel 'third passage' and the slave trade. But there is also the white grandfather. White and black are forever mingled in his blood, in which 'gritan, sueñan, lloran, cantan'. Perhaps one of Guillén's most important contributions to Cuban literature was his recognition of the importance of African myth and culture. In 'Sensemayá' and 'La muerte del Ñeque' he draws on African rite and belief as the Modernists had drawn on the classics, but unlike the French *négritude* writers, this did not imply a rejection of white culture. So in 'Son número 6' he writes,

> Yoruba soy, soy lucumí
> mandinga, congo, carabali,
> Atiendan, amigos, mi son, que acaba así.

but in the poem he also recognises that:

> Estamos juntos desde muy lejos
> jóvenes, viejos,
> negros y blancos, todo mezclado;

The 'negro' was a fashion in contemporary Europe, the symbol of spontaneity, of the superiority of vitality and instinct over reason. But in West Indian poets such as Guillén the negro theme marks a recognition that Cuba's roots are in slavery and slave culture, that both Africa and Spain are part of the past. Guillén's later poetry was less African and more political. In the thirties, he became a communist and published a collection of poems on the Spanish Civil War and ballads on 'simple themes'. However, his real originality is in the Afro-Cuban poetry.

Only one black poet emerged from Afro-Cubanism—not surprisingly since the black elements in the Cuban population were also the illiterates and the under-privileged. Marcelino Arozareno (1912-) was directly influenced by Guillén and like him declared his universality: 'Intento cantar desde negro pero con la porción de voz que nos toca en el canto universal'. His *Canción negra sin color* includes poems written in the thirties, many of them describing negro *santería* rites, as in 'Liturgia etiópica'; others satirical like the 'Canción negra sin color', which was written in 1939 but anticipates the defiant poetry of *négritude* writers:

> Somos lo anecdótico;
> lo eternamente beodo,
> de una embriaguez de látigo, de selva y de canción;
> en los bares del ritmo
> la rumba nos da rones batidos en cinturas
> y Trópico,
> el orate de las Islas Sonoras,
>   —charcos musicales en las amplias praderas del Atlántico—
> nos envasa en vitrinas de sextetos y sones
> para peinar la desmelenada curiosidad turística.

There has been some revival of this *négritude* in post-Revolutionary poetry, but mainly in an effort to find a new non-European mythology and in response to post-Revolutionary Third-Worldism.[12]

IV. MEXICAN POETS

Along with Buenos Aires and Havana, Mexico was the other major centre of activity of the avant-garde of the twenties. In the heady post-Revolutionary years, the *estridentistas* wrote Futurist poetry which, perhaps incongruously and in imitation of Russian Futurism, celebrated the machine and the city and man's release, through machines, from servile labour. *Estridentismo,* whose most important representative was Manuel Maples Arce (1900-), was short-lived. The great poetry of the twenties in Mexico was to be meditative, and influenced by English and North American movements rather than Futurism. The doyen was Alfonso Reyes (1889-1959), literary critic, scholar, thinker, a great believer in keeping open channels of communication with other cultures, particularly with Spain. A provocative and stimulating writer, he was preoccupied with Latin America's position in the world and was opposed both to narrow regionalism and slavish imitation. He believed that Latin American writers must deal with the archetypal human themes, though they had come late to 'the banquet of civilisation'. Some of his finest essays are devoted to the mythic vision of America.[13]

He had a lofty, 'Arielist' vision of culture. 'Ábrase paso la Inteligencia; reclame su sitio en la primera trinchera', he proclaimed in one of his speeches.[14] His poetry, which introduced the rhythms of English poetry into Castilian, reflects a cultured and erudite mind. Some of his best verse, however, is his evocation of places like Cuba, or the port of Vera Cruz where the sea is always at one's back though seldom in sight:

> La vecindad del mar queda abolida,
> Gañido errante de cobres y cornetas
> pasea en un tranvía.
> Basta saber que nos guardan las espaldas.
>
> (Atrás, una ventana inmensa y verde ...)
> El alcohol del sol pinta de azúcar
> los terrones fundentes de las casas.
> (... por donde echarse a nado)

The twenties and thirties were extraordinarily fertile periods for Mexican poetry. The magazine *Los Contemporáneos,* founded in 1928, brought together the work of a talented generation, which included Jaime Torres Bodet (1902-), Bernardo Ortiz de Montellano (1899-1949), Gilberto Owen (1905-52), Xavier Villaurrutia (1903-50), Carlos Pellicer (1899-), José Gorostiza (1901-), and Salvador Novo (1904-). Like Reyes, but unlike their contemporaries in the muralist movement, they were less concerned about Mexico's 'originality' and more with keeping open contact with the poetry movements of Europe and North America. *Los Contemporáneos* published an impressive number of translations of contemporary poets, including T. S. Eliot, but, apart from Salvador Novo, much of whose early poetry was ironic, mocking, and 'contemporary', the poets of the group were more concerned with the archetypal themes.[15] It is a poetry intensely concerned with the subconscious, with the polarities of Eros and Thanatos. And in Xavier Villaurrutia and José Gorostiza the movement produced two poets of extraordinary intensity and technical brilliance. Villaurrutia's greatest poems are the *Nocturnos* (1931), which invoke a dream-world in which certainties disappear, 'el latido de un mar en el que no sé nada, en el que no se nada'. The play on the word 'nada'—meaning either 'nothingness', or 'swims'—is characteristic, for his technique rested on verbal ambiguities. Many of his poems work on the principle of the Freudian slip, the almost unconscious association, the same phonemes signifying very different areas of experience. But Villaurrutia's night journeys always return upon themselves, to the inescapable image in the mirror, the journey to meet the self, the thirst, the lack of fulfilment, which is the essence of living, so that absence signifies presence and death life. In 'Nocturno amor', the poetry describes circles of frustration:

> y una sed que en el agua del espejo
> sacia su sed con una sed idéntica.

There is no escape from the cruel dialectic which only stops in death, like 'la estatua que despierta, en la alcoba de un mundo en el que todo ha muerto'. There is something 'fantasmal' about Villaurrutia's language, a constant pointing to the insubstantiality of words because of the ease of their transformation from one significance to another, as he himself indicates in the closing lines of 'Nocturno eterno':

> porque vida silencio piel y boca
> y soledad recuerdo cielo y humo
> nada son sino sombras de palabras
> que nos salen al paso de la noche.

If Villaurrutia betrays an awareness of the ghostliness of words, his friend and fellow-poet José Gorostiza is concerned with 'transparency', with purity. He wrote one of the finest poems of the period, 'Muerte sin fin',[16] which is about form and the tendency of all forms to disintegration; the image of the self is the glass of water in which the formless water takes on the form of the glass into which it is poured.

> un vaso
> que nos amolda el alma perdidiza,

Water is formless, flowing; it is like time which takes on form and
hence consciousness, becomes God, that which is pure consciousness
of itself. Form and substance can only exist when there is a consciousness to reflect them. But this is not life but death, a denial of the
nature of water which is to flow and terminate in a region of undifferentiated substance. To have form is to work against the essential
characteristic of the phenomenal world, but the formless cannot be
expressed. This is the complex antinomy of Gorostiza's poem:

> Porque el hombre descubre en sus silencios
> que su hermoso lenguaje se le agosta
> en el minuto mismo del quebranto,
> cuando los peces todos
> que en cautelosas órbitas discurren
> como estrellas de escamas, diminutas,
> por la entumida noche submarina,
> cuando los peces todos
> y el ulises salmón de los regresos
> y el delfín apolíneo, pez de dioses,
> deshacen su camino hacia las algas ...

It is interesting to compare this very sober, traditional language with
Neruda's and Vallejo's exploration of new forms and vocabulary at
the same period.

Two poets who were associated with the *Contemporáneos* group but
whose poetry was very different from that of Gorostiza and Villaurrutia
were Salvador Novo and Carlos Pellicer (1899-). Novo is far nearer to
the European avant-garde poetry of the time, and his first collection,
xx poemas (1925), had a self-conscious modernity:

> ¿Quién quiere jugar tennis con nopales y tunas
> sobre la red de los telégrafos?

But his poetry was urban and modern in a way that neither Villaurrutia nor Gorostiza could be. He was a poet, like the young Borges,
of city landscapes.

> Brochas de sol absurdo
> en la pared
> como en estantes hay
> vida en hogares interrumpidas.

In 1933, he published a poetic autobiography, *Espejo*, a series of lyric,
humorous poems, evoking his history lessons, the housemaids in his
home, and the books he read:

> ¿Qué se hicieron los gatos, los conejos,
> el Rey de la Selva, y la Zorra de las Uvas,
> los Cinco Guisantes, el Patito Feo?

Hace tiempos que no trato con esos animales
desde que me enseñaron que el hombre
es un ser superior, semejante a Dios.

The light mocking tone is characteristic of his early poetry, which was to turn bitter in *Poemas proletarios* (1934), although there was still a great deal of humour in his poem-pictures of 'Gaspar el Cadete', 'Roberto el Subteniente', and 'Bernardo el Soldado'. At the same time, he was writing the serious love-poetry of 'Nuevo amor' which is much closer in tone to the poetry of Gorostiza and Villaurrutia, but characteristically, in his fine poem 'La renovada muerte', he introduces the train as a modern image of absence and departure:

hay trenes por encima de toda la tierra
que lanzan unos dolorosos suspiros
y que parten
y la luna no tiene nada que ver
con las breves luciérnagas que nos vigilan
desde un azul cercano y desconocido
lleno de estrellas políglotas e innumerables.

In these lines, he situates himself outside the Romantic tradition and its concept of human destiny. The modern world is at once more complex, more enigmatic, and man's destiny infinitely less important and transcendental. In Carlos Pellicer's poetry, on the contrary, life prevails over death. His poetry is a poetry of nature, but a nature which is a reflection of the divine. Born in Tabasco, he transmits the colour and life of the tropics, which are present, even in the city:

En la ciudad, entre fuerzas automóviles
los hombres sudorosos beben agua en guanábanes.
Es la bolsa de semen de los trópicos
que huele a azul en carnes madrugadas
en el encanto lóbrego del bosque.

The reference to 'semen' is not gratuitous. For Pellicer, the tropics are a symbol of the inexhaustible creativity of God, regions of the earth where this creativity is still manifest because comparatively untouched by man:

La tierra, el agua, el aire, el fuego,
al Sur, al Norte, al Este, y al Oeste
concentran las semillas esenciales
el cielo de sorpresas
la desnudez intacta de las horas
y el ruido de las vastas soledades.

In these poems, the poet is the voice of the elemental, as Neruda was to be in his *Canto General,* but whereas Neruda is the poet of man's Fall, Pellicer still seems to inhabit a Paradise in which man and nature are not yet separated. In 'He olvidado mi nombre', he is completely identified with the landscape of Tabasco:

> El bien bañado río todo desnudo y fuerte,
> sin nombre de colores ni de cantos.
> Defendido del Sol con la hoja de tóh.
> Toda será posible menos llamarse Carlos.

There remains one thing to note in this Mexican poetry written in the first two decades after the Revolution, and that is the refusal of poets to write for anyone but an élite public. In the 1940s Neruda was to attack Mexican poets precisely on these grounds.[17] Except for certain poems of Salvador Novo, these are poems that divest language of history, that place themselves outside the historical flux, and this makes them quite different from the work of the two great poets of South America, Neruda and Vallejo.

V. CÉSAR VALLEJO (1892-1938)

César Vallejo is generally recognised as the greatest Spanish American poet; he achieved a personal style which, without being in any way regionalist, or local, was clearly American. He was a poet who rejected seduction. The flowing 'feminine' endings of Spanish poetry, the past participles—'ado', 'ido'—lend themselves easily to the rhythmic flow that Neruda was to adopt in his *Veinte poemas de amor,* in lines like:

> Mi alma no se contenta de haberla perdido

where the unstressed 'a's act like the rhythmic bass notes in a piano piece. If Vallejo ever feels the danger of seduction, he breaks the line. So one of his poems opens with:

> Tahona estuosa de aquellos mis bizcochos

in which the two first words seem to introduce a voluptuous rhythm which is quickly broken by the hard 'K' sound of 'aquellos mis bizcochos'. Some of his poems break up into a mishmash of letters and phonemes, as the limits of sense are reached and the poem passes over into dissolution.

Whereas much modern poetry stands up as an order in a chaotic world, Vallejo's verse excavates the ground beneath his own feet. Certainties crumble, familiar and comforting clichés are suddenly sinister. Thus, he ends one poem 'Hasta el hueso', which sounds similar enough to 'Hasta luego' to have a familiar ring until the reader receives the full impact of that alien 'hueso', which is isolated and bare as a skull on a monk's table. For the first time, we realise what we are saying when we utter the cliché 'hasta luego' and with realisation, we glimpse the abyss. Vallejo dislocated the Spanish language as never before, firstly because he wanted to make it express the inexpressible, but also because, like the *négritude* writers, he assumes an alien culture with the very language he is forced to use. The confrontation between the culture of Latin America and that of Europe is enacted in the linguistic tensions and in references such as the following:

Samain diría el aire es quieto y de una contenida tristeza.

Vallejo dice hoy la Muerte está soldando cada lindero a cada hebra de cabello perdido ...

The French poet Samain has his desperation under control, whereas Vallejo, the Peruvian, can only express his desperation in a sentence that hardly makes sense. But it is this quality of Vallejo, the rupturing of language and the piercing of convention, that makes him a truly outstanding poet.

César Vallejo was a *cholo,* of Spanish and Indian ancestry; a provincial born in Santiago de Chuco, which was some hours mule-ride from the town of Trujillo. He was very much the man of a marginal culture, a provincial, virtually self-educated as far as literature was concerned, for though he attended university and wrote a thesis on Romanticism, the cultural environments of Santiago de Chuco and of Trujillo were relatively poor. Vallejo was the youngest son of a large, modest, but united family in which the sense of traditional values was strong. The home and the church were important institutions in his young life, foundations of security that were drastically swept away from him when his mother and older brother, Miguel, died. These events cut at his roots and his ties with home, and helped to create in him that sense of the futility of the biological process in which life is carefully developed from seed to perfection for no discernible reason except the betterment of the species. To grow up was to greet the dawn of a senseless adult world:

> Y se acabó el diminutivo, para
> mi mayoría en el dolor sin fin
> y nuestro haber nacido así sin causa.

To call childhood 'the diminutive' deprives it of a human quality. Both 'diminutive'—a grammatical category—and *mayoría*—a legal one —deprive human growth of any transcendental purpose when the stages in growth become merely convenient categories.

Vallejo published four major collections of poetry. The first,

Los heraldos negros (1918), included mostly apprentice pieces in which the poet often used a traditional imagery (derived from Modernism), an imagery that was out of key with the kinds of sentiments he was trying to express. Christ on the cross is an inappropriately tragic image in some of the love-poems. And there are poems on Indian themes, the *Nostalgias imperiales* written in an objective, Parnassian style that is very alien to the dramatic mode of Vallejo's later poetry. Yet, even in this apprentice collection, there were anticipations of the mature Vallejo.

One group of poems included in *Los heraldos negros* were called 'Canciones de hogar' and in these, we have the foreshadowing of the imagery of *Trilce*. In these poems, Vallejo is already the observer or participant in his own drama. A helpless voyeur, he spies on the old age of his mother and father, watching their lives lose meaning:

> Mi padre es una víspera
> Lleva, trae, abstraído, reliquias, cosas,
> recuerdos, sugerencias.

The poetic lines here suggest a meaningless collecting of odds and ends, a pottering-about with no purpose, since purpose is simply pro-creation, the multiplication of the species in a future which the father will never see.

> Aún reirás de tus pequeñuelos
> y habrá bulla triunfal en los Vacíos

The determined optimism of this phrase in which the father still is given something to look forward to ends sharply and disagreeably on the noun 'Vacíos'.

In his next collection, *Trilce* (1922), Vallejo broke free of tradition completely, producing a poetry as startlingly new as anything being written in Europe. The poems use a scaffolding of 'positive' language —numbers, dates, places, scientific terms—but only to destroy the positive. Impossible structures are generated out of the linguistic system:

> 999 calorías
> Rumbbb ... Trraprrr rrach ... cha
> Serpentínica *u* del bizcochero
> engirafada al tímpano.

In the last two lines quoted, the structure is a possible Spanish structure, but there is no sense in speaking of a 'biscuit-vendor with a serpentine-like u giraffed onto the timpany'. And yet in a curious way there *is* meaning, for the expressive phonemes (Rumbbb, etc.) test the limits of language as does the distortion of sounds produced by the biscuit-seller whose 'u' is nothing like the sound we expect in 'bizcocho' and yet still conveys meaning.

Numbers are important in *Trilce*, but only because they indicate a sense of harmony and order which has been emptied of meaning. In cabbalistic terms, the one is symbol of wholeness, to Vallejo it is the symbol of the lonely individual; the two is the 'coupling' of male and female, to Vallejo it is the symbol of a purposeless dialectic; three is the symbol of the trinity and of perfection, to Vallejo it is a symbol of senseless generation; the four to the ancients represented the four elements, but for Vallejo it symbolises the four walls of the cell and man's limitations. There are other 'senseless' numbers too—the nine months of gestation, the twelve months of the year. But all alike are desacralised. Numbers are mere cyphers which, like the walls of the cell, either add stupidly to the same number or multiply into cyphers as empty as themselves.

The mathematical, the biological, the physical aspects of existence all tell the same story to Vallejo—that there is a disparity between the mental and spiritual drama of the individual and the biological and physical processes.

More tragic to Vallejo than the death of God is the death of the mother who was the source of his life. In the following poem, he contrasts the idea of the mother, origin of organic growth, with the abstract idea of transcending time and of unity.

Oh valle sin altura madre, donde todo duerme horrible mediatinta, sin ríos frescos, sin entradas de amor. Oh voces y ciudades que pasan cabalgando en un dedo tendido que señala a calva Unidad. Mientras pasan, de mucho en mucho, gañanes de gran costado sabio, detrás de las tres tardas dimensiones.
Hoy   Mañana   Ayer
(¡No, hombre!)

The fresh rivers and entrances of love refer to the human flux, and all attempts to transcend this lead to an abstract greyness, and hence to death. In this poem, Vallejo is seeing life from a God-like distance in which 'voices' and 'cities' are reduced to nothing and humanity is a mass of 'gañanes de gran costado sabio' (that is, of Adams from whom Eve sprang). These Adams are not scarce. They go by, 'de mucho en mucho', as if yoked to the three dimensions of time. The final 'No, hombre' rejects this abstract view (which would be that of a Schopenhauer, for instance), but the denial is a mere emotional response and in no way destroys the desolate vision.

For Vallejo, the physical confinement of prison life simply accentuated man's everyday existential situation. In *Trilce XVIII*, he does not simply use his cell as a primary image, but allows us to feel the irony of its religious connotations where cell was the place of retreat from the world and the threshold of salvation:

> Oh las cuatro paredes de la celda
> Ah las cuatro paredes albicantes
> que sin remedio dan al mismo número
>
> Criadero de nervios, mala brecha,
> por sus cuatro rincones cómo arranca
> las   diarias   aherrojadas   extremidades.

The 'albicante' (whitening) suggests the religious connotations, the cell as a place of purification or self-mortification which, however, does not offer any escape from the limitations of the four walls which always add up to the same number. Vallejo cannot escape through belief in God. Instead he appeals to the woman figure, the source of life:

> Amorosa llavera de innumerables llaves,
> si estuvieras aquí, si vieras hasta
> qué hora son cuatro estas paredes.
> Contra ellas seríamos contigo, los dos
> más dos que nunca. Y no lloraras,
> di, libertadora.

This is the return to the origins, to the source of life, but the limitations of the cell wall shift from a statement about space to one about time. The poet's attempt to form other more human combinations in order to break down his sense of separation cannot succeed. He is finally on his own; because separated by time from the source.

> Y sólo yo me voy quedando,
> con la diestra, que hace por ambas manos
> en alto, en busca de terciario brazo
> que ha de pupilar entre mi dónde y mi cuándo
> esta mayoría inválida de hombre

What the poet seeks is something beyond the limitations of extension (dónde) and time (cuándo). He transforms the interrogative adverbs into nouns, making them substantive and at the same time infinitely more suggestive of the human duration than if he had used the abstractions 'space' or 'time'. The poet's raised arm seeks but does not find the arm that will mediate for him, but the language skilfully suggests the monk's cell, once again, with the saint's arm raised towards a heaven. The poem thus moves between the two tensions of the limitations of earth and the impossibility of heaven which result in the final contradiction—the 'mayoría inválida'—where the idea of the 'majority' (maturity and adulthood and hence a kind of perfection) is qualified by the adjective 'invalid'.

What is original in this poem is not any 'theme' that can be isolated, since the conflict between eternal aspirations and existential situation is as old as time. The originality lies in Vallejo's entirely modern presentation, in the constant ironic reference to the values of the past and the dramatisation of the situation in the poet's own self.

Vallejo's posthumously published poems were given an ironic title, *Poemas humanos*, ironic since many of them convey a dehumanised, alienated humanity. From 1923 to the end of his life he had lived in Paris, with brief visits to Russia, to Spain, where he was forced to stay in 1931 when the French government would not allow him into France (because of his work as a militant). He was also in Spain for two short visits during the Civil War and wrote a number of Civil War poems, published posthumously under the title *España aparta de mí este cáliz*.[18] After joining the Communist Party in 1931, Vallejo's political activity was intense, and his articles on Russia written for the Spanish press in 1931 show that he shared the social and political ideals of the Marxists.[19] However, the *Poemas humanos* present an agonised view of the individual; they were written out of despair when the sum of individuals did not seem to him to make up a society.

> ¿Quién no se llama Carlos o cualquier otra cosa?
> ¿Quién al gato no dice gato, gato?
> ¡Ay, yo que sólo he nacido solamente!
> ¡Ay, yo que sólo he nacido solamente!

Indistinguishable individuals form the mass, but this mass cannot break down the sense of aloneness. The verb 'nacer' is surrounded by adverbs, but they are the same adverb, ringing the changes on 'only', 'alone', and isolating the idea of birth and loneliness.

This is why the title of *Poemas humanos* has an ironic ring. In *Trilce* the situation is generally subjective, with Vallejo at the centre of a drama, attempting to wrestle with abstractions like time, creation, eternity, death in meaningful language. But in *Poemas humanos* Vallejo *becomes* humanity, condemned to incarnate the Son; in these poems he and other individuals are reduced, become a bundle of habits, clothes, illnesses whose only power—absurdly—is that of reproduction. The title of one poem—'Sombrero, abrigo, guantes'—sums this up:

> Enfrente a la Comedia Francesa, está el Café
> de la Regencia; en él hay una pieza
> recóndita, con una butaca y una mesa.
> Cuando entro, el polvo inmóvil se ha puesto ya de pie.
>
> Entre mis labios hechos de jebe, la pavesa

de un cigarillo humea, y en el humo se ve
dos humos intensivos, el tórax del Café,
y en el tórax, un óxido profundo de tristeza.

Importa que el otoño se injerte en los otoños
importa que el otoño se integre de retoños,
la nube, de semestres; de pómulos, la arruga.

Importa oler a loco postulando
¡qué cálida es la nieve, qué fugaz la tortuga,
el cómo qué sencillo, qué fulminante el cuando!

The inner room turns into the 'thorax' of the café. Inwardness, from
being a spiritual state, becomes a physical one so that with Vallejo we
enter into a body with its accompanying associations of degeneration.
But now the poet turns to contrasting the café/body (that is, the human
environment) with the changing seasons. Seasonal change is 'important', a word that becomes, in the context, an absurd understatement.
On the other hand it is absurd to try and turn the back on the
seasons by stating that snow is hot, or by rhetorically defying physical
laws. The sonnet ends on a note of paradox with human life reduced
to the two main questions—the single 'how' and the final 'when'. What
has happened in the course of the poem is that the poet has demonstrated that all the supports of human life—tradition, culture, nature
—are simply the 'sombrero, abrigo, guantes' of the title, the essence
lying in that naked 'cuando'.

The 'thorax' of this poem leads us to one of Vallejo's major preoccupations—his obsession with the body which he constantly seems
to be examining as if it were an alien thing: [20]

Que es verdad que sufrí en aquel hospital que queda al lado
y está bien y está mal haber mirado
de abajo para arriba mi organismo.

It is this fragile body which stands between him and death. And in
certain moods, he feels that he wants life at any price.

Me gustaría vivir siempre, así fuese de barriga,

he declares, alluding to La Pasionaria's 'It is better to die on your
feet than to live on your knees'. In 'Dos niños anhelantes', he finds
'nada/en el orgullo grave de la célula,/Sólo la vida; así: cosa
bravísima'—which conjures up a vision of an unheroic, diminutive,
enslaved man, whose life is lived as a waiting for death:

luego no tengo nada y hablo solo,
reviso mis semestres
y para henchir mi vértebra, me toco.

The fact that many of the poems were written during the depression adds to their tragic tone. Vallejo is not simply seeing his own end as a man, but the end of progress, the termination of a certain kind of civilisation. In the apocalyptic poem 'Los nueve monstruos', the magic number nine points to the end of the world. The poet has a vision of hyperbolic suffering and evil. What progresses is not man, but unhappiness:

> Crece la desdicha, hermanos hombres,
> más pronto que la máquina, a diez máquinas, y crece
> con la res de Rousseau, con nuestras barbas;

The theory of progress based on the supposed goodness of human nature cannot take into account this vast recrudescence of evil in which even nature is crucified.[21]

In *Poemas humanos*, Vallejo glimpses the inadequacies of any view of progress which does not take into account that man is limited in space and time and is, in fact, anything but a superman. The difficulty comes about when man visualises progress towards future perfection, since progress itself obviously comes up against these limits. It is here that the depression, mass unemployment, starvation—i.e., public reality—invades the private world. 'The stoppage', the unemployed man seated upon a stone, are living symbols of the stopping of progress in both a social and an individual sense.

> Parado en una piedra,
> desocupado,
> astroso, espeluznante,
> a la orilla del Sena, va y viene.
> Del río brota entonces la conciencia,
> con peciolo y rasguños de árbol ávido:
> del río sube y baja la ciudad, hecha de lobos abrazados.

The contrast between man 'parado' and the flowing river is accentuated by the fact that the man has become a thing. It is the river which has consciousness, but it is a consciousness of an evolutionary progress and of the survival of the fittest. The city arises directly out of this natural law and epitomises the Darwinian struggle of 'wolves embracing'. The man who sits there is a 'parado, individual entre treinta millones de parados', a 'nothing' who sits alone with his body, his bugs, and:

> abajo
> más abajo,
> un papelito, un clavo, una cerilla.

The production of this 'ciudad' is merely this detritus—both human and the material rubbish of civilisation.

Poemas humanos thus deepen the sense of crisis between man and society. They demonstrate that man cannot find sense by projecting into a future when he might be different or society might be different. A society in industrial crisis offered only hopelessness to man; however, this did not mean that Vallejo himself was entirely without faith. His communism was not of a Utopian variety, because he did not believe in any mystical future, but he certainly believed strongly that injustices must be fought. It is therefore unfortunate that *Poemas humanos* should have been published separately from *España aparta de mí este cáliz* which is the other side of the coin.[22] In these poems, he finds the modern hero in men like Pedro Rojas:

> Lo han matado, obligándole a morir
> a Pedro, a Rojas, al obrero, al hombre, a aquel
> que nació muy niñín mirando al cielo,
> y que luego creció, se puso rojo
> y luchó con sus células, sus nos, sus todavías, sus hambres, sus
> pedazos.

The man who glimpses Apocalypse in 'Los nueve monstruos' now salutes 'el sufrimiento armado'. The mother who dies and leaves him without eternity is now resurrected, as Spain. Thus he addresses the world in the words of a mother addressing her children:

> si tardo
> si no veis a nadie, si os asustan
> los lápices sin punta, si la madre
> España cae—digo, es un decir—
> salid, niños del mundo; id a buscarla!

Vallejo's poetry operates as a dramatisation of destruction. Both *Trilce* and *Poemas humanos* are set in a nightmare region in which the poet solders fragments only to have them break again. The poem is like a shoring of a sea-washed dike. But perhaps the supreme paradox is that Vallejo was a communist who lived the crisis of individualism to its extreme limit.

VI. PABLO NERUDA (1904-)

Born Neftalí Reyes in Chile, son of a train-driver, Neruda came from a provincial background that at first sight seems similar to that of Vallejo. But, whereas Vallejo was brought up in a traditional community whose moral order centred on family and church, Neruda's boyhood was passed in the extreme south of Chile in a pioneer community. Vallejo's poetry turns against tradition, ruptures language, tears old myths apart; Neruda's, on the other hand, stems from quite a different relation to modern culture. His poetry is the direct expression of a natural force:

> La naturaleza allí me daba una especie de embriaguez. Yo tendría unos diez años, pero ya era poeta. No escribía versos, pero me atraían los pájaros, los escarabajos, los huevos de perdiz.[23]

Living in an area without traditions, where the 'first man to publish poetry south of the Bío Bío' was a friend of the family, growing up among workers who, as he later pointed out, were mostly irreligious, Neruda's childhood was unstructured whereas Vallejo's had been very strongly structured by a scaffolding of custom and belief. Whereas Vallejo desacralised words in order to bend them to his new conditions, Neruda used a vocabulary drawn direct from his experiences of nature to suffuse a crumbling society with pioneer energy and freshness.

His journey to Santiago at the age of sixteen and his lonely years in boarding houses and cafés were the traumatic events that probably made him a poet.

His first collection, *Crepusculario* (1920-23), was derivative. But in 1924, he published *Veinte poemas de amor* (1924), the book in which, as he later explained, he had solaced the loneliness of city life. The *Veinte poemas* and the 'canción desesperada' with which the volume ended constituted a diary of two affairs, his love for the dark girl he had left in Temuco, evocative of sadness and absence, time and loss, and the Santiago girl through whom he attempts to seize the present.[24] These are true poems of adolescence—aggressive and self-centred—and they shift restlessly between two lives, the one he had left and the one he was living with, between dark and light, absence and possession:

> En su llama mortal la luz te envuelve.
> Absorta, pálida doliente, así situada
> contra las viejas hélices del crepúsculo
> que en torno a ti da vueltas.
>
> Muda, mi amiga,
> sola en lo solitario de esta hora de muertes
> y llena de las vida del fuego,
> pura heredera del día destruido.
>
> Del sol cae un racimo en tu vestido oscuro.
> De la noche las grandes raíces
> crecen de súbito desde tu alma,
> y a lo exterior regresan las cosas en ti ocultas,
> de modo que un pueblo pálido y azul
> de ti recién nacido se alimenta.

> Oh grandiosa y fecunda y magnética esclava
> del círculo que en negro y dorado sucede:
> erguida, trata y logra una creación tan viva
> que sucumben sus flores, y llena es de tristeza.

The woman here is a daughter of time, is time's slave reflecting the night/death and sun/recreation cycle. The sun's fruit (*racimo*), the night's roots, the flowers of creation all have their origin in her. She is completely identified with the natural cycle, with birth and death, with phoenix-like creation out of destruction. And yet at the same time, we also have a visual picture of a woman sitting alone at twilight receiving the colour of the blazing sun while at the centre of gathering darkness. The poet is on the outside, the observer, who cannot break into the silence and solitude of the woman. A Schopenhauerian sadness on which this poem ends pervades many of the *Veinte poemas*.

Whereas Vallejo's poetry was slow to reach a public, the *Veinte poemas* were immediately acclaimed. The collection attracted by its freedom and naturalness. The rhythm comes from the skilful grouping of three- or four-syllable phrases, the use of easy internal rhymes, 'desbocado, violento, estirado', etc., or from repetition of words, 'el vaho del mar, la soledad del mar'. The mingling of colloquial expressions with a heightened imagery that came from the elements and from nature gave the poetry a spontaneous effect. Many young poets were to believe that they could write like Neruda and many tried, but none were able to reproduce the inexhaustible flow of his poetry, uninterrupted since childhood. In 1925 he published a collection of poetry, *Tentativa del hombre infinito*, and a novel, *El habitante y su esperanza*, which showed the influence of Surrealism. *Tentativa* is still reminiscent of *Veinte poemas*, though it is more experimental and there is less cohesion. The metaphors often seem to stand out on their own:

> cuando aproximo el cielo con las manos para despertar completa-
> mente sus húmedos terrones su red confusa se suelta.

or

> oh cielo tejido con aguas y papeles.

They are images without a theme, floating free from the poetic imagination. A few years later, during a period of intense solitude and isolation when he lived as Chilean consul in Rangoon, India, and Java, Neruda published his two volumes of *Residencia en la tierra*, in which images of great force and energy cluster around a single field. As he himself explained, *Residencia* was a collection that arose out of a single obsession 'Todo tiene igual movimiento, igual presión, y está desarrollado en la misma región de mi cabeza, como una misma clase de insistentes olas'.[25] In them, the poet expresses his awareness of dissolution, decay; entropy not growth is understood as the important law of nature. So in 'Unidad', he exclaims 'Me rodea una misma cosa, un solo movimiento'. In these poems a searching, microscopic vision monitors the passage of time whose touch contaminates even the most solid of objects. In 'El fantasma del buque de carga', the entire poem is a metaphor of this 'solo movimiento'. The cargo boat struggles to persist in its own being against the force of the waters, but the enemy is within and each object receives the invisible corrosive touch of the 'phantom':

> Observa con sus ojos sin color, sin mirada,
> lento, y pasa temblando, sin presencia ni sombra:
> los sonidos lo arrugan, las cosas lo traspasan,
> su transparencia hace brillar las sillas sucias.

But human identity is as fragile. In 'Caballo de los sueños', the poet cannot discover any essential 'I' in the trivial fragments that make up his everyday life:

> Innecesario, viéndome en los espejos
> con un gusto a semanas, a biógrafos, a papeles
> arranco de mi corazón al capitán del infierno
> establezco cláusulas indefinidamente tristes.

So life is dominated by this stately procession towards death; everyday life can only be grasped as triviality and absurdity. In these poems, Neruda is at his best, when he can extend and proliferate an analogy, as in 'El fantasma del buque de carga' or 'El sur del océano' where the moon, symbol of seasonal change and of the passage of time, becomes a kind of rag-picker, gathering the dispersed fragments of drowned men:

> cuando en el saco de la luna caen,
> los trajes sepultados en el mar,
> con sus largos tormentos, sus barbas derribadas,
> sus cabezas que el agua y el orgullo pidieron para siempre
> en la extensión se oyen caer rodillas
> hacia el fondo del mar traídas por la luna
> en su saco de piedra gastado por las lágrimas
> y por las mordeduras de pescados siniestros.

The moon attracts death, like the force of gravity. This nightmare image has an exactness and links scientific fact with literary tradition. The seeming chaotic imagery—'trajes', 'barbas', 'cabezas', 'rodillas'—reinforces the fragmentary impression. Death is not suffered integrally but simply as unimportant fragments. Neruda's vision of death in *Residencia en la tierra* is closely linked to his vision of the city. For it is in the city that organic growth, the life of nature which might counteract or alleviate despair, is absent.

Impressive as it was, *Residencia en la tierra* was only one aspect of Neruda's career as a poet. During the 1930s he was in Spain where he was appointed Chilean consul to Barcelona and here he edited the avant-garde poetry magazine *Caballo verde para la poesía* in which he called for 'impure poetry' that would smell of life, and would break away from the arid abstractions of pure poetry. At the outbreak of the Civil War in Spain he took an active part in appealing for aid and securing the evacuation of children. The poetic diary of these years is a third volume of *Residencia en la tierra* in which he wrote of personal anguish, his sense of aloneness, of being 'vegetalmente solo', of sexual love in 'Furias y penas', and of the Spanish Civil War in *España en mi corazón*. In 1939, he wrote a disclaimer to 'Furias y penas' in which he declared:

> En 1934 fue escrito este poema. ¡Cuántas cosas han
> sobrevenido desde entonces! España, donde lo escribí,
> es una cintura de ruinas. ¡Ay! si con sólo una gota de
> poesía o de amor pudiéramos aplacar la ira del mundo,
> pero eso sólo lo pueden la lucha y el corazón resuelto.

He was now moving from solitude and despair to militancy. In 1937 and 1938, he was active in the Popular Front movement, so much so that he had little time for poetry:

> Pero he avanzado por otro camino, he llegado a tocar el corazón
> desnudo de mi pueblo y a realizar con orgullo que en él vive un
> secreto más fuerte que la primavera, más fertil y más sonoro que
> la avena y el agua, el secreto de la verdad, que mi humilde, solitario
> y desamparado pueblo saca del fondo de su duro territorio ...[26]

At this moment, Neruda's past flows harmoniously into his present. He identifies the people with that subterranean, organic power that alone could withstand the forces of destruction; his membership of the Communist Party was the logical outcome of his position, and his epic poem, *Canto general*, begun in 1938 and finished in 1950, the supreme monument to this period of his life. It was a period in which he lived for three years in Mexico in the diplomatic service, became Senator, and, because of his defence of miners, fell out of favour with President González Videla and had to escape from Santiago.

Notwithstanding the enormous volume and the excellence of the poetry that Neruda has since written, the *Canto general* will remain his masterpiece. In it, the adolescent who came from the woods of southern Chile as the voice of nature, who suffered alienation in the city, becomes the voice of humanity itself. The construction of the poem reveals his new historical consciousness; it proceeds in fifteen cantos from the invocation of America before man—('La lámpara en la tierra' symbolises man's submerged consciousness)—to the final assumption of his own responsibility as a militant and a poet in the final section 'Yo soy'. In between this genesis and finale, the poet becomes the voice of the silent, anonymous oppressed victims of pre-Columban civilisations in 'Alturas de Macchu Picchu'; he recalls the 'Conquerors', the 'Liberators', and the 'Traitors' who have forged the history of America. In the sixth section, 'América, no invoco tu nombre en vano', he sums up this 'night' of America and invokes the dawn of workers' fraternity. The second part of the epic he calls the 'Canto general de Chile'; it is the celebration of his native land, of the anonymous worker and peasant heroes of 'La tierra se llama Juan'; and he includes a section, 'Que despierte el leñador', in which he pleads with the spirit of Lincoln to waken the North American continent and arouse them, 'contra el mercader de su sangre'. Sections 11 to 15 of the epic relate Neruda's personal experience—the strikes in 'Las flores de Punitaqui', the invocation of his 'patria en tinieblas', 'El gran océano,' and finally his own life and faith in 'Yo soy'.

The historical perspective of *Canto general* was new, but many aspects of the poem are in the tradition of the Spanish American epic, from Bello and Gutiérrez González to Lugones. The 'naming' of American nature, the praise of honest toil and the unassuming lives of ordinary people, already formed part of a literary tradition, although no other epic poem attained the magnificence and scope of the *Canto general*. Above all there is superb orchestration: the major themes are stated, developed, and then reappear in a new key. Again and again, world/country/individual, geography/land/the single plant or organism are joined in new connections. The cosmic and the microcosmic obey the same laws of growth and development; and tyranny and class are the evils of civilisation which destroy man and land and prevent their true fulfilment. One of the finest sections of the poem, 'Las alturas de Macchu Picchu', is a micro-epic within the epic, for it traces the growth of the political and historical conscious-ness of Neruda from an empty individualism to assumption of his role as the voice of the oppressed. Consisting of twelve sections, the poem describes a descent into the self, the ascent to the Inca ruins of Macchu Picchu, which is also a journey into the past, and the poet's vision of the anonymous builders of the city. The Neruda who had described himself as 'vegetalmente solo' in 'Bruselas' now faces the triviality of his life, which has not even the importance of the ever repeated natural cycle:

(Lo que en el cereal como una historia amarilla
de pequeños pechos preñados va repitiendo un número
que sin cesar es ternura en las capas germinales
y que idéntica siempre, se desgrana en marfil ...)

Neither individualism nor human suffering can give the poet the basis
on which to build his life:

> Entonces en la escala de la tierra he subido
> entre la atroz maraña de las selvas perdidas
> hasta ti, Macchu Picchu.

This is a 'pilgrim's progress' with the landscape serving as a moral
correlative. 'Macchu Picchu' symbolises man pitting himself against
nature, defying nature, 'una permanencia de piedra y de palabra', but
built 'de tanta muerte'.

To erect Macchu Picchu was to defy man's ephemerality and to
'contain' the silence of death, though, paradoxically, the fortress is
built on the death and exploitation of 'el esclavo que enterraste'; yet
the poet still believes that Macchu Picchu represents an 'aurora'.
With its construction, humanity emerged into history and hence into
time. This is why the poet seeks to see beyond the perfection and
beauty of the stones and resuscitate the human beings who had constructed them:

> Déjame olvidar, ancha piedra, la proporción poderosa,
> la trascendente medida, las piedras del panal,
> y de la escuadra déjame hoy resbalar,
> la mano sobre la hipotenusa de áspera sangre y cilicio.

The historical parts of the poem represent a revision of official history. Labourers, fishermen, carpenters, become the new heroes. The
heroes of history find their supremacy challenged. Valdivia, the conqueror of Chile, is described as 'el verdugo'; it is the Indian victims
of the conquerors, and Bartolomé de las Casas, their defender, who
are celebrated by the poet. Curiously the weakest parts of the poem
are those which deal with events that were very close to Neruda—
the death of the wife of the Brazilian leader Carlos Prestes in a gas
chamber, and his own persecution by González Videla, the 'Judas
enarbolado'. Here, the portentous vocabulary is often too weighty.
Events which seemed important in the 1940s have already slid lower
down the scale of historical evaluation. But this scarcely matters. So
much of the poem attains a grandiose vision unequalled in modern
times. The religious awe of nature whose purity informs the poem
is conveyed in the magnificent litanies of the 'Alturas de Macchu
Picchu' and 'Antárctica', in which he likens the frozen blocks of ice to
cathedrals.

> nave desbocada
> sobre la catedral de la blancura,
> inmoladero de quebrados vidrios ...

The vast poem is sustained by this religious sense of nature which the young Neruda had first absorbed in the countryside of Temuco and which had, for him, supplanted Christian indoctrination. Not surprisingly his vision of the good society which comes at the end of the section 'Las flores de Punitaqui' is of man's return to an organic life:

> Sobre esta claridad irá naciendo
> la granja, la ciudad, la minería,
> y sobre esta unidad como la tierra
> firme y germinadora se ha dispuesto
> la creadora permanencia, el germen
> de la nueva ciudad para las vidas.

In this section, work is not seen as a form of alienation but as an extension of man's relation with nature; like bread coming from corn, so will the country be 'kneaded' by the hands of workmen; its new order will be that of the fishermen 'como un ramo del mar'. Neruda's vision is a coherent one, and is, in short, that of a return to a society very near that of Temuco.

When Neruda was writing *Canto general*, he was already thinking of a public of 'simple people', as different as possible from the literary élite or the small, divided groups of Latin American avant-gardistes. One of the moving experiences of his life was his first reading of poems to a workers' meeting[27] in 1938 and his subsequent feeling that 'estaba en deuda con mi país, con mi pueblo'. As he was writing *Canto general*, he would read sections to audiences at political meetings. And in Mexico, arguing against the Mexican poet Octavio Paz, he declared his belief that 'Toda creación que no esté al servicio de la libertad en estos días de amenaza total, es una traición'. In *Canto general*, the political intention is clear, but the politics are subsumed under a broad human category. The language and style of the poem is less hermetic than the poetry of *Residencia*, though sections like 'Alturas de Macchu Picchu' could scarcely be referred to as 'simple'. Neruda borrows the techniques of rhetoric, using repetition, reiteration, litany-like naming of attributes, and a rhythmic verse line dictated by the breath-lengths of speech. After publishing *Canto general*, Neruda wrote *Las uvas y el viento*, about his political journeyings during the Cold War period. Yet his creativity was such that these new directions did not erase his old preoccupations and he published anonymously in Naples a series of love-poems, *Los versos del capitán* (1952), which celebrated his love for the woman who later became his third wife. He acknowledged the authorship a decade later after his marriage. *Los versos del capitán* represent a poetic diary of the passion and quarrels of that first meeting; far from being an aberration from his political poetry, they heralded a love-poetry of maturity which was to be one of his most persistent obsessions. However, it was not so much in the overtly political poems nor in the love-poems that the Neruda of the fifties reconciled the public and private spheres. This was, above all, the period of his *Odas elementales*, short-lined, buoyant poetry which celebrated wood, air, copper, poverty, laziness, but most of all the 'simple people', who in Neruda's eyes were nearly always represented, not by skilled factory-workers, but by the older trades:

> los que en la altura
> de la vertical cordillera
> pican piedra,
> clavan tablas,
> cosen ropa,
> cortan leña
> muelen tierra ...

Neruda had already expressed his joy in simple things in the 'Tres cantos materiales' which formed such a contrast to the tragic tone of *Residencia en la tierra*. In the *Odas elementales*, the poems to the artichoke, the onion, and the tomato express this sensual joy in the vegetable world. There is a tenderness in his description of the artichoke as there was in that of the celery:

> La alcachofa
> de tierno corazón
> se vistió de guerrero,
> erecto, construyó
> una pequeña cúpula.

One might object to the intention of these poems on the grounds that 'simple' people are not necessarily interested in such basic things, but the objection is irrelevant to the poetry. In a continent where poets are tempted by abstractions and generalisations, this careful observation of the material and natural world operated as a corrective. Besides, Neruda's humour in poems such as 'A la pereza' was also salutary. He was to allow it full rein in the most delightful of his collections, *Estravagario*, which as the title suggests is devoted to fantasy. In this collection, he harnessed the creative imagination, previously expressed in poems such as 'El fantasma del buque de carga', to a new theme. In these poems, Neruda is natural man, the enemy of convention, and one of the finest poems in the collection, 'Fábula de la sirena y los borrachos', could stand as an allegory for himself.

> Todos estos señores estaban dentro
> cuando ella entró completamente desnuda

ellos habían bebido y comenzaron a escupirla
ella no entendía nada recién salía del río
era una sirena que se había extraviado.

The mermaid is like an albatross, an image of the poet; she is outside
her natural element and subject to the hatred and scorn of those who
do not understand:

ella no hablaba porque no sabía hablar
sus ojos eran color de amor distante
sus brazos construídos de topacios gemelos
sus labios se cortaron en la luz del coral
y de pronto salió por esa puerta
apenas entró al río quedó limpia
relució como una piedra blanca en la lluvia
y sin mirar atrás nadó de nuevo
nadó hacia nunca más hacia morir.

In this strange allegory, the mermaid chooses purity and death rather
than the degraded tavern and misunderstanding. Natural and elemental
life conflicts with 'inmundicia' of the tavern. Once again the pioneer's
son from Temuco faces the city. After *Estravagario* Neruda's poetry
tends to repeat with undiminished vigour the patterns of his previous
verse. There is always the threefold interest—the odes about simple
things; love which he again celebrates in *Cien sonetos de amor*; and
nature in *Arte de pájaros*. But there is a new element. Neruda had
built a house by the sea in Isla Negra which he first visited in 1939.
Increasingly Isla Negra and the seascape dominate the later poetry.
In *Las piedras de Chile*, he evokes the rocky landscape around his
home:

Yo vine a vivir a Isla Negra en el año 1939 y la costa estaba
sembrada de portentosas presencias de piedras y éstas han
conversado conmigo en un lenguaje ronco y mojado,
mezcla de gritos marinos y advertencias primordiales.

and *Cantos ceremoniales*, in which he collected a miscellany on divers
themes, was also full of the ocean and the island. In 1964, Neruda
published his *Memorial de Isla Negra*, a 5-volume poetic biography
which recalled the whole of his life and which ended on a new note
of tranquillity, in 'El futuro es espacio' where the river flows into
the sea:

Adelante, salgamos
del río sofocante
en que con otros peces navegamos
desde el alba a la noche migratoria
y ahora en este espacio descubierto
volvemos a la pura soledad.

His later collections, *Una casa en la arena* and *La barcarola*, achieve an almost religious sense of resignation:

> Es tarde ya. Tal vez
> sólo fue un largo día color de miel y azul,
> tal vez sólo una noche, como el párpado
> de una grave mirada que abarcó
> la medida del mar que nos rodeaba,
> y en este territorio fundamos sólo un beso,
> sólo inasible amor que aquí se quedará
> vagando entre la espuma del mar y las raíces.

and in one of the most recent poems, 'La barcarola termina', he prefaces his verse with the words:

> (De pronto el día rápido se transformó en tristeza y así la barcarola que crecía cantando se calla y permanece la voz sin movimiento.)

Neruda's poetry has always followed closely the natural rhythms of human life. Aggressive in adolescence, obsessed by death in early manhood, political and social in maturity. Now, with the advancing years, the poetry flows unchecked, confronting the darkness of the time but still seeing hope in a general awakening or in perpetual sleep. Growing up as he did within the freedom of a pioneer community, imbued with a sense of freshness and purity of the environment, modern life was always measured against the organic power of vegetable life. Man, like trees and plants, must have roots and branches and contact with the four elements in order to survive and this is precisely what industrial society takes away, choking the human lifeline. For Neruda, communism was the restoration of this natural state, the most human of goals.

VII. OCTAVIO PAZ (1914-)

Octavio Paz, the other outstanding living Spanish American poet, is a Mexican; son of one of Zapata's representatives in New York, he has moved far from the revolutionary nationalism of his parents' generation. Yet his poetry, like Neruda's, has its roots in his childhood. In 'Soliloquio de medianoche', written in Berkeley in 1944, he wrote:

> mi infancia, mi sepultada infancia,
> inocencia salvaje domesticada con palabras, preceptos con palabras
> agua pura, espejo para el árbol y la nube,
> que tantas virtuosas almas enturbiaron.

One might summarise Paz's main achievement as the freeing of words from 'preceptos' and from 'domesticación'. Yet—and this may seem paradoxical—given his suspicion of precepts, of the major Latin American poets, he is the only one who has contributed much to the theory of poetry. He is an accomplished essay writer, author of a classic analysis of Mexican characters, *El laberinto de la soledad* (1950), of a work on the history and nature of poetry, *El arco y la lira* (1956), and of collections of essays on poets and poetic movements, which include *Los signos en rotación* (1965), *Cuadrivio, Las peras del olmo* (1958), and *Corriente alterna* (1967). In addition he has written works on the anthropologist Claude Lévi-Strauss, *Claude Lévi-Strauss o el nuevo festín de Esopo* (1969), on Marcel Duchamp, in *Marcel Duchamp or the Castle of Purity*, as well as *Conjunciones y disyunciones* (1969), a book that contrasted Eastern and Western notions of the body.

Paz's ideas on poetry are summed up in *El arco y la lira* and they derive from a tradition of modern poetry that includes the German Romantics, Rimbaud, Apollinaire, and the Surrealists. For him, poetry is the queen of the arts, and indeed of all human activities. The aim of poetry is not to control words and matter, but to free them and restore them to their primitive magic.

> Palabras, sonidos, colores y demás materiales sufren una transmutación apenas ingresan en el círculo de la poesía.[28]

The freeing of words consists in releasing them from 'usefulness', from their function as instruments of communication.

> Durante un momento la palabra deja de ser un eslabón más en la cadena del lenguaje y brilla sola, a medio camino entre la exclamación y el pensamiento puro. Lo poético la obliga a volver sobre sí misma, a regresar a sus orígenes.[29]

The central experience of poetry is to abstract the reader from duration and return to original time. Paz describes the experience thus:

> La experiencia poética, como la religiosa, es un salto mortal: un cambiar de naturaleza que es también un regresar a nuestra naturaleza original.[30]

Poetry even when we forget the actual words stays with us, the 'alta marea que rompió los diques de la sucesión temporal'.

It follows that Paz's view of poetry is totally different from that of a Neruda, 'the voice of nature', or of Vallejo who was not so much freeing words as dislocating them. *El arco y la lira* gives a detailed account of Paz's theory of poetry. In it he studies rhythm, linking poetic rhythm with universal and archetypal patterns, with

Yin and Yang, union, and separation. He equates poetry with religion and love as processes of revelation. 'El poeta revela al hombre creándolo'.

Paz does not ignore the historical and social aspects of poetry. His main interest is, however, in the modern movements from Blake, Hölderlin, Nerval, Rimbaud down to Surrealism, movements which considered the poet to be the outsider from society, holding values that are subversive to it.

Paz's opinions on poetry remained substantially unchanged and many of the assertions of *El arco y la lira* are found again, in a more epigrammatic form, in *Corriente alterna*:

> El ritmo es la metáfora original y contiene a todas las otras.
>
> Dice: la sucesión es repetición, el tiempo es no-tiempo.
> Cada lector es otro poeta; cada poema, otro poema.
> En perpetuo cambio, la poesía no avanza.
> La poesía es nuestro único recurso contra el tiempo rectilíneo—contra el progreso.
>
> La poesía es lucha perpetua contra la significación. Dos extremos: el poema abarca todos los significados, es el significado, de todas las significaciones; el poema niega toda significación al lenguaje. En la época moderna la primera tentativa es la de Mallarmé; la segunda, la de Dadá.

We are now in a position to understand the sources of inspiration of Paz's own poetry, his insistence that poetic 'time' is something other than lived time or duration, that poetry is ontological, that its language must subsume immense varieties and even the contradictions of experience. A perfectionist, he has defied the usual chronological approach to his poetry by ordering and changing different editions of his collection *Libertad bajo palabra*, which included poetry written between 1935 and 1957. (His earlier poems are included in the second edition, of 1968.) In 1933, he had published *Luna silvestre*, an apprentice collection, at a time when he was editing a number of poetic journals, including *Barandal* (founded in 1931) and *Cuadernos del Valle de México* (founded in 1933). In 1938, he founded the important magazine *Taller*, the title suggesting the careful elaboration which he brought to his poetry. *Libertad bajo palabra*, his first major collection, reflected his basic preoccupations with love, time, solitude, with poetry as revelation, and the word as the key to human freedom:

> Contra el silencio y el bullicio inventa la palabra
> libertad que se inventa y me inventa cada día.

But in so far as there has been a progression in Paz's poetry, one can note that the early poems grew out of an almost solipsistic view of experience, a sense of human solitude and that the poet has moved increasingly towards poetic revelation as the instrument of human liberation and change. Thus some early poems, 'Nocturno', 'Insomnio', 'Espejo', are clearly related to the poetry of the *Contemporáneos*. In 'La calle', for instance, included in the group of poems 'Puerta condenada', the poet writes:

> Es una calle larga y silenciosa.
> Ando en tinieblas y tropiezo y caigo
> y me levanto y piso con pies ciegos
> las piedras mudas y las hojas secas
> y alguien detrás de mí también las pisa:
> si me detengo, se detiene;
> si corro, corre. Vuelve el rostro: nadie.
> Todo está oscuro y sin salida,
> y doy vueltas y vueltas en esquinas
> que dan siempre a la calle
> donde nadie me espera ni me sigue,
> donde yo sigo a un hombre que tropieza
> y se levanta y dice al verme; nadie.

This poem reflects two absences—absence of progress, absence of communication. 'Todo está oscuro y sin salida/y doy vueltas' ... Yet the poem has a nightmare sense of following and being followed: and the moment the poet comes face to face with the 'other', the self has become 'nadie'. What strikes the reader is, however, the very abstract plane on which the transaction takes place. Paz's poetry, however, moves from the aloneness which comes from his rejection of the idea of a paradise in some hypothetical future to a grasping of the present. The change is already there in 'Soliloquio de medianoche', a poem written in 1944 in Berkeley:

> Dormía en mi pequeño cuarto de roedor civilizado,
> cuando alguien sopló en mi oído estas palabras:
> 'Duermes, vencido por fantasmas que tú mismo engendras,
> y en tanto tú deliras, otros besan o matan,
> conocen otros labios, penetran otros cuerpos
> y de sus manos nace cada día un mundo inagotable,
> la piedra vive y se incorpora,
> y todo, el polvo mismo, encarna en una forma que respira'.

The poem is one of the few Paz poems that directly reflects an autobiographical experience. In it, he passes beyond the empty rhetoric of adult life, 'Dios, Cielo, Amistad, Revolución o Patria', and returns to childhood, when 'una palabra mágica me abría cada noche las puertas de los cielos'; but this poem still ends on the conviction that life is a dream. In 'Semillas para un himno', written soon afterwards, the revelation is finally achieved:

> Hay instantes que estallan y son astros
> Otros son un río detenido y unos árboles fijos
> Otros son ese mismo río arrasando los mismos árboles

This revelation is a return to the lost paradise of childhood:

> Como en la infancia cuando decíamos 'ahí viene un barco cargado de ...'
> Y brotaba instantánea imprevista la palabra convocada
> > Pez
> > Álamo
> > Colibrí

In the moment of revelation, name and experience are identical. 'Por un instante están los nombres habitados'.

The poetry of the 1940s and '50s culminated in *Piedra de sol*, a long poem in which Paz uses the 'simultaneous' technique of 'Himno entre ruinas' and also uses the poem as the image of the 'no time' which is poetry. The number of lines (584) corresponds to the number of years in the Aztec calendar, the form is circular, with the poem contained within the image of the 'sauce de cristal, un chopo de agua/ un río de cristal que el viento arquea' which are the lines which open and introduce the end of the poem. The poem flows out of these initial images and flows back to them without a full stop to halt the flow. Both the 'other' and the external world apprehended through the senses are identified in the poem with a goddess figure, the Venus Aphrodite, goddess of life and death, symbol of dual aspects of human experience. The poet's identification of himself with this 'other' fragments the self and leads to his search for wholeness in memory and in the past.

> busco una fecha viva como un pájaro
> busco el sol de las cinco de la tarde
> templado por los muros de tezontle:
> la hora maduraba sus racimos
> y al abrirse salían las muchachas
> de su entraña rosada y se esparcían
> por los patios de piedra del colegio ...

But the attempt to realise himself through the other, to find meaning in the succession of events in the past, fails until finally he is left with nothing. The world is transitory; once again the poet evokes the hotel rooms of his past,

> trampas, celdas, cavernas encantadas,
> pajareras y cuartos numerados.

which can only be transformed when he finally gives himself totally
in love. Then all barriers are down:

> se derrumban
> por un instante inmenso y vislumbramos
> nuestra unidad perdida, el desamparo
> que es ser hombres, la gloria que es ser hombres

The poem culminates with the poet's experience of timelessness when
the walls crumble:

> todas las puertas se desmoronaban
> y el sol entraba a saco por mi frente,
> despegaba mis párpados cerrados,
> desprendía mi ser de su envoltura,
> me arrancaba de mí, me separaba
> de mi bruto dormir siglos de piedra ...

Piedra de sol carries Paz to the crossroads. Until then one of the
fundamental contacts of his life had been that with Breton and the
Surrealists in Paris, though he adapted 'Surrealism' in a very personal
manner. Soon after publishing *Piedra de sol*, he was appointed
Mexican ambassador to Delhi and there remained until his resignation
in 1968. Paz had, of course, already been interested in Eastern philosophy. He mentions the 'piece of unpolished stone' of the Taoists
in his introduction to the Mexican edition of *Piedra de sol*[31] and
his search for revelation has evident affinities with Buddhist and Hindu
practices. The sum of his Eastern experience is found in *Ladera
este*, a collection of poems written between 1962 and 1968, poems
which explore new areas of techniques, though the fundamental preoccupation is the same:

> Hambre de encarnación padece el tiempo
> Más allá de mí mismo
> En algún lado aguardo mi llegada.

The poems are more than ever now the 'surtidores' which he had
described in *Los signos en rotación*. So in 'Balcón', a series of colours,
adjectives, become the objective analogy of refraction:

> Blancas luces azules amarillas

while in 'Custodia', there is an approach towards concrete poetry. The
most ambitious poem in this collection, the *Piedra de sol* of a later
epoch, is 'Blanco' which was first published separately in Mexico in
1967. It is a poem which can be read in several manners, as a single
text, or, since it is written in three columns and has four parts, the
poem has another order—that of the separate columns in four parts.

There are thus a series of separate poems which establish different relationships between the themes which Paz describes as: a) the relation between word and silence, b) the elements, and c) sensation, perception, imagination, and understanding. Since publishing 'Blanco', Paz has also published rotating poems on discs, something like the 'frames of images' from which the *haiku* are constructed, and he also collaborated on a communal poem with three other poets, each writing in a different language.[32] Thus, in this later period, Paz's main efforts seem to be directed at making poetry more like music or painting.

Paz's ideas on poetry and his poetry have had a very profound influence, especially on younger Mexican poets. He has constructed a kind of poetic metalanguage and he tends more to abstraction than to quiddity. Though very different from Modernism, his poetry seems to arise out of similar tensions and to be constructed from a frame of images—elements, primary sense perceptions, colours, dualistic myths which subsume the phenomenal world. The new poetry that has emerged from Latin America since Modernism either follows very closely Paz's view of poetry or veers violently in the opposite direction into a poetry of ironic statement or commitment. On the one hand, there is the revelation of the world of objects, the emphasis on the liberation of language from functionalism. And there has also developed the kind of poetry in which the poet takes an ironic attitude towards the modern world and his own society.

VIII. OTHER POETS

After Modernism, the death of God had drained language of religious significance and poets began to turn towards the material world in order to perceive its quiddity. Sense perception became the most important and reliable door to knowledge. Characteristic of this new appreciation of the objective world was the poetry of the Ecuadorian Jorge Carrera Andrade (1903-), who stressed the visual impact of things and therefore the marvel of the eye, that 'window' onto reality. A diplomat, he lived in the East and adapted the *haiku* into Spanish, but Eastern poetry impressed him most because of its appreciation of the sensual world. He also lived in Europe, an experience which made him turn nostalgically to the sights and sounds of his native Quito:

> ese mismo sentimiento de aborigen arrancado del suelo natal, es el que me aprieta ahora la garganta, mientras ordeno estas líneas sobre el papel, cerca de esta ventana por donde se ve un cielo gris, horadado de chimeneas, y una muchedumbre de casas agrupadas

sin la gracia de esos puñados de casucas sencillas que se encuentran
por toda la anchura de nuestra Sierra.[33]

In his poetry, he explored the objective world, attempting to rid
objects of their value-loaded accretions. In 'El objeto y su sombra' he
writes:

> Arquitectura fiel del mundo.
> Realidad, más cabal que el sueño.
> La abstracción muere en un segundo:
> sólo basta un fruncir del ceño.
>
> Las cosas, o sea la vida.
> Todo el universo es presencia.
> La sombra al objeto prendida
> ¿modifica acaso su esencia?
>
> Limpiad el mundo—ésta es la clave—
> de fantasmas del pensamiento.
> Que el ojo apareje su nave
> para un nuevo descubrimiento.

The poet could not be a clearer statement of a poetic creed. However,
it is in his imagery that Carrera Andrade illustrates his belief that
the world should be cleansed of the 'phantoms of thought' and
especially in the compressed *haiku*-like *Microgramas*. Here, for
instance, is his description of the walnut:

> Nuez: sabiduría comprimida,
> diminuta tortuga vegetal,
> cerebro de duende
> paralizado por la eternidad.

And it is in these revelations of the objective world that the originality
of his poetry resides. Like Jorge Guillén of *Cántico*, Carrera Andrade's
poetry excludes the darker side of existence so that poetry becomes
an area of salvation in a degraded world. This attitude is found among
many poets writing in the period of the Second World War and the
Cold War period when public happenings were of such a horrifying
nature that many could not encompass them and took refuge in personal visions and private experience. In this period, Surrealism was
at the height of its influence, since it committed the poet to a personal
authenticity without committing him to an ideology or a political
stance. Furthermore, the movement stimulated poetic invention by
its emphasis on freeing the word from the chain of logic and the
attainment of inner truth. In Mexico, this inventiveness is reflected in
the poetry of Marco Antonio Montes de Oca (1932-) who, like Carrera
Andrade, opens his eyes to the marvellous. In his charming 'La

despedida del bufón' he sets out a kind of manifesto:

Damas y caballeros, piedras y pájaros,
es la hermosura de la vida lo que nos deja tan pobres
la hermosura de la vida
lo que lentamente nos vuelve locos.

The war and Cold War period were rich in poetic movements. In Chile the magazine *Mandrágora* published poems by Braulio Arenas (1913-) and Gonzalo Rojas (1917-) both of whose work has its origins in Surrealism. The former later broke with *Mandrágora* to found *Leitmotiv* (1942 and 1943). Meanwhile in Buenos Aires, Raúl Gustavo Aguirre (1927-) proclaimed:

el surrealismo, el creacionismo y su derivación en el inven-
cionismo, significan la culminación de un proceso histórico por
el cual el lenguaje poético alcanza el punto máximo de separación
con el lenguaje lógico convencional.[34]

And here too neo-Surrealism was highly important. The magazine *A partir de cero* marked a rediscovery of Surrealism which had been introduced into Argentina by Aldo Pellegrini years before.[35] Alberto Girri (1918-) was one of the poets who most successfully adapted Surrealist techniques and extended them, in order to express his inner vision.

In Havana during the forties, the *Orígenes* magazine was founded and became an influential review which published the work of three fine poets, José Lezama Lima (1912-), Eliseo Diego (1920-), and Cintio Vitier (1921-).

Surrealism was of course not the only source of inspiration. Lezama Lima drew on a tradition that went back to neo-Platonism and many poets at this period were in search of a classical purity, poets such as Ricardo Molinari (Argentina; 1898-) and the Mexican Alí Chumacero (1918-) who used language of almost ritual solemnity to describe everyday places and things; and Rubén Bonifaz Nuño (Mexico; 1923-)—an excellent translator of the classics—also repre-sents a 'neo-classical' tendency in modern poetry.

The poet during this period attained serenity in proportion to his withdrawal from the public order, but not all were able to follow the course of evasion. Public life intersected private experience at too many points. For the poet who must live in the present and could not accept either backward-looking nostalgia or the no-time of the poetry of revelation, irony seemed the only alternative. The ironic poet tended to stress, not to transcend, the corruption of language and the hollowness of rhetoric. The most notable of poets who chose this vein was the Chilean Nicanor Parra (1914-), who is savage in his assault on society. This, for instance, is his 'Autorretrato', where a school-teacher apostrophises his pupils:

> Considerad, muchachos,
> Este gabán de fraile mendicante.
> Soy profesor en un liceo obscuro.
> He perdido la voz haciendo clases.
> (Después de todo o nada
> Hago cuarenta horas semanales).
> ¿Qué les dice mi cara abofeteada?
> ¡Verdad que inspira lástima mirarme!
> ¿Y qué les sugieren estos zapatos de cura
> Que envejecieron sin arte ni parte?

Like many satirists, Parra finds the period in which he lives is the worst. In 'Los vicios de mundo moderno', he catalogues the 'gran cloaca' which is modern civilisation and in 'Las tablas' he relates a contemporary dream that is far too close to reality:

> Soñé que me encontraba en un desierto y que hastiado de mí mismo
> Comenzaba a golpear a una mujer.

The violent frustration of modern life is magnificently conveyed in this and in the autobiographical 'El túnel', in which he describes a childhood spent in the thrall of his aunts until one day he looks through a keyhole:

> Mi tía paralítica
> Caminaba perfectamente sobre la punta de sus piernas
> Y volví a la realidad con un sentimiento de los demonios.

This disillusionment is a continuing process. Parra exposes the moral blackmail imposed by tradition, age, custom, and the Establishment, and the weight of his satire is directed against this type of exploitation. There are times when his vision is apocalyptic, when he sees no need for society to continue:

> Señoras y señores:
> Yo voy a hacer una sola pregunta:
> ¿Somos hijos del sol o de la tierra?
> Porque si somos tierra solamente
> No veo para que
> Continuamos filmando la película.
> Pido que se levante la sesión.

Or in 'Socorro' where he suddenly finds himself bleeding on the ground:

> Realmente no sé lo que pasó
> Sálvenme de una vez
> O dispárenme un tiro en la nuca.

Another Chilean, Enrique Lihn (1929-), also adopts this ironic attitude
to the world and it is also a feature of much contemporary Argentinian
poetry, notably that of César Fernández Moreno (1919-).

In Peru, the theme of personal anguish is expressed with great
originality in the verse of Carlos Germán Belli (1927-), whose first
collection was appropriately named *El pie sobre el cuello*. Belli is deliberately archaic. His poetry recalls the forms and the language of
Golden Age Poetry, but whereas the conflicts of Quevedo and Góngora
were played out within a religious framework, Belli's sufferings are
senseless, absurd exercises for which there is no reward. His poems
reach depths of terror and despair, as in the following 'Plexiglas',
where the suffering is like that of meat cut up and wrapped in a
plastic bag at the butcher's.

> Este cuero, estos huesos, esta carne,
> días hay que no sufren por milagro
> el tenedor, las hachas, el cuchillo
> que el gerifalte tal un matarife
> limpia, agita y afila con primor,
> para hincar luego y dividir en trozos
> el mas avasallado de la tierra;
> pues veces hay que por ensalmo mil
> el cuerpo que hipa pasto no es del filo,
> sino de plexiglas cual res el alma
> de la que cortan y pesan y ponen
> en el seno de un turbio celofán
> el alón de la mente y el filete
> no de carne, no, pero si de aire.

What Belli is describing is mental anguish in terms of physical chop-
ping-up process. The abstract term 'fragmentation' is given physical
reality because the poet visualises pieces of his own being wrapped up
in cellophane, but these pieces are air not flesh. Belli's language is extraordinarily savage. He brings power even to a commonplace experience like being overworked:

> Ya descuajaringándome, ya hipando
> hasta las cachas de cansado ya,
> inmensos montes todo el día alzando
> de acá para acullá de bofes voy,
> fuera cien mil palmos con mi lengua,
> cayéndome a pedazos tal mis padres,
> aunque en verdad ya por mi seso raso,
> y aun por lonjas y levas y mandones,
> que a la zaga me van dejando estable,

ya a más hasta el gollete no poder,
al pie de mis hijuelas avergonzado,
cual un pobre amanuense del Perú.

We can understand why Belli finds archaic Spanish so appropriate. His language is of effort, torture, Inquisition, but applied to mental experiences, so that the style itself becomes a metaphor for the survival of ancient guilt and suffering in a contemporary setting. *Oh hada cibernética* is a collection of poems in which the old idea of inspiration symbolised by the 'hada' is linked to technology and hence desacralised. Belli is one of the most original voices in Spanish America today because of his extreme sensitivity to the way the modern world breaks into the private sphere. Although very different, one might see this originality as comparable to the 'confessional poetry' of Robert Lowell. Also in this category is the Mexican Jaime Sabines (1925-), who, however, is far more lighthearted than Belli despite the title, 'Autonecrología', that he gave to a selection of his poetry.

The Cuban Revolution in 1959 was a major influence on poetry. Some poets joined the guerrilla movements and one of the most promising—the Peruvian Javier Heraud (1942-63)—died with the guerrillas. The magazine which best captures the literary and political revolutionary fervour of the time is *El corno emplumado*, founded by a Mexican, Sergio Mondragón (1935-), and an American poet of the Beat generation, Margaret Randall. The magazine brought together European and North American Beat poetry and the new social poetry of Latin America.

El corno emplumado did much for the reputation of the Nicaraguan Ernesto Cardenal (1925-), a revolutionary and Catholic poet whose committed attitudes were very much in harmony with his 'Third Worldism' of the early sixties. His poetry is reminiscent of Ginsberg and, like Ginsberg, he likes simultaneity, collage, and poetry that springs from an immediate impression. In 'La hora O', he wrote a poem of denunciation, a more radical *Canto general* which described the suffering and exploitation of a banana republic. The poem ends on the prophetic note which was to characterise much of this post-Cuban Revolution poetry.

Todas las noches en Managua la Casa Presidencial
se llena de sombras.

Pero el héroe nace cuando muere
y la hierba verde renace de los carbones.

For a time Cardenal lived in a monastery in the United States and this refuge symbolised for him an island of reality in the midst of the neon-lighted, unreal modern city.

En la noche iluminada de palabras:
PALMOLIVE CHRYSLER COLGATE CHESTERFIELD
que se apagan y se encienden y se apagan y se encienden
las luces rojas verdes azules de los hoteles y de los bares
y de los cines, los trapenses se levantan al coro
y encienden sus lámparas fluorescentes
y abren sus grandes Salterios y sus Antifonarios
entre millones de radios y de televisiones
Son las lámparas de las vírgenes prudentes esperando
al esposo en la noche de los Estados Unidos.

Few writers have succeeded so well in capturing this combination of ancient and modern which is religion in the contemporary world. There is a slight air of absurdity in the poem which makes the burning vigil of the monks all the more pathetic.

In post-Revolutionary Cuba, there was an immediate upsurge of poetry which was now released from the imposed hermeticism of the Batista era. Among the new poets, there was an attempt to use African mythology and apply it to the new revolutionary situation, notably in *El libro de los héroes* (1963) by Pablo Armando Fernández (1930-). But perhaps this was rather an enforced position. In general the Revolution favoured, certainly in its early years, a more direct language which could at times develop into direct criticism, as in the poetry of Heberto Padilla (1932-), for whom the poet is the eternal wet blanket.[36] Revolutionary poetry outside Cuba during the sixties all too often became a matter of verbal brickbats.

The death of Che Guevara in 1967 had the effect of killing the hopes of quick guerrilla solutions. The rhetorical militant and social poetry has recently given way to a quieter tone and there is a great deal of self-criticism. This is especially true of the Peruvians, and Antonio Cisneros (1942-) has described this change in the fine 'In Memoriam' to his generation. For Cisneros the enemy is not the fascist jackboot but the all-pervading comfort of the bourgeois world which might even kill by kindness and smothers action in its furry embrace. It is symbolised by the city of Lima wrapped in its perpetual mist:

Y lo demás es niebla.
Una corona blanca y peluda te protege del espacio exterior.[37]

In Mexico, where commitment in poetry has been rare even when it was fashionable elsewhere, there has been a different development, from purity to a more critical stance. José Emilio Pacheco, for instance, has moved from the intellectual poetry of *Los elementos de la noche* (1963) to the more outspoken and critical poetry of *No me preguntes como pasa el tiempo* (1969). In the first collection, the poetry was almost classical in its evocation of the 'ubi sunt' theme:

Nada se restituye, nada otorga
el verdor a los valles calcinados.
Ni el agua en su destierro sucederá a la frente
ni los huesos del águila volverán por sus alas.

Only words could then act as a restorative, only poetry could bring
the poet back to paradise:

Vuelve a tocar, palabra, ese linaje
que con su propio fuego se destruye.
Regresa así, canción, a este paraje
en donde el tiempo se demora y fluye.

But in the later poetry, the poet no longer finds that his verse offers
a way of escape. He knows that language is historically limited:

La realidad destruye la ficción nuevamente. No me vengan con
cuentos porque los hechos nos exceden, nos siguen excediendo,
mientras versificamos nuestras dudas.

So the poet must now reject the rhetoric of the past:

y pensemos en serio en todas las cosas que ya se avecinan.

He is one of the poets of the younger generation, most aware of the
fact that suffering and politics are no longer national, that it is now a
question of the species. Few writers give such an impression of being
born in unfavourable times.

Quizá no es tiempo ahora:
nuestra época
nos dejó hablando solos.

His poetry shows awareness of imminent catastrophe and yet reminds
us that we are not the first generation to suffer this.[38]

This brief survey has taken little account of national differences
in Spanish American poetry. There is great contrast between the irony
and humour of the poets of Buenos Aires—a César Fernández
Moreno, a Francisco Urondo—for instance, and the confessional poetry
of the Venezuelan Rafael Cadenas (1930-). The Peruvians influenced
by the Beat generation are totally different from the Colombian
Nadaístas. Yet national differences should not be overemphasised.
Poetry is the most international of the literary arts, its manifestations
infinitely diverse. The purpose of this chapter has been to indicate a
few of the major trends. It cannot detail all the excellent younger
poets who are now emerging onto the scene.

NOTES

1. G. de Torre, *Literaturas europeas de vanguardia* (Madrid, 1925), *¿Qué es el superrealismo?* (Buenos Aires, 1955); F. Alquié, *Philosophie du Surréalisme* (Paris, 1955); Juan Larrea, *Del surrealismo a Machupicchu* (Buenos Aires, 1967). The essays of Octavio Paz listed in the reading list are also essential reading for anyone interested in Surrealism and Latin American poetry.

2. Jules Laforgue (1860-87), born in Montevideo, was one of the important figures of the avant-garde in Paris, a pioneer in the use of free association.

3. There is a useful short study of Huidobro and his ideas by Antonio de Undurraga, in *Vicente Huidobro. Poesía y prosa* (Madrid, 1957).

4. Gloria Videla, *El ultraísmo* (Madrid, 1963).

5. A. de Undurraga, 'Teoría del creacionismo', preface to *Vicente Huidobro. Poesía y prosa.*

6. 'Adán' is included in Book I of *Poesías completas* (Santiago, 1964).

7. For a brief discussion of concrete poetry see J. Reichardt, 'The Whereabouts of Concrete Poetry', *Studio International* (London, February 1966).

8. 'Arrabal' from *Fervor de Buenos Aires*, in *Obras completas*, I.

9. 'La mujer estéril', included in *Poesías completas* (Madrid, 1958).

10. 'La maestra rural', ibid.

11. R. Martínez Villena, *La pupila insomne* (La Habana, 1960), includes a biography of the poet by Raúl Roa.

12. For example, the poetry of Pedro Pérez Sarduy, a brief selection of which is to be found in José Agustín Goytisolo's *Nueva poesía cubana* (Barcelona, 1970). The selection is not very representative of the *négritude* trend and these poems are not easy to get hold of.

13. Alfonso Reyes, 'Última Tule', *Obras completas*, XI (Mexico, 1955-63).

14. A. Reyes, 'En el Día Americano', *Obras completas*, XI, 70.

15. Frank Dauster, *Ensayos sobre poesía mexicana* (Mexico, 1963).

16. Octavio Paz has an introduction and critical essay in the edition published in Mexico in 1952.

17. E. Rodríguez Monegal, *El viajero inmóvil* (Buenos Aires, 1966), pp. 106-8.

18. According to Mme Georgette Vallejo in her *Apuntes biográficos sobre 'Poemas en prosa' y 'Poemas humanos'* (Lima, 1968).

19. *Rusia en 1931. Reflexiones al pie del Kremlin* (Lima, 1959). See also Mme Vallejo, op. cit.

20. Many critics have commented on this. See, for instance, James Higgins, 'The conflict of personality in César Vallejo's *Poemas humanos*', *BHS*, XLIII (January 1960).

21. For some discussion of evil in Vallejo's poetry see X. Abril, *Vallejo. Ensayo de aproximación crítica* (Buenos Aires, 1958).

22. James Higgins, 'Los nueve monstruos de César Vallejo. Una tentativa de interpretación', *Razón y fábula* (Bogotá), 3.

23. See the short autobiographical essay in *Obras completas*, I, 3rd ed. (Buenos Aires, 1967), 26.

24. The biographical element of the poems is discussed by M. Aguirre, *Genio y figura de Pablo Neruda* (Buenos Aires, 1964), and in E. Rodríguez Monegal, *El viajero inmóvil.*

25. ibid., p.63.

26. M. Aguirre, op. cit., p.131.

27. Rodríguez Monegal, op. cit., pp. 97-8.

28. Octavio Paz, *El arco y la lira* (Mexico, 1956), p.22.

29. ibid., p.12.
30. ibid., p.132.
31. Published in Mexico in 1957.
32. 'Blanco' is included in *Ladera este* (Mexico, 1969).
33. J. Carrera Andrade, *Latitudes* (Buenos Aires, 1940).
34. Quoted F. Urondo, *Veinte años de poesía argentina 1940-60* (Buenos Aires, 1967).
35. Graciela de Sola, *Proyecciones del surrealismo en la literatura argentina* (Buenos Aires, 1967).
36. J. Franco, 'Before and After: Contexts of Cuban Writing'.
37. For a discussion of social protest poetry see R. Pring Mill, 'Both in Sorrow and in Anger: Spanish American Protest Poetry', *Cambridge Review* (20 Feb. 1970).
38. This is not a survey of contemporary poetry. Those who wish to read present-day work should look at the anthologies recommended in the reading list.

READING LIST

The best texts of the poetry of Neruda and Vallejo are expensive editions. There are also paperback editions of separate volumes published by Losada of Buenos Aires.

Anthologies
Caillet-Bois, Julio, *Antología de la poesía hispanoamericana* (Madrid, 1965)
Caracciolo-Trejo, E. (ed.), *Penguin Book of Latin American Verse* (London, 1971)
Goytisolo, J. A. (ed.), *Nueva poesía cubana* (Barcelona, 1969)
Paz, O. (and others; eds.), *Poesía en movimiento* (Mexico, 1966)
Paz, O. (ed.) and Beckett, S. (translator), *Anthology of Mexican Poetry* (London, 1959)
Pellegrini, Aldo, *Antología de la poesía viva latinoamericana* (Barcelona, 1966)
Peru: *The New Poetry* (London, 1970)
Tamayo Vargas, A. (ed.), *Nueva poesía peruana* (Barcelona, 1970)
Tarn, N. (ed.), *Con Cuba* (London, 1969)
Triquarterly (Winter/Fall 1968-69). Special issue devoted to Latin America

Texts
Belli, Carlos Germán, *El pie sobre el cuello* (Montevideo, 1967)
——, *Sextinas y otros poemas* (Santiago de Chile, 1970)
Borges, J. L., *Poemas (1923-58)* (Buenos Aires, 1958)
Cardenal, Ernesto, *Epigramas* (Mexico, 1961)
——, *Poemas de Ernesto Cardenal* (La Habana, 1967)
——, *Homenaje a los indios americanos* (Nicaragua, 1970)
Carrera Andrade, Jorge, *Registro del mundo: antología poética (1922-39)* (Quito, 1940)
——, *Edades poéticas* (Quito, 1958)
——, *Latitudes* (Buenos Aires, 1940)
Cisneros, Antonio, *The Spider Hangs too Far from the Ground* (selected poems with original Spanish text; London, 1970)
Gorostiza, José, *Poesía* (Mexico, 1964)
Huidobro, Vicente, *Poesía y prosa* (Madrid, 1957)
——, *Obras completas de Vicente Huidobro*, 2 vols. (Santiago de Chile, 1964)
Ibarbourou, Juana de, *Obras completas* (Madrid, 1960)
Lihn, Enrique, *La pieza oscura (1955-62)* (Santiago de Chile, 1963)
Mistral, Gabriela, *Poesías completas* (Madrid, 1958)

Neruda, Pablo, *Obras completas*, 2 vols., 3rd ed. (Buenos Aires, 1967)
——, *Selected Poems*, ed. Nathaniel Tarn (London, 1970)
——, *The Heights of Macchu Picchu* (London, 1966)
——, *20 poems by Pablo Neruda* (London, 1967)
Paperback editions of the separate collections mentioned in the text are published by Losada, Buenos Aires
Novo, Salvador, *Poesía* (Mexico, 1961)
Pacheco, José Emilio, *Los elementos de la noche* (Mexico, 1964)
——, *El reposo del fuego* (Mexico, 1966)
——, *No me preguntes como pasa el tiempo* (Mexico, 1969)
Parra, Nicanor, *Obra gruesa* (Santiago de Chile, 1969)
Paz, Octavio, *El arco y la lira* (Mexico, 1956)
——, *Libertad bajo palabra* (Mexico, 1960)
——, *El laberinto de la soledad*, 3rd ed. (Mexico, 1963)
——, *The Labyrinth of Solitude. Life and Thought in Mexico* (New York, 1961)
——, *Corriente alterna* (Mexico, 1967)
——, *Los signos en rotación* (Mexico, 1966)
——, *Salamandra* (Mexico, 1962)
——, *Ladera este* (which includes *Blanco*) (Mexico, 1969)
——, *Discos visuales* (Mexico, 1968)
Vallejo, César, *Poesías completas* (Lima, 1968)
——, *Human Poems*, translated by C. Eshleman (London, 1969)
    (separate collections published by Losada of Buenos Aires in paperback)
Villaurrutia, Xavier, *Poesía y teatro completo* (Mexico, 1953)

Historical and critical
Abril, Xavier, *Vallejo. Ensayo de aproximación crítica* (Buenos Aires, 1958)
Aguirre, Margarita, *Genio y figura de Pablo Neruda* (Buenos Aires, 1964)
Alonso, Amado, *Poesía y estilo de Pablo Neruda* (Buenos Aires, 1940)
Fernández Moreno, César, *La realidad y los papeles* (Madrid, 1967)
Flores, Ángel (ed.), *Aproximaciones a César Vallejo*, 2 vols. (New York, 1971)
Higgins, James, *Visión del hombre y de la vida en las últimas obras poéticas de César Vallejo* (Mexico, 1970)
Ortega, Julio, *Figuración de la persona* (Barcelona, 1970)
Rodríguez Monegal, Emir, *El viajero inmóvil* (Buenos Aires, 1966)
Torre, Guillermo de, *Literaturas europeas de vanguardia* (Madrid, 1925)
Urondo, Francisco, *Veinte años de poesía argentina 1940-60* (Buenos Aires, 1967)
Xirau, Ramón, *Octavio Paz: el sentido de la palabra* (Mexico, 1970)
Zilio, Giovanni Meo, *Stile e Poesia in César Vallejo* (Padua, 1960)

Chapter 9

CONTEMPORARY PROSE-WRITING

La novela deja de ser 'latinoamericana', se libera de esa servi-
dumbre. Ya no sirve a la realidad; ahora se sirve de la realidad
(Mario Vargas Llosa)

SPANISH-AMERICAN PROSE-WRITING at the present time represents a
rebellion and a liberation. The rebellion, initiated by the avant-garde
of the twenties, was directed against a concept of 'realism' and
'reality' which was too poor, which all too often gave rise to schematic
works in which writers were concerned more with formula than substance. By and large, Spanish American Realism lacked that density
of specification which Henry James thought the mark of the great
novel. But once writers got away from the idea that 'the novel'
implied 'the Realist novel', once they felt free to use Joycean stream
of consciousness, Proustian memory and time, Dadaist parody, Surrealist fantasy, a great burst of creative energy was produced and quite
new styles and techniques developed.

Buenos Aires played a special role in this process, especially during
the 1920s. Despite the cultural aridity of which Borges complained
on his return from Europe in 1921, it was a city that owed less to
tradition than almost any other city in the Latin American hemisphere
and was correspondingly more alive to the new. The boast of the
1920s intellectuals that they would make the cultural axis of the world
run through Buenos Aires may have been empty, but it also indicates
how sensitive their antennae were to the modern. They could not, like
Mexican or Peruvian writers, manufacture a cultural tradition out of
an indigenous past and so had to train their eyes on the future, on
creating their own modes. Besides this, the city was itself rich with
tension. It was full of Russians, Poles, Italians looking for Utopia and
hardly able to relate in any meaningful way to gauchos and cattle-
rearing. There was a wealthy oligarchy, legendary even in Europe for
their conspicuous spending, for their sophistication; and on the other
hand, the uprooted, poor immigrant population which made a kind
of poetry out of *lunfardo* (the dialect of Buenos Aires), the tango,
and the night-towns.[1] Buenos Aires was unique among Latin American

cities in that it had something of an intellectual life with *tertulias,* literary polemics, little magazines such as *Claridad, Proa, Prisma,* and *Martín Fierro,* the first of which was didactic, earnest, directed towards the less literary, while the other three were avant-garde, full of talk of new European writing, ironic and satirical in tone, and very much concerned with 'in'-group politics. Their favourite form of activity was the literary and artistic banquet. Pedro Figari, the painter, Jules Supervielle, Oliverio Girondo were some of the personalities they fêted 'a base de ravioles y buen humor'. Commitment was to art rather than to politics, although politics did erupt from time to time, to split groups and embitter polemics.[2]

It is against this background that we should see the work of Oliverio Girondo (1891-1965), Macedonio Fernández, Roberto Arlt, and the early writings of Jorge Luis Borges.

I. MACEDONIO FERNÁNDEZ AND ROBERTO ARLT

Macedonio Fernández (1874-1952) was the type of personality common in Latin countries, a man who spent most of his energy in discussion and projects and who seldom published. For this reason, people have been slow to recognise his originality, although his writings were to inspire Borges, Cortázar, and many others. For Macedonio Fernández, the novel was on trial. In his strangely-titled works, *No toda es vigilia la de los ojos abiertos* (1928), *Papeles de recienvenido* (1929), *Una novela que comienza* (1941), and *Museo de la novela eterna* (1967), he has characters without novels, parodies of newspaper articles, lectures, toasts, scraps of autobiography. Many of his ideas are still being utilised. Consider, for instance, his prologue 'Lo que nace y lo que muere' in *Museo de la novela eterna* in which he poses questions of evaluation which are never really faced. Complaining that while writing the 'última novela mala' and the 'primera novela buena' the pages got mixed, he exclaims:

> Tengo la suerte de ser el primer escritor que puede dirigirse al doble lector, y ya abusando de este declive me deslizo a rogar a cada uno de los que me lean, quiera comunicarme cual de las dos novelas le resulto la obligatoria. Si usted forma juicio de la obra, yo deseo formar juicio de mi lector.

This 'double' reader is certainly the progenitor of Cortázar's 'two' readers of *Rayuela.* And indeed the whole of Macedonio Fernández's work is full of such anticipations. Everything he wrote in prose went beyond conventions, often to destroy them, because he needed to get through the cliché in order to find the essence.[3]

Experiment of a different kind is found in the work of Roberto

Arlt (1900-42). He belonged to the earnest, didactic *Boedo* group and his novels show the influence of Dostoievsky, Gorky, and Nietzsche. Yet he too makes a very untraditional use of his influences and of the novel form. The son of immigrants, he had been brought up in the moral twilight of a city in which human beings are freed from constraints and social censorship and are left to struggle in a morass of uncertainties. His first novel, *El juguete rabioso* (1926), has many autobiographical elements but its protagonist, Silvio Astier, is also faced with moral dilemmas of a peculiarly complex and unprecedented type. There is no longer the rather simple proposal that loss of Catholic faith leaves the Darwinian struggle for life as the only alternative (the theme of *Sin rumbo*, for example). Astier's problem is far more complex. There has never been any faith in the first place. The environment offers him nothing, except the chance to play out the fantasies his reading provides him with. The bandits and outlaws of the penny dreadfuls are the only heroic matter available to him; and chance encounters and gang life allow him to enact his fantasies free from any restraint, except that of the law. At the same time the frustrating effects of the environment channel his possibilities into a single direction. He can only be a delinquent. There is nothing else. Even this comparative freedom is no longer available once he is old enough to work. Then he must enter into a life of sheer misery and drudgery, in the backrooms of the bookseller's shop where he labours for the whole day. The future is visible in those around him:

> En el futuro ¿no sería yo uno de esos hombres que llevan cuellos sucios, camisas zurcidas, traje color vinoso y botines enormes, porque en los pies ha salido callos y juanetes de tanto caminar, de tanto caminar solicitando de puerta en puerta trabajo en que ganarse la vida?

Society offers him nothing but frustration. He tries to set fire to Don Gaetano's bookshop and fails, attempts to join the army but is too intelligent for the training scheme, and he is finally caught up in an attempted robbery, which he denounces. His confused Nietzschean explanation for the denunciation only accentuates the picture of moral chaos. Astier escapes the fate that seemed inevitable by an act of disloyalty which turns out well for him since he is given the opportunity to leave Buenos Aires and go south, but all this simply reinforces the view that Christian morality or even a kind of socialist morality breaks down in the city. Urban society *de facto* obeys quite different conditions from those that operate in organic societies.

All this emerges on a grander scale in the two-part novel *Los siete locos* (1929) and *Los lanzallamas* (1931). *El juguete rabioso* still had the semblance of a structure. But now these novels are without organic development and obey a pattern of accident, of chance encounter, and sudden violence which is the pattern of urban living. The plot, such as it is, centres around Erdosaín, the inverted superman, the seeker after humiliation whose dialectical opposite is the Astrólogo. Erdosaín is accused of embezzling and his wife leaves him. Now an outcast and without family, he and the Astrólogo forge dreams and fantasies, plan to end capitalist society with gases and microbes and secret organisations, plan to save humanity. As part of their scheme, they kidnap the wealthy Barsut, Erdosaín invents a golden rose, they save a prostitute. All the characters in the novel are mad if one takes social norms for granted. Society makes its rules, legislates for robbery on a small scale while practising it on a large scale; legislates for murder while committing mass murders in wars. That is why, when Erdosaín is accused of embezzling money, he does not feel that the word 'thief' really applies to him, because this is only an unjust society's view of his crime. 'Quizá la palabra ladrón no estuviera en consonancia con su estado interior', the author remarks.

The novel explores the region between public life and private concern and shows how the former reacts upon the latter. At the beginning of the novel Erdosaín lives in a 'zona de angustia' because he tries to conform to society's institutions and is therefore merely 'una cáscara de hombre'. When he is accused of theft and when his wife leaves him, he is doubly disgraced in society's eyes and now becomes a rebel capable of any outrageous act which will show the absurdity of social institutions. He becomes engaged, for instance, to the twelve-year-old daughter of his landlady in order to demonstrate that marriage is a venal matter.

But the moral limbo in which the characters of Arlt's novels live is more especially the product of an urban environment which destroys organic relationships and acts as a centrifugal force. People are terribly mutilated by modern life, a mutilation which is reflected in the nicknames of characters—'La Bizca', 'La Coja' (identified by her lover as the Great Whore of the Apocalypse), and 'El Castrado' (the other nickname of Erdosaín's friend, 'El Astrólogo'). Once Erdosaín has decided to defy society instead of conforming to it, he finds himself in the company of other 'madmen'—pimps, killers, forgers. The Astrólogo who controls this strange underworld symbolises the random nature of urban living in which moral responsibility imposed by continuity in family life and work and community has been replaced by the casual relationships which encourage betrayal and violence.

Arlt's world is apocalyptic—the city reflects the jungle on a larger and more inhuman scale. And that city is above all Buenos Aires, a Buenos Aires that had frustrated the immigrant's dream of El Dorado and reduced him to a helpless automaton. The mutilation of an individual by urban living must result in the blind and violent rebellion of this human waste. Arlt's grotesque imagination thus separates his work spectacularly from the pedestrian Realism of other members of the *Boedo* group. Though less sustained, the weird situations encountered both in his short-story collections, *El criador de gorilas* and *El jorobadito* (1933) and a later novel, *El amor brujo* (1932), have few parallels before the novels of Günter Grass.

II. JORGE LUIS BORGES (1899-)

The career of Jorge Luis Borges as a writer was curiously and perhaps characteristically tortuous. He was the leading and the most energetic member of the twenties' avant-garde, a poet, author of the collections *Fervor de Buenos Aires* (1923), *Cuaderno San Martín* (1924), and *Luna de enfrente* (1925), he also helped to found *Prisma, Proa,* and *Martín Fierro,* the three avant-garde periodicals of that time, and he was the acknowledged avatar of Buenos Aires 'ultraísmo', a poetic movement which was not simply an offshoot of Spanish Ultraism. While the latter was very much concerned with literary fashion, Buenos Aires 'ultraismo' was, according to Borges, the natural development of Hispanic literary tradition:

> Nosotros, mientras tanto sopesábamos líneas de Garcilaso, andariegos y graves a lo largo de las estrellas del suburbio, solicitando un límpido arte que fuese tan intemporal como las estrellas de siempre. Abominábamos de los matices borrosos del rubenismo y nos enardeció la metáfora por la precisión que hay en ella, por su algébrica forma de correlacionar lejanías.

We are not here directly concerned with Borges's poetry, but the quotation is apt as regards his writing as a whole. Precision, cleanliness, and timelessness are the qualities of style he sought and was to perfect. But it was to be some time before he was to apply these to fiction. Instead, he approached the short story by way of the essays which he collected under the title *Inquisiciones* (1925) and in which his basic preoccupations are apparent—the nature of the self and of time, the attractions of solipsism for a man who has very little patience with objective laws that rule the physical world and who avoids the organic analogy. The essay is a significant genre in this respect. It abstracts and generalises, while the novel particularises and is concrete. The essay presents an argument. Borges's stories often take the form of an argument or thesis. They are analogous to logic but are often false logic and deliberately so. And curiously this is often true of his essays which simulate the exposition of a theory while hinting at a certain absurdity.

Borges is more attracted to Idealism than he is to Realism because it has greater imaginative possibilities. He believes that the universe is unintelligible to the human mind in many important respects and this being so, Idealism appears to him more fertile in creative speculations. Thus, in the story 'Tlön, Uqbar, Orbis Tertius', he declares that it is useless to argue that reality is ordered: 'Quizá lo está pero de acuerdo a leyes divinas, a leyes inhumanas—que no acabamos nunca de percibir'. The work of art gives man a possibility of creating 'a more human world'. But it was some time before Borges himself chose wholeheartedly the path of art. He was in fact to publish, besides *Inquisiciones, Discusión* (1932), and *Historia de la eternidad* (1936), and other essays before he definitively turned to the short story. When his first stories were published in the collection *Historia universal de la infamia* (1935), these were based on historical characters, on real although legendary criminals like Billy the Kid.

Borges, then, arrives at the story, by way of the essay, by way of his interest in Idealism and in metaphysical problems, by way of a view of art as intuition, by way of an interest in the cinema and through the practice of poetry. By 1935 and 1936, he was writing his first stories, although only in 1941 did he publish *El jardín de los senderos que se bifurcan*, a collection that was later included in the enlarged *Ficciones* (1944). He subsequently published *El Aleph* (1949) and *El hacedor* (1960).

Each of the stories to which he gave the name *ficciones* is a small masterpiece, whose deceptively limpid surface constantly knots the reader into problems. Saturated with literary references, often as near to essay as to the conventional idea of the short story, the *ficciones* nevertheless challenge print culture at a very deep level and perhaps suggest its impossibility. The words addressed to Leopoldo Lugones at the beginning of *El hacedor* are significant:

> Los rumores de la plaza quedan atrás y entro en la Biblioteca. De una manera casi física siento la gravitación de los libros, el ámbito sereno de un orden, el tiempo disecado y conservado mágicamente. A izquierda y a derecha, absortos en su lúcido sueño, a la luz de las lámparas estudiosas, como en la hipálage de Milton.

The library is abstracted from flux and if offers us an order, a human and understandable order, as he points out in the story 'Tlön, Uqbar, Orbis Tertius', which describes an imaginary planet whose language and habits of mind are Idealist and which reverse the postulates of our planet where language and culture combine to make Idealism unconvincing. Borges constructs a planet in which Idealism is feasible, then shows it to be a human construct, the practical joke of a group of philosophers which nevertheless acts on reality and alters it. Unlike a Marxist for whom the intellectual life and culture is always affected by the groundswell of history and its laws, Jorge Luis Borges is often concerned with the falsification of history and fact. And in this, print and the word are vastly important. Print suggests meaning. It is linear. The 'Biblioteca de Babel' is constructed of symmetrical rooms and shelves in which there are exactly the same number of books with lines of similar length and identical numbers of pages. Though the letters on the page only accidentally make sense, the mere existence of the books suggests meaning:

> Como todos los hombres de la Biblioteca, he viajado en mi juventud; he peregrinado en busca de un libro, acaso del catálogo de catálogos.

The linear structure of a book suggests that it is leading us somewhere—to an ultimate meaning—but in fact it is only leading us to its own end, to silence. Again and again the bait that draws a man into some mad search for the absolute is a book—the *Don Quixote* which Pierre Menard sets out to reproduce word for word in his endeavour to achieve the perfect interpretation (and therefore the perfect reiteration); the symmetrical novel that Herbert Quain attempts to write.[4] Is this kind of search the outcome of the human reverence for print? It would seem so. In 'La muerte y la brújula', a detective on the track of a murderer finds the message, 'La primera letra del Nombre ha sido articulado', which leads him to suppose (he is an expert on the Cabbala) that four letters must be pronounced to make up the mystic pentagram, four murders committed. But his ingenuity leads him into a trap, since the fourth victim is himself. The story is analogous to the reading of a book. We embark on our search with the first line and seek completion, fulfilment in our reading, but to end the book is to end our voluntary dream. Completion is a kind of death.

In Borges's imagination, the book is very similar to the labyrinth, although the latter is an even more wilful and arbitrary construct. The only purpose of a labyrinth is to reach the centre and the centre means nothing except the completion of the journey, the understanding of a pattern. There is an obvious analogy with human existence where the 'goal' is death. To achieve the goal and understand the pattern is to die. Most of Borges's stories culminate at this point when the protagonist 'understands' the whole and through his act of understanding knows himself to be doomed. The detective Lönnrot, in 'La muerte y la brújula', understands that the sequence of the murders is an elaborate trap just as he is about to be shot. In 'El jardín de los senderos que se bifurcan', the Chinese protagonist understands the purpose of his ancestor's great work at the moment when he must kill Albert, the man who has revealed the pattern to him. Understanding and death are often simultaneous. Thus in 'El muerto':

> Otalora comprende, antes de morir, que desde el principio lo han

traicionado, que ha sido condenado a muerte, que le han permitido
el amor, el mando y el triunfo, porque ya lo daban por muerto,
porque para Bandeira ya estaba muerto.

Suárez, casi con desdén, hace fuego.

Or again, from the ending of the 'Biografía de Tadeo Isidoro Cruz':

Comprendió su íntimo destino de lobo, no de perro gregario;
comprendió que el otro era él.

The words 'comprender' or 'sentir' often occur in these final para-
graphs where total lucidity means either the end or endless repetition
(which is like death).

The 'fiction' becomes the 'secret consolation' which, nevertheless,
cannot halt the time flow, as the author pointed out in an essay which
he called *Nueva refutación del tiempo* (1947):

Negar la sucesión temporal, negar el yo, negar el universo
astronómico, son desesperaciones aparentes y consuelos secretos.
Nuestro destino ... no es espantoso por irreal; es espantoso porque
es irreversible y de hierro. El tiempo es un río que me arrebata,
pero yo soy el río: es un tigre que me destroza, pero yo soy el tigre;
es un fuego que me consume, pero yo soy el fuego. El mundo desgraciadamente, es real; yo, desgraciadamente, soy Borges.

The realistic novel and short story accompany the flow, while Borges's
fiction abstracts from it. That is why early on in his career he declared
that a novel should be 'un juego preciso de vigilancias, ecos y afini-
dades. Todo episodio, en un cuidadoso relato, es de proyección
ulterior'.[5] The key word here is 'juego', not to be translated simply as
game but as 'set', whose elements can be broken down, recomposed,
and thus offer new insights.

If existence in time is not illusory, the same cannot be said of the
individuation principle which is the source of human illusion and error.
Like Schopenhauer, Borges believes that individual differences belong
to the world of will.

Lo que hace un hombre es como si lo hicieran todos los hombres.
Por eso, no es injusto que una desobedencia en un jardín contamina
al género humano; por eso no es injusto que la crucifixión de un solo
judío basta para salvarlo. Acaso Schopenhauer tiene razón; yo soy
los otros, cualquier hombre es todos los hombres.

The story from which this quotation is taken, 'La forma de la espada',
is about a man who relates a story as if he were the victim when he
was in reality the traitor. In 'Los teólogos' the two rival theologians
whose lives are spent in refuting each other's theories are, when they
reach heaven, discovered to be the same man in the eyes of God: 'el

ortodoxo y el hereje, el aborrecedor y el aborrecido, el acusador y la víctima' were one and the same.

Darkness, ignorance, the desperate constructs which individuals fabricate—these give the illusion of complexity and variety. 'El tiempo, en la oscuridad, parecía más largo', Borges writes in 'Abenjacán el Bojarí, muerto en su laberinto', and in 'La muerte y la brújula', the house that Lönnrot explores seems bigger than it is because of the symmetry, the mirrors, his own weariness. The labyrinth—the central image in so many Borges stories—in 'Abenjacán', 'El jardín de los senderos que se bifurcan', 'La casa de Asterión', is like spiders' webs, but webs constructed by men for their own deaths. They are programmes of existence in time, but they end with the constructors' death and only the reader, or the writer, knows the whole pattern.

The 'fictions' are the major achievement of Borges. *El hacedor* bears the same stamp, but the prose pieces are almost intolerably compressed, to the point where they become prose poems. In them, the ideal of fatal, useless repetition is even more intense. The mirror is the key symbol of *El hacedor* as the labyrinth was of *ficciones*. So in 'La trama', a gaucho unwittingly repeats Caesar's words on his assassination, *Pero, che*: 'Lo matan y no sabe que muere para que se repita una escena'.

In 'Los espejos velados', he writes:

> Yo conocí de chico ese horror de una duplicación o multiplicación espectral de la realidad, pero ante los grandes espejos. Su infalible y continuo funcionamiento, su persecución de mis actos, su pantomima cósmica, eran sobrenaturales entonces, desde que anochecía.

What the mirror reflects is the ephemeral, the day-to-day image which is easily erased. Out of the mass of ephemeral images, a few survive, are transformed into myth, become Don Quixote or the Inferno. 'Así mi vida es una fuga y todo lo pierdo y todo es del olvido, o del otro', he writes in 'Borges y Yo'. And throughout *El hacedor* there is a certain nostalgia for what is lost.

> ¿Qué morirá conmigo cuando yo muera, qué forma patética o deleznable perderá el mundo? ¿La voz de Macedonio Fernández, la imagen de un caballo colorado en el baldío de Serrano y de Charcas, una barra de azufre en el cajón de un escritorio de caoba?

And this is finally the importance of the fiction, for it shores up what otherwise would be gone, at least for the time that elapses during its reading.

The 1930s were a difficult period in Argentina. There was a right-wing oligarchy in power which only ceded in the forties to the populist movement of Perón. Many intellectuals felt themselves to be in an untenable position between an establishment they did not like and the threat of popular movements which were totally anti-intellectual. It was a time of desperate solutions. Ernesto Sábato became an anarchist. Leopoldo Marechal (1900-) and Eduardo Mallea embarked on inner 'spiritual' journeys, the former spending most of the decade at work on a great epic quest novel, *Adán Buenosayres,* which was not published until 1948. The social, political, and cultural problems of Argentina were here internalised in one microcosmic character, Adán, who between his awakening and his separation from the original unity and his sleeping, at the end of the novel, embarks on a search for a Platonic perfection. The novel falls into three parts: first, the sortie of the hero into the streets of Buenos Aires, where he enters into a multiplicity of experience. In this part, 'Platonic' dialogues follow one on the other, as the hero discusses life, literature, philosophy with an 'astrólogo', Samuel Hessler, and with a group of 'Martínfierristas' with whom he goes on an expedition to the outskirts of Buenos Aires. The author has pointed out how this expedition encompasses the whole history of Argentina from its geological formation onwards (and it includes the discovery of a dead horse). The second part of the novel is a spiritual biography which Adán calls his 'Cuaderno de Tapas Azules', in which it is revealed that perfection is, like Dante's supreme virtue, incarnated in the figure of a woman, the Solveig 'celeste'. In the final section of the novel, the author descends to the hell of Cacodelphia, in whose circles are all the inhabitants of Buenos Aires.[6]

Marechal's view is Christian and Platonic, and the structure of the novel deliberately imitates that of the *Divine Comedy* and the Greek epic. Classical references abound. Adán in his 'descent' to the city encounters Polyphemus, Circe, and the sirens, converted into inhabitants of Buenos Aires. He has his Beatrice—Solveig—who exists both as a terrestrial being and as an ideal. His disillusionment with the terrestrial Solveig is what releases him to search for the ideal and undertake the 'ascent'. This involves a 'juicio final' of his whole existence and the 'death' of his former selves.

Before the end of the novel, Adán is guided by the demiurge Schulze through the inferno of Buenos Aires where some of its typical characters—the political personalities of the oligarchy, 'El Gran Oracionista', 'Potenciales', etc.—are condemned. These latter are the might-have-beens, men like Don Brandán, who live in an illusory gaucho past.

¿Dónde están los establecimientos ideales, las estancias maravillosas que yo fundé o habría fundado en el sur, distribuyendo mis tierras entre los colonos que trabajaban como ángeles y proliferaban como bestias, no sin que una y otra función les dejara el tiempo necesario para leer a Virgilio y meditar la Política de Aristóteles?

The satire is perhaps a little heavy, yet the huge canvas, the vast array of personages, and the vision all make *Adán Buenosayres* an impressive experiment.

The Platonic scaffolding is essential to Marechal's work, for he regards the metaphysical as more important than the aesthetic or the social. In 1966, he published a novel which is, in reality, a continuation of the Socratic dialogues which are such a feature of *Adán Buenosayres* and which have always interested him. This was *El banquete de Severo Arcángel* (1966). The choice of the Socratic structure means that there is a dialectic rather than a plot, and the novel never descends from the remote world of intellectual conflict and resolution. Perhaps Marechal's novels represent that rare phenomenon, the religious or metaphysical novel.

IV. EDUARDO MALLEA (1903-)

Born in Bahía Blanca, 'una ciudad relativamente grande, de mucho movimiento comercial: tres puertos ofrece al mar, posee una base marina, silos, elevadores de granos y un tenue labio gris donde faenan los pescadores',[7] Mallea grew up in a period of radical rule which ended in 1930 with the restoration of a conservative oligarchy that lasted until the Perón era. As a member of a liberal and provincial family, he was critical of the specious, hollow society in which he lived. He had published his first collection of stories, *Cuentos para una inglesa desesperada*, in 1926, but his major work came much later and arose out of a feeling of tension:

Un libro solo existe en la medida de la resistencia que inicialmente provoca. En la pugna entre la obra y el desconcierto triunfa el más fuerte: un libro que resiste a esa prueba ordena poco a poco el desconcierto y acaba sometiéndolo a su ley.[8]

Intensely preoccupied by the nature of Argentina and by the relationship of the individual to social forces, Mallea wrote many essays and essay-type novels on these themes, including *Historia de una pasión argentina* (1935), *La vida blanca, Conocimiento y expresión de la Argentina*. His quest novels include *La bahía del silencio* (1940), *Las Águilas* (1943), and *La torre* (1951). The crucial division of categories which separates individuals he places between 'lo visible' and 'lo invisible', between the superficial and the profound; the 'visible' includes false commercial values and society life which prevent self-knowledge:[9] 'La vida blanca' he calls it in one essay:[10]

> nuestra caridad es una caridad blanca, y nuestra educación una educación blanca, y nuestra arquitectura una arquitectura blanca y nuestra devoción una devoción blanca, y nuestra literatura una literatura blanca, y nuestro pensamiento general de las cosas un pensamiento blanco también.

Because of this superficiality of national life, the quest for authenticity —pursued through literature—is a matter of urgent necessity and the subject of many of the novels. Characters like Tregua in *La bahía del silencio*, like Roberto Ricarte in *La torre*, are self-projections and must go through the process of rejecting a 'cosmopolitismo progresista y visible' because authenticity is not to be found in

> esa fácil prosperidad, en ese progreso amonedado que constituye la naturaleza de las napas turbulentas de la metrópoli, que constituye la voz adjetiva de hombres absolutamente desprovistos de gravitación sustancial.[11]

As against this he sets up the idea of a natural aristocracy of men not subject to vile material motivation:

> Sólo una elegancia me importaba, sobre cualquier otra, y era la elegancia del alma, esa forma de dignidad, esa forma de desprecio por la parte vil y predatoria de la vida, ese señorial desinterés en la lucha por la vida.[12]

He does not take into account that this aristocratic detachment often presupposes a substantial economic basis. However, despite this possible reservation, *La bahía del silencio* is explicable in relation to the history of a country like Argentina which get-rich-quick immigrants simply regarded as a convenient source of plunder. In such an environment, to be 'disinterested' was obviously a significant gesture of difference. Mallea, like his father, felt himself to be a civilising influence in a rude world.

In *Las Águilas* and *La torre*, two novels which deal with the landowning family of the Ricartes, there is a contrast between the material 'external' edifice of the *hacienda*, 'Las Águilas', and the spiritual 'tower' which Roberto Ricarte constructs.[13]

Mallea's most interesting novels, however, are those in which he is not so much projecting his own search for authenticity, as depicting more varied characters. In *Fiesta de noviembre* (1938), *Todo verdor perecerá* (1941), *Los enemigos del alma* (1950), and *Chaves* (1953), there is a break with the straightforward quest situation. *Fiesta de noviembre*, though one of the earlier works, is the most sophisticated in its structure (Mallea is little interested in formal experiment), for the novelist interleaves three stories: in the first Señora Rague (the visible Argentina) holds a party for society; in the second, her daughter Marta and the painter Lintas meet and converse (they represent the 'invisible Argentina'). The third story concerns the murder of a writer (Lorca) in an unidentified foreign country and reminds us that the novel was written when Fascism was triumphant in parts of Europe. The novel is a good example of Mallea's narrative style in which the past tense predominates. There is no attempt at immediacy. Instead events are related as history, as past. Here, for instance, is the opening of the novel:

> El treinta de noviembre, justamente a las ocho de la noche, las celosías que daban a los dos flancos, sobre las dos calles, fueron cerradas. La residencia quedó así como un continente de temperatura mucho menos elevada que el creciente sofoco de la ciudad, y el asedio exterior de esta ola calurosa pareció apretar, concentrar en el comedor, los salones, las habitaciones altas, el fresco olor costoso y señorial de las magnolias, los geranios, las fresias, los claveles, las 'rosa mundi' y los primeros jazmines de la temporada. Todavía sonaban las ocho en el ronco reloj Tchang del primeró piso.

The prose effectively delineates a geography of this 'visible Argentina' separated from the rest of the world, artificial, unnatural, and rich. Marta and Lintas are to separate themselves from it physically by leaving the party and thus exposing themselves to the outside world and its potential violence. In doing this, they will find themselves.

In *Todo verdor perecerá* and *Chaves,* Mallea broaches another theme which is central to his work and which he had already touched on in the stories published in the collection *La ciudad junto al río inmóvil* (1936)—this is the theme of isolation and lack of communication. Chaves, a naturally silent man, tries during the crisis of his life to break down the barrier between himself and others by talk, but talk fails to bring his dying wife back to life and he relapses into silence and isolation: 'bajó de las palabras a la llanura de su soledad'.

In *Todo verdor perecerá,* the theme of isolation takes on hyperbolic proportions in the story of Ágata Cruz, a woman who had been unable to communicate with her widowed father, whose unhappy marriage only increases a sense of solitude, and who on her husband's death has an affair with the shifty Sotero who abandons her. Plunged into despair, she faces her own essential solitude. 'Dios, ¿cuándo encontraré quien hable mi lenguaje?'. She ends in solitary madness, persecuted by the children of the town in which she lives.

Mallea is somewhat different from most contemporary novelists in that his novels are thesis novels and in some cases they border on the essay.

Both Mallea and Marechal, though very different writers—and Borges too—are characteristic in their eclectic erudition of a Spanish American literary tradition which began with Bello, which runs through Modernism, and which culminates in their work and in that of the Cuban Lezama Lima. They are men who, according to Borges, belong to Western culture and yet, like the Jews, are outside it.[14] Their erudition sometimes strikes the European rather oddly. Borges, for instance, claims a debt to a group of English writers who are very little-known among contemporary Englishmen—he quotes Stevenson, Sir Thomas Browne, Chesterton. Marechal's literary world belongs to the classical and medieval periods, from Homer to Dante, but with an admixture of James Joyce and the European avant-garde of the twenties. Mallea breathes a kind of European good taste which would not be out of place in Proust or Oscar Wilde. Quite apart from the merits of their work, there is this aspect in them of guardians of a culture that has come to them in books and which is separated from its origins. In rootless Argentina, this electicism is almost a way of life. In Cuba, the contrast between the erudition of a Lezama Lima and the semi-literate and illiterate pre-Revolutionary Cubans for whom print culture did not exist was even more flagrant.

V. JOSÉ LEZAMA LIMA

José Lezama Lima (1912-) belongs properly to the pre-Revolutionary period, though his major novel, *Paradiso* (1966), appeared after the Revolution. He was a poet, formed during the forties, during which period he edited the magazine *Orígenes* and wrote a hermetic poetry, imbued with Catholic mysticism. His was the 'hortus conclusus', the 'pradera oscura'. Cuba during this period was living violence and dictatorship. Many writers lived in exile. Those who remained, like Lezama Lima, felt themselves besieged. He himself shut himself in a world of myth and literary tradition constructed of random reading, especially in neo-Platonic literature. As against the limitations of an unjust society, he saw art as a sphere of liberty and the poet as the 'engenderer of images'—'El sujeto metafórico actúa para producir la metamorfosis hacia la nueva visión', he wrote.[15]

Like Marechal, Lezama Lima avails himself of myth and the title, *Paradiso*, that he gave to his novel is a reference both to Biblical innocence and to Dante's goal. The novel is about a childhood and adolescence, but the author refuses a biographical, evolutionary structure. Instead there is a dense, poetic text with no continuity other than its relation to the writer-protagonist José Cemí. The author shows him sweating with fever during a childhood sickness; now we are transported to Jacksonville in the United States where his

mother had lived as a girl; now we are in Havana when his mother
and father are courting. There are long dialogues, too, between Cemí's
student friends, Foción and Fronesis. But these incidents are simply
starting-points for the substance which is part poetic description
and evocation, part discussion of the creative process.

The novel constantly takes flight into the realm of the marvellous.
In one scene, for instance, a guitarist plays in the back of a car and
like Orpheus he transforms the whole of the natural world:

> La palabra eternidad aparejó un sopor, dando comienzo a un
> inmenso ejército de tortugas verdes en parada descanso. Tortugas
> con el espaldar abombado, durmiendo con algas y líquenes sobre el
> escudo. Dentro de una niebla de amanecer, los chinos aguadores
> comenzaban a regar las lechugas. El desprendimiento de los vapores
> hipnóticos de la lechuga, hacía que los chinos manoteasen la niebla,
> se recostasen en ella con una elasticidad de sala de baile o lanzasen
> sus palabras pintadas de azul. La inmensa legión de lechugas, mon-
> tadas en tortugas inmóviles; era el primer sembradío de la eterni-
> dad.

A simple popular song carries us into the fantastic world of creation
myth. Tortoises, lettuce, Chinese are words completely liberated from
day-to-day associations and are now freed to form a fantasy inspired by
the music. This world of the fantastic always lies just below the surface of the novel. It can be discovered at any moment by a chance
meeting, a sudden juxtaposition of words or events. Reality, on the
other hand, is very violent. As the guitarist sings and evokes the
fantasy, quoted above, the driver of the car in which he and Alberto
Olaya are travelling crashes into a sea-wall and Alberto is killed.
The novel opens with the illness of José Cemí; the Colonel, his father,
dies suddenly of influenza; his mother undergoes an operation to
remove a fibrome (which is minutely described); Alberto's brother,
Andrés, is killed in a lift after giving a violin recital; the dialogue of
Fronesis and Foción takes place against a background of violence with
troops attacking the university students. The violence of reality becomes
mythic and dreamlike. Dream informs the whole of reality, and the
novel constantly recalls a primitive unity before the division of the
world into categories and the separation of imagination from action,
the individual from the universal. As Cortázar was the first to point
out:

> A Lezama no le importan los caracteres, le importa el misterio
> total del ser humano, 'la existencia de una médula universal que
> rige las series y las excepciones'. De ahí que los personajes en los
> que el autor está mas comprometido vivan, actúen, piensen y hablen
> de conformidad con una poética total.[16]

Cortázar admires Lezama Lima for the 'innocence' and 'freedom' of his work and declares: 'A Lezama hay que leerlo con una entrega previa al fatum, así como subimos al avión sin preguntar por el color de los ojos o el estado del hígado del piloto'. It follows that a new critical attitude is necessary to cope with a work which like *Tristram Shandy* or *The Anatomy of Melancholy* occupies a mysterious zone beyond the normative categories of literature.

VI. LO REAL MARAVILLOSO

Writing of a journey to Haiti in 1943, Carpentier declared:

> A cada paso hallaba *lo real maravilloso*. Pero pensaba, además, que esa presencia y vigencia de lo real maravilloso no era privilegio único de Haití, sino patrimonio de la América entera donde todavía no se ha terminado de establecer, por ejemplo, un recuento de cosmogonías. Lo real maravilloso se encuentra a cada paso en la historia del Continente.[17]

'Lo real maravilloso' is not so much a 'school' of writing as a conviction held by a number of authors that American 'reality' is of a different order from that of Europe. The main representatives of this trend—the Cuban Alejo Carpentier, the Guatemalan Miguel Ángel Asturias, and the Paraguayan Augusto Roa Bastos—all come from smaller Latin American countries which had never known the mass organisation of people into factories, the categorisation of humans into an efficient workforce. They came from pre-industrial areas and this factor makes it important to distinguish them from the European Surrealists, who also celebrated 'the marvellous' but did so in reaction to an industrialised society which had imposed its own grey, mechanistic standards. Both Asturias and Carpentier were in Paris during the Surrealist movement, but both interpret the 'marvellous' in a way that is substantially different from the Surrealists or from the 'real maravilloso' of the Futurist Massimo Bontempelli.[18]

VII. ALEJO CARPENTIER (1904-)

Alejo Carpentier is a second-generation Cuban of French and Russian stock, a trained musicologist who wrote a history of Cuban music and who has always been interested in musical composition, an interest reflected in the musical *leitmotif* of several of his novels and stories. He was one of a group of Cuban intellectuals involved in the political militancy of the twenties, for which he was briefly imprisoned in 1928. During this period, he was associated with the

Afro-Cuban movement, wrote some Afro-Cuban poems, a black 'passion' which was performed in Paris, and a documentary novel on Afro-Cubanism[19] which was published with photographs in 1933. This was *Ecué-Yamba-O*, a work which is still of documentary interest though quite uncharacteristic of his later style. For several years after the publication of *Ecué-Yamba-O* he seems to have written little. When he began to write again, his novels and stories were based on journeys and had quest structures. The first of these to appear was the *nouvelle, Viaje a la semilla,* which reverses the usually chronological, biographical order and relates the life of a Cuban landowner from deathbed to birth and then back to the origins before human existence. The story is a lighthearted one, an extended joke, though it already showed a loving regard for catalogues and detail which was to become characteristic. In 1943 Carpentier visited Haiti, became interested in the story of the slave revolts at the end of the eighteenth century and in Henri Christophe, the black king. In 1949 he published *El reino de este mundo*, which, though set in the period just before and after the French Revolution, was not a historical novel in the ordinary sense. To begin with, great liberties were taken with history. The novel jumped drastically from the Mackandal rebellion to the story of Henri Christophe without mentioning the rise and fall of Toussaint Louverture. The novel falls into four periods which are chosen to stress Carpentier's criticism of alien 'orders'—the 1760s when Mackandal rebelled against the French; the beginning of the French Revolution up to 1802; the fall of Henri Christophe in 1820; and the period just after the death of Christophe. The unity between these periods is thematic, but they are also linked together by the fact that the negro house-slave, Ti Noël, appears in each of them. In this way, events are subordinated to the author's pattern, the novel shifting between the 'European' and the 'African'; the events are filtered through the consciousness of Ti Noël who is on the margin of both worlds—that of the Lenormand Mézy family, whose house-slave he is, and the 'African' world of the fugitive rebel, Mackandal. But from the first pages, it is the rational, cerebral world of French culture that is presented in the most critical light. Thus, Ti Noël looks at four waxen European heads outside the barber's shop:

Aquellas cabezas parecían tan reales—aunque tan muertas, por la fijeza de los ojos—como la cabeza parlante que un charlatán de paso había traído al Cabo, años atrás, para ayudarlo a vender un elixir contra el dolor de muelas y el reumatismo. Por una graciosa casualidad, la tripería contigua exhibía cabezas de terneros, desolladas, con un tallito de perejil sobre la lengua, que tenían la misma calidad cerosa, como adormecidas entre rabos escarlatas, patas en gelatina, y ollas que contenían tripas guisadas a la moda de Caen.

By the very contiguity, the heads of the fashionable wigs and the sheep's heads are identified. A few years later, the European revolutionaries would sever the heads of their enemies as if to strike off the seats of reason.

The Revolution triumphs and dreams of spontaneity, of imitating the noble savage, but this dream, too, is seen as grotesque. Paulina Bonaparte, married to General Leclerc, arrives in the island, her head full of romantic novels;

> Y así iba pasando el tiempo, entre siestas y desperezos, creyéndose un poco Virginia, un poco Atalá, a pesar de que a veces, cuando Leclerc andaba por el sur, se solazara con el ardor juvenil de algún guapo oficial.

Violence and death break into this dream and send Paulina hurrying back to France. Finally there is Henri Christophe's dream, his empire and castle of San Souci, which are mere reflections of Louis XIV and Versailles, mechanical imitations, built on the forced labour of his black subjects and as remote from their beliefs as the old régime. All that is left of Henri Christophe's empire after his death and the looting that follows is the king's green coat carried off by Ti Noël who delivers commands to the wind. The novel ends with Ti Noël's return to the now empty estate of Lenormand and the arrival of the new mulatto class who will take over.

El acoso (1958) is the novel which most closely reflects the atmosphere of the Cuba of the fifties, the stifling circle of repression and violence. Yet it is as far as Carpentier's other novels from being a documentary novel. The symphonic score imposes a pattern which is analogous to the web in which the main character, 'el acosado', is caught. The symphony ends, the 'acosado' is shot by the students he has betrayed, quite unable to avoid his fate.

Los pasos perdidos, published in 1953, returned to the quest theme, though it was not a historical novel. Based on a journey that Alejo Carpentier made while staying in Venezuela, it is, like *El acoso*, a work that reflects the claustrophobia and frustrations of the Batista régime. And, like all Carpentier's novels, it is very close to allegory. The story is that of a sophisticated musician who works on film scores in a large industrial country; of his wife, a successful actress, acting in an interminable play; and of his mistress, Mouche, who makes her living out of astrology. This triad represents the corruption of art in the Western world. The musician undertakes a journey to a nameless Latin American country in search of primitive musical instruments. This will be his retracing of lost steps and will take him first to the revolutionary upheaval of a Latin American capital where, during a strike and fighting, the jungle once again invades the city; to an artist's refuge away from the revolution in the hills where the alienated native painters nostalgically talk of Paris; and lastly into the jungle itself, accompanied by an expedition seeking for a place so remote from civilisation that they can build Utopia there. The three unnamed points on the musician's compass are Europe and the European culture to which the musician belongs (he is writing a setting to Shelley's *Prometheus Unbound* and is haunted the while by memories of Beethoven's Ninth); North America, whose urban rhythms are so different from the organic rhythm, where culture has become a mere collage of fragments.

Thirdly, there is the world of the jungle, not a primitive world, for even so-called 'savage' life is highly complex, but one which still conserves creative vigour and variety. But unlike other members of the jungle expedition—the woman Rosario with whom he falls in love, the Adelantado (the Pioneer), the missionary—the musician cannot stay away from 'civilisation'. He is taken out of the jungle by helicopter and when, months later, he tries to return to find Rosario, he cannot rediscover the opening in the forest wall that will take him to her. He recognises that he is divided from her by history. She knows nothing of history; the 'Adelantado' wants to begin again at the beginning; but the musician must situate himself not in the past but in his own time and even a little beyond it. He must, in short, be an 'avant-garde'. But the conflict occurs when the avant-garde has lost touch with the organic and the archetypal. Both Europe and America represent dangers in this respect. The Europe the musician recalls is not simply that of Beethoven, but that of the Second World War. Feeling and art have been divided from action and reason. North America is a sterile urban and commercialised culture quite cut off from creativity. But to retrace 'lost steps' cannot be the whole solution either, since the artist cannot live in the past. The problem is not solved at the end of the novel. And perhaps it is not solved because it was Carpentier's own dilemma, and particularly the dilemma of the Cuban. Havana at this period was a replica of a North American city, with strong links with Europe and with the pervasive underground culture of the African slave. The latter still had creative vigour, and perhaps *Los pasos perdidos* was, in one sense, Carpentier's own warning, administered to himself, that creative vigour must be preserved without returning to prehistory. A few years after its publication, Cuba was on the verge of a change so radical that the structures of the past would be swept away, North American and European influence virtually eliminated by the blockade, leaving the Cuban artist with only his own resources.

In this post-Revolutionary period, Carpentier published his finest novel, *El siglo de las luces* (1962), which was set in the French Revolutionary period. In common with many of his other novels, it has a quest structure and like *El reino de este mundo*, the theme is the breakdown of the 'siglo de las luces' with the French Revolution. But the historical events are also related to the adventures of a single family—the son, daughter, and nephew of a Cuban merchant, left orphaned by his death, just as the French were left without authority on the collapse of the monarchy. The young people—Carlos, Sofía, and their cousin, Esteban—find themselves in sole possession of their father's goods and, delighted at their liberty, they plunder Europe for their enjoyment, buying anything that comes to their fancy and storing it in the huge house. At the point where liberty is becoming license, a saviour appears—the Haitian freemason Victor Hugues, who takes them under his control. On the outbreak of the French Revolution, he sets off to Haiti with Sofía and Esteban, but Sofía is forced to turn back by the violence of events and the two men go to Europe without her. Esteban seeks meaning in the French Revolution, but soon sees the degeneration of the Revolutionary movement into lifeless bureaucracy. And Victor Hugues degenerates with the Revolution. When he again embarks for the West Indies with Esteban to become the new Governor of Guadalupe, he takes the guillotine with him, justifying this on the grounds that he is also taking a decree which emancipates the slaves. Even with the fall of Robespierre, the position does not change. Victor Hugues becomes uncrowned king of the island, living off buccaneering, and holding a more and more disillusioned Esteban in his thrall until the latter is released by being sent on a mission to Cayenne.

Esteban does not find a social Utopia in the French Revolution. Chaos is followed by authoritarianism, institutions arise out of the ashes of the old. Only when he journeys through the islands with the buccaneers and sees the marvellous and enigmatic creativity of nature do human events seen in the time-scale of creation fall into their true significance. Towards the end of his adventure with Victor Hugues, Esteban situates himself in the time-span of natural history, moving out of the narrow spirals that circumscribe a single life to observe with a God's eye-view the Oceanic life, the slowly changing clouds, or the shells. In the second part of the novel, Sofía undergoes a similar experience of hope and disillusion.

There is no psychological analysis in Carpentier's novels because his view is too wide to span a minute human life. He is concerned less with the individual than with the archetype—the Liberator, the Oppressor, the Victim—less with a life than with a historical span. The very style in which the novel is written represents the reference of the particular to the universal pattern. Thus, for instance, the globe with which Esteban and Sofía play becomes 'el símbolo del Comercio y la Navegación'. Carpentier is constantly reordering the world into categories under which he subsumes the many names of things. Hence, the lists of objects with which the novel is loaded, like this view of Havana at the beginning of the novel:

> extrañamente parecida, a esta hora de reverberaciones y sombras largas, a un gigantesco lampadario barroco, cuyas cristolerías verdes, rojas, anaranjadas, colorearan una confusa rocalla de balcones, arcadas, cimborrios, belvederes y galerías de persianas.

and just as the vast variety of perceptions can be crammed into a single sentence, so can great historical experiences. The second of May is related in four lines:

> Reinaba, en todo Madrid, la atmósfera de los grandes cataclismos, de las revulsiones telúricas—cuando el fuego, el hierro, el acero, lo que corta y lo que estalla, se rebelan contra sus dueños—en un inmenso clamor de Dies Irae.

In a recent *nouvelle*, *El camino de Santiago* (1967), the period of Counter-Reformation and religious war is similarly compressed, with untold human suffering conveyed in a single stroke:

> De Holanda, de Francia, bajan los gritos de los emparedados, el llanto de las enterradas vivas, el tumulto de las degollinas, la acusación, en horrible vagidos, de los neonatos atravesados por el hierro en la matriz de sus madres.

The effect is to change the reader's perspective from that of a single man with a single life to a much wider vision and time-span. With Carpentier we are in cosmic time and this has the effect of making individual tragedy seem a mere detail in a great and rather simple pattern.

VIII. MIGUEL ÁNGEL ASTURIAS (1899-)

Like Carpentier, the Guatemalan novelist and Nobel prizewinner Miguel Ángel Asturias also structures his novels around myth, although he usually starts from pre-Columban Indian myths rather than from the Western myths. As a student, he wrote on the Guatemalan Indian and studied anthropology at the Musée de l'Homme in Paris. His first imaginative work was *Leyendas de Guatemala* (1930), a poetic recreation of Maya and colonial folk-tales. During the dictatorship of Jorge Ubico, he began work on the novel that many people regard as his masterpiece, *El Señor Presidente*. The novel was published in 1946, after the fall of the dictatorship, but the style and treatment remove it from documentary. In fact, though based on the dictatorship of Ubico and that of a predecessor, Estrada Cabrera, it is the novel of Dictatorship rather than of one particular historical character.

El Señor Presidente introduces us into a caricature world of an oppressed city. All organic relationships are distorted, families broken up, associations except those that bind the citizens to the Dictator are shattered. The old natural world in which human life developed and grew to fruition has disappeared to give way to the city, which is particularly susceptible because of its very structure to total control by the Demiurge-Dictator. The novel thus reflects the change, which Asturias certainly feels to be disastrous, from an organic community to the modern urbanised community which in Latin American conditions immediately becomes the prey of an irrational madman. This is Dr Strangelove in the microcosm of a Latin American republic.

Like Carpentier, Asturias structures his novel on a mythic pattern, on the age-old struggles between the powers of light and the powers of darkness, which is reflected in universal myths but also in Latin American and more particularly Maya myth. The novel opens with church bells ringing through the city, booming 'lumbre de alumbre' and 'Luzbel de piedralumbre'. Luzbel (Lucifer)—in the novel the Dictator's favourite, Cara de Ángel—will arise against the demiurge in order to assert his individuality and will be destroyed. The novel presents us with a world of darkness and indeed begins at night with the city beggars sleeping in the shelter of the arcades; among them is an Idiot, haunted by memories of a Mother from whom he feels an eternal sense of separation. Thus against the masculine powers of oppression and darkness, against the demiurge who has created the evil world in which society lives, there is the ideal of a Mother, of the earth, and of the organic. The Idiot, deprived of the light of reason, nevertheless feels this subconscious truth, and in its name kills Colonel José Parrales, thus setting in motion the tortuous web of crime that is the plot. For the Dictator decides to use the killing not to punish the real murderer, who in any case will be shot by an over-zealous policeman, but in order to hunt down a suspected traitor, Eusebio Canales. And the instrument of Canales's overthrow will be Cara de Ángel.

The chain of rational cause and effect which forms the structure of the Realist novel is here deliberately broken. The beggars are tortured, not so that they will confess the truth that the Idiot killed Parales, but so that their words will confirm the President's own paranoia. Those who will not share his paranoia, like 'el Mosco', are tortured to death. With the support of the rational taken away, the inhabitants of the novel are victims of darkness and unreason.

The style of the novel gives this dark vision its maximum effect. Short chapters jump from incident to incident, person to person, with the only unity, the common fear of 'El Señor Presidente'. Even the faithful are not exempt from punishment, since irrationalism is carried to the point of the absurd. One of the President's own clerks, docile to the point of idiocy, is beaten to death for a minor fault. It is in this light that we must see Cara de Ángel's rebellion. By falling in love with Camila, the daughter of General Canales, whom he allows to escape, he commits the gravest sin of all. Not only has he disobeyed 'El Señor Presidente', but he dares to marry Camila and hence tries to substitute a natural relationship for that with the President. The second half of the novel is concerned with the trapping of Cara de Ángel, the cruel illusion he is offered of escape, and his slow depersonalisation in a concentration camp where he becomes a mere number. He dies at last when falsely informed that Camila is unfaithful to him. And the man responsible for his capture and torture is a Major Farfán whom he himself had once helped to survive.

Asturias uses a process of caricature, exaggeration, reduction of persons to animal or puppet level in order to achieve a grotesque nightmare effect. But what we witness in the novel is not simply a case history of a dictatorship. It is a demonstration of what happens to man when his relationships cannot develop naturally; when as substitute for a family unit or for religious faith, there is only attachment to the state, which is embodied in the person of a madman. But it is the environment of the modern city which makes this possible. Like the Idiot, people and things are snatched out of the matrix and hence become mere objects to be used and cast aside. The photograph and the moving picture substitute human contact; the telephone—so easily tapped—supplies communication; the brothel supplies love; and the prison becomes the only place where men, though kept in darkness, can communicate, dream the only area of freedom in which they know the truth about themselves. But outside the city is 'el campo', a place of hope, the idyllic valley where Camila and Cara de Ángel spend their honeymoon, where her father takes refuge and starts a revolution, where she herself finally hides in order to bring up her child. El Señor Presidente thus oscillates between the city and country, between darkness and light, between nightmare and dream, with thematic images as much as plot being responsible for the unity.

Asturias's other major novel is Hombres de maíz (1949) which, though totally different in theme, has much in common with El Señor Presidente. Like the previous novel, Hombres de maíz is structured around the antinomies of light and darkness, closed and open eyes, sleeping and waking, dreaming and insomnia. The theme of the novel is also similar, being the destruction of an organic way of life—this time that of the Indians—by the ladinos who invade Indian communal lands in order to grow maize for profit. The Indians cannot defend themselves against the overwhelmingly powerful forces of the army and against the treachery of the Machojón family; but they have weapons which the white man and the mestizo do not dream of.

These are the weapons of magic and myth. The Indian chief who resists becomes a mythic hero, and a curse descends on the Machojón family who had betrayed them.

But the destruction begun by the *maiceros* cannot be stopped. They have committed a kind of original sin by introducing an element of imbalance into nature. The Indian world is organic, integrated:

> Al sol le salió el pelo. El verano fue recibido en los dominios del Cacique de Ilóm con miel de panal untada en las ramas de los árboles frutales, para que las frutas fueran dulces; tocoyales de siemprevivas en las cabezas de las mujeres para que las mujeres fueran fecundas; y mapaches muertos colgados en las puertas de los ranchos, para que los hombres fueran viriles.

The *maiceros* release the demon when they upset this balance. With the appearance of this original sin, the Golden Age is over. The communities decline, though myth and magic still allow them to transform reality. The blind man Goyo Yic loses his wife, María Tecún, and has his blindness cured so that he can find her, only to discover that sight cannot help him find a woman he has never seen. The myth of the lost María Tecún is the myth of the Indian's loss and separation. Goyo Yic's drunken journey to sell clandestine *aguardiente*, and on which he and his friend drink the liquor and end in jail, symbolises the Indian inability to understand the world of commerce. And the story of the postman, Nicho, who turns into a *coyote* and so once again gains possession of ancestral wisdom, illustrates the inability of the Indian to come to terms with the modern social organisation for Nicho burns the letters that have been entrusted to him.

But in the eyes of the state, these Indians are not myth figures but simply criminals who end far from their native hills serving sentences in the coastal penitentiary. And finally it is the state which wins. Life loses organic significance.

Asturias has written a whole series of novels since *Hombres de maíz*, though he has found it difficult to wed the theme of social protest successfully to a lyrical and mythic presentation. His works include a trilogy about the banana plantations which he was probably inspired to write during the brief democratic interregnum of the Arévalo and Arbenz governments. The trilogy comprises *Viento fuerte* (1950), *El Papa verde* (1954), and *Los ojos de los enterrados* (1960). He also published a fictionalised account of the invasion of Guatemala and the fall of the Arbenz government, *Weekend en Guatemala* (1956). One of his most recent works, *Mulata de tal* (1963), is a renewed attempt to create modern myth. The chapters have titles like fairy stories, 'Gran Brujo Bragueta convertido en enano por venganza de su mujer', 'La danza de los gigantes y la guerra de los esposos', etc.

But whereas in *El Señor Presidente* and *Hombres de maíz* style and theme are wedded, *Mulata de tal* is a virtuoso piece. Asturias can create new mythic figures, having learned the procedure of myth, but in doing so, he has severed the 'marvellous' from the 'real'.

IX. REALISM IS NOT PROSAIC: AUGUSTO ROA BASTOS AND JOSÉ MARÍA ARGUEDAS

Augusto Roa Bastos (1917-) is a Paraguayan writer, José María Arguedas (1911-69) was a Peruvian. Both of them have written novels which remain close to 'reality', which are accurate observations of the society in which they live; yet the harshness of the events they describe is tempered by a lyrical style. And in both authors this lyricism of style derives in some measure from their use of Indian words and the rhythm of Indian languages.

Roa Bastos uses *guaraní* expressions freely in his outstanding novel, *Hijo de hombre*.[20] This is a novel which covers a hundred years of Paraguayan resistance to dictatorship, from the middle years of the nineteenth century to the Chaco war of the 1930s. The events are not told in strict chronological succession, but are grouped around figures or events. The unity of the novel centres on two symbols—a Christ carved by a leper which has become the symbol of rebellion among the inhabitants of Itape; and the railway line, the modern symbol of rebellion, since it was here on the station at Sapukai that two thousand Paraguayans were killed by a government bomb during an armed rebellion. Each generation is decimated, but the fight never entirely ends. The central figure of this resistance is the almost mythic Crisanto Jara, who survives the train explosion and survives the suffering of the *maté* plantations, and whose son carries on the bitter struggle.

Superficially this material would seem to make *Hijo de hombre* a protest novel of the *Huasipungo* type. But the style in which it is written removes it from any such comparison. The incidents even when cruel or brutal are recounted with tenderness, and the human dimension is never sacrificed to theology. Here, for instance, is the account of Jara's mad journey in a railway carriage for which he lays down the sleepers himself, and whose journey nobody betrays:

> ... en el caso del vagón todos se callaron. El jefe de estación, los inspectores del ferrocarril, los capataces de cuadrillas. Cualquiera, el menos indicado habría podido alzar tímidamente la voz de alerta. Pero eso no sucedió. Una omisión que a lo largo de los años borronea la sospecha de una complicidad o al menos un fenómeno de sugestión colectiva, si no un tácito consentimiento

tan disparatado como el viaje. Es cierto que el vagón ya no servía para nada; no era más que en montón de hierro viejo y madera podrida. Pero el hecho absurdo estribaba en que todavía podía andar, alejarse, desaparecer, violando todas las leyes de propiedad, de gravedad, de sentido común.

The passage indicates how Roa Bastos adopts a conventional symbol of progress—the railway train—and converts it into something totally different. The train had brought death during rebellion, but Crisanto Jara makes it into the vehicle for a marvellous journey in which the whole of the Paraguayan populace act as accomplices. And its miraculous survival, despite its ruined state, is symbolic of the persistence of people even beyond hope.

José María Arguedas, like Roa Bastos, draws on popular myth and uses Quechua expressions. Indeed in his early work, the short stories of *Agua* (1935), he tried to devise a Spanish on the basis of Quechua modes and constructions. His first novel, *Yawar fiesta* (1941), though far more lyrical, was related to the social protest and Indianist novels, and it was not until his two major novels, *Los ríos profundos* (1958) and *Todas las sangres* (1964), that he wedded the lyricism of popular sources with major themes.[21]

Los ríos profundos was based on biographical material and is a first-person account of Ernesto's adolescence, much of which is spent in a Catholic boarding school at Abancay. Ernesto is torn between the Indian and Spanish cultures and feels that he belongs to both. From the first, the reader is aware of two different systems of values below the surface of life. At the outset of the novel Ernesto and his father visit the house of an avaricious but pious old man, 'El Viejo' who lives in Cuzco. El Viejo sends them to sleep on a trestle bed normally reserved for Indians and thus classifies them socially before he has even addressed a word to them. This social classification is only the surface manifestation of deep patterns of racial sensitivity, which are manifest in the very stones and buildings of the very town.

> Era estático el muro, pero hervía por todas sus líneas y la superficie era cambiante, como la de los ríos en el verano, que tienen una cima así, hacia el centro del caudal, que es la zona temible, la más poderosa.

The Inca remains are nearer to the vitality of nature; Hispanic culture, in contrast, seeks to hold motion and stem the flux. There is a type of spirituality associated with Inca belief just as there is with Spanish Catholicism, but they are somehow incompatible. It is evident that Arguedas is searching for differences at far deeper levels than those of the Indianist novel. Ernesto is in touch with a spiritual world 'cargado de monstruos de fuego, y de grandes ríos que cantan con la música más hermosa al chocar contra las piedras y las islas'. This spiritual life can be grasped in broad patterns of motion and rest, river, stone, and on a cultural level in the songs and music and even of the playthings of the Indian children. Ernesto's world is full of invisible and half-perceived correspondence between a world of nature and that of Indian institutions and culture. The *cholos* (part-Indian, part-Hispanic), who preserve the harp music and who have instinctive communal feeling, are part of this world of hidden but deep relationships. It is the white Catholic, Hispanic world whose culture and spirituality are more ambiguous. Arguedas does not draw a division between Indian and cruel Spaniard, for there are moments when the Catholic too attains depth and understanding; but the very structure of the boarding school is symbolic of their outlook on the world. It is shut off from the life of the town, dark, enclosed, and somewhat sinister. Sexuality becomes perverted and the boys give vent to their repressed sexuality on the person of an idiot kitchen maid. Meanwhile life goes on outside—there is an uprising of *cholo* women, the army arrives in the town, there is an outbreak of plague —and the school cannot entirely cut itself off from these, though its relationship to the town is a paternalistic one. That is why Ernesto always evokes rivers as a magic charm against the stagnant rotting atmosphere within.

Los ríos profundos has much in common with the novels of Asturias in evoking a myth world, but in one respect, it is different. Arguedas does not resolve contradictions. Throughout the novel, Ernesto's attitude to the school and the director are ambiguous. The headmaster is part of the landowning establishment, but Christian mercy also works within him and at times converts him into the substitute father whom Ernesto needs. The Church, the school, and its discipline offer a masculine side to existence, but deprive the boys of the feminine world of instinct and feeling. Ernesto attempts to balance these two worlds as he attempts to balance the two cultures within him. Hence, though the novel has a roughly biographical structure, its attention to the deep truths lifts it out of any psychological or social sphere. Ernesto's responses are aesthetic—to colour, music, song, language, and natural life, and when he responds, he is indifferent to social class or race. As in Wordsworth, this aesthetic response is also moral and natural. Thus, listening to the song of the larks, Ernesto declares:

> Los hombres del Perú, desde su origen, han compuesto música, oyéndola, viéndola cruzar el espacio, bajo las montañas y las nubes, que en ninguna otra región del mundo son tan extremadas.

And he adds that he himself is made of 'la materia' of the lark's song, for it belongs to 'la difusa región de donde me arrancaron para lanzarme entre los hombres'.

It is in this profound sense that the maternal Indian side of Ernesto must triumph. Separation, orphanhood find some satisfaction in Catholicism, but wholeness and integrity belong to the realm of the maternal.

X. A NEW VISITATION OF HELL. COMALA, MACONDO, AND SANTA MARÍA

Comala, Macondo, and Santa María are fictional places, invented by Juan Rulfo (Mexico; 1918-), Gabriel García Márquez (Colombia; (1928-), and Juan Carlos Onetti (Uruguay; 1909-). Lost in a nameless wilderness, the three places are located somewhere at the frontier of reality and fantasy, on the map first drawn by Dante. Juan Rulfo's Comala resembles the mouth of hell:

> Aquello está sobre las brasas de la tierra, en la mera boca del infierno. Con decirle que muchos de los que allí se mueren regresan por su cobija.

Macondo, at first a Garden of Eden, turns into a barren hell. Santa María occupies a grey intermediate zone between hell and purgatory. People go there:

> para usar el tiempo restante en el ejercicio de venganza sin trascendencia, de sensualidad sin vigor, de un dominio narcisista y desatento.

In other respects, the inhabitants of Comala, Macondo, and Santa María are as different from one another as inhabitants of different continents. Each author has created an imaginative world that is totally distinct, consistent, and recognisable as his own.

XI. JUAN RULFO

Rulfo was born in the Mexican province of Jalisco, an area of barren lands and of sad and deserted villages. He has published one collection of short stories, *El llano en llamas* (1953), and one novel, *Pedro Páramo* (1955), and the mythical town of Comala is the setting for both the novel and some of the short stories. The landscape is constant—a Great Plain on which rain never falls, hot valleys, distant mountains, remote villages inhabited by solitary people who nurse guilt and vengeance, living in a purgatory of suspense. Life is never here and now for these people, but somewhere in the future or the past, or somewhere over the plain or the mountains. His characters are perpetually either pursued or pursuing. In these villages, time takes on different dimensions, as it might for a man in a cell or for the sick. In the story 'El hombre' different streams of time are conflated, so that a man who has tracked down an enemy and killed him and his family, only to be tracked down in his turn, is seen simultaneously as pursuer and pursued as he dialogues with an invisible avenger. The story is like a brief nightmare, for the man flees but never gets away. The horizon is never closer. The ravine he tries to swim down sends him back. And time too casts him back in the same way because there is no future for him, no horizon. It is the fate of Rulfo's characters to be caught in this way, not so much by society but by the net of their own guilt. In 'Talpa' an adulterous pair, who allow the woman's husband to die while they sleep together, will never be free of their guilt. The dead man will always be between them. In 'Díles que no me maten', a man expiates a murder he has committed thirty-five years before. His avenger is just as much trapped by events as he himself and has to have his victim shot even though he no longer feels any hatred of him.

The loneliness of the haunted and hunted man finds an outlet in the monologues and the confessions which are often the framework of the stories. The reader is like the ear of the confessor, leaning to catch the last words of the condemned, scarcely able to unravel the meaning of events whose original motivation is lost in time or obscurity. This obscurity is often physical. In 'En la madrugada', for instance, a mist shrouds the village as Esteban begins his confession. He tells what he remembers—his boss Don Justo who has beaten him, a calf that did not want to be separated from the mother—but the event for which he is imprisoned—the killing of Don Justo—he cannot remember at all, although he is assured that it is true: '¿Con qué dicen que lo maté? ¿Que dizque con una piedra, verdad?' The truth is that violence wells up from an unconscious zone and it is useless to look for motivation or explanation. The violent men are peasants, unused to verbalising. It is the outside world which judges their actions as crimes or categorises them as violent. In 'La cuesta de las comadres', the narrator is the only man in the village who can live under the shadow of the bandits, the Torricos brothers, but even he turns on them one day and when he least expects it. One of the Torricos brothers falsely accuses him of killing:

> Por eso, al pasar Remigio Torrico por mi lado, desensarté la aguja y sin esperar otra cosa se la hundí a él cerquita del ombligo. Se la hundí hasta donde le cupo. Y allí la dejé.

This gulf between what is said and what is done always exists in Rulfo's stories as an unbridgeable chasm. Hence the need for confession though the confessions can never clarify. Even a halfwit, Macario, feels the need to confess, to tell of the comforting feel of darkness, the breasts of Felipe, and his fear of crude light, of the outside world where he is stoned and insulted. Inside, there is a certain security and comfort; outside there is a world that judges and categorises. 'Outside' is also society, though one that is scarcely ever just. In 'Nos han dado la tierra', even the post-Revolutionary government is alien to the deep feelings of the peasantry. They know, without having to utter the words, that the land they want is in the valley, but they are given the waterless plain.

For the men and women of Rulfo's stories, social order is an abstraction. For them, life is organised not according to social class but according to relationships—family relationships in which intimacy frequently gives rise to hatred or guilt, or the feudal relationship of the 'compadrazgo', the protection of the strong man who is both feared and yet regarded as 'good' insofar as he is effective as a protector. In 'El llano en llamas', the leader Pedro Zamora is more of a bandit than a revolutionary leader, but he is regarded as good precisely because he affords protection:

> Si él nos cuidaba. Ibamos caminando mero en medio de la noche con los ojos aturdidos de sueño y con la idea ida; pero él, que nos conocía a todos, nos hablaba para que levantáramos la cabeza. Sentíamos aquellos ojos bien abiertos de él, que no dormían y que estaban acostumbrados a ver de noche y a concertarnos en lo oscuro. Nos contaba a todos, de uno en uno, como quien está contando dinero.

This is the primitive relationship between men and the charismatic leader or protector. Rulfo is unique in recognising this attraction, for generally speaking, the Realist novel had painted a black/white picture of oppressor and oppressed. But Rulfo's intuitive knowledge enables him to appreciate the deep need of the poor for the powerful father figure, so much more real than the vague 'cielo' or 'horizonte' in which they also pin their hopes, but which they never reach. In 'Es que somos muy pobres' this horizon is a very limited one. Tacha simply wants to live a decent life and not become a prostitute like her sisters. But the cow which is her dowry is swept away in a flood and the inexorable rise of the waters are like the inexorable forces which will swamp her own life:

> y los dos pechitos de ella se muevan de arriba abajo, sin parar, como si de repente comenzaron a hincharse para empezar a trabajar por su perdición.

'¡Perdición!' The pull of hell is so much stronger than the pull of heaven because 'nature' is on the side of damnation. Whole villages and landscapes are damned in Rulfo's universe. Luvina, for instance, is a ghost village where flowers die, a village where the air is blackened and it is always dark, so that people lose count of time and live in a purgatory of waiting.

Nunca verá usted un cielo azul en Luvina. Allí todo el horizonte está desteñido; nublado siempre por una mancha caliginosa que no se borra nunca.

It is a place in which 'sadness nests', the streets are deserted, hours infinitely long. Young men leave so that only women and old people are to be found in the streets.

Me sonaba a nombre de cielo aquel nombre. Pero aquello es el purgatorio. Un lugar moribundo donde se ha muerto hasta los perros y ya no hay ni quien le ladre al silencio.

On Rulfo's map, Luvina is in purgatory. Heaven is distant and invisible; so the waiting can only be interminable or lead to damnation. But Rulfo's world has many places of this kind, places which are deserts until shaken by sudden tragedy or violence.

Rulfo's language is a stylised regional language, but he is not a regional writer any more than Tolstoy was. His landscapes are real landscapes, but are also moral analogies. His characters are Jalisco peasants, but their inability to communicate their real urges and feelings is universal. Perhaps the most regional aspect of his stories is a characteristic black humour which illuminates even the most horrifying moment. The revolutionary bandit Pedro Zamora bullfights with prisoners as a grotesque variation on executing them. And the most humorous of the stories, 'Anacleto Morones', has the grimmest of backgrounds, for the narrator, the murderer of Anacleto Morones, is hiding the body in his own yard where he receives a group of women who come to ask for his help in securing the canonisation of Anacleto, the village soothsayer, of whose murder they are unaware. Despite this grim background, the story is a funny one, very much in the mood of Mexican death jokes. The black-clad women, most of them ugly and middle-aged, had adored the 'saint', because he had pandered to their sexual needs under the guise of his witch-doctor's craft. The humour arises from the disparity between the women's adoration of the dead man and the narrator's rankling memory of a cheat and hypocrite. In the following dialogue, between one of the 'beatas' and the narrator, the latter's disabused comment is sandwiched in between her own fervent beliefs.

— Está en el cielo. Entre los ángeles. Allí es donde está, más que le pese.

— Yo sabía que estaba en la cárcel.

— Eso fue hace mucho. De allí se fugó. Desaparecido sin dejar rastro. Ahora está en el cielo en cuerpo y alma presente. Y desde allá nos bendice. Muchachas, arrodíllense. Recemos el 'Penitentes somos, Señor', para que el Santo Niño interceda por nosotras.

This humour, however, serves to accentuate the sadness of the scene, not to alleviate.

Rulfo's stories are totally original. They are a vision not of a region of Mexico, but of a moral universe as recognisable as the pitfalls, valleys, and Vanity Fairs of *The Pilgrim's Progress*.

Juan Rulfo's major work is his novel *Pedro Páramo,* the story of a search for Paradise which ends in the hell of Comala. The narrator, Juan Preciado, has been sent back to her native village by his dying mother who remembers a place of green fields and abundance. Dante-like, Preciado is guided to the village by a mule-driver, Abundio, who conducts him into the burning hot valley of Comala, the 'mouth of hell' where all men are the sons of Páramo, where all the inhabitants including Páramo are dead, and where life is only memory. But it is some time before Preciado recognises the deadness of the village. Only gradually does he learn that Abundio the mule-driver is dead and that Eduviges, in whose house he stays, has committed suicide. Stifled by the noises of the past, Juan Preciado dies in his turn and shares a grave with Dorotea, a woman whose whole life had been spent longing for a child and whose hope is only crushed when she visits heaven in a vision and learns that it will never be fulfilled. Dorotea's unfulfilled life and wasted hope is the common pattern in Comala, where people see themselves not as they are but as they want to be. Dorotea sees herself as a mother. Pedro Páramo, who extorts, kills, steals, and thus rises from being a poor boy to wealthy *hacendado,* never recognises that he is an unjust oppressor, but always sees himself as the romantic young man, dreaming of Susana San Juan, the woman he finally marries but never really possesses. Dreams separate men and women, make communication impossible between them, make it impossible for them to attend to the suffering and injustice on this earth. Padre Rentería, the priest, who refuses absolution to the moneyless and absolves Miguel Páramo despite the fact that he is suspected of seducing his niece, epitomises the trust in heaven that leads his flock astray.

In this novel, Rulfo abandons the conventions of chapter arrangement in favour of an orchestration. Short, sometimes unconnected, sections are intercalated; snatches of dialogue or monologue, the voices of people whose identity the reader can only guess, form the substance of the book. The structure is poetic rather than logical, the links between the sections being often a matter of mood, an echoed word, or a memory association. Layers of time, of mood, of events have settled on the village like dust. In the opening chapter, for instance, Comala is imagined by Juan Preciado as the paradise his mother had remembered, 'una llanura verde, algo amarilla por el maíz maduro. Desde ese lugar se ve Comala, blanqueando la tierra, iluminándola durante la noche'. But in Abundio's eyes it is 'la mera boca del infierno'. The novel constantly vacillates between people's hopes and what is actually present. Thus the bustling life of Preciado's dream is contrasted to the deserted village he actually sees on his arrival:

> Fui andando por la calle real en esa hora. Miré las casas vacías; las puertas desportilladas, invadidas de yerba ...

> Al cruzar una bocacalle vi una señora envuelta en un rebozo que desapareció como si no existiera. Después volvieron a moverse mis pasos y mis ojos siguieron asomándose al agujero de las puertas.

The physical world seems to exist quite independently of this world of dream and imagination. Thus in the passage quoted above, Juan Preciado's feet carry him along, his eyes look, even though his imagination is unwilling to grasp this reality. But the world of illusion kills the real world. Preciado finds himself suffocated.

> No había aire. Tuve que sorber el mismo aire que salía de mi boca, deteniéndolo con las manos antes de que se fuera. Lo sentía ir y venir, cada vez menos; hasta que se hizo tan delgado que se filtró entre mis dedos para siempre.

Once Juan Preciado is dead, it is Dorotea who becomes his guide and identifies the voices for him. She is one character in the book who has visited heaven in a dream and therefore knows that belief and hope in this other world is nonsense. From the shelter of their grave, she and Preciado relive the final years of Páramo's life. They see his dreams of marrying Susana San Juan finally realised and they witness Susana's refusal to give herself to him, for in dream she is still bound to her first dead husband. When she dies, Páramo's reason for living has gone. He is the dying king who allows the countryside to go to waste and who, to the last, refuses to give. He is killed by his own son, Abundio, who has been refused money for his wife's funeral, but the murder, too, is dreamlike. Neither Pedro nor Abundio seems really to be 'there' during the killing and the reader only guesses what has happened from the reactions of the servant Damiana. The section is a fine example of Rulfo's technique, with its superimposition of planes of memory, imagination, reality, and the shifting focus as attention moves from one figure to the next.

> [Abundio] trató de ir derecho a su casa donde echó a andar calle arriba, saliéndose del pueblo por donde lo llevó la vereda.

> Damiana—llamó Pedro Páramo—Ven a ver qué quiere ese hombre que viene por el camino.

Abundio siguió avanzando, dando traspiés, agachando la cabeza y a veces caminando en cuatro patas. Sentía que la tierra se retorcía, le daba vueltas y luego se le soltaba; él corría para agarrarla, y cuando ya le tenía en sus manos se le volvía a ir, hasta que llegó frente a la figura de un señor sentado junto a una puerta.

Here we have Abundio's drunken attempt to go home, the sudden cut to Pedro Páramo, and then Abundio's attempt to control his movements, which is exactly analogous to the characters' attempts throughout the novel to seize their hopes, to grasp their illusions. The road carries Abundio fatally to Páramo, whom he kills without realising it. The dark forces of passion, greed, envy, resentment are what rule lives, whereas the forces of light exist only in illusion.

The regions of ambiguity, of planes of perception ironically juxtaposed, are impossible in the linear narrative, but they are what give Rulfo's work its real significance.

XII. JUAN CARLOS ONETTI (1909-)

Onetti's novels, like Rulfo's work, constitute a moral geography. Some, though not all, of them are set in Santa María, a remote river port, decaying but self-sufficient, a place where hope seeps away, where people are dedicated to mediocrity.

Lo importante a decir de esta gente es que está desprovista de espontaneidad y de alegría; que sólo puede producir amigos tibios, borrachos inamistosos, mujeres que persiguen la seguridad y son idénticas e intercambiables como mellizas, hombres estafados y solitarios. Hablo de los sanmarianos; tal vez los viajeros hayan comprobado que la fraternidad humana es, en las coincidencias miserables, una verdad asombrosa y excepcionante.

This passage indicates an important difference, between Onetti's world and Rulfo's. Rulfo's characters are damned because they refuse to live in the here and now, Onetti's are damned insofar as they subscribe only to a vulgar materialism. To have a dream is to be in some sense (perhaps only temporarily) saved.

Onetti's stories and novels have a remarkable consistency, for both deal with characters on the edge of despair. They put up a losing fight on the verge of the grave, make a last gesture of humanity in the grey desert of loss.

Onetti's first novel, *El pozo*, was published in 1939 and concerned a lonely man, attempting to write, to communicate his visions—to the woman he loved, to a prostitute, or a friend. 'Sólo y entre la mugre', 'Encerrado en la pieza', he is already the archetypal Onetti hero who has reached the stage where self-deception and hope are coming to an end. All he can narrate are the successive failures of communication. There is nobody to share his dreams, he has no ideal to realise, unlike his friend, the militant, Lázaro, unlike the poet, Cordes. At the end of the story he can only recognise his total solitude.

Man's enemies are dirt, age, prostitution, routine, money. But worst of all is loss of hope. When men and women lose hope, they turn desperately against one another in order to destroy. In the *nouvelle* *Tan triste como ella*, a husband deliberately destroys the garden, the symbol of love and communion, and covers the ground with cement so that his wife, in desperation, commits suicide. In the short story 'El infierno tan temido', a faithless wife persecutes her husband with pictures of herself in pornographic postures and when finally she sends one to their daughter, he too commits suicide.

How do people sink into this pit of hatred and desperation? Onetti does not offer explanations, only mirrors of degradation. The prose is like a magnifying glass held up to the tissue of decay.

Onetti's stories and novels fall roughly into two cycles. *El pozo, Para esta noche* (1943), *Tierra de nadie* (1941), *La vida breve* (1950) belong to a first cycle in which the characters attempt, though unsuccessfully, to realise themselves in society. *Para esta noche* (1943) dealt with a dictatorship and the attempted flight of Osorio, which is, in reality, a dream flight. But there is still an illusion of dealing with real people, of problems in a real world. *Tierra de nadie* is also set in a 'real' moral desert, that of Buenos Aires, with its rootless, amoral inhabitants. *La vida breve*, as many critics have pointed out,[22] marks a transition point, for in this novel, the central character, Brausen, realises himself in dream and not in the real world. Onetti had already sketched out a similar situation in a short story, 'Un sueño realizado', in which a madwoman pays two actors to act out a dream for her. In *La vida breve* (1950) this germ grows into a complex structure in which the central character, Brausen, is a voyeur for whom life is not his own dull existence with Gertrudis, the faithful wife who has just been operated on for breast cancer; but it realises itself next door in the noisy apartment of 'La Queca'. Brausen is the incarnation of routine:

> Juan María Brausen y mi vida, no eran otra cosa que moldes vacíos, meras representaciones de un viejo significado mantenido con indolencia, de un ser arrastrado sin fe entre personas, calles y horas de la ciudad, actos de rutina.

But by assuming the name Juan María Arce and penetrating the next-door apartment, he becomes his 'other', a violent, more masculine character who plans murder. However, there is a third plane of fantasy in the shape of Dr Díaz Grey (a 'real' person in some of Onetti's later novels) who becomes another of Brausen's *personae* and who eventually dreams his creator. The search for a different *persona* constitutes a search for liberation from the horrors of physical existence, which Gertrudis's severed breast horribly reminds Brausen of.

Onetti's later novels are set in the fictional town of Santa María. *Una tumba sin nombre* (1959), *El astillero* (1961), and *Juntacadáveres* (1964) as well as some short stories are set in this community whose invention freed the author from any possible documentary interpretation.[23] Santa María is a web of despair, a geography of obstacles to authentic communication and existence. Larsen, Onetti's most impressive creation, is the human entity, the 'individual', as Santa María is the 'social'. Both are, in a sense, abstractions.

Larsen is the protagonist of both *Juntacadáveres* and *El astillero*. The first of these was written last, but refers to events earlier in time when Larsen, though middle-aged, still hoped to achieve his dream of organising a brothel in Santa María. The population of Santa María is divided between those who want the brothel (the chemist, Barthé) and those who reject it (the priest, Bergner); between the 'good' (the daughters of María) and the 'bad' (the prostitutes whom Larsen imports). The town is a moral battlefield on which old causes (positivism versus religion, purity versus lust) are apparently fought, but in reality the lines which people want to draw cannot be drawn. The pure are impure, the impure innocent. But the town nevertheless attempts to keep this distinction. The prostitutes are kept shut away in their brothel and run a gauntlet when they try to visit the town on their free afternoon. In this society, where people try to align themselves according to faiths or ideologies in which they no longer believe, the real polarisation is between the complete disillusion of Larsen and the inexperience (not purity) of the adolescent Jorge, who is irresistibly attracted to degradation and corruption and resigned to the horrors of adulthood when he finally penetrates the forbidden region. Thus at the end of the novel he describes himself as going away:

> me alejaba para bajar, sin remedio, hacia un mundo normal y astuto, cuya baba nunca se acercó a nosotros.

Santa María in this novel is a moral miasma in which people never fit the categories into which they are placed and in which legislation (the town council votes for the brothel) or the Church's institutionalisation of morality are both irrelevant. That is why the geography of bar, brothel, houses, and streets objectifies the falseness of all that is given form, since these forms then become immutable symbols of our existence: the brothel of corruption, the Church of purity. This is the 'mundo normal', the world of norms into which Jorge Malabia resignedly walks.

Onetti's finest novel is *El astillero*, the story of Larsen's return after a long absence to Santa María. It is his 'end as a man', but he fights to the last gasp, by creating one last illusion. The 'shipyard' which belonged to Petrus, a man who is charged with embezzlement, is empty and decaying, and Larsen undertakes to set it on its feet. He undertakes, too, to court the mad daughter of Petrus. The projects are those of the Balzacian opportunistic hero, but the scene is that of a ghost town:

> Larsen quedó solo. Con las manos a la espalda, pisando cuidadosos planos y documentos, zonas de polvo, tablas gemidoras, comenzó a pasearse por la enorme oficina vacía. Las ventanas habían tenido vidrios, cada pareja de cables rotos enchufaba con un teléfono, veinte o treinta hombres se inclinaban sobre los escritorios ...

Here is meaningless activity carried to the point of absurdity, for Larsen, in an office that is empty except for the two last employees, Kunz and Gálvez, will read old files, read the itinerary of ships that had passed long ago. He is at the heart of a great modern enterprise which exists only in a dream which is shattered the minute he realises that Petrus is imprisoned for embezzlement. Larsen is, of course, no innocent. He has been a pimp and is a criminal. Yet out of 'el astillero', he creates the pattern of his whole existence—a project (the shipyard), a pure love (Petrus's mad daughter), communion with another (Gálvez's wife), satisfied love (with a maid), though each is a grotesque caricature, as the shipyard itself is a mockery of a real enterprise. Nonetheless, Larsen's story is true tragedy. For it is finally the grotesque repetition of his failures which kills. As Larsen leaves Santa María just before his death:

> pudo imaginar en detalle la destrucción del edificio del astillero, escuchar el siseo de la ruina y del abatimiento. Pero lo más dificil de sufrir haber sido el inconfundible aire caprichoso de setiembre, el primer adelgazado olor de la primavera que se deslizaba incontenible por las fisuras del invierno decrépito.

The renewal of spring is so different in nature. In human life, and most particularly in the lives of Onetti characters, development is irrevocable, the pure die young. There is no cycle which allows man to start life afresh.

One of the most difficult aspects of Onetti's work is his prose style, which is dense, opaque, indirect. He favours indirect speech. 'Pensé entonces, no que estaba loco, sino que su voluntad era suicidarse'; it is the stance of the voyeur, like the Larsen who peers through the windows of a hut and sees Gálvez's wife bearing a child but will not go in to help. It is a style which is always approximating to discovery and comprehension and as personal and as fitting to his vision as his creation of Santa María.

XIII. GABRIEL GARCÍA MÁRQUEZ (1928-)

It is no exaggeration to say that García Márquez's *Cien años de soledad* has become as popular in the Spanish-speaking world as *Don Quixote*. It was the culmination of a long apprenticeship in which the creation of the imaginary town of Macondo was slowly elaborated. In *La hojarasca* (1955), *El coronel no tiene quien le escriba* (1962), *La mala hora* (1963), in the short stories of *Los funerales de la Mamá Grande*, a remote, solitary town torn by internal dissensions and hatreds, breeding-ground of eccentricity, is the protagonist. And from the first novel, *La hojarasca*, Gabriel García Márquez liked to imagine a lonely and proud figure living out a life in defiance of the society around him. In this first novel, the doctor whose funeral provides the framework of the story is still an ambiguous figure. He is an outsider who arrives in the small town to practise medicine, only to find that the clientele fade away when the Banana Company arrives, bringing more up-to-date medical practitioners. The doctor shuts himself away in voluntary isolation and when the Banana Company abandons the town and civil war breaks out, he refuses to treat the wounded, and for this is sent to Coventry. Thus resentment is nursed, long after the original causes are forgotten, and even extends beyond the grave. Like Onetti, García Márquez's main preoccupation is this question of individual authenticity within an unjust society. It is a theme which recurs in short stories, such as 'La siesta del martes' which was written about 1948 and based on an incident the author remembered from his childhood.[24] A woman whose son has been shot as a thief arrives in town during the siesta hour and goes to lay flowers on the son's grave, while the inhabitants gather in hostility at the doors and windows of their houses. The woman's dignity and integrity is unshaken. She is one of the prototypes of the colonel in *El coronel no tiene quien le escriba*, a story that is a minor masterpiece. In *El coronel*, all rhetoric is stripped away and we are left with the starkness of the colonel's isolation. Veteran of a civil war, he has for fifteen years been awaiting a pension. Each week when the post arrives, his hopes are dashed. His one son, Agustín, has been shot for distributing illegal leaflets and has left the colonel with no source of income other than a fighting cock which he cannot afford to feed. Moreover, the town is controlled by political enemies, leaving him absolutely no option, no escape, except into his own dignity and integrity and the pride which he hangs on to with ferocious persistence. The pride becomes incarnated in the fighting cock which he sees as a symbol of the crushed forces of the town and which he finally refuses to sell. At the end of this novel, he is left without prospects, starving but with his dignity untouched. 'Se sintió puro, explícito, invencible'.

Cien años de soledad has been called by Mario Vargas Llosa the *Amadís* of America.[25] All García Márquez's early themes come to fruition in this novel. It is a mythic work, dealing as myths always do with a migration and the founding of a city. Isabel and José Arcadio Buendía are first cousins and fear that their marriage will give birth to monsters. They leave the town of their birth in order to found Macondo in an inaccessible region and though for the first years of its existence, Macondo lives in primeval innocence and ignorant of history, its innocence and ignorance are based not on natural goodness but on original sin:

> Macondo era entonces una aldea de veinte casas de barro y cañabrava construidas a la orilla de un río de aguas diáfanas que se precipitaban por un lecho de piedras pulidas, blancas y enormes como huevos prehistóricos.

For some time Macondo's only contact with the outside world comes about through the visits of gypsies with their tribal leader, Melquíades, who introduces the inhabitants to the wonders of false teeth, ice, and the magnet, and arouses in José Arcadio an ambition to attain the scientific knowledge of the outside world. All the Buendía men are to be born with a self-destructive thirst for realisation, for breaking out of their limits, while the women are absorbed by birth and death, by houses and shrouds.

Macondo's isolation does not last. Its relationship with the outside world always remains anachronistic, but progress does arrive—a *corregidor* makes an appearance, the town is dragged into a civil war, a railway is built, a Banana Company is installed with foreign managers; thousands of strikers are massacred, a rainstorm destroys the plantations, the Banana Company withdraws and leaves Macondo in isolation again. In miniature, this is a reflection of Spanish America's isolation and the cycle of progress and neo-colonialism.

But Macondo also represents tragedy at a deeper level than the social. At the end of their history, the last of the Buendía family begins to decipher the manuscript that Melquíades has left and finds that he is reading the history of the family and that this history will last only as long as the reading:

> todo lo escrito en ellos era irrepetible desde siempre y para siempre, porque las estirpes condenadas a cien años de soledad no tenían una segunda oportunidad sobre la tierra.

The act of reading is itself an act of solitude and death which can never be repeated. The ending suddenly brings the reader face to face not with comedy (for on the surface the novel appears comic) but with tragedy. Life is unrepeatable, lives are irreversible. The dead are dead. And this realisation should make the reader go back and reconsider. For despite the marvellous humour of these grotesque characters, they are suddenly revealed to have tragic dimensions. They are 'alone in their dreams' and these dreams are vast smoke-screens between them and oblivion, like the gold fish which the Buendías manufacture in their workshop. The real terror of life is that it cannot be repeated and the only way to bear this terror is through humour. Hence death is constantly presented in a magical way—flowers rain down on José Arcadio when he dies, Remedios la Bella is assumed into heaven hanging onto a sheet, a massacre during a carnival leaves a wake of dead Pierrots and Columbines and Chinese empresses. The novel thus becomes a magical attempt to confront death. Characters paradoxically are monstrously alive precisely because of the hyperbolic individualism which isolates them, rather like the feats of saints which divide them off from ordinary mortals. Remedios la Bella has no sense of guilt and walks around without clothes, quite unafraid of sexual aggression. Fernanda is the epitome of Catholic purity:

> llevaba un precioso calendario con llavecitas doradas en el que su director espiritual había marcado con tinta morada las fechas de abstinencia venérea. Descontando la Semana Santa, los domingos, las fiestas de guardar, los primeros viernes, los retiros, los sacrificios y los impedimentos cíclicos, su anuario útil quedaba reducido a 42 días desperdigados en una maraña de cruces moradas.

Her husband's mistress is yet another remarkable woman—Petra Cotes whose love 'tenía la virtud de exasperar a la naturaleza' and who makes cows reproduce as rapidly as rabbits. The men too are exaggeratedly eccentric, the José Arcadios being dreamers, the Aurelianos men of action. But this abundant life has tragic undertones, for even the grand eccentrics are condemned to oblivion.

One of the most remarkable aspects of *Cien años de soledad* is that the novel breaks away from Realism by going back to the sources of fiction in myth and romance. The very prose in which it is written has a traditional ring, announcing its intentions with the formulae of the storyteller:

> Muchos años después, frente al pelotón de fusilamiento, el coronel Aureliano Buendía había de recordar aquella tarde remota en que su padre lo llevó a conocer el hielo.

It is the 'past mythic' tense, the demonstrative 'aquella' referring to something which only the story-teller can reveal through his magic.

XIV. ANALYSING THE PAST: AGUSTÍN YÁÑEZ AND CARLOS FUENTES

If García Márquez magically re-creates the past, Agustín Yáñez (1904-) and Carlos Fuentes (1928-), two Mexican writers, analyse it and confront it with the present. Agustín Yáñez, a prolific novelist whose first work was *Flor de juegos antiguos* (1942), has published a series of novels which cover Mexican provincial and metropolitan life before, during, and after the Revolution. The most successful of these is *Al filo del agua* (1947), in which, using a technique of stream of consciousness, he portrayed the collective life of a small town in Jalisco, a place as remote as Macondo, and living in a period of pre-history just before the Revolution. It is 'prehistorical' because the forces of the town are directed against change. The church, under a puritanical priest, Father Dionisio María Martínez, is the principal force of order and through the Daughters of María imposed 'rígida disciplina, muy rígida disciplina en el vestir, en el andar, en el hablar, en el pesar y en el sentir de las doncellas, traídas a una especie de vida conventual, que hace del pueblo un monasterio'. The town's rhythm is that of the liturgical year which endows the place with timeless stability. Or so it seems, until Micaela, a girl from the capital, arrives to disturb its rigid attitudes. She and another outsider, Damián, a native son who has lived in the United States, represent the external forces which are about to disrupt the town. The appearance of the Haley comet is seen as a portent of disaster and the novel ends with the approach of the Revolutionary army which will free the town not only from tyranny but also from the artificial 'innocence' that the Church had imposed.

Agustín Yáñez's novels, along with those of José Revueltas (1914-) and Juan Rulfo, marked a transition in the Mexican novel, away from social protest and Realism, and towards experiment. There has been no more fertile creator than Carlos Fuentes (1928-), novelist and short-story writer, with interests in the cinema and the theatre, whose writing develops out of a perpetual sense of irritation with the country of his origin. As a child he travelled from one country to another, since his father was a diplomat, and he became sophisticated, multilingual, and, by the fact of living abroad, highly critical of his own environment.[26]

Fuentes is an accomplished short-story writer who has published *Los días enmascarados* (1954), *Cantar de ciegos* (1964), and a *nouvelle*, *Aura* (1962), but his main contribution has been to the novel. Here all his effort is directed at breaking the linear narrative. Only one of his works, *Las buenas conciencias* (1959)—the story of the rebellion of a young provincial against false social values and his ultimate conformism—has a conventional evolutionary structure. His first novel, *La región más transparente* (1959), in which the protagonist was the city of Mexico and which he described as 'una síntesis del presente mexicano', attempts to link the diachronic and synchronic by mixing the lives of all classes of Mexico City at a single brief period in time. A mythic character, Ixca Cienfuegos, is the force that synthesises the distinct elements, a group of typical Mexican characters: opportunists like Roberto Régules and Librado Ibarra; a *nouveau riche* banker, Federico Robles; his snobbish wife, Norma Larragoiti. Fuentes's difficulty in this novel arises from his critical attitude. He asks the question, 'Who killed the Mexican Revolution?', and to answer this he must plunge into the past, show us how his characters came to be as they are, how Mexico came to lose truth and authenticity through aping the outside world:

> México se ha convertido en una especie de basural para todo lo que trae la marea de otras partes del mundo.

This is one of the intellectual characters speaking, ineffectual like many of Fuentes's characters, yet gifted with a clairvoyant sense of what things ought to be: 'Hay que crearnos un origen y una originalidad'. The characteristic of Fuentes's major work is this critical eye which sees defects pitilessly but no easy solutions, in which characters are caught in a web of lies and boredom from which it is too late to escape.

La muerte de Artemio Cruz illustrates that self-analysis does not necessarily lead to action. The protagonist, a millionaire and one of the most powerful 'new men' of post-Revolutionary Mexico, lies pinned to his bed from the beginning to the end of the novel, able to see, relive, and correct his vision of the past, but quite impotent to change it. At the outset of the novel, old and ill, he is not even able to recognise the image he glimpses in the reflection from his wife's handbag. The bloodshot eye he glimpses is an alien thing, as is his voice on the tape-recorder and the strange, new personality of the sick man who has not even the authority to get his wife to open the window. He has lost control, too, over his bodily functions. Only his lucidity remains. As he awaits the operation, unwillingly receives a priest and the visits of his family, perception, memory, and understanding split apart. The 'yo' that is Artemio Cruz leads him back to his moments of success and triumph—the time when he escaped from execution during the Revolution; his marriage to the wealthy landowner's daughter, Catalina, after the Revolution; his successful bid to remain in the President's favour during the Calles period; his rapidly growing fortune which is injected with North American capital. Each of these triumphs and survivals is, however, made at the cost of love, friendship, relationship with his son, personal happiness. These losses are recorded by an *alter ego* who addresses Artemio as 'tú', and a parallel third-person narrative records another aspect, not the subjective 'yo', nor the accusing conscience, but the objective decline of Artemio Cruz as a man.

This multiple and cinematic view gives us insight into the different forces at war for Artemio's soul and shows us why his 'survival' ethic triumphs over less egoistic feelings. His need to survive is stronger and more ingrained than either love or compassion. Survival implies the raping of the other, the treating of the 'other' as object. And as sexual virility grows weak, there is sublimation of this into other forms of power. Appropriately the woman who becomes his mistress and remains with him to the end of his life is Lilia, a girl he buys and whom he watches flirting and eventually making love to a boy of her own age as he lies on the beach. This conversion of the *macho* into the voyeur is significant, for the *voyeur* depends on the life of others. This makes Cruz (and his name—Cross—is a deliberate symbol) an incarnation of post-Revolutionary Mexico, in which the spontaneous young revolutionary turns into the impotent, wealthy old man whose wealth ultimately comes from foreign sources. Fuentes makes us ask where personal and social responsibility converge and suggests that society cannot be mature if man himself still clings to the adolescent *macho bravura* instead of growing up to accept the more feminine qualities of openness and self-sacrifice. But he is too clever a writer to suggest that there is any easy solution for this. Artemio dies at the end of the novel. The 'tú', 'yo', and 'él' become one in death.

Fuentes has since published two short novels, *Zona sagrada* and *Cumpleaños* (1970), and one long novel, *Cambio de piel* (1967), which also has a 'structure of impotence'. Four characters, a Mexican professor; his mistress and pupil; his wife, Elizabeth; and a German friend Javier are together on a car journey from Mexico City to Cholula, in a hotel room in Cholula, in a pyramid which collapses on them. Fuentes's intention was evidently to write an abstract novel with interchangeable characters, but he cannot free himself from his basic preoccupation which is, as in *Artemio Cruz*, with decay. His best passages are those which describe physical discomfort, crumbling towns, ageing bodies. *Cambio de piel* sets out to be a happening, but turns into the microscopic examination of a decayed relationship.

XV. MARIO VARGAS LLOSA

The Peruvian novelist Mario Vargas Llosa (1936-) is one of the best examples of the novelist for whom experiment is vital.[27] His novels deal with one of the major conflicts of our time, the antinomy between the historical and the structural. What is more, the devotion to the craft of writing shown by the author is exemplary in a continent where speedy achievement has all too often been valued over craft.

The titles of Mario Vargas Llosa's novels—*La ciudad y los perros* (1962), *La casa verde* (1966), *Conversación en la catedral* (1969)—all refer to structures, and there is something in the nature of structure which deeply obsesses the author. In each of these novels, buildings represent systems and order of ideas in such a complex fashion that the over-used term 'symbol' is plainly inadequate. The city and the school of *La ciudad y los perros*, the brothel, the island, and the convent of *La casa verde*, the bar called 'La Catedral' of *Conversación en la catedral* are all analogous to certain ways of structuring experience. They are highly disciplined systems in which variant elements are forced to act in a uniform manner. They deprive people of their personal histories in order to convert them into working elements of the whole. The determinism which many critics refer to when speaking of these novels is therefore something far more complex than the nineteenth-century understanding of this term. In Mario Vargas Llosa's institutions, the organic and the structural, the evolutionary processes and the synchronic relationships, are antithetical. Consider, for instance, *La ciudad y los perros*, a novel set in the Leoncio Prado military academy.

The anecdote is quickly told. A group of cadets, *los perros*, are identified by one fact only—the fact that they are all in the same year. Organised by 'Jaguar', they steal the questions for the chemistry examination. The 'Slave', an outsider in the group, denounces the thief in order to get a free Saturday and is mysteriously killed on manoeuvres. The mystery is not solved, but it brings about a confrontation between 'Jaguar' and the 'Poet', Alberto, who in turn has denounced Jaguar as the 'Slave's' killer. This anecdote is the scaffolding; the theft, the killing, the denunciation form a linear and chronological sequence, but this is like a series of beams or struts. The substance of the novel is a much denser substance, composed of the convergence of the individual histories of cadets and their masters with the discipline and routine of the school, the convergence of an organic development with family relationships, and the military academy with its timetable, rules, parade-ground which determine the patterns in which the individual students with their individual histories may fit. The impersonal synchronic structure of the academy has a distorting effect on instincts and a limiting effect on students' choice. They can become bully ('Jaguar') or bullied (the 'Slave') or a clown like the poet, but whatever they become, natural development will be violated. To survive the academy and still exist as a person means to break rules, but to break rules means to recognise their existence. The novel's 'inner history' is the moulding of a group to the exigencies of the academy and the group's disjunction. An arbitrary order (the novel opens with the number four called by Jaguar as they throw dice to see who will steal the question papers) substitutes natural order. And this man-made order is carefully laid out, delimited:

hacia la izquierda, se yerguen tres bloques de cemento: quinto año, luego cuarto; al final, tercero, las cuadras de los perros. Más allá languidece el estadio, la cancha de fútbol sumergida bajo la hierba brava, la pista de atletismo cubierta de baches y huecos, las tribunas de madera averiadas por la humedad. Al otro lado del estadio, después de una construcción ruinosa—el galpón de los soldados—hay un muro grisáceo donde acaba el mundo del Colegio Militar Leoncio Prado y comienzan los grandes descampados de La Perla.

The school is seen as a structure that is totally man-devised, a product of an ideology which, to be accepted, must first brainwash the boys, break them of their former loyalties, and induce the new code which Alberto, the poet, sums up:

aquí eres militar aunque no quieras. Y lo que importa en el Ejército es ser buen macho, tener unos huevos de acero.

The 'baptism' of the new boys is an initiation rite into the tribe: 'aquí uno se hace más hombre—aprende ... a conocer la vida'; but this involves losing individual freedom and taking on a group identity. All this constitutes a violation of individual and of 'natural' life. The officers violate the recruits—keep them shut in, kick them as part of the discipline; older boys violate younger boys, by making them go through the humiliating baptism; the boys violate one another, fight, masturbate, rape other boys, and even animals. The material of *La ciudad y los perros* might easily form the basis of a novel of social protest, but the technique of the author transforms the basic material into a far denser view of human motives. He uses not only a multiple viewpoint and different time planes, but intercalates different degrees of consciousness and awareness. 'Boa' represents a kind of collective subconsciousness, violence at its most primitive and instinctive level, and appropriately expresses himself in an undifferentiated stream of consciousness. The 'Poet' is the most coherent and articulate, and one of the most corrupt, members of the community, motivated by fear, need for self-preservation, and saleable, a man who conforms to the rules of the college as he will later conform to the society outside. 'Jaguar', who turns out to be one of the most individual and authentic members of the community, is a thwarted individualist. The variety of viewpoints suggests the complexity of the moral positions, the constantly shifting relationships of one cadet to another and the points at which system prevails over the individual.

In Mario Vargas Llosa's second long novel, *La casa verde*, the destruction of chronological sequences is even more drastic. In effect, we have a number of parallel life histories—that of Bonifacia, who is a 'selvática', a girl from the jungle, educated at a convent, expelled from it, married to an army sergeant, and finally inmate of a brothel; that of the Sergeant, a slum boy disciplined by the army, returned to civilian life where his *macho* code gets him into trouble, so that he ends in jail and on his release finds his wife in the brothel; that of Fushía, an escaped convict who has led a group of bandit rubber-stealers from his headquarters on an island, who falls sick, and goes to a leper-colony; that of his wife Lalita, who marries a corporal, Nieves, and later marries a third time. But the originality of the novel is not in these interweaving lives, but rather in the manner in which they are connected. Each chapter of the novel falls into a number of subsections on different time-levels. By breaking up chronological order, Mario Vargas Llosa achieves a new perspective on lives, for we are constantly shown people both through their own eyes and in the eyes of others, from the present and from some time in the future and in the past. The effect is that of a relief map in which we see as from a height the convergence of life-rivers around islands, houses, towns, and from our height we can appreciate what the participants cannot—the way the present will slot into some future pattern and how its significance will change with the passing of time. And this is achieved not only through the slotting-together of different time planes, but also through the shifting points of view and tenses within the prose. Here, for instance, the Nun Madre Angélica, gives orders to the Sergeant.

> La Madre Angélica alza la cabeza: que hagan las carpas, Sargento, un rostro ajado, que pongan los mosquiteros, una mirada líquida, esperarían a que regresaran, una voz cascada, y que no le pusiera esa cara, ella tenía experiencia. El Sargento arroja el cigarrillo, lo entierra a pisotones, qué más le daba, muchachos, que se sacudieran.

The reader seems to be placed between the two, monitoring each reaction—the words of the Mother Superior, punctuated by the un-complimentary reactions of the Sergeant, the Mother Superior's intuition of the Sergeant's thought, the Sergeant's suppressed violence as he grinds the cigarette into the earth.

This detailed perception of people's thoughts and reactions is accompanied by a very broad overview in which river, convent, town are not simply specific historical places but have a mythic significance. The Marañón is The River, Piura The City, the 'casa verde' is not only a brothel of that name but also symbolic of the jungle. And these symbolic places correspond in the novel to the division between structures—(army, convent, brothel, town)—and 'life': the river. The author thereby draws a kind of existential map.

The unstructured external world is the object of man's violation, of his appropriation. In choosing the setting of the jungle, Vargas Llosa sets his novel in an area where there is little social order. Yet man still acts in response to the code of the system he is in. The opening of the novel shows the clash of three systems—Church, army, and Indians, none of whose members can really communicate with the others. La Madre Angélica speaks the language of the *aguarunas*, but their responses are beyond the bounds of her comprehension. Those who free themselves from one system, soon find themselves in another. Fushía runs away from prison, takes refuge on an island, but ends in a leper colony. Bonifacia leaves the convent, marries, and ends in a brothel. *La casa verde* is thus a very thorough exploration of what institutions do to human beings and how they structure men's lives.

The 'overview' has been applied by Mario Vargas Llosa in *Conversación en la catedral* to a most difficult theme—that of the historical and political past of the country. The 'conversation' takes place between a journalist (ex-communist and rebel businessman's son) and the black bodyguard of a dictator. The novel presents us with the 'world behind the news', the corruptions and betrayals of ministers, businessmen, and public figures; but it is not in any sense an *exposé* novel. It is a minute and detailed drawing of a process of corruption.

Mario Vargas Llosa has said that he considers himself to be a Realist, 'pero tengo un concept ancho, no mezquino, del realismo':

> En el mundo de la ficción, la verdad se llama autenticidad y es subjetiva. El escritor debe ser, ante todo auténtico, es decir, fiel a sí mismo, fiel a sus propias obsesiones, a sus fantasmas, a sus demonios, a su locura, aun a su mugre.[28]

What raises him above the level of many Realist writers is the density with which this 'authenticity' is presented.

XVI. THE NOVEL IN QUESTION. JULIO CORTÁZAR

In one of his best-known short stories, 'Las babas del diablo', which first appeared in *Las armas secretas* (1959), the story takes the form of an 'agony', the writer/photographer, Cortázar/Michel, writes/records what seems to be 'reality', though the recording is hedged in by questions: 'me pregunto por qué tengo que contar esto'; 'nadie sabe bien quién es el que verdaderamente está contando'; writer and photographer are concerned with the 'lying' nature of their craft. The writer and the photographer interfere with reality by recording it. The faithful reproduction can only represent nature without man, like the blown-up photograph he is finally left with on which rain and sunshine succeed one another

> quizá sale el sol, y otra vez entran las nubes, de a dos, de a tres. Y las palomas, a veces, y uno que otro gorrión.

It would be misleading, however, to convey the impression that Cortázar's short stories and novels are entirely concerned with the problem of perception and aesthetics. Like Mario Vargas Llosa his passion is for authenticity and precisely because of its nature, art stands at a borderline region where authenticity all too speedily becomes corruption. This is obviously so in 'El perseguidor', in which Johnny, the jazz musician, is observed by Bruno who has written a best-selling biography of him. Johnny's vital experience, his shunning of commercial success, his spontaneity, is constantly put in danger by Bruno's need to interpret, explain, 'save' (and finally to destroy). Aesthetic perception is fragile, constantly exposed to destruction, and must be purified, freed from accretions. Hence Cortázar's work is often a kind of preliminary burning which will clear away the mess of cliché. As he writes in 'Las babas del diablo': 'Ahora mismo (qué palabra, *ahora*, qué estúpida mentira)'.

Cortázar's art was slow in developing. Until he was thirty-seven, he lived mostly in Argentina (though he had been born in Brussels), and here wrote some poetry, essays, and other works, often using the pseudonym of Julio Denis. His first important work was the collection of short stories *Bestiario* (1951) and he has since published three other collections, *Final del juego* (1956), *Las armas secretas* (1956), and *Todos los fuegos el fuego* (1966), and a kind of burlesque manual, *Historias de cronopios y de famas* (1962), a guide to the 'inauthenticity' he wishes to destroy.

It would be absurd to try and present the complex and subtle world of Cortázar's stories in a few lines. But they are concerned with 'this side' and 'the other side', with what is structured and categorised and with what might broadly be termed 'imagination' or 'freedom'. The 'other side' is a world of unstructured creativity, like Johnny's music in 'El perseguidor', 'una construcción infinita cuyo placer no está en el remate sino en la reiteración exploradora, en el empleo de facultades que dejan atrás lo prontamente humano sin perder humanidad'. The problem becomes one of creating without destroying, constructing without over-structuralising. The problem is complicated by the existence of the reader or observer and perhaps this is the most variable element of all. In the story 'Axolotl', the narrator watches tropical fish through the glass of an aquarium and by dint of perception becomes an *axolotl*, seeing himself from the other side of the glass. But this is like the finished work of creation, looking back on the creator as a foreign and alien body. Once created:

> los puentes están cortados entre él y yo, porque lo que era su obsesión es ahora un axolotl, ajeno a su vida de hombre.

The relation between creator, creation, and public is also the subject of 'Final del juego', a story in which three little girls play 'statues' near the railway track. They have made their rules, but the game becomes more complex when they know that they are observed by a boy, 'Ariel', from the train. The existence of 'audience' changes the game, makes one of the girls use real instead of artificial jewels for the statue, but it also finally kills the game forever. There is undoubtedly a quest for purity which goes very deeply through Cortázar's work, a purity which might easily be upset and stultified.

Cortázar's short stories move in the direction of much greater self-consciousness with regard to the writer's role. In *Bestiario*, the stories still retain much anecdotal material. The 'self-consciousness' about language in 'Las babas del diablo' becomes the predominant preoccupation in many later stories, a preoccupation that is directed against all cliché, all routine. The reader is deprived of any opportunity to identify with characters, confuse art and reality, to 'use' literature. There is a clearing-away of accretions, a tendency towards purification and abstraction. This same process is evident in the novels. In the epilogue to the first of these, the author already disclaims interpretation, but the disclaimer is an appendage, not an integral part of the book. Yet a careful reading already betrays a self-conscious attitude to formula, and the novel begins with a reference to the phrase 'La marquesa salió a las cinco', a reference to what a novel is *not* about. The language and structure of *Los premios* has much to do with cliché. It relates the fortunes of a group of passengers who win a cruise on a lottery, embark in Buenos Aires, and encounter unexpected difficulties—the mysterious illness of the captain, a door to the stern which they are not allowed to open, a division of the boat into 'this side' and the 'other side' and of the passengers into those who accept the boat's destination and those who question and explore. A group of passengers try to reach the 'other side' and one of them, the dentist Medrano, is killed, whereupon the cruise suddenly ends and the passengers return to Buenos Aires. The journey-return structure and the cross-section of Argentinians would seem to put the novel in a common category. The journey acts as a bait to the reader, who wants to follow the passengers to a destination. In fact, there is no progression. The journey is the unaccustomed, the chance happening; the passengers act and react according to formula and to stale attitudes that the language exposes. The significant factor is not that people change, but that they remain almost entirely within the limitations of their personality. The exception is Medrano, who penetrates to 'the other side' both literally and psychologically, although to do so means death. But before his death, Medrano has a revelation of himself which shows him what he looks like from the 'other side':

> le dejaba solamente una sensación de que cada elemento de su vida, de su cuerpo, de su pasado y su presente eran falsos, y que la falsedad estaba ahí al alcance de la mano, esperando para tomarlo de la mano y llevárselo otra vez al bar, al día siguiente, al amor de Claudia, a la cara sonriente y caprichosa de Bettina siempre allá en el siempre Buenos Aires.

One other character remains outside the game. This is the 'astrologer', Persio, the only person who does not have a ready-made structure to escape into, one who allows reality to form its own patterns and delights in 'la perfect disponibilidad de las piezas de un puzzle fluvial'. This observer is the prototype of many, a man who sees the complexity of things:

> una infinidad tan pavorosa de simultaneidades y coincidencias y entrecruzamientos y rupturas que todo, a menos de someterlo a la inteligencia, se desploma en una muerte cósmica y todo, a menos de someterlo a la inteligencia, se llama absurdo, se llama concepto, se llama ilusión, se llama ver el árbol al precio del bosque, la gota de espaldas al mar, la mujer a cambio de la fuga al absoluto.

In *Rayuela* (1963), the entire form of the book is a questioning of literature and indeed art in its relation to reality. The structure no longer conforms to any traditional novelistic form. Instead the novel falls into three parts: 'Del lado de allá', 'Del lado de acá', and 'De otros lados' (*Capítulos prescindibles*), which consist of scraps of quotations, the meditations of an apocryphal writer, Morelli, and other matters. After *Rayuela*, Cortázar was to separate this 'scrapbook' side of the writing from his invention. In *62 Modelo para armar* we have the pure invention, in *La vuelta al día en ochenta mundos* and *Último round* (1969) we have the scrapbooks.

Rayuela earned a certain amount of notoriety on its first appearance because the author pointed out that there were two ways of reading the novel, either in the order it was printed or in the order he himself indicated. But once the initial novelty of being offered two (or more) readings wears off, it becomes obvious that the structuralisation of the novel into movable sections is only one aspect of the author's questionings about literature and its relation to reality. The artistic vanguard has, since its inception, been exercised by two paradoxical problems—the underlying structures and patterns of experience which abstract art seeks to isolate; and getting to the heart of the flux. In *Rayuela*, we have a third stage, a repeated demonstration and questioning of both these paths. In a sense, *Rayuela* is the *Encyclopédie* turned upside down. That is to say that whereas the *Encyclopédie* was the eighteenth-century manner of ordering reality and bringing all phenomena into the circle of the light of human reason, *Rayuela* represents the disintegration of all that constitutes culture and morality, and the demonstration of the conventional nature of thought, action, and literary activity. The basic paradox is that this must be done with language, and language is suspect in that it generates the conventions by its very nature. The central character of the novel, Oliveira, has reached the stage of questioning all verbalisation:

> Toda tentativa de explicarlo fracasa por una razón que cualquiera comprende, y es que para definir y entender habría que estar fuera de lo definido y lo entendible.

Like many other Cortázar characters, therefore, Oliveira is constantly questioning the words he has to use, aware that they are leading him in directions he does not want to go:

> Poner el día, vaya expresión. Hacer. Hacer algo, hacer el bien, hacer pis, hacer tiempo, acción en todas sus barajas. Pero detrás de toda acción había una protesta, porque todo hacer significaba salir de para llegar a, o mover algo para que estuviera aquí y no allí o entrar en esa casa en vez de no entrar.

Literature is simply one more deceptive ordering of disorder. This is the Maga's fascination for Oliveira because she grasps intuitively while he can only be ironic about her intuitions:

> Ah sí, el tacto que reemplaza las definiciones, el instinto que va más alla de la inteligencia. La vía mágica, la noche oscura del alma.

In one sense, then, *Rayuela* is the response to Oliveira's own command, 'No hagamos la literatura'.

The hierarchies of values that literature, language, and philosophy have imposed are continuously attacked, directly, through parody, through the invention of a new language, *gliglich*, through 'incidents' in the novel. Though there is no plot in the ordinary sense and no progression, the novel clusters around two geographical points. Paris (Oliveira's affair with Maga and Pola, the meeting of Oliveira's friends in the Club de Serpientes, the death of Maga's child, Rocamadour); and Buenos Aires (Oliveira's friendship with Traveler and Talita, his affair with Grekeptken and the circus and mental asylum in which they work). In the incidents and conversations which make up these clusters, parody, irony, and the constant questioning of the language not only act as a destruction of convention, but at the same time form a dike against the atrocious fragments of reality that are glimpsed. Paris is described as a metaphor. Oliveira feels that any corner of the city offers an analogy to life and its absurdities, but the humour and the parody seem an almost necessary weapon to stave off a tragic realisation that could only end in suicide. In the 'Paris' part of the book, for instance, the concert of Berthe Trépat, the death of Rocamadour are surrounded by layers of parody. Berthe Trépat is an avant-garde composer and pianist whom Oliveira goes to hear because it is raining and whose concert is given to a diminishing audience. Her 'compositions' are musical equivalents of what *Rayuela* is about —the breaking-down of traditional structures, the introduction of silence into the work, etc. And the whole 'invention' floats gratuitously free of any possible 'interpretation'. Berthe Trépat's concert and Oliveira's responses are clichés, mutual misunderstandings. Oliveira finds himself telling her he had enjoyed the concert, walking home with her, becoming involved in her sordid and pathetic life. The terror comes from the void that lies behind the meaningless and absurd structures. When Rocamadour dies, it is during a conversation between Oliveira and Ossip; unable to break the news to Maga, they go on talking about death and reality while friends arrive, gramophone records are put on, and the old man upstairs bangs on the ceiling. The decomposing baby's body impregnates the whole scene, and the jokes are more desperate than ever: little wonder that Oliveira compares the activities of the group to those of flies:

> todo eso va tejiendo un dibujo, una figura, algo inexistente como vos y como yo, como dos puntos perdidos en París que van de aquí para allá de allá para aquí, haciendo su dibujo, danzando para nadie, ni siquiera para ellos mismos, una interminable figura sin sentido.

Yet Oliveira does feel that there is a goal, though it is not 'upwards', not geographical. By the banks of the Seine, he lies down with the tramp, Emanuèle, is arrested, and taken off to the police station with her and with two homosexuals. In the police car, they look at the colours of the kaleidoscope that one of the homosexuals carries. For Oliveira this is the image of our knowledge of reality, as the game of Hopscotch with its 'cielo' or goal is the image of endeavour. But the goal will only be reached, the kaleidoscope will only achieve its most brilliant combinations when our way of structuring reality is totally transformed.

In one of the 'dispensable chapters', Morelli imagines a last sentence of a novel that would be like a wall. 'En el fondo sabía que no se puede ir más allá porque no lo hay'. *Rayuela* stands as one of the great tragic novels of our time, because it is erected as a barrier against a situation too desperate to contemplate.

While *La vuelta al día en ochenta mundos* and *Último round*, the two collections of essays and criticism, constitute—to use Ginsberg's phrase—*Reality, Sandwiches*, Cortázar's third novel, *62 Modelo para armar*, is wholly concerned with the point at which life becomes literature, and with the hazards and chances which the act of creation involves. But the book also arose out of the conviction that the writer has at his disposition more than he consciously knows. Cortázar confesses that he did not know how the novel would develop. In any case, in writing it he was also concerned with changing the relationship of author and reader. It is a 'model to make' in which there are people elements—Marrast, Polanco, Calac, Hélène, Nicole; cities—London, Paris, Vienna; ways of communications—roads, trains, underground. These are presented as schemata and it is expected that the reader himself will be there in the interstices—creating, suggesting, exploring. Cortázar is therefore not only concerned with the web he has made, but also with the holes in between.

The reader, however, must ask why this preoccupation? The abdication of form, the supply of a kit from which the reader may make his own novel, seem to reflect a conviction that there is no overview, that each man is alone with his individual experience. But finally this must seem a solution more tragic than *Rayuela*. In *Rayuela* the author offered us his shield against the horror of living, but he also allowed the horror to be glimpsed. In *62* he seems to offer only scraps and pieces of his notebooks, which we are intended to put together. Certainly the novel can be seen as the logical outcome of transferring the novel's interest from creator and created object to the reader.

XVII. GUILLERMO CABRERA INFANTE (1929-)

Cabrera Infante's novel *Tres tristes tigres* (1967) represents yet another development of the contemporary novel—the inventions of language systems as a parody on society. The author is a Cuban who published *Así en la paz como en la guerra* (1966), a series of short stories set in the Batista period. In 1964, he won the Biblioteca Breve prize for the novel *Tres tristes tigres*. Editor of the literary supplement *Lunes de la Revolución* during the early years of the Castro period, he was unable to fit into the austerities of the post-Revolutionary régime and now lives abroad. The novel *is* the language of Cuba spoken in 1959, just before Castro came to power, its substance a series of conversations among people in Havana, most of whom belong to the marginal world of nightlife—they are television personalities, singers, jazz musicians, the sons and daughters of the rich, photographers—all nightlife characters. They speak jazz slang, Afro-Cuban, *petit bourgeois*, and a myriad of other languages. At their centre is a group of intellectuals. All this would be merely a game if it did not give us a picture of what Cuban culture actually consisted of in 1959—the bastard culture of an island dependent on North Americans, with Spanglish as one of its idioms, with instant commercialisation and with a consumer culture overlaying any other aspirations. There are parodies of the 'literary men'—of Carpentier, Lezama Lima, and Guillén—whose 'cultured' style seems absurdly at odds with degraded reality. One of the central characters, Arsenio Cué, is an adept at punning, transforming words; through his mediation, European culture takes on a degraded Cuban mask. So in one passage, he lists 'great men':

> Américo Prepucio y Harun al'Haschisch y Nefritis y Antigripina la madre de Negrón y Duns Escroto y el Conde Orgazmo y William Shakeprick o Shapescare o Chasepear y Fuckner y Scotch Fizzgerald y Somersault Mom ...

So far from being simply a joke, Cabrera Infante illustrates literary underdevelopment, the swamping of the island in the consumer culture while lip-service is paid to the great names of history and world culture which, however, *are* simply names and not substantial parts of people's lives even when these people are intellectuals. One culture is imposed through the United States economic hegemony, the other is a weak attempt to resist this hegemony. There is no Cuban language and hence no Cuban culture. There are only alien influences and slang.

Brilliant as it is, Cabrera Infante's novel illustrates an attitude that contemporary novelists have inherited from the Modernists—a sense of a cultural gulf between them and their public. Cabrera Infante's novel suggests that there is no Cuban culture except as a grotesque reflection of European and North American civilisation, an attitude that can ultimately lead only to despair.

XVIII. THE REAL AND THE FANTASTIC

In the vast variety of the contemporary Spanish American novel, two aspects stand out: firstly, the almost universal need that writers have felt to break with the linear narrative; and secondly, the use of myth, fantasy, humour, and parody. As we have seen, this fantasy and humour may act as a shield between the writer and a reality too dreadful and hopeless to be contemplated direct. García Márquez's humour, Vargas Llosa's manipulation of time, and Cortázar's irony are in the nature of signals to the reader, warning him of what might happen without the mirror of Perseus.

It would be wrong, however, to give the impression that all modern writers have abandoned verisimilitude. If we turn to Chile, Uruguay, and some other countries, we find similar preoccupations among writers, but a manner of presentation which stays closer to Realism with the notable exception of Fernando Alegría who makes use of science fiction techniques in *Amerika Amerikka Amerikkka* (1970). In Chile, Jorge Edwards (1931-) and José Donoso (1925-) have taken the family situation of the traditional bourgeois novel in order to expose the weakness and inauthenticity of bourgeois society. Donoso uses conventional structure with great effect in *Coronación* (1959), in which servants take over a moribund middle-class household.[29] In Uruguay, too, the middle-class family tends to be used as a symbol of national institutions in the work of Carlos Martínez Moreno (1917-) and Mario Benedetti (1920-). Benedetti is the author of several collections of short stories and several novels, of which two, *La tregua* (1960) and *Gracias por el fuego* (1964), depict human relations in conflict with social structures. His outstanding work is the short-story collection *Montevideanos* (1959), in which he depicts the lives of office-workers, underpaid clerks, and secretaries of a Latin American city. He has a good ear for language and captures the surface quality of ordinary people's speech, as in this monologue of a footballer in 'Puntero izquierdo':

> le quise demostrar al coso ese que cuando quiero sé mover la guinda y me saqué de encima a cuatro o cinco y cuando estuve solo frente al golero le mandé un zapatillazo que te le bogliodire y el tipo quedó haciendo sapitos pero exclusivamente a cuatro patas.

Martínez Moreno's novels are frequently on political themes, though the political theme is expressed through personal and family relationships, notably in *El paredón* (1962). One of the most skilful political novels is that of the Argentine writer David Viñas, author of *Cayó sobre su rostro* (1955), *Dar la cara* (1963), *Los dueños de la tierra* (1959), *Un dios cotidiano* (1954), and *Los hombres de a caballo* (1968). Many of these are structured around events which have been significant in Argentina's history, notably *Los dueños de la tierra*, which is set during the Yrigoyen period. And in *Sobre héroes y tumbas* by Ernesto Sábato, the decline of the Argentine élite and the anarchism and oligarchy of the thirties is evoked through the history of a family whose heroic qualities have degenerated in modern Argentina.

In Venezuela, the contemporary novel also has centred on political themes. Miguel Otero Silva, in *Casas muertas* (1955) and *Oficina número 1* (1961), described the change from a provincial, rural society to the Venezuela of industry and oilfields. In *La muerte de Honorio*

(1968), he wrote the novel of political oppression, a theme which also recurs in the stories of Guillermo Meneses and in the *País portátil* (1969) by Adriano González de León which introduces the theme of urban guerrilla warfare into the novel. Another Venezuelan writer, Salvador Garmendia (1924-), reflects the new urban Venezuela in novels whose theme is often the frustrated and sordid lives of the petty bourgeoisie. His main works include *Los pequeños seres* (1959), *Día de cenizas* (1964), *Los habitantes* (1968), and *La mala vida*.

The Spanish American writer of forty or less has now an extraordinarily rich novelistic tradition on which to draw, a tradition that includes works such as *Rayuela*, *La casa verde*, and *Cien años de soledad*. Although it is too early to detect general trends, there has already developed a sophisticated urban novel in Mexico and Buenos Aires, and writers such as Manuel Puig (Argentina), Nestor Sánchez (Argentina; 1935-), Gustavo Sáenz (Mexico; 1940-), Salvador Elizondo (Mexico; 1932-), and José Agustín (Mexico; 1944-), whose technical skill is very high. At a moment when many European countries are going through a dead period in the novel, the genre has attained totally new dimensions in Spanish America.

NOTES

1. David Viñas, *Literatura argentina y realidad política* (Buenos Aires, 1964).
2. *El periódico Martín Fierro 1924-49* (Buenos Aires, 1949).
3. César Fernández Moreno, *Introducción a Macedonio Fernández* (Buenos Aires, 1960), pp. 16-20.
4. The stories referred to are 'Pierre Menard, autor del Quijote' and 'Examen de la obra de Herbert Quain', both in *Ficciones*.
5. 'El arte narrativo y la magia', in *Discusión* (Buenos Aires, 1932), pp. 119-20.
6. 'Descenso y ascenso del alma por la belleza', in *Revista de la Universidad de Buenos Aires* (April-June 1950), 521-46.
7. 'De la soledad', in *Odas para el hombre y la mujer* (Buenos Aires, 1929).
8. John H. R. Polt, 'The writings of Eduardo Mallea', *University of California Publications in Modern Philology* (Berkeley and Los Angeles, 1959).
9. E. Mallea, *Notas de un novelista* (Buenos Aires, 1954), p. 103.
10. *La vida blanca*, 2nd ed. (Buenos Aires, 1960).
11. *Meditación en la costa* (Buenos Aires, 1939).
12. From *La bahía del silencio*, and quoted Polt, op. cit.
13. Mallea has come under attack for 'mystification' from younger Argentinians. For some discussion of his critics, see E. Rodríguez Monegal, *Narradores de esta América*, I (Montevideo, 1969), 258-69.
14. J. L. Borges, *The Spanish Language in South America: A Literary Problem* (London, 1964).
15. 'Mitos y cansancio clásico', in *La expresión americana* (Madrid, 1969), p. 15.
16. Julio Cortázar, 'Para llegar a Lezama Lima', in *La vuelta al día en ochenta mundos* (Mexico, 1967).
17. In an essay printed as an introduction to *El reino de este mundo*

(Mexico, 1967) and included in a collection of essays, *Tientos y diferencias* (Mexico, 1964).

18. Massimo Bontempelli, *La avventura novecentista. Selva polemica 1926-38* (Firenze, 1938), used the term 'magic realism'. For a thorough interpretation of *El reino de este mundo*, see an article by Emil Volek, 'Análisis e interpretación de "El reino de este mundo" de Alejo Carpentier', in *Ibero-Americana Pragensis* (Año 1, 1967).

19. *Santería* is a Cuban form of transculturation of African religion.

20. *Guaraní* was preserved as the current language during the days of the Jesuit missions and survives as the main language in rural areas.

21. Mario Vargas Llosa, 'Ensoñación y magia en José María Arguedas', Preface to *Los ríos profundos* (Santiago de Chile, 1967).

22. Mario Benedetti, 'José Carlos Onetti y la aventura del hombre', in *Literatura uruguaya del siglo xx* (Montevideo, 1963).

23. *Juan Carlos Onetti* (La Habana, 1970) is part of a series of 'valoraciones múltiples' which collects the critical essays on this author.

24. Luis Harss, 'Gabriel García Márquez o la cuerda floja', *Los nuestros* (Buenos Aires, 1968).

25. The title of an article first published in *Amaru* (No. 3, 1967) and reprinted in *García Márquez* (La Habana, 1970) in the 'valoraciones múltiples' series. See also the same author's *García Márquez. Historia de un deicidio* (Barcelona, 1971).

26. See the interview with Fuentes in *Confrontaciones: los narradores ante el público* (Mexico, 1966), pp. 137-55.

27. His critical articles have not been collected, but they have appeared in a wide variety of magazines. Apart from those in the reading list see, for instance, 'Realismo sin límites', in *Índice* (Madrid, 1967)

28. ibid.

29. He has since published *El obsceno pájaro de la noche* (1971), a work with a gallery of grotesque characters that is totally different from his earlier novel.

READING LIST

Anthology

Alegría, Fernando, *Novelistas contemporáneos hispanoamericanos* (Boston, 1964)

Texts

Alegría, Fernando, *Amerika Amerikka Amerikkka* (Santiago, 1970)
Arguedas, José María, *Yawar fiesta* (Lima, 1941)
——, *Los ríos profundos* (Buenos Aires, 1958)
——, *Todas las sangres* (Buenos Aires, 1964)
——, *Amor mundo y todos los cuentos* (Lima, 1967)
Arlt, Roberto, *Novelas completas y cuentos*, 3 vols. (Buenos Aires, 1963)
Asturias, Miguel Ángel, *Obras escogidas*, 3 vols. (Madrid, 1955)
Borges, Jorge Luis, *Obras completas*, 2 vols. (Buenos Aires, 1966)
——, *Ficciones* (Buenos Aires, 1961)
——, *El Aleph*, 3rd ed. (Buenos Aires, 1961)
——, *El hacedor* (Buenos Aires, 1960)
Carpentier, Alejo, *El acoso* (Buenos Aires, 1956)
——, *El reino de este mundo* (Mexico, 1967)
——, *Guerra del tiempo* (Mexico, 1958)
——, *Los pasos perdidos* (Mexico, 1959)

——, *El siglo de las luces* (Mexico, 1952)
——, *El camino de Santiago* (Buenos Aires, 1967)
Cortázar, Julio, *Ceremonias* (Barcelona, 1968)
——, *Las armas secretas* (Buenos Aires, 1959)
——, *Rayuela* (Buenos Aires, 1963)
——, *Final del juego* (Buenos Aires, 1964)
——, *Los premios* (Buenos Aires, 1965)
——, *La vuelta al día en ochenta mundos* (Mexico, 1967)
——, *Último round* (Mexico, 1969)
——, *62 modelo para armar* (Buenos Aires, 1968)
Donoso, José, *Coronación* (Santiago de Chile, 1957)
Fernández, Macedonio, *No toda es vigilia la de los ojos abiertos* (Buenos Aires, 1967)
——, *Papeles de recienvenido* (Buenos Aires, 1966)
——, *Museo de la novela eterna* (Buenos Aires, 1967)
Fuentes, Carlos, *Las buenas conciencias* (Mexico, 1961)
——, *La muerte de Artemio Cruz* (Mexico, 1962)
——, *La región más transparente* (Mexico, 1965)
——, *Cantar de ciegos* (Mexico, 1967)
——, *Cambio de piel* (Mexico, 1967)
——, *Aura* (La Habana, 1968)
García Márquez, Gabriel, *La hojarasca* (Montevideo, 1965)
——, *La mala hora* (Esso Colombiana, 1962)
——, *Los funerales de la Mamá Grande* (Xalapa, 1962)
——, *El coronel no tiene quien le escriba*, 2nd ed. (Mexico, 1963)
——, *Cien años de soledad* (Buenos Aires, 1967)
Lezama Lima, José, *Paradiso* (La Habana, 1966)
Mallea, Eduardo, *Obras completas*, 2 vols. (Buenos Aires, 1961)
Marechal, Leopoldo, *Adán Buenosayres*, 3rd ed. (Buenos Aires, 1966)
Onetti, Juan Carlos, *Novelas cortas* (Caracas, 1968)
——, *Tierra de nadie* (Montevideo, 1965)
——, *La vida breve* (Buenos Aires, 1950)
——, *Juntacadáveres* (Montevideo, 1965)
——, *El astillero* (Buenos Aires, 1961)
Roa Bastos, Augusto, *Hijo de hombre* (Buenos Aires, 1965)
Rulfo, Juan, *El llano en llamas* (Mexico, 1953)
——, *Pedro Páramo*, 4th ed. (Mexico, 1963)
Vargas Llosa, Mario, *La ciudad y los perros* (Barcelona, 1963)
——, *La casa verde* (Barcelona, 1966)
——, *Conversación en la catedral* (Barcelona, 1969)
——, *Los cachorros* (Barcelona, 1967)

Historical and critical

Alegría, Fernando, *Historia de la novela hispanoamericana* (Mexico, 1965)
Barrenechea, Ana María, *Borges, the Labyrinth Maker* (New York, 1965)
Benedetti, Mario, *Letras del continente mestizo* (Montevideo, 1968)
Books Abroad, vol. 44, *The Latin American Novel Today*
Flores, Ángel (ed.), *La nueva novela hispanoamericano actual* (New York, 1971)
Fuentes, Carlos, *La nueva novela hispanoamericana* (Mexico, 1969)
García Márquez: *Asedio a García Márquez* (collection of essays on his work; Santiago de Chile, 1969)
Harss, L., *Los nuestros* (Buenos Aires, 1966)
Lafforgue, Jorge (ed.), *Nueva novela latinoamericana*, 2 vols. (Buenos Aires, 1969)

Loveluck, J., *La novela hispanoamericana* (Santiago de Chile, 1966)

Ortega, Julio, *La contemplación y la fiesta. Ensayos sobre la nueva novela hispanoamericana* (Lima, 1968)

Oviedo, José Miguel, *Mario Vargas Llosa. La invención de una realidad* (Barcelona, 1970)

Rodríguez Monegal, Emir, *Narradores de esta América*, I (Montevideo, 1969)

Sommers, Joseph, *After the storm* (on the Mexican novel; Albuquerque, 1968)

Valoración multiple. Series published by the Instituto de Investigaciones literarias in Havana. These are collections of critical essays. So far volumes have appeared on Juan Rulfo, García Márquez, and on Juan Carlos Onetti

Vargas Llosa, Mario, *García Márquez. Historia de un deicidio* (Barcelona, 1971)

Chapter 10

THE THEATRE

'Hay que vivir peligrosamente'

(Rodolfo Usigli)

EXCEPT FOR THE CINEMA, the dramatic arts in Latin America have never reached the heights of its poetry and novel. It is not easy to account for this except by considering the sociology of the theatre and the relation of the writer and actors to the public. In most Spanish American countries, the theatre is an amateur or at best a semi-professional affair and commercial theatre only exists in the bigger cities (especially Mexico and Buenos Aires) and, even here, on a scale more modest than in Europe. Runs of plays tend to be very short and many are translations.

The existence of a commercial theatre in Europe and North America with a devoted and mainly middle-class public has acted as an indirect stimulus to the avant-garde, and forms the inert mass against which 'new theatre', at least from the time of Jarry, has always reacted. And over the last fifty years, much theatrical experiment has been concerned directly or indirectly with the involvement of the audience. In Spanish America, however, conditions are very different in that a commercial theatre (except possibly for the *sainete* theatres in Buenos Aires) has hardly attained enough volume to be attacked or reacted against. The emergent national drama of the twenties and thirties was outstripped in popularity by the cinema before a mass audience could be built up, with the result that writers often created works in a vacuum. The Mexican Rodolfo Usigli, for instance, wrote plays that, because of their political content, could not be staged at the time they were written. Because of the popularity of the cinema, which even replaced the theatre as the middle-class social occasion, the drama was left in an uneasy position of either searching for the non-existent mass audience or attacking a non-existent bourgeois public. To some extent this social vacuum must account for the relative poverty of the genre. Even so, over the last two decades much talent has been poured into theatrical experiment and there is a small but dedicated theatre public in many Spanish American countries.

Unfortunately this development is occurring at a time when theatre elsewhere has been turning away from verbalisation towards spectacle, away from the 'work of art' towards the 'happening', so that the emergence of good dramatists at this stage seems only remotely likely.

Curiously, despite the dearth of modern theatre, the genre has a long history in Latin America, for there were dance dramas in the pre-colonial period.[1] In the century after the Conquest, Spanish Golden Age drama reached its heights, a fact that was reflected throughout the Spanish dominions. Unlike the novel, colonial governments did nothing to prevent the importation of plays to the colonies and, indeed, in the form of *autos* and *loas*, theatre was the handmaid of religion. Plays were used for the purpose of indoctrinating converts. Secular drama flourished equally. Thomas Gage, the English Jesuit who visited Central America as a missionary in the seventeenth century, tells that plays were staged on the boat during the voyage to relieve the tedium of the long journey.[2] And some of the best talents of colonial America—Sor Juana Inés de la Cruz and Pedro de Peralta Barnuevo —wrote both religious and secular dramas. And in Lima in the eighteenth century, the theatre was an important social centre of the viceregal Court, the meeting-place of the Hispanic aristocracy with the lower orders, especially during the late eighteenth century when the legendary Pericholi—the subject of some of Palma's *tradiciones* —was both the Viceroy's mistress and the leading actress.

It was in Lima that one of the most interesting plays of the colonial period came to be written. This was *Ollantay*, a Quechua drama which fused pre-Columban tradition and Hispanic conventions and is a truly *mestizo* work. The play dramatises a love affair between the warrior Ollantay and the daughter of the Inca, Qoyllur, an affair which is thwarted by the opposition of the Inca. When Ollantay flees to join a group of rebels, Qoyllur is imprisoned and only rediscovered ten years later on the death of her father when she and Ollantay are once again united. The play incorporates many traditional Quechua songs and verse forms such as the following chorus:

> No devores, avecilla,
>   Tuya mía
> El plantío de mi princesa,
>   Tuya mía
> No lo consumas,
>   Tuya mía
> Su maíz golosina,
>   Tuya mía
> Su fruto es blanco
>   Tuya mía
> Y es tanto su dulzura

> Tuya mía
> Su corazón aún es tierno
> Tuya mía
> Sus hojas aun son débiles
> Tuya mía.

Here the poet draws on traditional metaphors, the *tuya*, the ear of wheat—and this source in oral tradition extends also to the dramatic dialogues. Thus Ollantay protests the staunchness of his love in these words which balance both Quechua lyricism and the passion of the Hispanic *galán*:

> Aún de la dura roca,
> Libremente el agua manara;
> Lágrimas el fuego llorara
> Y yo, no por eso
> Dejaré de ver a mi Qoyllur.[3]

Both in language and theme, then, there is an astonishing balance between two traditions, with Quechua lyricism and Spanish structure harmonised. The authorship is not known, but it is thought to have been the work of the *mestizo* priest Antonio Valdés writing at the end of the eighteenth century. Unfortunately it stands alone as an outstanding but unique work of art.

After Independence, the theatre continued to be an important meeting-place of the aristocracy and middle classes, and prestige buildings in the nineteenth century very often took the form of opera-houses or theatres like the Colón in Buenos Aires and Bellas Artes in Mexico. However, the existence of these theatres, far from helping native drama, seemed to discourage it, since the audiences almost invariably chose to watch foreign performers and foreign plays. Yet both in Mexico and in Lima, native drama did not entirely die out. In Mexico, there was the romantic historical drama of Fernando Calderón, and in Lima, there were the didactic and satirical dramas of Felipe Pardo y Aliaga (1806-68) and Manuel Ascensio Segura (1805-71). Pardo y Aliaga's work included *Frutos de la educación* (1829) and *Una huérfana en Chorrillos* (1833), but as a comic writer, he was surpassed by his rival, Segura, author of fourteen plays and the best of nineteenth-century Latin American dramatists. His three outstanding works are *El sargento Canuto* (1839), *La saya y manto* (1842), and *Ña Catita* (1845; revised in 1856). His targets are the traditional targets of comedy—hypocrisy and pomposity—and he chooses characters who are types like the bullfight *aficionado* of *El sargento Canuto* or the bawd, Ña Catita, who descends from a long line of pious Celestinas. A consummate hypocrite, she always claims that her life is irreproachable:

No conozco en Lima más
Que a Fray Juan Salmaqueja
Y Fray Rufo, a una monjita
De allá de las Nazarenas.

Like Palma, Segura likes to use colloquial expressions and as in Palma, though the characters are local, their character defects are universal. But whereas Palma invented something new in the *tradición*, Segura was content to work in a genre already developed in Spain in the school of Moratín and brought nothing new to this genre except Limeñan local colour.

Buenos Aires with its boom conditions after the 1870s was one of the first cities in Latin America to develop a genuinely popular drama. While the imported play and opera dominated the Colón season, there was also a popular theatre which showed melodramas based on gaucho types. The most famous was *Juan Moreira*, originally a novel by Eduardo Gutiérrez (1853-90) but adapted in 1884 to pantomime theatre and later converted into a melodrama, thanks to the initiative of Podestá, the actor who did most to promote a native Argentine theatre. After the turn of the century, there also grew up a theatre of ephemeral *sainetes*: short farcical interludes often written in *lunfardo*, the dialect of Buenos Aires, and addressed to a working-class audience. In the year 1924, when the *sainete* was at the height of its popularity, about 370 were produced. They formed the inspiration for the more durable dramas of working-class life written by Armando Discépolo (1887-). These popular *barrio* theatres of Buenos Aires had no equivalent in other countries except perhaps in the street entertainments and cheap vaudevilles of Mexico, in which the comedian Cantinflas got his training, or the rhumba theatres in Cuba.

The conscious attempt to create national theatres and encourage national playwrights stems from the *criollista* period at the turn of the century. This is also the period when the Naturalist drama of Ibsen was most influential and many novelists of the Latin American Naturalist and Realist schools also contributed to the theatre. Roberto Payró of Argentina and Federico Gamboa of Mexico are two examples of these novelist-dramatists. But the outstanding dramatist of the period, the Uruguayan Florencio Sánchez (1875-1910), devoted himself wholly to the theatre in Buenos Aires. In his youth, he was involved in Uruguayan politics and was an early member of the anarchist movement, but soon after settling in Argentina, he turned to the theatre and wrote successful plays which depicted the conflict between progress and new ideas on the one hand and traditional attitudes on the other. His first success dates from 1903 when *M'hijo el dotor* was performed at the Comedia theatre. Deterministic in structure, the play presents a series of insoluble conflicts—between youth and age, between the educated (the university-trained 'dotor' of the younger generation) and the uneducated creole, between urban sophistication and rural simplicity, between modern and traditional morality. The 'dotor' is the son of a creole farmer who wants to break with tradition. He refuses to conform to the old honour code by refusing to marry a woman he has seduced and only bows to tradition when his father is on his deathbed. Though more rational, the new morality is more inhuman than older ways, and 'El dotor' is coldhearted and repellent. In *La gringa* (1904), the 'new' is represented by an immigrant Italian family who slave in order to accumulate money, in contrast to the easygoing old creole Don Cantalicio whose lands they take over. Peace is made when Próspero, Cantalicio's son, falls in love with the immigrants' daughter, Victoria, but it is clear that Florencio Sánchez considers the old ways of life to be doomed. The cutting-down of the *ombú* tree, symbol of the old Argentina of the *gaucho*, spells the beginning of a new age, an age that will be dominated by work and progress. In *Barranco abajo* (1905) Sánchez wrote a Lear-like tragedy. The old creole farmer Zoilo is deprived of everything and even his family turns against him, leaving him with suicide as his only option. He is a blameless victim of forces beyond his control, doomed to cede to the new Argentina. He himself cannot understand why a 'moral' life in the old sense should meet with such deserts:

> Si hubiera derrochao: si hubiera jugao: si hubiera hecho daño a algun cristiano, pase; lo tendría merecido. Pero fui bueno y servicial; nunca cometí una mala acción, nunca ...

But this 'goodness' is meaningless in the society which judges by material success, not by moral virtues. Zoilo is without a future and hangs himself.

These three works by Florencio Sánchez, though old-fashioned to the modern taste, reflected the conflict between the immigrant and the creole Argentina which became acute at the turn of the century. The whole nature of the country underwent a transformation which is mirrored in these plays, though the formulation of the problem is oversimplified.

Sánchez also wrote a number of dramas centring on family life and dealing with moral failings. Among these are *Los muertos* (1905), *En familia* (1905), *El pasado* (1906), *Nuestros hijos* (1907), and one play in *lunfardo* and dealing with the lower depths, *Moneda falsa* (1907).

Florencio Sánchez was representative of a period when the theatre appeared to be on the point of development, when national drama reflecting local problems and conditions and even language was in its early stages. But this drama had hardly begun to develop when it was outstripped by a powerful rival—the cinema, which penetrated with ease to the most remote provincial towns and transformed the social habits of millions of Latin Americans. The cinema was the great popular attraction. It drew the middle classes who made a visit to the movies a Sunday afternoon outing and it drew the peasants and working classes. Large film industries developed in Mexico, Argentina, and Cuba, though the majority of the films were of poor quality. Yet with the emergence of the 'Indio Fernández' in Mexico, the presence of the Spanish director Luis Buñuel, and of Leopoldo Torre Nilson in Argentina, a quality cinema came into being. Against this the theatre has never been able to compete. One should remember that in London and Paris, there was a very well-established theatre which was not shaken by the advent of the cinema, although even in these cities, the music-halls and popular theatres were mostly forced to close sooner or later. In Latin America, without an established theatre, there was nothing to resist the triumph of the new art.

The theatre survived very largely, in fact, by becoming an avant-garde project, the domain of dedicated experimenters, many of whom had made their reputations in other fields. Outside the big theatre centres such as Mexico City and Buenos Aires, it was often a semi- or wholly an amateur affair and often run by universities. In some countries, notably Uruguay, Mexico, and Argentina, there were state theatres financed by the government but with limitations inherent in state-supported drama. The commercial theatre where it existed continued to be dominated by foreign importation.

Argentina, as we have seen, was the one country to possess a flourishing popular genre in the *sainete*, a genre that more ambitious writers like Discépolo utilised as a source of inspiration. In the thirties an attempt was made to create a theatre of more originality and a higher artistic level by the novelist Roberto Arlt (1900-42). A member of the progressive and didactic Boedo group, Arlt's first theatrical work, *Trescientos millones*, dates from 1932 and was written for a group organised by Leonidas Barletta. In this first play and in many others, Arlt fills the stage with figments of the imagination. In *Trescientos millones*, the brutal realities of a servant's life, the son of the house who seduces her, her miserable existence, can only be made bearable by the world of fantasy. Her imagination is filled with the characters of cheap novels and fairy stories: Cinderella, Rocambole, the Queen of Byzantium. Arlt developed this interplay of imagination and reality in many plays, but especially in *El fabricante de fantasmas* (1936), the story of a playwright who murders his wife, re-enacts the murder in his plays, and then executes judgement upon himself. The work of art is thus seen as a form of self-knowledge. In *Saverio el Cruel*, which was not staged until 1956, fantasy turns to madness. Susana tries to play tricks on the simple Saverio by pretending to be mad and asking him to enter into a fantasy. She is queen and he is to be her colonel. His imagination released, Saverio spends his time daydreaming, until Susana's own fantasy turns into reality and she falls in love with Saverio. Saverio now believes Susana really to be mad and refuses to 'play the game', whereupon she shoots him. Saverio and Susana never manage to share the same area either of reality or fantasy. They are always out of key with one another—and this too is a favourite theme of Arlt, developed particularly in *Prueba de fuego*, which, though published in 1932, was only staged in 1947. He also wrote an Arabian-nights-type fantasy, *África* (1938), and a powerful political allegory, *La fiesta del hierro* (1946), in which the child of an arms manufacturer is immolated on the very day that war is declared and the prosperity of the father's factory assured.[4]

Arlt's plays show evidence of great power and talent, but he was limited by the environment in which they were produced.

Samuel Eichelbaum (1894-) was an Argentine playwright who worked within the Naturalist and Realist conventions rather than breaking with them as Arlt had done. *Tejido de madre* (1936) and *El gato y su selva* (1936) were among the early works, but it was in 1940, with *Pájaro de barro* and *Un guapo de 900*, that he began to explore more extreme cases. In the latter, he explored the character of a professional killer and his loyalty to the *cacique* to the point of killing the wife's lover on his behalf. And in *Un tal Servando Gómez* (1942), the author attacked conventional reactions to the eternal-triangle problem. The play concerns a woman who goes to live with her lover, though pregnant by her husband. Her husband jealously pursues her for years until her son, now grown-up, makes peace between them and shows how absurd *macho* jealousy had been. A more poetic and imaginative drama was initiated at this period by Conrado Nalé Roxló (1898-), author of *La cola de la sirena* (1941), in which a man marries a mermaid, cuts off her tail, and then is disappointed when she turns out to be like any other woman. Men want the marvellous but then find that they cannot live with it. Roxló's themes are more universal than those of Eichelbaum and for this reason he eschews the regional or local setting. The historical drama permits him to transcend regional associations. Thus in *El pacto de Cristina* (1945), he gives his play a medieval setting. Cristina sells herself to the devil for love of Gerardo who is a crusading knight. When she finds out that the devil really wants the son of the marriage, she commits suicide before the marriage can be consummated. As in *La cola de la sirena*, fulfilment of the dream pollutes it.

Two of the most successful of Argentina's younger dramatists are Agustín Cuzzani (1924-), author of *El centro forward murió al amanecer* (1955), and Osvaldo Dragún (1929-), whose *Heroica de*

Buenos Aires (1966) won a prize awarded by the Cuban Casa de las Américas. However, the more extreme avant-garde of Buenos Aires has moved away from 'literary' drama towards balletic drama and happenings. They are influenced by North American avant-garde movements in the theatre, notably by the work of Merce Cunningham and John Cage.

In Mexico, which, after Buenos Aires, has seen the most active development of the modern theatre, the emergence of modern drama dates from the activities of the *Contemporáneos* group. Of these Celestino Gorostiza devoted himself almost wholly to the theatre. The poets Salvador Novo and Xavier Villaurrutia turned increasingly to the theatre in their maturity. The plays of Novo and Villaurrutia are, however, less experimental than one might expect, given the group's interest in contemporary European literature. Villaurrutia's plays bear some resemblance to those of Eugene O'Neill and often present archetypal Greek myth situations in a contemporary setting. His interest is in the psychological drama, particularly those dramas that develop out of family relationships. In *El yerro candente* (1944), for example, Antonia devotes intense love and loyalty to her father. But unknown to herself, she is the daughter of her mother's first lover, Román, whom she detests. When the real situation is revealed to her, she cannot change her sentiments and continues to be loyal to the man whom she had always believed to be her father.

Villaurrutia likes to show that real relationships have little to do with the family structure. In *La hiedra* (which glosses the Phaedra theme), Hipolito hates his stepmother Teresa, to the point where he has to be sent away. When he returns as a man, he sees her not as a stepmother but as a woman he can love.

The plays of Villaurrutia are more literary than dramatic. There is little colloquialism in the dialogue. Classical associations abound and even the stage directions are more akin to novelistic description than to practical theatrical instructions. Thus, for instance, he describes Teresa in *La hiedra*, exactly as a novelist might have done:

> Teresa tiene unos treinta y cinco anos. Es alta y fuerte. Se diría que bajo su piel de un color vegetal circula savia en vez de sangre. El aire y la luz la turban y la hacen sentir más profundamente. Se diría tambien que de todos los objetos que toca, que de todos los seres que abraza, extrae, insensiblemente, algo que la enriquece. Y se adivina que la oscuridad y la soledad completas la empobrecerían definitivamente.

One of the first Latin Americans to claim for the theatre a special critical role among literary genres was Rodolfo Usigli (1905-), who began writing plays in the thirties in Mexico during the period when the country was dominated by ex-President Calles. Influenced by George Bernard Shaw, he wrote plays with epilogues and essays,[5] plays which often could not be staged because they were too critical of contemporary political life. The *Tres comedias impolíticas* published at this period exploit a great variety of techniques in order to satirise the absurdity of Mexican political life, but they could not be staged. In 1938 Usigli became head of the theatre section of the government department of Fine Arts and in 1940 he was able to create his own semi-professional theatre, *Teatro de Media Noche*. He also translated plays. His dedication to the theatre was partly responsible for the upsurge of the Mexican theatre after the 1940s. His own plays fall into two classes—dramas centring on middle-class life which push problems of family relationships to much more daring limits than the plays of Villaurrutia; and plays which explore problems of *mexicanidad*. Of the first type, a good example is *Jano es una muchacha* (1952), in which a respectable schoolgirl doubles as a prostitute. And in *El niño y la niebla* he explores problems of instinct and suggestibility. Marta hates her husband so much that she tries to get her son, who walks in his sleep, to kill him, but her attempts at insinuating this suggestion bring about such a conflict that the son kills himself.

Usigli's two most famous plays on Mexican themes are *El gesticulador* (1937) and *Corona de sombra*. The first of these suffered the fate of *Tres comedias impolíticas* and could not be staged for some time because it was too critical of Mexican politics. The play concerns the fate of a failed university teacher, César Rubio, who has the same name as a general who has been missing since the years of the Revolutionary war. Rubio knows him to be dead and when a North American scholar, investigating the General's disappearance, identifies him with César, the latter decides to continue the deception. He becomes the General, is immediately made a candidate for the governorship, and he assumes a new and more forceful personality. 'Estoy viviendo como había soñado siempre' he declares. But the General had too many political enemies. César is assassinated and now the myth can never be separated from the man. His son's attempt to be honest and prove that Rubio was not the General cannot succeed because myth is stronger than reality, especially in Mexico where political life feeds on it.

Corona de sombra (1943) is not Usigli's only historical drama, but it is his most outstanding one. In this play, he imagines what might have happened if the Empress Carlota, who went mad, had recovered her sanity long enough to tell the story of the Emperor Maximilian and herself and their Mexican adventure. The drama is one of ambition. Maximilian represents a new and better strain than the existing European monarchs and his stay in Mexico transforms him, but tragically he is executed before he can use his new knowledge and awareness. For the author, he represented the death of 'la codicia europea' and the birth of 'el primer concepto cerrado y claro de la nacionalidad mexicana'.

The historical drama on Mexican themes is a popular genre among Mexican writers who are concerned with the problem of *mexicanidad*, a problem that is a central theme of their essays and of many novels. Celestino Gorostiza chose the subject of Doña Marina, Cortés's mistress and one of the great Mexican myth figures, as protagonist for his drama *La malinche* (1958) and she is also the central figure of *Todos los gatos son pardos* (1970), a play written by the Mexican novelist Carlos Fuentes. And the pre-Columban theme has not been neglected. The talented woman dramatist Luisa Josefina Hernández (1928-) has successfully based a play on the Maya Bible in her *Popol Vuh* (1966).

As in Argentina, the theatre in Mexico has increasingly moved away from verisimilitude in the direction of fantasy. Juan José Arreola (1918-) and Elena Garro (1917-) have brought poetry back into the theatre, the latter being author of a delightful black comedy, *Un hogar sólido* (1958). And two of the most successful contemporary dramatists, Emilio Carballido (1925-) and Jorge Ibargüengoitia (1928-), are primarily satirical writers. Carballido is author of a satire of the press, *Las noticias del día* (1968), and a play which deals satirically with the life and love of provincial Mexico in 1919, *Te juro Juana, que tengo ganas* (1966). Two of his best plays, *Rosalba y los Llaveros* and *La danza que sueña la tortuga*, both have provincial settings.

Mexico has also seen the production of the works of a Guatemalan dramatist, Carlos Solórzano, who is also author of important works on the Latin American theatre and has been instrumental in getting many plays published.

Outside the major centres, it is Chile which has most successfully developed a theatre over the last decades, although her first successful dramatist, the popular Armando Moock (1894-1943), worked mostly in Buenos Aires. More recently, the university theatres have played a decisive role in encouraging experiment and there are two outstanding dramatists—Egon Woolf (1926-) and Luis Heiremans (1928-). Woolf's plays reflect preoccupations similar to those of contemporary Chilean novelists, such as José Donoso. In *Los invasores* the theme is indeed remarkably similar to that of Donoso's novel *Coronación*, in that both are about the fear and guilt of the middle class. In *Los invasores*, the house of Lucas Mayer is gradually taken over by beggars who make him confess that his wealth has been earned by unscrupulous means and who humiliate his haughty daughter, Marcela, and his left-wing student son, Bobby. The weakness of the play is that it turns out to be a dream which lessens its effectiveness, but as a depiction of the crisis of middle-class guilt it is very effective. Luis Heiremans, author of *Cuentos para teatro, La jaula en el árbol* (1957), and *Moscas sobre el mármol*, died just when his work was reaching maturity. He had already shown great imagination and sensitivity in his plays, in which he often used fantasy and illusion.

Uruguayan theatre is subsidised by the government, so that there are regular seasons of both classical Spanish and foreign dramas, and of new plays, though talent tends to be drawn off to Buenos Aires. In Peru, where drama was badly eclipsed by the cinema, the outstanding playwright of this century has been Sebastián Salazar Bondy (1924-). In Venezuela, a new drama has developed out of drama festivals.

In smaller Latin American countries, theatrical production tends to be very modest indeed and largely dependent on amateur or semiprofessional groups. The exceptions are Puerto Rico, which has an outstanding dramatist in René Marqués, and Cuba.

René Marqués is very much concerned with the problem of Puerto Rican identity, especially in relation to the United States. One of his first plays, La carreta (1952), had dealt, on realistic lines, with the problem of the Puerto Rican immigrant who goes to the United States and then, on his return to his native land, finds readaptation difficult. In later plays, Marqués made use of symbolic techniques. In Los soles truncos, for instance, a decaying house symbolised the decay of a class and of the old social order. In La muerte no entrará en palacio (1957) he wrote a play which is also a political allegory. A leader comes to power on a reform programme, but quickly abandons any idea of agrarian reform and instead of ridding the country of foreign influences, he prepares to sign a treaty with 'the North'. The country of which he is ruler is never named, nor is the United States, but the references to Puerto Rico and the United States are explicit enough. It is his own daughter who, at the end of the play, assassinates her father in order to save the country from betrayal, the women in the play acting as symbols of grassroots nationhood.

In Cuba, the Revolution brought about the complete reorganisation of the theatre and, more important, a displacement of much theatrical activity from the former centre in Havana to the countryside. One of the most original developments of post-Revolutionary drama has been that of a marionette theatre for which scripts have been written by the leading authors such as Antonio Arrufat and Virgilio Pineyra.

The most original developments in the Cuban theatre have been in the direction of a non-literary style, in which music, mime, and dance are incorporated into the spectacle. There has also been experimentation by a marionette theatre which uses both puppets and live actors and which has staged some Afro-Cuban myths. Of the younger dramatists, the most successful has been José Triana (1933-). His Noche de los asesinos (1965) was a symbolic family drama, centring around three characters—Lalo, Cuca, and Beba—who 'kill' their mother and father in the first act, then enact the trial as accusers and accused, and finally re-enact the murder of their parents. It represents human beings caught in the limitations of their own natures, unable to accept freedom without guilt.

Whether a major Latin American drama will emerge must remain doubtful. In Europe and North America, both commercial and underground theatres are flourishing, but it is a theatre in which the spoken word is becoming less important. It is possible that theatre will cease to be a literary art and will move in the direction of ballet and spectacle, in which case its place will not be in a history of literature. Latin American culture reached maturity at a time when the novel was declining in other parts of the world and has already made an outstanding contribution to the genre. The importance of its poetry is undeniable. But as far as theatre is concerned, there would need to be some radical new element for this to attain real significance as a genre. Here and here alone can it be said that Latin America does not have a distinctive voice.

NOTES

1. One example is the *Rabinal Achí*. Adaptación de José Antonio Villacorta (Buenos Aires, 1944).
2. Thomas Gage, *The English American: His Travels by Land and Sea* (London, 1648).
3. *El drama quechua. Apu Ollantay*, versión de J. M. B. Farfán (Lima, 1952).
4. R. H. Castagnino, *El teatro de Roberto Arlt* (La Plata, 1964).
5. For example, the essay 'Epílogo sobre la hipocresía del Mexicano', included in the second edition of *El gesticulador* (Mexico, 1944).

READING LIST

Anthologies
Leal, René (ed.), *Teatro cubano en un acto*, 2 vols. (La Habana, 1963)
Saz Sánchez, Agustín del, *Teatro hispanoamericano* (Barcelona, 1963)
Solórzano, Carlos, *El teatro hispanoamericano contemporáneo* (Mexico, 1964)
Latin American Theatre Review, published by the University of Kansas since 1967, regularly publishes complete plays

Texts
Arlt, Roberto, *Teatro completo*, ed. Mirta Arlt, 2 vols. (Buenos Aires, 1968)
Brene, José R., *El gallo de San Isidro* (La Habana, 1964)
——, *Teatro* (La Habana, 1965)
Cuzzani, Agustín, *Para que se cumplan las Escrituras* (Buenos Aires, 1965)
——, *El centro forward murió al amanecer*, 2nd ed. (Buenos Aires, 1956)
——, *Teatro* (Buenos Aires, 1960)
Díaz Díaz, Oswaldo, *Teatro*, 2 vols. (Bogotá, 1965)
Dragún, Osvaldo, *Heroica de Buenos Aires* (La Habana, 1966)
Eichelbaum, Samuel, *Pájaro de barro* (Buenos Aires, 1965)
——, *Un guapo de 900* (Buenos Aires, 1940)

——, *Un tal Servando Gómez* (Buenos Aires, 1942)

Heiremans, Luis A., *La jaula en el árbol y dos cuentos para teatro* (Santiago de Chile, 1959)

Three one-act plays are published by *Mapocho*, III (1965)

Ibargüengoitia, Jorge, *La conspiración vendida*, in *Cuadernos de Bellas Artes* (Mexico, 1965)

Magaña, Sergio, *Moctezuma II*, in *Cuadernos de Bellas Artes* (Mexico, 1963)

Maggi, Carlos, *Teatro* (Montevideo, 1960)

Marqués, René, *Teatro* (Mexico, 1959)

Novo, Salvador, *La culta dama* (Mexico, 1951)

Ollantay: El drama quechua. Apu Ollantay, versión de J. M. B. Farfán (Lima, 1952)

Piñera, Virgilio, *Dos viejos pánicos* (La Habana, 1968)

Rabinal Achí, new translation in the spring 1968 issue of the *Latin American Theatre Review*

Sánchez, Florencio, *Teatro* (La Habana, 1963)

——, ——, ——, ed. Walter Rela (Montevideo, 1967)

Triana, José, *La noche de los asesinos* (La Habana, 1965)

Usigli, Rodolfo, *Teatro completo* (Mexico, 1966)

Villaurrutia, *Obras*, 2nd ed. aumentada (Mexico, 1966)

Historical and critical

Castagnino, Raúl, *Esquema de la literatura dramática argentina* (Buenos Aires, 1950)

——, *El teatro de Roberto Arlt* (La Plata, 1964)

Ordaz, Luis (ed.), *Breve historia del teatro argentino*, 2 vols. (Buenos Aires, 1962-64)

Reyes de la Maza, Luis, *El teatro en México durante el Porfirismo*, 3 vols. (Mexico, 1968)

Richardson, Ruth, *Florencio Sánchez and the Argentine Theatre* (New York, 1933)

Solórzano, Carlos, *Teatro latinoamericano del siglo xx* (Buenos Aires, 1961)

——, *Teatro guatemalteco* (Madrid, 1967)

Suárez Radillo, Carlos Miguel (ed.), *Autores del nuevo teatro venezolano* (Caracas, 1971)

Usigli, Rodolfo, *Anatomía del teatro* (Mexico–Ecuador, 1966)

INDEX

*Printed in Great Britain by Richard Clay (The Chaucer Press) Limited,
Bungay, Suffolk*